VERTICAL ACADEMY

VERTICAL ACADEMY

Tom Briggs

ISBN 978-1-300-64403-3, 978-1-300-37968-3

Contents

Chapter 1   Professional Standards...2

Chapter 2   Organizing 8

Chapter 3   Communications 16

Chapter 4   Safe Practices 24

Chapter 5   Scene Management 44

Chapter 6   General Rigging 56

Chapter 7   Pulleys & Mechanical Advantage............................128

Chapter 8   Pulley Systems 140

Chapter 9   Personal Competencies 172

Chapter 10   Anchoring...230

Chapter 11   Portable Anchors...264

Chapter 12   Belaying...284

Chapter 13   Rescue Baskets 322

Chapter 14   Climbing Up 342

Chapter 15   Team Competency...374

Preface

Target

Vertical Academy is intended as a reference to support formal teaching sessions led by technically competent vertical rescue experts. It is never safe to use this or any other reference in order to 'self-learn' or practice with vertical rescue equipment and techniques. Always seek instruction from technical experts before using any kind of vertical rescue equipment.

Basic Content

The strategies used to deal with vertical rescue emergencies have changed little over the last couple of decades. Two ropes and belaying climbers have been in common use since the 1980s. The equipment changes and improves almost monthly. Standards evolve to keep up with favored practices and equipment changes. *Vertical Academy* attempts to guide readers through practices that have been proven and are rendered down to the most basic equipment choices. These practices have relevance with teams using basic caches of equipment and with those lucky enough to be using cutting-edge technical tools. Advanced teams will easily recognize the strategies and techniques in this book and understand how to integrate more specialized equipment.

Format

Vertical Academy is arranged with firefighters in mind. The compact dimensions are intended to facilitate carrying and using the book on the training ground. Fonts are chosen to aid reading in low light and moving vehicles. Many of the self-supporting illustrations are clustered rather than inserted into the text as the content progresses. Grouping makes illustrations more accessible, similar to the comfortable feel of a field operations guide (FOG). The text provides detailed information about each chapter topic. The FOG-style illustration clusters support the written content but can also be used on their own to understand the chapter subject(s). Fonts used in Chapter Five were enlarged for field operations use. Hopefully, this simplified design improves usability during outdoor teaching and learning events.

Legend

Readers will notice a number of recurring banners, badges, and pictograms throughout the book. Diagrams and pictograms are used to simplify recognition and understanding. Badges and banners are used to highlight special points of importance or preference. The following definitions will help readers understand this non-text information:

 "Remember" banners point out information that will improve skill and judgement in the long term.

 "Caution" banners highlight areas that require special consideration, close inspection, or the need for risk-benefit analysis.

 "Warning" banners signal situations that can impair operations, damage equipment, or injure personnel.

 "Danger" banners alert readers to conditions that may cause equipment or systems to fail and cause personal injury or death.

 "Best Practices" badges identify the safest or most effective methods to rig equipment or carry out maneuvers when several choices are illustrated or described.

 "Caution" badges identify areas that require special consideration, close inspection, or the need for risk-benefit analysis.

 "Danger" badges alert readers to conditions that may cause equipment or systems to fail and cause personal injury or death.

 "Load" pictograms represent any object (usually a rescue climber) that weighs on rescue rigging or levers.

  "Anchor" pictograms represent anchor objects and locations of various types.

"Bomber" banners added identify anchors able to support loads significantly greater than needed.

Acknowledgments

Technical references are acknowledged wherever they appear in the book. Tables are derived from relevant standards identified by the table title. In several instances, "Anecdotal Observations" are cited. Anecdotal observations are based on formal manipulative training events or actual emergency incidents. Anecdotal observations are not based on scientific research or testing. These anecdotal statements are included to relate subject matter to real world applications.

The expertise and approach in this reference guide comes from a long fire service career and exposure to many teachers and influential people along the way. Special thanks to the following people: Bruce Suenram, Rich Klinke, Jim Segerstrom, Barry Edwards, Jay Bowdler, John Brenner, Reed Thorne, Dave Odgers, Dave Nettle, and Tom Neville.

1 Professional Standards

NFPA

Why You Should Care about NFPA Rescue Standards...

Aside from the fact that using the National Fire Protection Association (NFPA) rescue standards will help ensure that you provide good rescue service, there are a number of other compelling considerations.

Anyone tasked with putting a fire department technical rescue service together may encounter a few misconceptions. Protectors of the budget or defenders of comfortable working conditions will likely have input. Sometimes that input is based on a superficial understanding of important industry standards. Don't be surprised to hear things like "NFPA Standards aren't regulations; they're only recommendations," or "We ignore other NFPA standards; what's the big deal?" Everyone from the Engineer, who is dreading the future drills, to the Special Operations Chief, who doesn't want to deal with the headache of keeping a team well honed, will make those points.

The truth is: they're right. However, 1670 and 1006 aren't your garden-variety NFPA standards. For one thing they're relatively new, published shortly after the turn of the twenty-first century following some influential civil liability cases. These standards define in black and white the baseline of competency for each firefighter and for the department. Even though the focus should always be on providing the safest and most effective rescue service possible, you can't ignore the issue of liability. You also can't ignore the levels of good performance that NFPA makes known to the public. You can't just hope that there will never be an incident on the vertical hazards within the jurisdiction. Imagine a doctor or dentist sitting on a witness stand declaring that he or she ignores the American Medical Association or the American Dental Association because their standards are only "recommendations." Those professionals would be civil liability sitting ducks. Fortunately, many government entities provide great compliance motivation by adopting these standards as codes and linking them to licensing. Now, put a firefighter on the stand. How would that person answer the question, "How long has that vertical hazard been in your jurisdiction?" If the answer is forever, he can stick his head in the guillotine. How about, "Did you ignore the rescue proficiency standards of the National Fire Protection Association, the only rescue competency standard for your own industry?" Unless the agency having jurisdiction (AHJ) has an equal or better operating standard...ka-ching! It's payday for the attorneys. Even though an AHJ may not have adopted NFPA standards, they're the only professional rescue standards against which fire agencies can compare themselves. When deciding whether your fire department did a good job on a rescue or not, NFPA standards 1670 and 1006 are what they'll be compared to—like it or not.

Every professional firefighter understands that even when everything goes well on a call, sloppy attention to industry standards opens the "deep pockets" door to anyone wishing to cash in. "Contact Accident Injury Attorneys" pops up on the flat screen while the vertical rescue subject you snatched from the clutches of the grim reaper a few days prior recuperates. Next thing you know, he's got his attorney's number in his contact list. From that point on, it's a matter of going through the "ambulance chasing" process to sniff out the path to the easiest money. Once an attorney catches the scent of a department ignoring professional standards, it can be a real bloodbath. Even though NFPA standards are not law, they carry the weight of law because the penalties can be so severe. A civil liability judgment from a sympathetic jury, or even a pre-court settlement, will pack more financial sting than any Occupational Health and Safety Administration (OSHA) fine.

Some wealthy fire organizations do intentionally flout NFPA standards. Many have been dealing with rescue hazards well before 1670 and 1006 were penned. But "ignore" is not the best word to describe their approach. It might be better to say that they understand NFPA standards, but feel that their own operating standards meet the agencies' needs better. Variables like climate, staffing, availability of repair, and fabrication facilities (advanced resources like crane, aviation or marine companies) may lead some organizations to develop procedures and equipment that exceed NFPA standards. My guess is that they can describe in court how their own standards are better. Many departments probably meet or exceed many NFPA standards without even trying. Teaching organizations and equipment manufacturers usually keep a keen eye on 1670,1006, and other standards because they're under the same kind of legal microscope. It benefits manufacturers and schools to cater to industry standards, whether it's construction safety or vertical rescue.

The one area where fire organizations often stumble when it comes to complying with 1670 and 1006 is manipulative practice. There's no getting around it. To stay sharp enough to keep up with NFPA rescue standards, you have to engage in frequent high-quality and meaningful practice. Whether you are interested in NFPA compliance or not, practice is key. Attending a weeklong vertical rescue training course is good but should only be considered as a means to get started by learning what you must practice on a regular and frequent basis. Anything less just does not work, period. It's not uncommon to witness veteran rescue teams struggling to carry out the simplest of evolutions, even though their members can produce any kind of vocational training certificate you require faster than a gunslinger from the old west. Not because they weren't trained, but simply because they put off practicing regularly. That kind of approach is just plain backward. A team might be better off not attending a training course at all if they frequently practice using systems they invent themselves. Realistic and meaningful practice in locations where real rope rescue incidents occur is crucial for success.

NFPA 1670 establishes competency standards for fire agencies in the field of technical rescue. Rescue disciplines included in this standard are rope rescue, confined space rescue, search, water rescue, ice rescue, collapse rescue, mechanical disentanglement and extrication rescue, hazardous materials rescue, and trench rescue. 1670 is the "Bar" of competency for any United States fire agency, referred to by NFPA as the Agency Having Jurisdiction (AHJ).

In the past, fire organizations responded to emergency rescue calls and provided service based on a wide range of factors, the least of which included well thought-out forecasting, preparation, and practice. Some of the most well-prepared agencies that respond to technical rescues had to suffer embarrassment, or even legal action, before making an effort to plan, train and gear up adequately. 1670, published shortly after the turn of the twenty-first century, provides guidance to fire and rescue agencies by identifying how to determine needs, how to meet those needs, and how to keep their technical rescue program working adequately. In short, how to assess their potential to respond to technical rescues, train and equip their personnel, and how to monitor and maintain proficiency.

NFPA 1006 establishes competency standards for individuals in the field of technical rescue and is closely associated with standard 1670. Standard 1006 defines several levels of expertise for rescue individuals. Think of these as the different color belts identifying varying levels of expertise in karate. Individual capabilities are defined in detail for each of these classifications. The levels of expertise can be described as:

- **Awareness Level**: Individual possesses the ability to recognize technical rescue situations and any associated hazards and can provide support during rescue operations. These folks can tell when they're in over their heads and when to call for more specialized help. They also know enough to keep anyone from getting hurt.

- **Operational Level**: Individual possesses the ability to utilize tools and assemble systems designed to mitigate technical rescue situations. Ops people are the workhorses on most rescue teams. They've been shown how to assemble and use rope systems, and they practice regularly with an assigned cache of equipment.

- **Technical Level**: Individual possesses the ability to design systems, make repairs, or solve problems in technical rescue situations. These people usually develop standard operating procedures or policy and decide what kinds of equipment and systems will be used in an AHJ. Often you'll find techs in leadership or teaching roles.

NFPA 1983 establishes standards of durability for rope rescue equipment used by firefighters based on two measurement benchmarks. These benchmarks are:

- **15 to 1 Safety Factor:** Vertical rescue systems and components within Standard 1983 require a minimum capacity of supporting 15 times the static working load. The actual 15:1 factor was calculated and defined in the earliest versions of Standard 1983, but has been left out of later editions as the content has changed. Load capacity values in the latest edition of the standard line up with this 15:1 figure.

- **One Person Load:** NFPA considers 300 pounds to be the maximum static weight and 20 kilonewtons (kN) to be the maximum dynamic force of one person on a rope system. If the load goes to 301 pounds, even if it's one big rescuer, your rope system should be assembled with equipment and methods that will support 600 pounds of static weight and 40kN of dynamic force.

> One-person load of 300 lbs. x 15 = 4,500 lbs.
> Two-person load of 600 lbs. x 15 = 9,000 lbs.

A rating system defined in NFPA 1983 helps rescue workers choose the right tools for the job. To help ensure that durability standards are practical to for use in the field, or when making purchases, NFPA offers a listing schedule to manufacturers. Rope rescue equipment bearing NFPA rating markings makes it easy to know if you're hooking into a component designed and built for a one-person load or a two-person load.

- **NFPA-T:** Equipment designed and built for a one-person load meeting 1983 standards can be marked "NFPA–T" to signify "Technical Use."

- **NFPA-L:** You may find equipment capable of supporting a one-person load marked "NFPA–L" for "Light Use." The term "Light" was changed to "Technical" in later editions of 1983. Same standard, different name.

- **NFPA-P:** You may also find equipment capable of supporting a one-person load marked "NFPA–P" for "Personal Use." The term "Personal" was changed to "Light" in later editions of 1983. Same standard, different name.

- **NFPA–G:** Equipment designed and built for a two-person load meeting Standard 1983 can be marked "NFPA–G" to signify "General Use."

It's important to understand that any given piece of equipment may be durable enough to meet the 15:1 safety factor of Standard 1983 for light or general loads without being marked as such. It's often a cost or marketing issue for manufacturers. You must know the capacities and limitations of unmarked equipment to make sure it meets your organization's working standards.

Comments about the 15:1 Safety Factor, Training, and Practice

Many non-fire service groups are critical of the NFPA 15 to 1 safety factor. Some firefighters claim that the heavy-duty factor is industry driven and ensures more profits for manufacturers. Hands down, it is the toughest standard for rope rescue equipment. Standards around the world go as low as 6 to 1. Non-fire service professions in the U.S. that use rope systems for high access or fall protection are often 10 to 1, as with the Society of Professional Rope Access Technicians (SPRAT). National and state OSHA regulations are also lower. So why should you support such a lofty safety factor? Consider that the modern fire service is much more diverse than it was just a short time ago. Not long ago it was considered progressive to respond to first aid calls with nothing more than American Red Cross First Aid expertise. Now firefighters respond to every kind of call imaginable and provide every kind of service, from putting out neighborhood fires to hazmat spills, dive rescues, vehicle extrication, and excavation and building collapse. You name it. Add on non-emergency routine services like inspections, community outreach, and education, and some firehouses are so busy that they hardly have time to eat, let alone train. Today's firefighter has to be "pretty good" at a large number of skills and carry a wide variety of equipment to do all those different jobs. Rigging oracle Reed Thorne, Lead Instructor for Ropes That Rescue, affectionately refers to firefighters as "plate spinners," referring to the circus act where multiple plates spin atop vertical rods for the entertainment of the audience, to explain how tough it is for a firefighter to be technically skilled in any one discipline, like ropes. He's right. It's very tough. It's a tall order to expect a firefighter to be an expert with rope rescue systems. The dependence on public funding compounds this by influencing when you can purchase things like ropes, training courses, etc. People in the private sector may not understand that because their ability to buy supplies depends on revenues and the budget process. There are also large variations in how different fire departments work. Across the U.S., you can find departments that consist of a few public service minded volunteers and departments with thousands of uniforms and huge budgets. All those points show that the 15 to 1 safety factor may make better sense for its fire service application than it first appears. Making the equipment super strong and durable might be a good thing for the firefighter who's only "pretty good" with rope skills and uses equipment that is a little older and dog-eared than it would be if there were more money in the budget. A more sobering point might be that there exists the potential for firefighters to work in not-so-sanitary environments with sharp and falling objects, such as building collapses. California US&R Task Force 7 used rope systems daily during their service at the Oklahoma City and World Trade Center disasters. The teams depended on strong rope equipment for access and support while using power-cutting tools. Much of that rope equipment returned home ruined from heavy wear and exposure to contaminants. It wasn't removed from service until <u>after</u> returning home. You learn to appreciate a wide margin of safety in the fire service.

2 Organizing

Organizing Your Rescue Program

Hazards Assessments

To develop any kind of successful program, a needs assessment must be completed. NFPA acknowledges the importance of this planning tool and refers to it as a **Hazards Assessment**. A comprehensive hazards assessment attempts to forecast and quantify the potential for and severity of future fires and EMS and rescue events in a jurisdiction. If training of personnel or purchasing of equipment takes place before a hazards assessment is completed (which is often the case), a rescue program is likely to start out with a bang, but then fizzle or even fade away when the subject becomes less sexy sometime down the road when administrators focus on the next craze. You also run the risk of starting out assessing in piece meal fashion and falling short of your actual needs, or prioritizing inappropriately, or spending more than is really needed. Without a hazards assessment, you're shooting without a target. Put your horse squarely in front of the cart by carefully evaluating your agency's rope rescue needs before you start sending troops to classes or buying expensive equipment. A clear understanding of your needs will make it easy to know how many people to train and what levels of expertise they must have. A good hazards assessment will also influence policy, response plans, staffing, operational procedures, and budget planning. A hazards assessment is sometimes a wake-up call enough for agency leaders to rethink priorities and approve spending, or even to shift policy. The hazards assessment can be a powerful tool for anyone trying to get a technical rescue program off the ground or up to standard. With or without NFPA, a hazards assessment will serve to make your agency better, no question.

A hazards assessment can be a major project involving highly expert and expensive consulting groups that result in flashy caches of charts, graphs, aerial photographs, media presentations, and meetings. But it stands to reason that any firefighter working the job for a few years probably already has a reasonable ability to forecast the AHJ's potential to respond to technical rescues. It shouldn't be too daunting a task to review call data and assess workload trends. Other information like natural and man-made hazards is probably already common knowledge among the ranks. It may just be a matter of gathering, organizing, and formatting the information so to reasonably predict the potential and severity of relevant technical rescue incidents. Once that's done, formalize it within the organization.

Agency Capability

Now, put the hazards assessment to work. Use it to determine what is needed for your agency to adequately respond to calls and mitigate related incidents. With respect to rope rescue, it can be pretty easy to figure out what abilities your agency must possess. If the assessment shows your agency has a strong potential to respond to people stuck on vertical cliffs, antennae towers, light poles or tall buildings, then a well-trained and equipped group will need to be developed, outfitted, and maintained. On the other hand, if the assessment shows little potential for vertical rescues aside from the occasional carnival ride accident, it may be better to focus on developing codes and ordinances restricting the height of Ferris wheels whenever they set up within jurisdictional boundaries.

The tough thing about this kind of forecasting and preparation is the "All-In or All-Out" factor associated with the technical rescue field. Kind of in the same way a woman can't really be *"kinda"* pregnant. Like most rescue disciplines, any rope rescue operation can result in disaster if not done well. Gravity works very reliably. It only requires one small mistake to mess up. If an AHJ doesn't respond to vertical rescues very often, that is no reason to downplay the potential for dangerous rescue events and "kinda" gear up for vertical rescues. These kinds of "Low Probability, High Risk" situations are the areas in which fire agencies probably need the most practice. When that once-in-a-career call comes in, all eyes will be on the first responding agency (usually the fire department) to deploy their NASA-like Special Ops team and make things go as smoothly as a TV show, much like they do on a daily basis for routine chest pain calls for which they're well equipped, well trained and well practiced. Firefighters on a vertical rescue scene will feel the pressure to make a successful rescue. This is the worst time to invent a vertical rescue plan. Unless an AHJ has automatic aid agreements with neighboring agencies that are well prepared for vertical rescues, there may be a need to assemble a full-on program, even though vertical rescue incidents are rare. Full-on means establishing operational procedures for every foreseeable vertical incident and engaging in regular and meaningful practice with specialized equipment. Even when an AHJ decides to defer risk coverage to well-trained neighbors (not a bad thing), it is important that staff be trained to adequately recognize when they're in over their heads.

Whatever the case, if the assessment shows a need for a vertical rescue resource, there are several broad capability categories from which to choose when determining how your agency should develop.

1. <u>Over The Side Incidents</u>
2. <u>Overhead Incidents</u>
3. <u>Below Grade Incidents</u>
4. <u>Traverse Across Incidents</u>

Over The Side means situations on a cliff or structure where rescuers set up above the subject and lower a climber. Sometimes referred to as "Top Down" mode. The subject is then captured, secured, and either lowered the rest of the way to the bottom or raised topside.

Overhead means situations, usually on a structure like a tower or bridge, where rescuers set up below the subject and climb up. Sometimes referred to as "Bottom Up" mode. The subject is then captured, secured, and lowered to the ground.

Below Grade means situations where a rope system is used for access into and out of openings such as manholes, wells, tanks, etc. These rope systems are often arranged directly over an opening with portable anchor devices such as davits, gantries, tripods, or multi-pods as "Artificial High Directionals" (AHDs).

Traverse Across means situations where a rope is used to cross a vertical or steep face horizontally, or to span a chasm for the purpose of either getting from one side to the other or maneuvering a climber below the span of rope. Rope systems where the working line is anchored on each end with the load traveling along the length between the anchors are known as "Static Systems." Static systems, such as highlines and tyroleans, are considered advanced and require high levels of skill to assemble and use safely.

Operational level ability to deal with Over The Side, Overhead, and Below Grade incidents meets the needs of most fire agencies. An Operational level approach for these categories will be the focus of this book. Traverse Across Systems will not be covered in depth.

Staffing

Systems presented in this book will be based on a seven-person team of operationally trained and equipped firefighters, combining a three-person Engine Company and a four-person Truck or Rescue Company. A vertical rescue group staffed with seven people can cover the tactical and safety positions needed to assemble and operate simple, reliable rope rescue systems capable of handling NFPA General loads. Though seven-person teams will be featured in the book, it must be understood that full back-up resources should be part of any emergency response or training exercise.

Depending on how your agency works on a daily basis, it can be a real nightmare to keep a rescue company staffed with qualified vertical rescue personnel. Administrators sometimes misunderstand the depth of expertise and ability needed to safely run a vertical rescue call and feel comfortable weighing the odds of covering a rescue assignment with an under-trained firefighter. Vacation leave or sick leave at role call is one cause of this. If this is not the case where you work, consider yourself very lucky. Today's fire service is about getting more done with fewer resources. Daily staffing coverage can get pretty complicated and creative.

With this dynamic in mind, it's a must to keep flexibility a part of any vertical rescue staffing plan. Anticipate the need to operate normally even when regularly-assigned, skilled professionals are on leave. Build a backup into your staffing plan by training and drilling extra personnel so that they can occupy vacant rescue positions on short notice. This can be accomplished by layering companies selected for response to vertical rescue hazards.

Example:

Rescue 1 and Engine 1 are the primary response vertical rescue group for the agency. Engine 2 and Truck 2 are the secondary responders and back-up resource for Engine 1 and Rescue 1. Station 2 personnel are operationally trained and equipped for the hazard. Engine 2 and Truck 2 also participate in vertical rescue practice sessions with Engine 1 and Rescue 1. Personnel from 2's are able to occupy Engine 1 or Rescue 1 assignments on short notice. Adding layers as needed can carry this further.

As an additional backup, create a rescue staffing pool from interested personnel assigned throughout the agency. Include those people in initial qualification training and regular practice sessions. This approach will not only ease daily staffing headaches, but also can better prepare the agency for large-scale events like earthquakes or floods.

Training

Shop wisely when deciding on training courses for team members. Don't be distracted by dramatic course titles, flashy websites, or government accreditations. Make sure the actual content of any training course meets the needs of your program. Watch out for teaching organizations that use exotic or proprietary equipment that isn't carried in your own cache. Evaluate prerequisite skill levels for participants before they attend a course and what skill level they will possess once they have completed the course. Make sure the curriculum includes an evaluation phase. Will a task book or skills sheet documenting the particular skills demonstrated by each student be provided? Make sure the skills and evolutions you need for your hazards are taught in the course. Determine what standards, if any, the course attempts to comply with. Clarify whether participants are trained to Awareness, Operational, or Technical levels of expertise. Beware of courses that provide certification in vertical rescue in only one or two sessions. This is the case in some long-standing curriculums because many administrators don't understand the difference and continue to use the training in their organizations. To provide for enough instruction, demonstration, manipulative application, and evaluation for a class of a dozen entry-level students, it takes about a week to achieve Operational competency. There is not really any way to get around this without a time machine.

Whenever possible, continue to make training opportunities available to team members. Host guest trainers. Send members to training courses that add depth and expertise to the team. Almost certainly, some members will develop an interest in further training and higher levels of competency, including achieving Instructor status. Enabling these people can be a real force-multiplier by providing the opportunity to establish internal education and training programs.

Remember: training is only a means to show your team how to practice safely on its own in the future.

Practice

Here's where the rubber meets the road. The importance of practice cannot be emphasized enough when it come to rescue competency, especially vertical rescue. It's no stretch to say that skills tend to erode over time. The longer the time, the more severe the erosion. Once personnel have been trained, it's time to hit the ground running and start ingraining the skills and evolutions they've learned with realistic and challenging practice sessions. There's no doubt about it, excellence is reserved for those who practice.

So how should you practice and how often?

Think of the initial training sessions in which your team participated to become qualified to safely operate at your hazards. If, for example, the rope ops training course(s) required 60 hours of intense participation to bring them to technical understanding and manipulative ability, use that figure to gauge a sufficient amount of practice. Lay out plans to repeat that number of training hours (60) over a time window that supports skill retention. NFPA and many teaching organizations nationwide regard 3 years as the maximum length of time a person can go unpracticed and still retain adequate skills. That's a very optimistic figure. Fortunately, the fire and rescue service recognizes more and more that old training doesn't cut the mustard. The solution is to factor in practice frequency. Waiting for 2.99 years and then sending everyone off to basic ops school again is costly and doesn't work very well. A better approach is to arrange regular (more frequently than every 3 years) practice sessions that include the topics contained in the initial training course. Using the 60-hour figure over the span of 36 months, you end up carrying out a 3.5-hour drill every other month. This is easy to do, and it's a good start. Compressing the schedule will build a cushion that allows personnel to take time off without falling short of practice hours. Example: fit that same 60-hour schedule onto a 2.5-year calendar and keep the 3-year window as a deadline. You end up practicing 4 hours every other month and allow for more success in your program, all while keeping up with standards of excellence.

Practice sessions should be manipulative in nature and involve the entire team. Instead of breaking down skills such as knot craft or anchoring each time you practice, try to arrange subject matter into manipulative exercises that not only include those personal skills but also team competency. As an example, there are a couple of ways to approach the topic of litter rigging and management. One is to lecture to the group as an audience in ground school fashion and then have personnel rig the basket while it's on the ground. This is not entirely without value, but consider the benefits of putting a full-weight mannequin in the basket and having personnel take turns manipulating the rigging while suspended off the ground. The entire team gets involved with litter tending and rigging a raising and lowering system. This is much more meaningful, and a lot more fun.

A large part of the practice schedule should be devoted to evolutions or scenarios. Carry out sessions as if they were actual incidents. Place your full-weight mannequin over the side in a precarious position, allowing it to fall if not handled properly. Once the dummy is in position, start the event. Operate as you would on a real call. The Drill Master can correct safety mistakes or make learning points by taking "training timeouts" any time during the session. Follow up with a genuine debriefing to review what went well and what areas need improvement. Over time, everyone learns what's practical and effective. You'll also notice a developing team style and pride.

You eventually want each team member to be comfortable operating in any position. Rotate assignments each time you practice evolutions and scenarios. This strategy will bolster the team's ability to function even when some members are on leave. Avoid the pitfall of heavy dependence on one or two highly-skilled individuals.

Repetition is a virtue. Even if you plan a variety of scenarios, systems used to deal with them will be more similar than different. Usually operations start with the same basic rope system, but use a different rig at the end of the main line. Team members may start experiencing

REMEMBER

Amateurs Practice Until They Get It Right.

Professionals Practice Until They Can't Get It Wrong.

boredom or begin questioning the need to set up the same systems over and over. Repetitive practice improves performance and cements cognitive understanding. It also provides the opportunity to rotate assignments to make each team member well rounded. Professionals practice repetitively. Check any pro sports team, for example. It also ensures that equipment is working properly and is set up and cached as it should be, kind of like regular apparatus checks. Amateurs practice until they get it right, pros practice until they can't get it wrong.

Finally, practice at levels slightly more intense than what the team routinely encounters in the field. Work all the tools carried in your cache into your practice sessions. Include worst-case situations when planning scenarios. Always use a heavy mannequin. Carry out sessions at locations where vertical incidents have occurred in the past. Challenge the team by setting up conditions encountered by other agencies about which you may have read in trade journals. When the actual call for a vertical emergency does come in, your team will have no problem dealing with a situation that is somewhat easier than that for which they've practiced. The reverse is obviously less desirable.

Records and Tracking

The validity of a rescue program relies on the ability to review qualification requirements and the history of practice and experience. Over time a rescue team and its members attain more and more competency as they train, practice, and experience rescue incidents. When outsiders like OSHA or an attorney evaluate your competency and credibility, they're not going to take your word for it. You can brag about it until you're blue in the face, but if your history of preparation isn't documented, you may as well have staffed the recliners. Whether it's the agency or an individual's credibility that's being questioned, the story is the same: if your training, practice, and experience are not documented, it didn't happen. To measure credibility, a formal system of recovering information about training and practice must be added to your department's records management system.

Start by formalizing a qualification policy for rescue team members. Identify necessary training along with practice requirements to maintain qualification. Next, secure and organize training documents like certificates, task books, and skills sheets for each team member. Develop a practice plan that complies with adopted standards. Closely track company and individual practice, and enter the related information into the training records management system. Make that information readily available to each member. Companies can enhance the record by making entries in station logs. And finally, encourage individuals to keep personal logs documenting their own training, practice, and experience. Logs that chronicle a long personal history of development often become sentimental treasures to their owners and a valuable document of expertise.

Measuring Success

Taking stock and regular evaluations are essential parts of measuring the ability to perform competently in the future. NFPA Standard 1670 compliance, for example, requires that agencies annually demonstrate awareness and operational or technical abilities to competently perform various rescue-related actions. Whether trying to keep pace with NFPA or not, regularly checking the ability to deal with hazards is elemental for success.

Regularly schedule readiness exercises that simulate real rescues in the presence of competent, third-party observers whose mission is to judge performance. Make sure everyone involved is aware of the desired outcome before starting the exercise. Use realistic settings, preferably simulating conditions from past or predicted incidents within the jurisdiction. Provide an evaluation form to observers that breaks down and grades key elements, such as safety procedures, skills, and effectiveness. Debrief immediately following the exercise, focusing on what went well and identifying any needed changes. Include the evaluation forms as part of the records documenting training and practice.

Evaluating regularly in this way can dramatically improve a developing team or fine tune highly accomplished teams.

3 Communications

Communications

Everything revolves around good communication. The need to use techniques and language that are easily recognized and understood is essential for operations where so much is at stake. When one of your own is hanging in harm's way, the last thing you want is delay or confusion caused by communication problems.

Organized Communications

There are a few communication rules you can follow to keep your rescue or practice event on track and flowing smoothly.

1. **Formal Briefing:** Huddle up for a formal briefing after sizing-up and locating the rescue subject.

2. **Assign Designators & Objectives:** Divide the labor at hand as described in the chapter 'Managing The Rescue Scene.'

3. **Minimize Chatter:** Demand "All Quiet" whenever a Rescue Climber is hanging dependent on the rope system.

4. **Follow Proper Communication Lines:** Demand that all tactical and safety personnel strictly adhere to proper communication lines as described in the chapter 'Managing The Rescue Scene.'

5. **Use One Set Of Commands & Signals:** Practice with a defined default vocabulary of clear, concise commands and hand and whistle signals.

6. **Parrot Commands:** Confirm that commands are correctly received by repeating them back to the sender.

7. **Develop Hand & Whistle Signals:** Practice using whistles and hand signals as a backup to communicate over long distances or in noisy conditions.

8. **Secondary Briefing:** Quickly verify all systems are a go before committing a Rescue Climber above ground.

Formal Briefing

When enough information has been gathered to formulate a plan, inform all involved through a formal briefing. This is a required step in many OSHA jurisdictions. Announce the chosen strategy and tactics. Make sure the Safety Officer signs off on the plan and adds his or her input to explain travel restrictions. Hopefully, the team is well practiced and the actual briefing goes much like a football huddle between plays. This is the best time for members to ask for any clarification.

Designators & Objectives

Assign each safety and tactical position a name and set of marching orders to set the plan in motion. A well-practiced team of people will understand their particular objectives once they've been assigned a designator. Teams with little practice will require detailed instructions for setting up, operating, and communicating. Skipping this important step will lead to overlapping effort, mistakes, and delays.

Minimize Chatter

Whenever someone is hanging his or her life on the line on a rope system, it's time to get deadly serious. Demand quiet on the worksite until all climbers are on level ground and off belay. When everything is rigged and safety checked, formally announce, "All quiet, commencing operations!"

Social interaction and chatter can be distracting and cause team members to miss or react more slowly to commands. It's easy for minds to wander and for personnel to get bored during periods of calm. Maintain discipline and limit conversation to commands as much as possible.

Follow Proper Communication Lines

It's usually easy for haul team and belay personnel to overhear radio or verbal communication between the climber and the leader. It may sometimes seem as if routing communications through the leader adds a needless layer of management. Nevertheless, lowering or raising communications must filter through whomever is assigned the responsibility for controlling the entire operation whenever it is possible. Because the climber is often out of view and unable to visualize the entire worksite, he or she may make requests that some topside team members are not ready to carry out. The same is true for topside team members unable to see the climber. With the leader controlling commands, messages are interpreted and translated in a manner that is best for the entire operation. It can be a challenge, and it may take practice for some people to resist reacting to commands and signals that are within earshot but not directed to them. However, safety and efficiency depend upon it.

NOTE: Any participant in the operation is permitted to command the team to STOP! If an issue like dangerous rigging, damaged equipment, members not ready, etc., presents itself, the operation must cease immediately to make any necessary corrections. In these cases, communication needs to shortcut directly to the leader and all team members at the same time. Whoever observed the problem has the responsibility to loudly and clearly command the team to STOP and then immediately describe the problem to the leader.

In some situations, like vertical, confined-space entries, additional tactical and safety positions are added for adequate safety and control. This sometimes puts the leader in a position that is less suited for relaying commands. In cases like these, the communication chain between the topside team and the climber is routed to the most appropriate position. In the case of confined space ops, that usually means the entry attendant.

Use One Set Of Commands

Practice a vocabulary that is concise and clear for operational commands. One-syllable words without the element of subjective interpretation are best. Example: "Up rope" compared to "Take up tension on the slack." Simple measurement terms can be added to control lowering or raising speed. Example: "Up rope–quarter speed" or "Down rope—full speed." Whatever words or phrases are chosen by the team, practice using them consistently during practice sessions.

The terms listed below have proven to work well in practice and emergency incidents. They work well for both radio and direct verbal communication. The meaning is clear for each, and they are short and to the point.

"Stop" Loud, clear command that directs the haul team and/or belay to stop motion and securely hold position.

"Stop & Lock Off" Command that directs the haul team or climber (not belay) to stop motion and tie the rope in a way that allows them to remove their hands from the system. Usually so haul team members or the climber can use their hands for other tasks.

"All Stop" Command tells the team that conditions are such that all operations can come to an end and that lowering or raising and belay systems can be set down.

"Up Rope" or "Up" Command that directs the haul team and/or belay to begin hauling in their respective ropes.

"Down Rope" or "Down" Command that directs the haul team and belay to begin letting out their respective ropes.

"Quarter-Speed" Such as "down quarter-speed." Directs haul team and belay to let out or haul in rope at about one-quarter the normal operating pace. This command is used in situations when the climber needs to maneuver over tricky sections like cornices, sharp edges, brush, etc.

"Half-Speed" Such as "up half-speed." Directs haul team and belay to let out or haul in rope at about one-half the normal operating pace. This command is often used to better enable the belay person to employ optimum form and keep up with the progress of the main line.

"On Belay" or "I'm On Belay" Loud, clear announcement by the climber that he or she has tied onto the belay rope and needs the belay system to go fully operational. This informs the belay person and the rest of the team of the need to go "hot" and operate the belay system to protect the life-load attached to it. The announcement should prompt a loud, clear response from the belay person.

"Belay On" or "Belay Is On" Loud, clear response from the belay person indicating that he or she has their hands on the belay system and that it is fully operational and ready to catch a life-load.

"Ready" or "Ready?" Announcement or inquiry confirming readiness. Example: Leader asks, "Belay ready?" Belay person replies, "Ready."

"Climbing" Loud, clear announcement and request to maneuver over the edge or to climb above ground. Announcement from the climber informs all team members, and at the same time requests permission from the leader to proceed.

"Climb On" Phrase used by the leader to grant permission to a climber to commit their center of gravity over the side.

"Two Block" Announcement from haul team members indicating that the pulley system has fully contracted and needs to be reset.

"Set Brake" or "Set The Brake" Command that directs whichever haul team member is closest to securely apply the main line brake.

"Brake Set" or "Brake Is Set" Loud, clear announcement confirming that the main line brake has been securely applied.

"Reset" Acknowledgement that the pulley system is fully contracted and that haul team members are taking steps to fully extend it.

"Slack" Usually used during lead climbing operations. Used by the rescue climber to inform the belay person of the need for less tightness on the belay rope. Typically, more slack is needed when the climber is lifting the belay rope up to clip it into a running anchor attachment.

"Rock" Loud, clear announcement that something is falling toward the climber or rescue subject.

"Falling" Loud, clear announcement from anybody who feels like they're about to fall or falling.

"Hot" Term meaning the rope system is supporting a life-load. For example, "We're ready to go hot."

Parrot Commands

Ensure message clarity and understanding with all team members by routinely echoing commands as they're given. If the leader gives the command "Up Rope," the haul team leader should acknowledge with something like "Up Rope" or "Copy Up Rope." This technique reinforces accuracy and keeps the machine running smoothly. It also benefits all team members by keeping them informed about what's going on while they keep their eyes on their own jobs.

Hand & Whistle Signals

Communication via whistle and hand signals works very well in environments with loud background noise. Rushing water, heavy traffic, construction noise, and weather can all make radio communication impractical. Signals are a good backup for portable radios. It only takes a dead battery or a dropped radio to completely kill communications. Simple whistle and hand signals are a good, low-tech solution.

Whistle & Hand Signals	
Stop	One whistle blast
Attention	Arm extended with fisted hand
Up	Two whistle blasts
Up Rope	Arm extended up with hand rotating
Down	Three whistle blasts
Down Rope	Arm extended down with hand rotating
OK	One hand tapping top of head
10-4	Grasp hands above head to form an "O"
Help	Three whistle blasts - Repeated
	One hand waving above head

Secondary Briefing

A short check to make sure all players are ready for off-the-ground operations is a must. In some OSHA jurisdictions, it's required. Much like covering the checklist of monitoring stations at mission control before lift off, making sure all rope system workers are ready before the climber commits his or her center of gravity over the edge is prudent. Once the safety officer has completely checked the rope systems and the leader has announced, "all quiet," it's time for a quick secondary briefing. Keep it brief and include the strategy.

Secondary Briefing Example	
Leader:	*"All quiet, prepare to go hot to lower the subject all the way to the bottom."*
Leader:	*"Climber ready?"*
Climber:	*"Ready" or "No"*
Leader:	*"Belay ready?"*
Belay:	*"Ready" or "No"*
Leader:	*"Haul team ready?"*
Haul Team	
Leader:	*"Ready" or "No"*
Leader:	*"Safety ready?"*
Safety:	*"Ready" or "No"*

Putting It All Together

Once things are underway, almost all communication can be carried out using the above list of terms and phrases. There are a few communication techniques that add even more clarity and help avoid some typical pitfalls associated with using rope systems.

Command Cadence: It can be beneficial to fill gaps between commands during operations. It's weird, but simply verbalizing "down" one time at the beginning of a long lowering operation sometimes leads to fluctuating speeds or even the occasional unwanted full stop. The same is true for long raises. This is hard to explain and probably just a human behavioral tendency. It's easy to keep things running smoothly by filling long breaks between commands. Calmly repeating the command that's appropriate to the moment keeps team members focused and working the tools as needed. Announcing "down" and then regularly repeating "down," "good down," "a little faster down," etc., keeps all members on track and instills that warm, fuzzy feeling when things are going along nicely without having to watch.

Stop Command Shyness: For some reason there seems to be a general reluctance to use the stop command. It may be that it feels rude to use the word for anything less than dire emergencies. You can quickly point out the seasoned veterans of any group because they've come to grips with how well the command works compared to common alternatives. It's very common to hear "hold on" or "hang on." Often, it comes out more like, "hold on...Hold On!... HOLD ON!...**STOP, STOP, STOP!"** Find a way to help the people on your team feel comfortable replacing "Hold On" with the stop command any time a pause is needed. It's brief; it's clear; and it makes evolutions go better.

"Hold On" or "Hang On" does not work well and frequently increases reaction time.

Haul Team Flow: There's also a tendency to "over-formalize" some communications and bog down the workflow. Example: During a raising operation the Haul Team has been given direction for "Up Rope." When the pulley system is fully contracted they announce, "Two Block," "Set Brake," "Brake Is Set," and then "Reset." This is all good, but once the pulley system has been fully extended, there is a tendency for the Haul Team to wait for a command from the Leader before continuing with the raising operation. This can make the overall operation choppy and slow. Once the Haul Team has been given their marching orders for "Up Rope," they can proceed with those orders between resets without direction from the Leader. It's still necessary to loudly and clearly announce all the actions associated with resetting the pulley system to keep all personnel informed about the situation. The Leader can pick up his or her command cadence between resets.

Backup Radios: If portable radios make good sense for the terrain you're working in, have a back up communication plan. Always plan for what happens if the Climber has radio failure. In addition to whistle, hand, and flashlight signals, rigging for radio failure is smart. Dropped radios and dead batteries are common. Use portables equipped with remote microphones and secure them using chest or fanny packs. If remote mics aren't an option, tether handhelds to the Climber's harness. Carry spare batteries. When possible, carry a backup radio. Civilian handhelds are inexpensive and very small, making them a great choice for a backup. Mobile phones can work well and can be used to relay pictures to topside workers.

4 Safe Practices

Safe Practices

There's no question about it.: above ground work using rope systems is dangerous. Operational integrity begins with an overall safety culture that develops from good planning and strict attention to safety details. Problem-free operations depend on a disciplined approach to safety management and compliance. Personnel using vertical rope systems must keep their heads in the game and understand that safety rules and efforts serve their own best interest. Operational safety increases with practice.

Default Safety Plan

There are some general safety premises that should be included in any vertical rescue operation. Use a default strategy that includes these elements to maximize worksite safety.

Personal Protective Equipment	All team members don PPE, including harnesses, at the start of any event.
Assign Safety Officer	Assign Safety Officer responsibilities to someone on scene for every event.
Complete A Safety Survey	Visualize the worksite to plan for safe operations.
Provide Fall/Drop Protections	Mark off dangerous areas; assemble travel-restraining leashes; and tie off equipment as needed.
Carry Out A Safety Briefing	Include safety plan information in the formal briefing.
Safety Check All Rigging	Certify all anchors, connections, and rigging configurations before committing a life-load above ground.
Belay Everything	Provide a redundant rope system to arrest accidental falls.
Use Safe Equipment	Use equipment that meets the specification standard your team has determined appropriate. Avoid using the gear that the rescue subject is connected to.
Prevent Shock & Abrasion	Systems should be engineered to minimize bouncing, heaving, and damage from friction.
Climbers Carry Etrier	Anyone working above ground must carry a means of transferring weight from their harness to their feet.
Staff & Equip A Backup Plan	Always develop and rig for an action plan to deal with an injured or disabled Climber.
No Rigging By Leader & Safety	Prohibit the Leader and Safety Officer from assembling rope systems.

Personal Protective Equipment

Just like responding to a fire, vertical rescue personnel should gear up and be ready to go to work before setting up the worksite. This includes donning harnesses and wearing them throughout the operation. This is the first step in addressing the top two priorities that protect personnel on the worksite. It also enables more flexibility in dealing with backup situations. When all personnel are wearing PPE and harnesses, assignments can be shifted and additional Climbers can be deployed for dealing with emergencies. With harnesses in place, personnel can easily clip into travel restraining leashes and enter exclusion zones.

At a minimum, each Team Member must have protection from injury and must be able to tie themselves or others off. Brimless or small-brimmed helmets are best for rock fall and perpendicular impact. Keep headlamps in place during daylight hours in case operations extend toward sundown. Headlamps are also good for working in shadows. Keep eye protection close at hand. Eyewear will prevent the loss of a worker caused by a twig or falling sand in the eyes. Flying splinters caused by hammering pickets into the ground is also a danger. Tether good, crisp sounding whistles onto harnesses for back up communications. Long sleeves and pants enable personnel to work more aggressively in uncomfortable, brushy, or abrasive conditions. Gloves are mandatory and must be well suited for the job. Thick, bulky, fire-protective gloves can be more of a hazard than a help. Snug, well-fitted, and supple gloves are more practical for rigging and tying knots. Fingerless gloves add dexterity necessary for rigging in tight quarters or awkward positions. Boots should strike a balance between low weight and sturdiness. Pick a boot or shoe that allows aggressive movement without sacrificing agility.

Every vertical rescue worker should carry a set of offset triple 8-millimeter prusik loops suitable for a 2-person brake. Carrying prusiks enables personnel to quickly tie off, relieve harness discomfort, ascend out of harm's way, trim rigging, or apply a shock-absorbing brake. The value of carrying these small, lightweight tools is beyond measure.

Assign Safety Officer

The responsibility of checking and monitoring for safety must be assigned to someone at the scene on every vertical rescue incident, vertical training, or practice event. Assigning these responsibilities is a requirement in many OSHA jurisdictions. Whenever possible, dedicate Safety as a stand-alone position. Avoid assigning safety checking and monitoring to someone as an additional set of responsibilities. Example: don't ask a Haul Team Staff Member to do safety surveys, safety checks, safety briefings, or safety watches. Assigning these responsibilities randomly as they need to be addressed should also be avoided. Pick the best person for the Safety position and dedicate him or her to it. The 7-person team approach described throughout this book includes one person dedicated to the Safety position with the responsibility of carrying out safety surveys, conducting safety briefings, completing safety checks, and monitoring operations for safety related problems.

The person assigned as Safety should not assemble any of the rigging. This creates the risk of getting too close to the work and developing the "Can't See The Forest For The Trees" phenomenon. The person assigned as Safety should have a high level of expertise and should be very familiar with the equipment cache and the methods used by the team. Safety should locate in a position that enables a view of the overall worksite and close access to each part of the rigging. If Safety cites a problem, corrections are best made via communication with the Leader. Safety should avoid handling the rigging as much as possible.

Minimum Personal Protective Gear

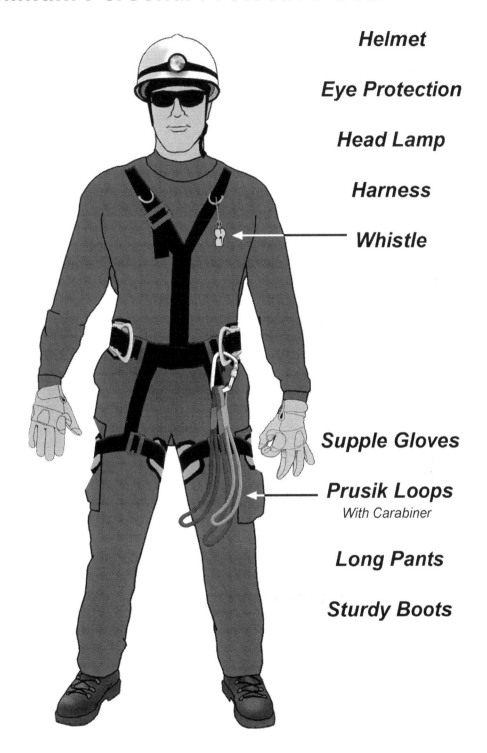

Helmet

Eye Protection

Head Lamp

Harness

Whistle

Supple Gloves

Prusik Loops
With Carabiner

Long Pants

Sturdy Boots

Safety Survey

Initial size-up efforts must always include surveying the scene for a worksite safety evaluation. This usually involves a physical inspection of the work area immediately after arriving on scene by the person assigned as Safety. Typically, Safety and the Leader move to the work area at the same time, while remaining team members gear up and begin moving equipment. Site inspection should generally evaluate the need for fall protection and travel restrictions. Additionally, environmental hazards created by weather conditions, animals, insects, plants, and terrain should be evaluated. Relay an assessment of these hazards in the formal briefing.

Fall & Drop Hazard Protection

Standing Orders for Fall Pro: All Vertical Rescue Team Members should understand and comply with standing safety orders to remain at least 6 feet from vertical edges unless they are connected to fall protections. Curiosity and the desire to unnecessarily hang out at the edge must be discouraged. Team members should increase safety by standing clear of "Drop Zones" where overhead climbers may dislodge rocks, drop hardware, or where rescue subjects may fall.

Travel-Restricting Leashes: Any downward vertical elevation change within the work area, like a cliff edge or hole, exceeding six feet should be considered dangerous. Fall protections such as barriers or "Exclusion Zones" delineated with flagging tape or other markers should be established to limit entry only to those connected to travel-restricting leashes. Assemble leashes so that personnel connected to them are unable to approach any fall hazard edge close enough to accidentally stumble off. When correctly assembled, leashes prevent falls from occurring and should need not to be engineered for impact forces. Anchors and rigging do not need to be as bomb proof as those used for vertical operations.

It can make good sense to leash objects carried into the exclusion zone. Setting up a large multi-pod or ladder near an edge can turn really bad if it gets fumbled and dropped over the side. Losing the equipment over the side is trouble enough, but this pales in comparison to harpooning the rescue subject. It's easy to connect a travel-restricting leash to large pieces of equipment until they're set up and securely in place within the exclusion zone.

TRAVEL RESTRAINT

RESTRICTS APPROACH DISTANCE TO PREVENT FALLS

6 FEET

EXCLUSION ZONE

Fall Arrest Lanyards: When working in tight areas where travel-restricting leashes are impractical and a misstep will result in falling over the edge, protections must be rigged to support impact forces and adequately absorb shock. Example: setting up a rescue system on a small catwalk with no hand railing. Anchor fall protection lanyards at an elevation slightly higher than where it connects to workers harnesses. Integrate adequate shock absorbing components into the rigging between the anchor attachment and the harness connection. Minimize slack in the lanyards. The dorsal connection ring located on the upper rear of the harness is best for fall arrest.

Shock-absorbing links and lanyards used to limit peak impact forces are highly engineered and must be used according to manufacturer directions.

Hazard Zones: Establish borders for areas where personnel are required to keep helmets or other forms or personal safety equipment securely in place. Any part of the work site where ropes are under tension, where overhead materials or equipment may fall from above, or where equipment can fall over the side should be identified as hazard zones. Hazard zones do not necessarily need to be flagged or marked as long as workers understand what areas require they have PPE on. Helmet straps should be securely fastened within hazard zones for effectiveness and to prevent falling helmets from injuring climbers below.

Drop Hazards: Cordon off areas with overhead loose materials such as rocks, soil, logs, ice, or equipment. Place barricades or mark the areas inside the worksite where these materials could fall. In some cases, it may be most practical to tie off or drop overhead loose materials before setting up the worksite. Describe travel precautions related to these hazards during the formal briefing. Block areas underneath precariously-perched, heavy training mannequins during practice sessions.

Basic Worksite Zoning

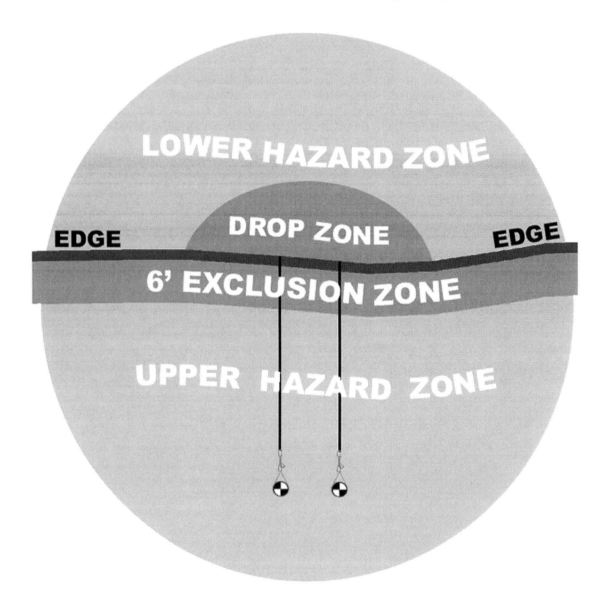

LOWER SAFE ZONE

LOWER HAZARD ZONE

DROP ZONE

EDGE

EDGE

6' EXCLUSION ZONE

UPPER HAZARD ZONE

UPPER SAFE ZONE

Safety Briefings

Relay information gathered during the Safety Survey to remaining team members as soon as possible. As workers enter the area, guide them toward safe travel routes and away from hazards.

The Leader and the person assigned to the Safety position should coordinate and agree on a safety plan. Deliver the safety plan information to all team members during the formal briefing. Reinforce standing safety orders, identify hazards and safe areas, and describe safety measures chosen for the operation during the Safety Briefing.

If the incident operation or practice session is already underway when additional participants arrive, these people must be briefed as well. Intercept new arrivals and make sure they're adequately informed. A written Safety Briefing for every event is also practical. Safety concerns related to vertical rescue events lend themselves to a simple form that's easy to fill out and review. It can be beneficial to create and distribute written Safety Plans in advance of training or practice events. Event Action Plans (for training) and Incident Action Plans (for real incidents) usually include sections for a General Safety Plan.

Safety Checks

Even the most accomplished rope technician is capable of rigging mistakes or oversights. It happens. Knots incorrectly tied, open connectors, hardware incorrectly threaded. It's the little things that can get you. There must be a systematic way of backing up the construction of systems to minimize human error.

Whether it's checking an elaborate high-line system over a raging river or making sure your descender has been threaded correctly, you want a fresh set of eyes looking at whatever has been assembled before risking a life above the ground. The 7-person team approach provides for a second opinion mechanism by dedicating a Safety Position to carry out Safety Checks.

Safety Checks are necessary any time equipment is rigged or altered for the purpose of supporting a human life. So, once the rope system of choice is assembled, it must be "certified" by Safety before the Climber moves his or her center of gravity over the edge or off the ground. The Safety Officer must certify alterations before the weight of the Climber is shifted to any alteration of the rope system as well. Example: when assembling and applying a brake on the main lowering line for the purpose of changing to a pulley system, the Safety Officer must check the brake before the weight of the Climber is transferred onto it. Once the brake has been deemed safe, the weight of the Climber can be loaded and the descent control device can be removed and replaced with a pulley system.

Systematic Approach: Safety Checks themselves should be systematic in nature. Using the same basic plan of attack each time will help ensure everything gets adequately checked. Prioritizing elements of vertical rescue systems will help the execution of safety checks. Prioritize belay systems, and check them first. Whatever method you use to complete a Safety Check, do it the same way every time.

Touch & Talk Method: Just as pilots touch control gauges with their fingers as they verbally go through pre-takeoff checklists, physically touch rope system components and verbalize observations as you inspect each of them. Grab and squeeze connectors to make sure they're closed. Describe findings out loud as you progress as if someone is listening. Pull tension on ropes and webbing to make sure they're secure and laid correctly. This "Touch & Talk" method encourages the inspector to crouch down for a closer look and compels a more continuous, beginning-to-end inspection. The vocal element aides clear thinking and enables other team members to confirm thoroughness. Be wary of people carrying out safety checks from a standing position with their hands in their pockets.

Safety Check Example

Prioritize Belay Systems: When checking a two-rope system, begin with the belay component first. When checking an individual, check his or her belay connection first.

Begin At The Anchor: Whether checking the belay system or the main line, start where the system connects to the earth. Make sure the anchor itself is a good choice and solid. Consider any degrading effects such as rust, rot, insect damage, etc. Make sure movable anchors, such as vehicles, are secured in their positions and lock-out-tag-out measures have been taken. Inspect any back up components like back-ties to make sure they're sound. Consider that many OSHA jurisdictions require a capacity of 5000 pounds for anchors used in vertical rope system work.

Anchor Connections: Next, make sure the materials and methods used for tying to the chosen anchor are appropriate. Check to make sure knots and/or connectors are secure and appropriate for the application. Make sure protections for abrasion and cutting are in place as needed. Ensure back-ties are integrated into anchor connections. Test any equalizing engineering to make sure it is working.

Rope System: Next, trace the path of the rope and rigging from the anchor connection all the way to where it connects to the Rescue Climber. Squeeze carabiners to see if they're closed, locked, and oriented properly. Look at and feel the knots and hitches. Check pulleys and other hardware to see if they're of the appropriate type and correctly placed. Look and feel for potential abrasions or tangle problems along the working path of the system, and check edge pro.

Directionals: Next, inspect any directionals used to alter the path of the rope system. Check anchoring and appropriateness of the components. Make sure high directionals are correctly assembled, suitably angled, and anchored for the job.

The Climber: Last, see if the Climber is well connected, and then do a head-to-toe check of his or her PPE, harness, and rigging. Ensure a capability of at least 2 forms of communication with topside operations and 2 sources of light.

Remote Safety Checks: In some cases, it will be impossible to do an independent, hands-on check. When climbers assemble or alter rigging while they're alone over the side or overhead, it will be necessary to conduct Safety Checks from a distance. This can be accomplished by verbally confirming each step of a normal Safety Check as the Climber manually carries it out. The Safety Officer verbally proceeds through each segment of a systematic check as the Climber touches, checks and verbally confirms each segment.

REMOTE SAFETY CHECK EXAMPLE	
SAFETY	**CLIMBER**
➡	*I've changed to my descender and need a Safety Check*
Copy. Let's do a remote check.	Copy.
Ropes clear above?	Rope are clear.
Belay knot good?	Knot is good.
Belay carabiner locked and oriented properly?	Biner is good.
Descender threaded properly?	Descender is good.
Descender carabiner locked and oriented properly?	Locked and oriented.
Ropes free below?	Ropes are free.
Safety Check Complete	

Partner Checks: As the team gears up, members can rely on each other to check PPE. Using a head-to-toe format, manually check each element of the PPE ensemble. Make sure helmet straps are in place, lights work, harness is on properly, and straps are tucked in. Verify that whistle, eye pro, and gloves are at hand.

At times, it may be practical for the Safety Officer to extend authority to other team members to carry out safety checks. Example: a Climber over the side has made rigging changes and needs a Safety Check before proceeding. The Safety Officer is topside and unable to conduct a close-up inspection of the changes. A second Climber is close by and in a position to do a hands-on Safety Check. The Safety Officer directs the second Climber to do the check. Carry out this Safety Check just as it would be done topside. Proceed systematically and use the "Touch & Talk" method.

Self-Checks: Occasionally, Climbers may find themselves alone and unable to get assistance with a safety check. Radio failure or overwhelming ambient noise may cut off communication with the team. Climbers must understand that they're in a red flag situation if communication is down and they have assembled or altered rigging after the last Safety Check. In cases like these, Climbers are forced to check their own work. Falling back to the routine use of systematic checks that proceed from the anchor to the Climber optimizes safety as much as possible in these less-than-desirable situations.

If a Climber is compelled to check his or her own work, it helps to mentally pause before starting a Self Safety Check. Remove hands from the rigging, and drop them to the side. Look away, and take a deep breath. Now, check the connections to the earth, and then work back all the way to the harness. As with a normal Safety Check, use the touch method and verbalize as you go. Proceed slowly and deliberately. Consider doing the check twice to bolster confidence.

Pre-tensioning: The final step of organized safety checking prior to suspending a Climber off the ground is to apply 'False Tension' on the fully assembled system. When Safety Checks and the Final Briefing are complete, direct the Climber to sit down on the main line until it is tight without maneuvering over the edge. Pre-tensioning in this way will usually expose operating problems in the rigging like twists or cross-loaded carabiners. It can also reveal weak anchor choices, poorly placed guy lines, or unstable high directionals. Pre-tensioning also serves to meter a safe pace and put everybody on the team at ease before going hot.

Belay Everything

'Belay' fundamentally means to provide rigging that will protect from an unwanted fall. In vertical rescue, a belay should work much like the self-adjusting seat restraints in your car. You wear restraints any time you're in a moving car, but they automatically adjust to allow enough freedom of movement to be comfortable and to operate the vehicle. They only react to restrain you when a sudden stop occurs. Same with a belay system. Belay rigging should allow freedom of movement, but must catch Climbers if there is a sudden loss in the main means of support.

Unless you're an arborist, you'll be hard pressed to find a professional standard or safety regulation that doesn't require work-at-height professionals to back up their main means of vertical support. Climbers must be connected by at least two

WARNING *Climbers Must Be Connected By At Least 2 Points*

points at all times. It's a very prudent premise for the rescue business. Rescue Climbers often find themselves working in environments that have already caused at least one casualty, but they must also direct their attention to another person and work hands free at a rescue pace. These factors quickly add up to a high-risk state. Every Rescue Climber must be belayed.

Vertical support is not always provided by ropes. There are rescue situations where firefighters can climb hand and foot on structures, such as towers, ladders, bridges, or light poles, as their main means of vertical support. In cases like these, a single rope system can be used to provide fall protection for Climbers that might lose their footing. However, they cannot lean back or otherwise rely on the belay for work-positioning support. A Climber maneuvering on a tower maintains one point of connection as long as he or she is balanced and standing upright. A second fall protection connection, such as a belay line or double lanyard, must be maintained at all times. This kind of belay can be tended by a team member or by the Climber, as would be the case if a double lanyard or fixed line is used. When the Climber leans back on the rigging, one point of connection (feet and hands) is compromised. In these situations, an additional connection, such as a flip line, must be established before leaning back.

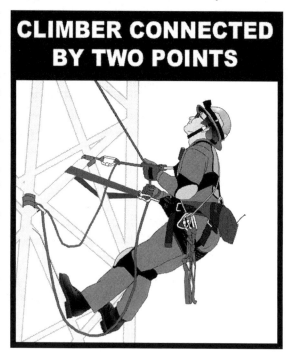

CLIMBER CONNECTED BY TWO POINTS

Belay Types: There are many ways to assemble belay systems, but they all fall into two general categories and several descriptive varieties. Belays are considered to be either

"Independent" or "Conditional," and their operation can be described as "Tended," "Self-tended," "Mechanical," or "Combination." Each has its own set of benefits and limitations. In some cases, various types of belays can combine to adequately protect the climber.

Independent Belays

Any belay system that is attached to its own anchor. In cases where the anchor is considered to be completely bomb proof, as with a large concrete freeway overpass pillar, the belay can use the main anchor and be considered independent as long as the attachment is separate from any other rigging.

Independent belays are the safest because of the built in redundancy. The downside is the need for additional equipment and appropriate anchors.

Conditional Belays

Any belay system that is not attached to its anchor separately from other rigging.

Example 1: Main line lowering and belay ropes using a common anchor attachment. Failure of the single anchor attachment would result in both the main line and belay systems failing.

Example 2: Belay device is attached to the main line and travels with the Climber.

Conditional belays are less safe because they lack redundancy. They use the main anchor and require less equipment to assemble.

Tended Belays

Any belay system that requires manipulation and is operated by anyone other than the Climber is considered a tended belay.

Tended belays are the system of choice because they free the Climber from having to operate his or her own backup. The downside is that they require additional staffing.

Self-Tended Belays

Any belay system that requires manipulation and must be operated by the Climber is a self-tended belay.

Self-tended belays can be a good choice when staffing is short, as when activating a backup plan to assist an injured Rescue Climber.

Mechanical Belays

Any belay system that adjusts automatically and is self-operating is considered mechanical.

Mechanical belays can be a good choice when staffing is short, when overhead anchors are available, or in confined space operations where access openings are limited.

Combination Belays

Rigging sometimes forces the combination of belay types in a way that requires tending from above and self-tending from below. Example: Some litter rigs connect to the belay via a gathering plate or ring with an extended tail down to the climber. Even though the belay is tended from above, the Climber must self-tend the slack on the belay between his or her connection and the gathering plate.

Belay Staffing: The belay position is not suitable for on the job training. The gravity of mishandling the belay system is far too great. Assign properly-trained personnel to the belay position. Proper training should include main line failure exercises that provide the opportunity for participants to arrest the fall of a full-weight mannequin. Never assign belay responsibilities to someone who has not demonstrated an ability to use the belay system of choice to catch falls.

Use Safe Equipment

Build a cache of equipment that is suitable for the work you do. Sticking to NFPA Standard 1983 is a good start. As teams work together over time, the equipment inventory tends to expand. Practice sessions shed light on solutions that are fine-tuned with additional cache components. Whatever equipment your team needs, keep it simple and stick to industry standards as much as possible.

Train and practice in a manner that enables your team to routinely use their own cache of equipment for any rescue situation. Using equipment found on the rescue scene can lead to problems. Recreational climbers, arborists, and rope access workers all look to lesser standards for their own equipment and rigging choices. In the case of an emergency operation, the equipment that may be in place when firefighters arrive has already fallen short of keeping the subject out of trouble. Civilian equipment on scene may look good, but may be poorly maintained or out of date.

It can be helpful to familiarize yourself with the equipment used by other professions. Knowing a little about what others use to work at height can aid in making good decisions about clipping onto a lineman's harness.

Prevent Shock and Abrasion

Hardware used for vertical rescue is engineered to strike a good balance between strength, compactness, and low weight. Software needs to be strong and highly flexible. Vertical rescue equipment is tough, but there are limitations. The human body is not well designed to tolerate impact and instant deceleration forces. Preventing shock loads and unwanted abrasion are an extremely important consideration when designing, assembling, and operating vertical rescue systems. Friction in the wrong place at the wrong time can cut ropes. Impact forces created by drops as short as a foot can blow out anchors, equipment, and spinal cords.

Shock: Rope and climbing systems must rule out or dampen shock. If a belay system is managed well, it will catch the Climber before he or she falls far enough to develop harmful impact force. If a firefighter using a fall arrest lanyard stumbles off of a catwalk, the shock-absorbing component will unfold and dampen the impact force he or she experiences. The amount of shock or impact force an anchor or human body experiences at the end of a rope can be reduced either by shortening the potential fall or by lengthening deceleration.

Belay Slack: A poorly-tended belay line with excessive sag can allow a climber to fall and accelerate long enough to develop substantial impact forces. It doesn't take much of a drop to get hurt or pop out some anchors. Everyone has accidentally stepped off of a curb stiff-legged and experienced the surprising abrupt impact at the bottom. Every inch of drop accelerates toward a bad ending.

Force = Mass x Acceleration

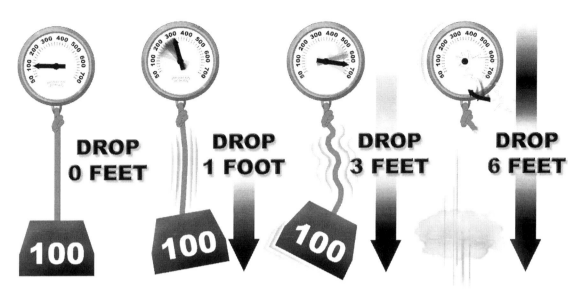

If the main means of climbing support fails, a properly tensioned belay system should take over. It should support the load before the load is allowed to fall, no more than a foot. Belay systems should not share the load during normal operations. Keeping belay slack to a minimum greatly reduces the potential impact force when things go wrong. Shock absorbers probably won't even deploy if fall-arrest lanyards are anchored high to minimize slack.

High Directionals: Avoid rigging belay ropes with high directionals like tripods, ladders, multipods, gin poles, etc. Failure of rigging that runs the belay rope above the edge will contribute to a significant fall and impact. Whenever possible, place abrasion protection, and run belay ropes over the edge at ground level.

Smooth Operation: Build rope systems that can be easily operated by the crew you have available. Pulley systems that require coordinated, rhythmic waves of pulling force to move the load can lead to bouncing on the anchor. Inexperienced workers may keep too much friction on descent control devices in a way that compels them to push rope through and cause bouncing as well. Bouncing is bad. Take another look at your system if the Haul Team sounds like a rowing crew or a chain gang. *One, two, three, PULL...one, two, three, PULL.* This is a very solid clue that your system requires more mechanical advantage to smooth out its operation. Practice has shown that hauling systems with 5:1 or greater mechanical advantage work well for 3-person haul teams. Hoisting a 2-person load with less mechanical advantage usually results in a heave-ho effort and bouncing. Adjust friction on lowering devices to reduce choppy rope release. The appropriate mechanical advantage and silky operation of lowering devices also improves belay performance. It can be very difficult for Belay to keep up and manage slack when the main line moves erratically.

Rope Grabs: Consider accidental shock loads when assembling rope systems. Imagine a 500 lb. dirt clod breaking off and falling into your litter. The equipment in your cache is very, very strong, but you can't rely on minimum breaking strength capacity alone. Putting the wrong component in the wrong place for the wrong reason can intensify and concentrate forces in a bad way. This can result in cut rope or anchor failure. Think about that big dirt clod when deciding what kind of brake is best for the main line and belay line in your operation. Both have the potential to catch the accidental heavy load. They can either stop the drop instantly by clinching hard on the rope, or they can more gradually apply

friction and slowly bring the load to a stop. Components like mechanical ascenders that use toothed or crushing cams to grip the rope will focus the impact force they bear onto a very small part of the rope. These kinds of devices tend to severely damage the rope they're attached to when a shock load occurs. Do not use mechanical ascenders for brakes. Some hardware devices are engineered to disperse shock force by allowing the rope to slip before catching. Prusik brakes using appropriate cord do the same. Prusiks are easy to use and work very well for main line and belay brakes.

Load Releasing Hitches: One means to add shock-absorbing capability to a rope system is to integrate a load-releasing hitch (LRH) between the anchor and the load. LRHs can add flexibility and enable rigging changes under a full load. Most of the time you'll find LRHs connected to prusik brakes in anticipation of locked-up knots, as can happen following an accidental shock load. LRHs can make knot passing easier and can be a safe option for dislodging jammed up rigging. Some LRH forms also add a degree of shock dampening.

California US&R Teams have tested and successfully used commercial and improvised versions of the Mariner's LRH for many years. Rope systems used by US&R Teams are built very simply. Clipping in a Mariner's Hitch adds options and increases shock safety.

Abrasion: Whenever software makes surface contact with anything else, the potential for damage must be evaluated. In most cases, that assessment has been considered ahead of time. In other words, you don't have to get the microscope out to do an inspection every time you clip a loop onto a carabiner. You already know that the cache is checked regularly and that the biner has a low abrasion risk. But whenever software runs over an edge, rubs on itself, connects to an anchor, etc., risk of abrasion and cutting damage must be eliminated. Nylon and polyester software are not very resistant to abrasion and heat. Rope and webbing under tension will cut surprisingly quickly when subject to lateral abrasion.

Edge Protections: Though protection of the edge is often a consideration, "edge protection" usually refers to measures used for dealing with preventing damage to the rope caused by running over an abrasive or sharp edge. Think of it more as rope protection. Whenever rope or webbing is extended over a lip, wall, edge, etc., some kind of protective barrier or space must be fashioned to protect the software. The most basic means of accomplishing this is to position a heavy form of sheeting made from compatible material on the edge. Heavy canvas tarps folded several layers thick work very well in this kind of application. Commercial rollers and gutters are also available and work great. These kinds of protections also preserve whatever material the edge is made of and can reduce rock fall.

Check out some of the rope wraps and jackets used in industry for abrasion prevention. Many can easily be carried by the Climber for over-the-side hot spots. Commercially supplied anchor attachments come in a wide variety of styles, and many have integrated edge protection or are weaved in a way that reduces cut failure.

Another means of protecting software is to lift the rope or web away from an edge or surface. Routing a rope through a directional and away from an edge or around an obstacle can be a very simple and effective solution for eliminating the chance of abrasion damage. In general, rigging systems up off the ground makes them more ergonomically favorable and less prone to abrasion problems.

Fixed Lines: Ropes or webbing rigged as a stationary part of any load-bearing system are especially prone to abrasion hazards. A loaded stationary line that is in contact with an abrasive or sharp surface needs very little vibration or movement to sustain serious damage. This problem is related to many rappelling accidents. Fixed ropes used for self-tended belays can also lead to serious abrasion dangers. Make sure any abrasion on these lines is eliminated. Abrasion hot spots on any software is bad, but when a rope moves over an edge, as with a lowering line, it can distribute friction damage and heat along its length. A stationary rope, such as a rappel line, concentrates abrasion and heat and accumulates the damage at a single point.

Simple pulley systems with mechanical advantage that calculate to even numbers will have a section of rope that remains stationary. Be on high alert whenever your rigging has a stationary leg. Example: a pulley system with 4:1 mechanical advantage that is used to move a Climber in and out of a manhole will have a stationary leg that can rub on the edge. Pulley systems with mechanical advantage that calculate to odd numbers do not have a stationary leg.

Nylon Chainsaws: Think of how a chainsaw works: a flexible, abrasive linear medium that continuously rubs against a stationary object. The chain concentrates friction onto a small area of the wood resulting in the rapid removal of material to produce a cut. Any firefighter who has changed a chain at the scene of a fire knows that this friction also produces serious heat. Now, think about a length of rope running against a stationary object like another piece of software or your skin. The same principles that make a chainsaw work so well also make running ropes a cutting and burning hazard. Nylon and polyester melt at very low temperatures, compounding these hazards. Pay close attention to the ropes that move in your system. Lowering and raising lines can quickly cut deeply into soil cliff edges or wooden windowsills. Rope slipping through unprotected hands will quickly burn and cut skin, causing the handler to let go. A speedy rappel on a long run-out with the rope rubbing against a strap on your harness is bad juju.

Understand that a rope running over soft material is a hazard. Engineer systems to work normally without nylon chainsaw problems. Wear gloves when handling ropes with a life-load on them. Maintain adequate space between running elements, and place friction reducing protections where needed. Anticipate rigging failures that might result in intense friction on software.

Climbers Carry Etrier

Whenever someone goes over the side or climbs up off the ground, they should be able to make rigging adjustments to rescue themselves. When it hits the fan, and topside operations are delayed with problem solving, rigging adjustments or maneuvers to get out of harm's way must be an option for the Climber. Soft tissue injuries and pathology related to blood and lymph circulation can result from being suspended in a harness for long periods of time. Harness Induced Pathology (HIP), as it is sometimes called, can occur when extremities are constricted while hanging dependent and immobile. To prevent HIP, and to routinely relieve harness discomfort, a Climber must be able to transfer his or her weight from the harness to his or her feet at will. This can be accomplished with a rope grab that enables the climber to attach an etrier or foot loop to the rigging.

Fancy sewn etriers are available, but all that's needed is a loop of cord that can be hitched to a rope with a prusik. Simply resting a foot on a stirrup fashioned with a prusik loop can increase comfort tremendously. Improvising a foothold can also assist with difficult work positioning or can increase reach. With the right combination of loop lengths, a few prusik or purcell loops can provide the means to safely ascend or descend a system with jammed up ropes.

Staff and Equip a Backup Plan

Every operational plan should be developed at least two layers deep. Plan A should always include plan B. Anticipate who needs to go where, and how they're going to get there if deploying a second Climber becomes necessary. Set up the equipment needed to safely deploy a Backup Climber while assembling the main system. Don't wait for something to go wrong to rig for a backup. Preplanning operational positions and attaching backup rigging to anchors ahead of time make it easy to deploy a Backup Climber when the Rescue Climber gets conked on the head with a softball sized dirt clod.

Staffing: Shifting someone from the Haul Team is probably the easiest way to staff the Backup Climber position. Using a Haul Team Member has the least impact on the operation. Using the right tactics, the shortfall on the Haul Team can usually be overcome easily with the addition of mechanical advantage when using a haul system.

Tactics: For over the side operations, deploying a Backup Climber on a rappel line that uses a self-tended belay that is attached to either the established belay or the main line can work well. Climber 2 obviously must possess all minimum over-the-side skills.

For overhead lead climbing operations, it may be necessary to use a different belay means when deploying a single Backup Climber. Double lanyards can enable the Backup Climber to independently protect him or herself while climbing up.

Rapid Intervention Strategy: A good default strategy is to continue with the access tactic already underway. Example: the operation was in lowering mode at the time of the emergency. The default emergency strategy would be to access the Rescue Climber and continue lowering to the bottom.

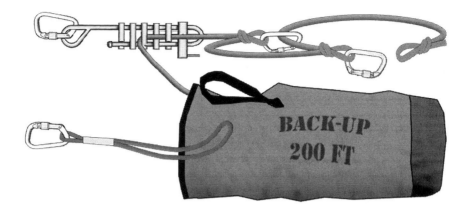

No Rigging by Leader or Safety

Safety positions must remove themselves from rigging any part of the rope system. The Leader and Safety positions have responsibilities that conflict with working closely with the equipment.

Safety is tasked with evaluating and checking the rigging. Anyone participating in the assembly of the system will be less able to evaluate the rigging from an objective perspective. When problems are found and adjustments are needed, Safety can direct rigging changes via communication with the Leader.

When the Leader helps set up rigging, his or her attention is focused too narrowly for the job they hold. The Team needs someone with a broad perspective to keep all parts of the operation coordinated and moving safely. The Leader must maintain a "big picture" perspective. Working on the rigging hampers the ability to monitor the entire worksite. The Leader should be able to verbally communicate rigging instructions to other team members.

Expertise shortfalls that occur when staffing is thin may force companies to compromise on this safety guideline. Whenever this condition arises, try to minimize "contaminating" whoever is responsible for safety checks and monitoring as much as possible. Regard this situation as a red flag condition and proceed very carefully.

Additional Safe Practices

Falling Rocks: Falling rocks are a fact of life in the vertical rescue world. Personal protective equipment can only do so much. A softball-size dirt clod zinging down and striking a climber can do real damage. Vigilant attention and reaction to the hazard of falling materials can be a matter

LEAN IN TO AVOID FALLING ROCKS

ROCK

of life and death. All personnel on the site bear responsibility to alert everyone when they see

dangerous materials dislodge and fall. Loudly call out "Rock!" to warn others of the hazard. Announce it loudly and sharply enough to get the attention of the entire group. Do the same for any falling material: soil, equipment, logs, ice chests, etc. Use the term "rock" for these hazards as well. No further explanation is needed when notifying others of the hazard. People get it when you use the term "rock."

The best warning system only works if people react appropriately to it. Team members need to know what measures to take when they hear "Rock!" Anyone working on a cliff face, or any area below suspended materials, should take a look and become familiar with the landscape above them as they set up and go to work. This tiny amount of personal preplanning can go a long way toward preventing a really bad headache. It may influence where you decide to stand, anchor, etc. It can also help you react effectively by moving toward safety when someone shouts "Rock!" Some simple personal practices can minimize or prevent injury if a rock is falling in your direction.

- Don't look up. Looking up takes your helmet out of play and exposes your face to impact.
- Lean in to the cliff face. Press your face against the cliff, and act like wallpaper. Generally, falling materials tend to arch away from the cliff face.
- Listen. You can get a feel for whether the materials are still on the way or if they have passed you. Listening may also let you know if the material is directly overhead or on one side. Teammates may announce an all clear before standing down.
- Give it time. Hold your water. Pause long enough for that silently flying flake to whiz by.

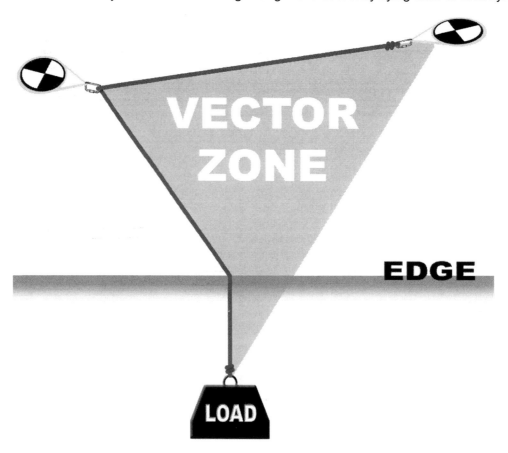

Recognize and Avoid Vector Zones: As ropes are extended and angled to assemble rescue systems, vector zones develop. A vector zone is an area of potential hazard that may suddenly strike if an anchor that supports a directional fails. Any redirect that pulls a loaded rope out of line builds kinetic energy in the rope. If the redirect suddenly fails, that energy is released to explosively return the rope to its natural orientation. The sharper the angle, the higher the energy. Think of pulling back on a bowstring. Anything inside the triangle created by the anchor, the directional, and the load will be in harm's way if the directional fails. Vector zones exist wherever directionals are in play. Horizontal vectors have the potential to sweep people and equipment over the edge. Vertical vectors have the potential to mousetrap and injure workers. A low-energy variation of this hazard can occur when an unloaded rope falls over the edge. A length of rope that is laid out can drag equipment and possibly even people over the side if it falls over. Example: a heavy 600-foot bag of rope that has part of its length laid out drags the entire cache container off of the catwalk when the bag is accidentally kicked over.

Vector zones deserve your respect. Avoid spending time in vectors, and position equipment caches uphill of rope systems whenever possible.

Ladder Trucks: Aerial Ladders can be a convenient means of positioning a directional above difficult access problems. However, using aerial ladders for high directionals must be undertaken with extreme caution and an expert understanding of the apparatus limitations. Generally speaking, routing raising or lowering systems through a directional attached to the tip of a fully extended aerial is very dangerous. Tip capacity usually ranges around 600 to 900 pounds. Directional pulleys can compound load forces wherever they are attached. Depending on the angle at the directional pulley, a two-person load on a raising/lowering system rigged to the ladder tip can almost double to 1200 pounds. The ladder may still hold, but you're really pressing your luck and betting that bouncing or an accidental shock load doesn't occur. If aerials are used for directionals, keep the ladder extension as short as possible and connect to suitable structural elements. When purchasing ladder trucks, specify anchor attachments that are positioned appropriately for directionals.

Aerials used for directionals should never be moved, and they require lock-out, tag-out measures. The risks involved in maneuvering ladders that have raising or lowering systems routed to directionals at the tip are extreme. Tip loads can be easily exceeded. Ropes and connectors can be stretched and snapped.

Static line and short haul operations can be more safely employed to move loads much as a crane would. Anchor short static lines directly to the tip and move the load using the ladder controls. Keep the ladder extension as short as possible for the situation. Tag lines attached to the load can be used to control spinning or reduce contact with a vertical face. Maneuver slowly to avoid bouncing and shock.

5 Scene Management

Rescue Scene Management

There's a lot to set up for a vertical rescue incident. Getting people to play from the same sheet of music, to quickly assemble and operate relatively complicated rope systems for the purpose of carrying team members safely over the side, can be a tall order. A little organizing before you get started and a clear understanding of priorities go a long way to making things run smoothly and professionally.

There probably isn't a firefighter alive that hasn't observed the dynamics of a disorganized group, either during training sessions or on real incidents. Often, the mission is self-evident. But if the rescue operation begins without dividing the labor, establishing a common plan of action, and using a good system of communication, a shotgun approach ensues. In this kind of situation, firefighters feel comfortable working shoulder-to-shoulder taking on tasks one at a time in a linear fashion as a group. It may be warm and fuzzy, but it is an extremely slow way to get things set up and working. Most likely, the mission will be successfully accomplished, but in a much slower and sloppier manner.

With a little planning and regular practice, a small team of firefighters can carry out just about any vertical rescue operation quickly, efficiently, and safely. A 7-person team of well-prepared firefighters can safely divide the workload of a vertical incident. Six tactical and safety positions make up the core of the Vertical Rescue Group. This core force can quickly organize, gear up, and begin the actual rescue before support resources such as back-up teams, recon observers, and medical transport arrive. If the group is well practiced in using these six tactical and safety positions, things will almost certainly go well.

Priorities

Priorities associated with vertical rescue incidents are virtually the same as they are for fire incidents. Just as with a burning house, firefighters need to take care of themselves and their co-workers while preventing further damage. When it comes to choosing who is taken care of first on a vertical rescue incident, use the following algorithm:

> **Priority 1 = SELF**
>
> **Priority 2 = TEAM**
>
> **Priority 3 = BYSTANDERS**
>
> **Priority 4 = RESCUE SUBJECT**

Priority 1

It may sound selfish, but self-preservation should be every team member's highest priority. When team members keep their heads in the game, use personal protective equipment, follow safety rules, and stay well practiced, they've done a lot to protect themselves from harm. A team member who takes safety and self-preservation seriously doesn't have to be closely watched by the team.

Priority 2

When individual members are geared up and trained to be safe, they can begin focusing on the safety of the team. In the event of a site safety incident, such as a rockslide, members should come to the aid of teammates once they themselves are out of harm's way. Disciplined communication and safety rules keep all members as safe as possible. Safety checks on systems before applying life-loads are a must and keep the entire group safe. It's easy to fudge on safety checks when a team feels pressure to get over the side to save someone clinging by their fingernails. A well-coordinated and practiced team can carry out all the safety procedures needed to prevent problems without causing time delays.

Priority 3

Unfortunately, everybody wants to watch. And everybody wants the best seat in the house. It doesn't take long to get a large crowd of people hanging out near the worksite trying to gawk over the edge. Most are passive, but some may be critical or try to take action on their own. Civilian bystanders can increase the risk of rock fall. The worst case is the possibility of compounding your rescue problem if a bystander falls over the side. Take steps to control bystanders as soon as possible, even before arriving. Mobilize law enforcement, set out caution tape, and have safety personnel monitor bystanders.

Priority 4

When we're set up to prevent further harm by attention to priorities one, two, and three, it's time to get to the Rescue Subject. Do whatever is possible to communicate with the person in trouble. Provide instructions and encouragement while the team sets up. If appropriate, lower a helmet, water, food, or clothing.

Core Rescue Team   *Tactical & Safety Positions*

Leader   **WARNING: Leader Does Not Assist With Assembly Of Rope Systems**

- The Vertical Rescue Group Leader should possess a high level of expertise and be very familiar with the cache and the methods routinely practiced by the team.
- Sizes up and pinpoints the fall line (the exact vector the main line must follow to carry out the operation).
- Assigns remaining tactical and safety positions to team members.
- Determines operational strategy and chooses tactics.
- Determines the back-up plan of action.
- Determines communication plan.
- Carries out initial briefing to set plans in motion.

- Carries out secondary briefing just prior to deployment of Rescue Climber.
- Directs the operation of the rope systems to meet the needs of the Rescue Climber.

Communicates Directly With: Overhead Staff, Rescue Climber, Safety Officer, Belay Person, Haul Team Leader, Backup Team Leader, Recon

If the Company Officer is not well qualified as a rope systems practitioner, it may make good sense to assign the Rescue Group Leader position to a more suitable member. The Leader should exercise a strong command presence and clearly assign identifiers (designators) and tactical objectives to team members early in the incident. This will divide the labor and set things in motion. Many OSHA jurisdictions require two briefings. If the team is well practiced, it may simply be a matter of announcing, "The usual set-up." It is important that the Leader closely supervises and maintains communication discipline. It should be considered a safety hazard if the Leader physically assists in assembling the rope systems.

Safety Officer

WARNING: Safety Officer Does Not Assist With Assembly Of Rope Systems

- The Safety Officer must possess a high level of expertise and should be very familiar with the cache and methods routinely practiced by the team.
- Performs the initial scene safety survey and recon.
- Establishes operational "Exclusion Zones" limiting entry to personnel wearing fall protection leashes only.
- Constructs travel-restricting leashes to prevent accidental falls over the working edge.
- Places fire line tape, flagging, barricades, etc. to restrict unauthorized access.
- Carries out safety briefing (part of the initial briefing).
- Carries out safety checks on systems before they are used to support any life-load.
- Monitors the scene and operation for safety issues and provides corrective direction via communication with the Leader.
- Is the final authority for clearance to place life-load on rope systems.

Communicates Directly With: Leader, Overhead Staff

At the direction of the Leader, the Safety Officer should be part of the initial survey of the work scene and development of a site safety plan. The Safety Officer provides protections as soon as possible. Work site hazards and safety rules, such as the use of fall restricting leashes and other protective measures, should be included in the initial briefing. The Safety Officer monitors the operation on the work site and provides corrective direction via communication with the Leader. All rope systems must be thoroughly checked by the Safety Officer before a life-load is applied. For this reason, it should be considered a safety hazard if the Safety Officer physically assists in assembling the rope systems.

Haul Team Leader

- Haul Team Leader must possess an operational level of expertise and should be very familiar with the cache and methods routinely practiced by the team.
- Organizes and selects the location of the forward cache of equipment.
- Chooses or assembles anchors to be used for the main lowering/raising system.
- Assembles the main line lowering/raising system with the assistance of Haul Team Staff.
- Assembles any portable anchors needed with the assistance of Haul Team Staff.
- Operates the main line lowering/raising system with the assistance of Haul Team Staff.

Communicates Directly With: Leader, Haul Team Staff

The Haul Team Leader directs the Haul Team Staff and is the point of communication with the Leader. The Haul Team Leader and Staff assemble the main line lowering/raising system on the fall line after briefings from the Rescue Group Leader and Safety Officer. Lowering or raising the system is coordinated via communication between the Leader and the Haul Team Leader only.

Haul Team Staff (*2 People*)

- Haul Team Staff members must possess an operational level of expertise
- Organizes the forward cache of equipment as directed by Haul Team Leader.
- Assembles anchors to be used for the main lowering/raising system as directed by the Haul Team Leader.
- Assembles the main line lowering/raising system as directed by the Haul Team Leader.
- Assembles portable anchors as directed by the Haul Team Leader.
- Operates the main line lowering/raising system as directed by the Haul Team Leader.

Communicates Directly With: Haul Team Leader, Haul Team Staff

Haul Team Staff members manage the equipment cache and assemble and operate the main line lowering/raising system as directed by the Haul Team Leader. Personnel with basic expertise can safely function as Haul Team Staff when closely supervised by the Haul Team Leader.

Belay Operator ▐ WARNING: Must have previously demonstrated proficiency

- The Belay Operator must possess an operational level of expertise.
- Must have previously demonstrated an ability to correctly operate the chosen belay system to catch a fall.
- Selects or assembles belay anchors.
- Assembles belay system.
- Operates the belay system in coordination with the main line lowering/raising system.

Communicates Directly With: Leader

The Belay Operator assembles and operates the belay system. Personnel who have successfully operated belay systems to catch full-weight falls in training situations are qualified to occupy the Belay Operator position. Never assign the Belay Operator position to a person that has never practiced catching full-weight falls.

Rescue Climber

WARNING: Must have previously practiced in this position

- The Rescue Climber must possess an operational level of expertise.
- Must be able to rig him or herself and climb to safety independent of the Rescue Group.
- Assembles and attaches equipment needed over the side.
- Connects him or herself to the main and belay lines.
- Directs the raising or lowering of the main line via communication with the Leader.
- Operates equipment and rigging to capture and secure the rescue subject.

Communicates Directly With: Leader

The Rescue Climber assembles and connects rigging such as litters and pick-off appliances to the main and belay lines. The Climber captures and secures the subject for relocation. Personnel who have successfully descended or climbed to capture and secure rescue subjects in training conditions are qualified for the Rescue Climber position. Never assign the Climber position to a person without this kind of experience. The Climber must have the skills and equipment to independently climb out of harm's way if the lowering/raising system fails or jams.

Work Flow: To better understand how a 7-person team can efficiently set up and deploy for a vertical rescue, the following breakdown of a simple litter recovery identifies how members communicate and go to work.

Leader	Safety	Haul Team	Belay	Climber
The rescue team is mobilized to assist an Engine Company on the scene of a subject over the side at a vertical cliff hazard within the jurisdiction.	The rescue team is mobilized to assist an Engine Company on the scene of a subject over the side at a vertical cliff hazard within the jurisdiction.	The rescue team is mobilized to assist an Engine Company on the scene of a subject over the side at a vertical cliff hazard within the jurisdiction.	The rescue team is mobilized to assist an Engine Company on the scene of a subject over the side at a vertical cliff hazard within the jurisdiction.	The rescue team is mobilized to assist an Engine Company on the scene of a subject over the side at a vertical cliff hazard within the jurisdiction.
Information is gathered en route. Tactical and safety positions are assigned. Ideally, the Rescue Team has practiced many times at this hazard location. If this is the case, assigning positions may simply be a matter of announcing "the standard operation."	Receives instructions from Leader.	Receives instructions from Leader.	Receives instructions from Leader.	Receives instructions from Leader.
Rescue Team arrives.	Rescue Team arrives.	Rescue Team arrives.	Rescue Team arrives.	Rescue Team arrives.
Moves to the work area along with the Company Officer already on scene. Carry radios, binoculars, fire line tape, and travel-restricting leashes to the work area. Add thermal imagers and portable lights if after daylight.	Moves to the work area along with the Company Officer already on scene. Carry radios, binoculars, fire line tape, and travel-restricting leashes to the work area. Add thermal imagers and portable lights if after daylight.	Dons personal gear and begin moving equipment to the work area.	Dons personal gear and begin moving equipment to the work area.	Dons personal gear and begin moving equipment to the work area.

Leader	Safety	Haul Team	Belay	Climber
Surveys the scene with the first-in Officer. The rescue subject is positively located either visually or by sound. If not positively located, take steps to deploy available personnel on scene or incoming units to locations with a better vantage point. Whenever possible, the subject must be located prior to setting up the scene.	Surveys the scene with the first-in Officer. The rescue subject is positively located either visually or by sound. If not positively located, take steps to deploy available personnel on scene or incoming units to locations with a better vantage point. Whenever possible, the subject must be located prior to setting up the scene.	Continues moving equipment to work area.	Continues moving equipment to work area.	Continues moving equipment to work area.
Once the subject is located, the Leader marks the fall line or point at the edge where the main line must go over. Fire line tape is good for this purpose. Mobilize any additional resources that may be needed, such as backup teams, law enforcement, medical transport, boats, helicopters, PIO, overhead management, etc.	Now that the work area has been identified, Safety provides fall protections by marking off the exclusion zone that requires the use of travel-restricting leashes to enter. Safety then assembles at least two travel-restricting leashes.	Continues moving equipment to work area.	Continues moving equipment to work area.	Continues moving equipment to work area.
Leader informs the Haul Team Leader about the fall line.	Continues placing fall protections.	Haul team leader begins providing directions for where cache of equipment should be dropped.	Continues moving equipment to work area.	Continues moving equipment to work area.
Leader and Safety quickly coordinate and assemble the group for the initial briefing. Non-rescue team members can continue to carry equipment to the work area if needed.	Leader and Safety quickly coordinate and assemble the group for the initial briefing. Non-rescue team members can continue to carry equipment to the work area if needed.	Assembles for the initial briefing. Non-rescue team members can continue to carry equipment to the work area if needed.	Assembles for the initial briefing. Non-rescue team members can continue carrying equipment to the work area if needed.	Assembles for the initial briefing. Non-rescue team members can continue carrying equipment to the work area if needed.
Leader announces the strategy and tactics to lower a litter and Climber over the side to capture and secure the subject and then continue lowering to the bottom where a boat company will transport to safety.	Safety identifies the exclusion zone and reinforces the requirement to use fall protections. Safety points out scene hazards and identifies minimum protective equipment to be used.	Receives instructions from Leader and Safety.	Receives instructions from Leader and Safety.	Receives instructions from Leader and Safety.

Leader	Safety	Haul Team	Belay	Climber
The Leader establishes the means of communication and lays out the back-up plan should something happen to the Climber or the system.				
Takes position in a safe location that allows a view over the edge and communication with the topside team.	Takes position in a safe location that allows a view of overall scene and the edge.	Haul Team Leader directs staff members to lay out the equipment cache in a suitable location. Haul Team Leader chooses the main line anchor and directs a Haul Team Staff member to attach a lowering system. Haul Team may need to assemble the needed anchor. Haul Team Leader and a staff member don travel-restricting leashes and set up the high directional and edge protections within the exclusion zone.	Belay Person chooses anchor and attaches belay system. Belay person may need to assemble the belay anchor.	Climber prepares litter and rigging.
Confirms the main line and belay systems are assembled and ready.	Completes safety checks on main line, high directional and belay systems. Safety checks Climber when connected.	Confirms ready. Stands-by for direction from Leader.	Confirms ready. Stands-by for direction from Leader Vocalizes, "Belay is on," once climber is connected.	Connects to belay line in preparation to enter the exclusion zone. Vocalizes, "On belay," after connecting. Inside the exclusion zone, connects to main line and litter system.
Confirms the main line and belay lines are safety checked.	Announces that the set-up and Climber are safety checked.	Confirms ready. Stands-by for direction from Leader.	Confirms ready. Stands-by for direction from Leader.	Confirms ready. Stands-by for direction from Leader.

Vertical Academy

Leader	Safety	Haul Team	Belay	Climber
Carries out secondary briefing. Quick confirmation that everyone understands the operation and all positions are ready.	Confirms ready.	Confirms ready.	Confirms ready.	Confirms ready.
Directs Climber to put weight on the system without going over the edge.	Observes.	Holds tension. Makes adjustments.	Operates belay.	Hangs full weight on the main line to test the system.
Determines that system is good.	Observes.	Stands-by for direction from Leader.	Operates belay.	Stands-by for direction from Leader.
Leader announces: "Down quarter-speed."	Observes.	Repeats: "Down quarter-speed." Operates lowering system.	Operates belay.	Keeps tension on main line. Maneuvers over the edge.
Leader continues vocalizing commands to keep the main line moving at a speed suitable to the climber.	Observes.	Operates lowering system.	Operates belay.	Maneuvers down to a position ten feet above and to the side of the subject. Minimizes rock fall.
Receives direction from Climber to stop. Directs Haul Team to stop.	Observes.	Repeats: "Stop." Stops lowering and holds position.	Operates belay.	Directs Leader to stop the main line when in position above subject. Sizes up the situation. Climber repositions him or herself low on the litter rigging.
Receives direction from Climber to go down quarter-speed.	Observes.	Repeats: "Down quarter-speed."	Operates belay.	Directs Leader to go down quarter-speed.
Directs Haul Team "Down quarter-speed."		Lowers main line at quarter-speed.		
Receives direction from Climber to stop and hold position.	Observes.	Repeats: "Stop."	Operates belay.	Directs Leader to stop lowering as soon as the subject is within reach of the rigging used to capture the subject.

52

Leader	Safety	Haul Team	Belay	Climber
Directs Haul Team to "Stop and hold position."		Stops main line and holds.		Begins attaching subject to main and belay lines with pick-off appliances. Places protective equipment. Maneuvers subject into the litter and secures.
Receives info from Climber that the subject is attached to the main and belay lines. Leader informs team. Receives info from Climber the subject is secured in the litter. Leader informs team.	Observes.	Holds main line position.	Operates belay.	Informs Leader when the subject is secured to the main and belay lines. Informs Leader when the subject is in the litter and secured.
Receives direction from Climber to go down. Directs Haul Team to go down.	Observes.	Repeats: "Down." Operates lowering system to go down.	Operates belay.	After making final adjustments to the litter and rigging, informs Leader ready for down.
Leader continues vocalizing commands to keep the main line moving at a speed suitable to the climber.	Observes.	Operates lowering system to go down.	Operates belay.	Continues down. Minimizes rock fall.
Receives communication from Climber that he and the subject are on the ground. Directs Haul Team to stop and hold.	Observes.	Repeats: "Stop and hold." Stops main line and holds position.		Informs Leader the rescue package is on the ground. Directs Leader to stop and hold.
Leader receives communication from Climber that belay is disconnected and ready for "Stop, all stop." Leader directs team to "Stop, All Stop."	Stop, all stop.	Repeats: "Stop, all stop." Stop, all stop.	Stop, all stop.	Informs Leader, "Off belay." Directs Leader, "Stop, all stop."
Directs members to safe area and debriefs as a group.	Directs members to safe area and debriefs as a group.	Participates in debriefing.	Participates in debriefing.	Participates in debriefing.
Inspects equipment and completes records.	Inspects equipment and completes records.	Inspects equipment and completes records.	Inspects equipment and completes records.	Inspects equipment and completes records.

Support Positions   *Resources Not Part Of The Core Rescue Team*

Recon Spotters
- Mission: Make a visual search for rescue subject and report conditions to Rescue Group Leader
- Assess climbing route and associated hazards, report conditions
- Monitor the rescue subject and periodically report conditions

Communicates Directly With: Leader, Overhead Staff

Highly mobile units equipped with optics for long distance viewing like binoculars, telescopes, or thermal imagers. This position is very suited to operational supervisors such as Battalion Chiefs. Specialized resources like hazmat companies equipped with telephoto mast-cams and recording equipment are an excellent choice for this assignment. If you have a problem with administrators responding to your incident as "lookie-loos," you can make them useful and clear them from your immediate worksite by assigning them to multiple recon vantage points.

Backup Teams
- Mission: Rapid Intervention Team in place to assist injured Rescue Climber
- Additional Vertical Rescue Team able to set up and deploy a RIT Climber
- Set up for immediate deployment

Communicates Directly With: Leader

Additional team with vertical rescue capability on scene and ready to immediately deploy a Rapid Intervention Climber to help the Rescue Climber if he or she is injured or becomes incapacitated. The mission of this resource does not include deployment to assist the Rescue Climber with the rescue effort. Keep the Backup Team in place to provide for the safety of your Rescue Climber. The Backup Climber position should be initially assigned to one of the Haul Team members to maintain system functionality. Additional mechanical advantage can be rigged to make up for lost hauling manpower if a rapid intervention deployment occurs.

Transportation Units
- Mission: Move the Rescue Subject, Rescue Climber, and equipment as needed
- Boats, 4x4 vehicles, helicopters, or foot teams
- Monitor the rescue subject and periodically report conditions

Communicates Directly With: Leader, Overhead Staff

Used to access the bottom of the rescue site and transport the Rescue Subject, Rescue Climber, and equipment. Vertical rescue operations often occur in areas without roads or trails and may require specialized transportation vehicles or a team of personnel to carry out the litter. Mobilize transportation units early to have them in place when you need them.

6 General Rigging

General Rigging Considerations

Connecting your cache equipment together to assemble strong rescue systems that work efficiently requires an operational understanding for how each piece is designed to carry a load. This chapter will take a close look at how typical NFPA cache components properly connect together to work well, to safely carry your rescue load, and to survive reasonable amounts of shock.

Basic Rigging Considerations

The overall premise for rigging and operating vertical rescue systems depends on a 2-rope approach for over-the-side rescues and belay systems for overhead operations. Whether it's a practice session or the real thing, there are core elements of rigging and procedural safety that apply to any rope or climbing system your group uses. No matter how simple or exotic a rope or climbing system may end up being, the following basic rigging considerations must be addressed:

Load Limiting	Lowering/raising rigging must carry a rescue package, but slip before it bears enough load to break component parts.
Backup	Belay rigging must be in place to instantly support or help support the load if the lowering/raising system slips or completely fails, or if a lead climber falls.
Prevent & Absorb Shock	Main line and belay systems must be assembled and operated in a way that they limit and absorb enough shock to prevent injury to climbers and to protect components from breakage.
Avoid Abrasion	Rig equipment in a way that eliminates or sufficiently reduces abrasion on software components.
Avoid Torque	Rig equipment in a way that eliminates twisting forces on hardware components.

Topics within this chapter will be described and diagramed with the above core elements in mind. Knots and hitches, anchor attachments, connector rigging, harness connections, pulley systems, belays, etc. will all be chosen and arranged to eliminate component failure and injury by minimizing the risks of shock, abrasion, and torque.

Component Considerations

The following focuses on cache component rigging considerations for efficiency and safety. Each piece of equipment in the cache has its own list of performance abilities and limitations, depending on how they are integrated into the overall system. Careful attention to how and where each piece is placed in the overall system is crucial. The ability of a team to quickly assemble cache components into a safe, over-the-side or climbing system depends heavily on a clear understanding of the functionality, strengths, and weaknesses of each component. It's also extremely important to develop set-up skills through regular, realistic practice that involves assembling systems.

Life Safety Rope and Cord

The life safety rope and cord are principle elements of vertical rescue systems. There are important rigging considerations for life safety rope and cord. Ropes used in the fire service today are engineered to be very strong and durable. The same load specifications and safety factors that address hardware components apply to fire service rescue ropes. NFPA standards specify that 2-person rescue ropes have a capacity to hold a dynamic load of 40kN, comparable to a static load of 9000lbf (8,993 lbf). That's about a ton more weight than a full-sized pickup! And it has to be supple and tough enough to tie knots and endure abrasion and other kinds of abuse.

Design And Construction: Modern ropes used for rescue are generally made of synthetic fibers (usually nylon or polyester) and are kernmantle in design. This design is comprised of an inner core (the kern) and an outer sheath (the mantle). The kern is made of very fine continuous filament fibers that are fashioned into small cords providing most of the rope's strength. The mantle provides some strength, but mainly serves to

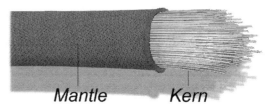

Kernmantle Construction

Mantle   *Kern*

contain and protect the core fibers. The mantle also compresses and holds the core fibers together when the rope is taut. This can actually increase the collective strength of the core fibers. Think of those Chinese handcuffs you played with as a kid.

NFPA STANDARDS - LIFE SAFETY ROPES				
Intended Use	Minimum Diameter	Minimum Breaking Strength	Elongation *Loaded To 10% MBS*	Heat
Tech	9.5mm - 3/8"	20kN - 4496lbf	min. 1% max 10%	min 400°F
General	12.5mm - 1/2"	40kN - 8992lbf	min. 1% max 10%	min 400°F
Escape	7.5mm - 19/64"	13.5kN - 3034lbf	min. 1% max 10%	min 400°F

Each core fiber runs the entire length of most rescue ropes. If you were to locate the tiny end of a single continuous filament fiber and follow it inside the sheath, it would continue all the way to the other end of the rope. Known as block-creel construction, this design makes a rope very strong and compact. Kernmantle ropes that have cores formed from straight block-creel fibers are strong and flexible with very little stretch. Ropes with cores formed from kinky or curly block-creel fibers have more stretch.

Strength: Minimum breaking strength (MBS) values established in NFPA Standard 1983 ensure that fire service ropes used for vertical rescue are very strong and have optimum amounts of elongation under load. Rope testing parameters for light use, general use, and escape use are designed to provide firefighters with ropes that will be bomber strong and durable, with enough elongation and suppleness to allow for efficient handling and impact absorption to reasonably prevent bodily harm. The Cordage Institute strength standards for life safety rope currently match NFPA 1983.

Stretch: Fire Service Rescue Teams need high-stretch (dynamic) ropes and low-stretch (static) ropes in their caches. At most top-down worksites, vertical rescue systems take a 2-rope approach to dealing with the potential for accidental falls and preventing harmful impact forces. Jobs that are overhead sometimes use a single rope to provide fall protection for the Climbers. Top down ops use low-stretch ropes. Overhead ops use dynamic ropes. During over-the-side rescues, the main line carrying the Climber and rescue load does not intentionally go slack and should not need shock absorbing deceleration properties. In fact, using a stretchy rope for over-the-side ops presents problems like spongy hauling systems and excessive rope elongation and drop when making pick-offs. Dynamic ropes are needed for those overhead rescue situations where Lead Climbers are going up with a single rope for fall protection. NFPA establishes stretch (elongation) standards to categorize rescue ropes as low stretch.

Low-Stretch (Static) Ropes: Rescue ropes that elongate less than ten percent when subjected to loads equal to 10% of their minimum breaking strength (MBS) are referred to by NFPA Standard 1983 as low-stretch ropes. Most synthetic low-stretch ropes used for rescue today actually elongate less than 10% depending on construction and materials. Some modern polyester ropes are very rigid with elongation figures below 2%. Nylon stretches more and actually continues to stretch as long as it is under load, kind of like pulling taffy. For precision operations like high-lines, it may be necessary to pre-stretch nylon ropes before rigging.

In reality, typical rescue loads are lighter than 10% of the MBS of rescue rated ropes, and people working with them will experience less linear stretch under normal working conditions. Example: a 1/2-inch (12mm) synthetic rope engineered to meet NFPA Standard 1983 must have a MBS of 40kN or roughly 9,000 lbf. A load equal to 10% MBS would weigh 900lbs for a 2-person rescue rope, much heavier than the NFPA maximum of 600lbs.

Low-stretch ropes are mainly necessary for rescue ops to minimize position changes as loads change. Picture a Climber over the side and 200 feet down tying onto a rescue subject and then moving him or her off the cliff and onto the rope. Even if the rope stretches 2%, the Climber and the subject can drop several feet because of elongation. A secondary reason is that hauling systems and ascending maneuvers work much better with static ropes. If a pulley system has a lot of stretch in the rope, gaining and capturing upward progress will be much less efficient. You may haul up 10 feet, only to give back 4 feet when you set the brake to reset.

The downside to hanging people on rigid ropes is the hard landing at the end of an accidental fall when things go wrong. At shorter rope lengths, falls caught by static lines can cause serious bodily harm. Low-stretch ropes should always be backed up with 2-rope techniques. Slack should be minimized with good rigging and management. Anticipate and eliminate conditions that create the potential for falls to occur on static ropes, especially shorter ones.

High-Stretch (Dynamic) Ropes: Usually used as fall protection for overhead situations, dynamic ropes stretch and softly decelerate a falling Climber to minimize impact. The rope absorbs the impact energy instead of the Climber. In general, dynamic ropes

REMEMBER

Use Dynamic Ropes To Belay Climbers Working Overhead

should be used for single person belays. Dynamic ropes are not ideal for use in pulley systems.

Moderate Elongation Laid Life Saving Ropes specified by NFPA are not suitable as dynamic climbing ropes. The standard, most widely referred dynamic rope specifications are the UIAA or Union International des Associations d'Alpinisme *(English translation: International Mountaineering and Climbing Association).* Another professionally respected standard is from the European Committee for Standardization (CEN). Concerned mainly with mountaineering and climbing, the UIAA and CEN are not in step with NFPA, but they do establish clear performance standards for dynamic climbing ropes. UIAA provides rope manufacturers with a schedule to rate the breaking strength and shock absorbing characteristics of dynamic climbing ropes. The UIAA Falls Rating System determines the number of worst-case scenario falls (fall factor of 2) a rope can withstand before breaking, while keeping impact forces below 12kN (2,700 lbs.). The testing uses a 176lb load to create the fall scenario. Look for the UIAA Falls number when purchasing dynamic ropes for your cache. A rating of 6 means that the ropes tested withstood 6 worst-case falls before breaking. In general, lower numbers equate to a lighter rope, more elongation, and a cushier impact. A higher number can mean the rope is beefier with less elongation and may result in a rougher impact at the bottom of a fall. Manufacturers make ropes that meet the needs of recreational climbers to be used as single lines, double lines, and twin lines. Each has its own set of performance variations and testing protocol.

Recommended: Choose a dynamic rope designed for use as a single line with a high UIAA Falls number and employ tactics that keep Climbers conservative to minimize the potential for accidental falls. Lead climbing methods described in this book are consistent with using single-line dynamic ropes with high UIAA Falls numbers.

Rope Life: Ropes, cords, and other software do not last forever. Wear and tear along with degradation of the synthetic materials over time affect the minimum breaking strengths of life safety and dynamic ropes. Every manufacturer provides decommission guidelines and requirements for ropes, but there are conditions that are common to all ropes used for vertical rescue that warrant removing them from service. It's a good idea to study manufacturer information to establish predetermined service life criteria for the ropes and cords in your cache.

Throwing a new rope into your cache without establishing decommission criteria is a mistake. Predetermined decommission benchmarks like maximum age, maximum wear, maximum shock exposure, and contamination tolerances are critical to keeping rescue ropes and cordage safe. Many organizations simply "time out" ropes and cords with replacement schedules that rotate new stock into each cache at regular intervals. It simplifies budget planning and keeps fresh rope coming to the rescue crews. Old rescue ropes make good utility lines for other companies. Don't wait until the rope is damaged to consider decommission standards. Have a plan that all participants are familiar with so everyone recognizes when it's time to replace the rope.

DECOMMISSION CONDITIONS - LIFE SAFETY ROPES	
• Harmful Contamination	• Excessive Fraying - Sheath
• Severe Impact - Fall Factor >0.5	• Internal Bulging - Core
• Exposed Core Fibers Mid Rope	• De-gloved - Loose Sheath
• Severed Sheath Cords	• Retirement Age
• Excessive Heat Exposure	• Excessive UV Exposure
Coordinate With Manufacturer Guidelines	

Age can have an effect on the flexibility and elasticity of the materials that make up modern life safety ropes, but it's difficult to establish hard schedules for determining when a rope is too old for service. A young and apparently undamaged rope that gets frequent heavy use may be worn beyond its years when you consider breaking strength and service life. A pristine-looking rope that has been in its bag for five years may have become brittle. There is a confidence factor to evaluating the service life expectancy of your own rope, absent any obvious damage. Many times it's a judgment call based on what you know, or don't know, about a rope. Think about it. Is it easier to decide whether to keep a rope in service if you know its history? Even if the rope is months old, it would be hard to make a sound safety judgment if you don't know how it has been used. Follow manufacturer guidelines to establish the maximum age of the rope, and then reduce the service life as wear and tear accumulates. Forecast wear, shock, and contamination limits that would cause you to take the rope out of service. Keeping meaningful records is the only way to evaluate accumulated wear for the purpose of determining service life.

Records: Retain instructions and guides provided by manufacturers. A good method is to keep these documents in the equipment log or to develop a computer file. Most manufacturers provide access to instructions and guides on their websites. Downloading and storing instructions and guides in the member-accessible computer system is great for training and maintenance reference. Protect and preserve NFPA compliance labels as much as possible. Maintain sections in your cache log that are dedicated to each individual rope. Avoid keeping rope log documents in the rope bag.

Label Ropes
And Identify Ends
With Different Colors

Documents stored in the bag, or in a bag pocket, do not hold up well enough against weather and wear. Assign agency identification/tracking numbers, and record lot and serial numbers. Marking rope ends with different colors (one end black, one end red) helps when making notations about wear and damage. Record the dates when ropes are put in service, and make pertinent entries after regular inspections and any use. No notation is too insignificant. Some organizations even log exposure to sunlight.

Rope Log Entry Examples

Rope # 15B	Diameter: 1/2"	Color: Orange	Length: 600ft	
Manufacturer: Sterling HTP Lot# 0401120101-12.5-266				☒Static ☐Dynamic ☐Nylon ☒Polyester

DATE	USE	In Service?	Current Location
5-19-10	☐Rescue ☐Practice ☒Inspection	☒Yes ☐No	RQ 99
	Description / Comments: *Recieved from Logistics, inspected and placed in service*		
5-24-10	☐Rescue ☒Practice ☐Inspection	☒Yes ☐No	Rq 99
	Description / Comments: *Ascending; Used as the main line, 3 hours exposure full load C-Shift*		
6-14-10	☐Rescue ☒Practice ☐Inspection	☒Yes ☐No	Rescue 99
	Description / Comments: *Lowering & raising 2-person loads, 2 hours full load w/ 6:1 MA Minor abrasion wear 10' from black end*		
7-6-10	☐Rescue ☒Practice ☐Inspection	☒Yes ☐No	RQ99
	Description / Comments: *Rigging practice; 3 hours light use, no load* B Shift		

Maintaining MBS: There are a few rigging considerations that help maintain rope strength. Ropes are strongest when pulled straight along a single linear axis. Tension is distributed unevenly as ropes turn within knots and around hardware and edges, the same way turns in the road affect the speed of your car. The tighter the turn, the more you have to slow down the car. Eliminating tight turns along the path the rope follows will help maintain rope strength within your rigging. Limiting the diameter of turns to at least 4 times the diameter of the rope will generally maintain minimum breaking strength. Compare the inside diameter of a ½-inch rope as it rounds a carabiner and a 2-inch pulley sheave. Of course, the bend around the carabiner is much tighter compared to the pulley. Since the 2-inch pulley is 4 times the diameter of the ½-inch rope, it preserves the MBS enough for field estimations. The larger the pulley sheave, the lower the strain on that section of the rope. Understanding these mechanics are important to clean, strong rigging and critical for advanced teams using very high-tension systems. It may sometimes be better to clip in a 2-inch pulley to lift a rope over or around an edge than it would be to run the rope through a carabiner.

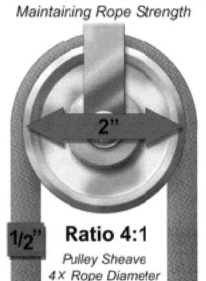

Turn Diameter Ratios
Maintaining Rope Strength

2"

½" **Ratio 4:1**
Pulley Sheave
4X Rope Diameter

Belt and drum friction principles also affect tensioned ropes that make turns around stationary objects. Riggers can take advantage of these principles to fashion knotless anchor attachments that maintain full rope strength. Knots degrade the breaking strength of rope. While some knots create less strain on rope, it's impossible to knot ropes without reducing the minimum breaking strength. Tensionless hitches and capstans are examples of ways to combine belt friction principles with minimum diameter ratios to anchor or control rope tension without degrading strength. These methods are often applied with rope systems used for river rescues and boat handling.

In general, dry ropes maintain strength better than wet ropes. Tensile strength is significantly reduced when ropes become soaked. Ropes also elongate more when wet. Treatments applied to some ropes by manufacturers reduce deep soaking to improve performance in wet or icy conditions. Dry-treated ropes are common, and they are a good choice for rescue caches. It's important to understand that dry treatments degrade as the rope is used more and more. Refer to manufacturer guidelines for maintaining the protective treatment of your ropes.

Rope Handling: Keeping ropes tangle free and organized on the job can mean the difference between a quick and smooth operation and a real cluster. A few simple tricks to storing and laying out ropes can help keep rope-handling hassles to a minimum. All it takes is a little forethought and some easy set up.

• **Bagging:** Storing ropes in bags is a good way to go for fire service users because of the way equipment is carried in tight vehicle compartments. Color indexing rope bags to distinguish life safety ropes from utility ropes is important. Choose bags that are fitted with compression straps and that are larger than the bulk of the rope they contain. Often, bags are tailored to barely fit a specified rope size, which makes reloading difficult. Stuffing a rope into a tight bag is slow, aggravating, and just plain NO FUN. Order bags with capacities that are about 20% larger than the bulk of the rope you intend to store in them. For a rope that is 400 feet long, order a bag for a 500-foot rope. This will make stuffing much more user friendly and will allow room for any pre-rigged equipment that may be added later. Bags with adjustable compression straps can tighten up any unwanted slop and shrink the overall size of the package after the bag has been stuffed with rope.

Tying a knot onto the rope end to make it easier to locate inside the bag sounds petty, but really makes a big difference, especially in a large, loose bag. When you're trying to reduce set-up times, these kinds of small rigging assists can really add up. Some teams tie the rope end to an attachment point on the outside of the bag for the same reason.

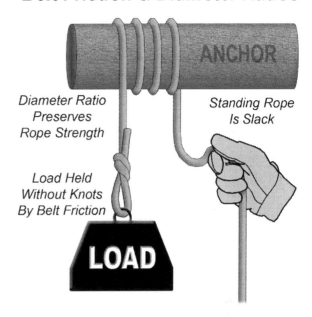

Belt Friction & Diameter Ratios

Diameter Ratio Preserves Rope Strength

Standing Rope Is Slack

Load Held Without Knots By Belt Friction

LOAD

Wet Ropes Lose Significant Strength

And

Elongate More

As Much As 50% Decrease In MBS

LOAD

Life Safety Rope Bags

Color Coded

Plenty Of Room

**Easy-Carry Handles
Or Pack Straps**

Knots On Rope Ends

Compression Straps

- **Stacking:** Everyone who has tangled up a rope after extending it by pulling on one end knows that everything comes to a screeching halt until the big spaghetti pile is unraveled. Any time a rope end is pulled from a disorganized pile, you have a snowball's chance in Havana of not suffering this punishment. Take the time to adequately organize your ropes so that they will be easy to extend for your rigging. Many times you'll see teams laying ropes out into picture perfect rows of overlapping figure eights. Pretty, but very time consuming. During training sessions, try to keep in mind that your team is in the rescue business, not spelunking, rope access, or recreational climbing. Setting ropes out in neat figure-eight layers eats up valuable time and is not practical for rescue operations.

A better approach is to simply stack the rope into a compact pile. Start by laying one end of the rope out about 4 feet from where you intend to place your pile. This will prevent burying the end under the pile. Now, pull the rest of the rope hand over hand and let it collect into a compact pile. When you run out of rope, place the second end a few feet off of the pile as you did with the first end. This will make the ends at the top and bottom of the pile easy to distinguish. This handling method can also be used to create 2 piles with both ends at the top of a pile. Once the rope is stacked, do not allow anyone to tidy up, step on, or move the pile. If the pile of rope is disturbed, the rope will tangle when you need to extend it. To extend the rope without tangles, grab the end that connects to the top of the pile. Pulling rope from the bottom will result in tangles.

To relocate the stack, carry the top end of the rope to the new location and re-stack it. It may seem like a hassle, but it's quick and much easier than any other method. Stack ropes whenever you need to extend or move them out of the bag.

Stacking Rope

*Feed Into Compact Pile With Ends
Positioned Several Feet Out*

Do Not Disturb The Pile

Extend Rope By Pulling Top End

Compatibility: As your cache of equipment grows, or as old ropes wear out and get replaced, it's important to make sure the rope and cord you use is compatible. Various combinations of materials and rope construction perform differently when rigged together. Example: Kernmantle cord with a core made from Kevlar does not work well when used as a prusik rope grab on nylon or polyester ropes. Make sure the rope and cord in your cache is suitable for the applications for which you use it.

Cautions

1. Store ropes away from engine exhaust and hydrocarbon vapors as much as possible. Exposure to these contaminants degrades the material that makes up life safety ropes. Other than clean water, materials that stick to ropes should be considered contaminants. Any solid, powder, dust, liquid, gas, or mist should be a suspected contaminant until proven otherwise. Remove life safety ropes from service if they have been contaminated until it can be definitively determined that the exposure was harmless.

2. Avoid walking on rope and keep them clean and dry. Imagine a small sticker, piece of glass, or grain of sand stuck on the sheath of the rope, and then getting stepped on or traveling through a pulley where it gets smashed into the core. Any individual continuous filament fiber that gets cut reduces the overall strength of the rope just a little. Particles that penetrate the mantle and remain lodged within the core will continue to wear on the fibers as the rope is used.

3. Remove ropes from service if they have been exposed to temperatures above 130°F or direct flames, or if there is obvious spot damage from a hot object or spark. NFPA life safety rope standards require ropes to endure temperatures of 400°F without signs of damage. The difficulty is determining how much degradation a rope has sustained when there are no obvious signs of damage after exposure to high temperatures below 400°F. In general, if your rope has been exposed to conditions that would burn your skin, it's time to question its life safety integrity.

4. Low-stretch life safety ropes exposed to impact loads should be removed from service. Impact loads of 0.5 on the Fall Factor scale or greater warrant immediate decommissioning of life safety rope. Impact loads less than 0.5 on the Fall Factor scale warrant close evaluation of the rope and its history by a technically competent person. Refer to manufacturer guidelines.

5. Dynamic ropes exposed to impact loads must be closely evaluated by a technically competent person to determine future safe use. Depending on the history and engineering specifications of a particular dynamic rope, it may be safe for future use following an impact load. Compare use records and the UIAA Falls Rating number assigned to the particular rope with the Fall Factor of the impact(s) to determine remaining service life. If there are doubts about the ability to sustain a worst case fall in the future, the rope should be removed from service.

6. Ropes with visual physical damage must be removed from service until inspected by a technically competent person. Refer to manufacturer guidelines.

Carabiners

Biners come in a huge variety of styles and strengths to suit a wide range of applications. NFPA classifies carabiners as either tech use or general use. Generally in the field, carabiners are described as either steel or aluminum and non-locking or locking. Manufacturers have established several broad operational categories to identify application and safety characteristics.

It's important to understand that biners must be loaded the way they are designed. A rescue service biner is engineered to be strong, but as is true with any connector, it must be loaded correctly. Torsion forces, side loading, and incorrect load distribution weaken carabiners significantly. Look for markings that identify load capacities. If marked, the information is usually located on the spine and identifies major axis and minor axis capacities of the particular carabiner. Sometimes markings identify the strength of the biner when the gate is open. If the biner meets NFPA standards, it may be marked as such. Look for NFPA markings that distinguish either general or tech use. It's common in the fire service to see caches containing only general use biners to help avoid confusion or to compensate for varying levels of operating expertise among the Rescue Team.

CARABINER CLASSIFICATIONS	
Type 1	Non-Locking Gate. Usually Used By Sport Climbers.
Type 2	Manual Locking Gate. Usually Screw Lock. Commonly Used In The Fire Service.
Type 3	Single-Action Auto-Locking Gate. Spring-Loaded Lock Requires Manipulation In One Direction.
Type 4	Double-Action Auto-Locking Gate. Spring-Loaded Lock Requires Manipulation In Two Directions. Commonly Used In Industry For Rope Access Work.

Application: Used as connectors to interface software and hardware, carabiners have a lot of applications. Carabiners provide a means of strong mechanical software connection to things like pulleys, brakes, anchors, rigging plates, harnesses, etc. Biners can even be used as descent control devices or brake mechanisms. Carabiners also connect hardware components together. Veteran firefighters will remember the old saw, "Never connect hardware to hardware." They meant well, but hardware often links to hardware. Avoid chaining biners together under a load. Biners connected in this way will bear torsion forces that significantly weaken them. Pulleys, plates, and brake racks all connect to the system with biners.

Strongest On Major Axis

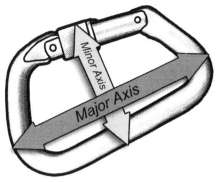

Loading Considerations: Always rig carabiners to carry loads along the strong axis. Diagonal or multi-directional loads on carabiners can be very dangerous. Because the gate opening creates an area of weakness, the overall strength of carabiners depends on directing load forces along the spine. The spine creates a solid, uninterrupted bridge that transfers load forces back to the anchor. Carabiners are strong and tough, but riggers should always consider shock loads as part of the equation. Carabiner closure mechanisms can fail if load forces vector toward the gate. This is especially true in shock-load situations. Loads from multiple directions (sometimes referred to as "triple loading") create stresses that can deform or even burst carabiners. Think of how internal pressure causes a popcorn kernel to pop open. For this reason, biners should not be used as gathering points unless they have been engineered for this kind of application. It's better to fall back on knot craft skills or clip in a rigging plate or ring.

NFPA Minimum Breaking Strength - General Use

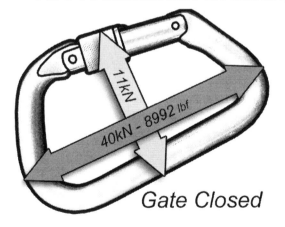

Gate Closed

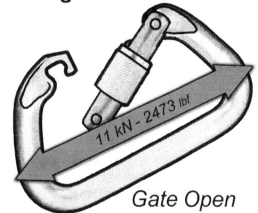

Gate Open

NFPA Minimum Breaking Strength - *Tech Use*

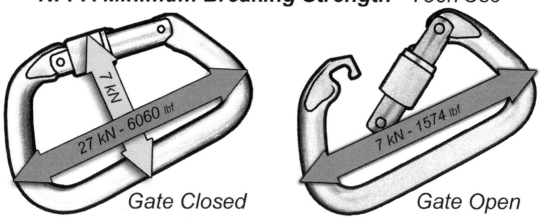

Gate Closed   Gate Open

While biners make connections simple, they should also be considered as one more point of potential failure in the overall system. In other words, it's another opportunity to make a rigging mistake or for a fall to occur if the biner connection fails. Riggers should value simple design and fall back onto knot crafting abilities to make connections whenever it is appropriate to do so.

Carabiner Positioning: Take engineering strengths and weaknesses into account when you clip on a carabiner. Consider how the load, gravity, and vibration will affect the biner for the duration of an operation. Make sure carabiners are rigged to remain stable and prevent unwanted rotation, keeping the load squarely on the spine. Anticipate how running ropes that are threaded through biners affect locking mechanisms. Forecast the potential for any biner to scrape against hard surfaces as the climber moves. Take these influences into account, and position carabiners accordingly.

Vibration and gravity *will* cause a poorly positioned screw gate to unlock. Running ropes *do* unscrew locks and open carabiners. Side loading and cross loading of carabiners *does* cause damage and failure. Poorly oriented harness connections *can* cause carabiners to unlock and open or sustain enough damage to stick closed. It will not always be possible to optimally orient carabiners. It may be necessary at times to position a biner with the lock and gate exposed to gravity, vibration, or scraping. In these situations, monitor the connection integrity closely. It may be necessary to apply tape to locking mechanisms to prevent unwanted creep and opening.

Carabiners - *Gravity Orientation*

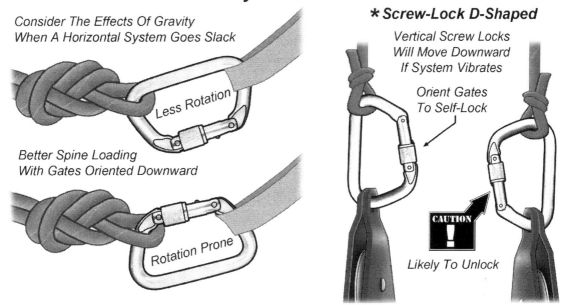

*Consider The Effects Of Gravity
When A Horizontal System Goes Slack*

Less Rotation

*Better Spine Loading
With Gates Oriented Downward*

Rotation Prone

✱ Screw-Lock D-Shaped

*Vertical Screw Locks
Will Move Downward
If System Vibrates*

*Orient Gates
To Self-Lock*

CAUTION !

Likely To Unlock

One of the most common types of carabiner used in fire service rescue caches are steel "D" or offset "D" shaped with screw lock gates. The following diagrams depict positioning and loading considerations for steel "D" and offset "D" shaped biners equipped with screw lock gates.

Carabiners - Loading Considerations

Good

- *Load Forces Are In Line With The Spine*
- *Gate Locks Are Oriented To Gravity*
- *Offset Shape Used Appropriately*

BEST ★ PRACTICE

Less Good

- *Load Forces Closer Toward Gate*
- *Gate Locks Not Oriented To Gravity*
- *Offset Shape Used Inappropriately*

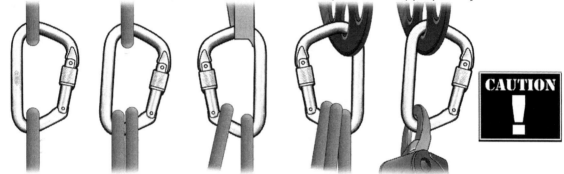

CAUTION !

No Good

- *Load Forces Contrary With Spine*
- *Running Rope On Gate And Lock*
- *Gate Unlocked*

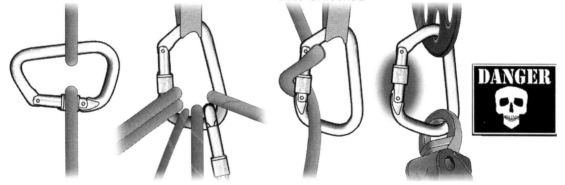

DANGER

Carabiners are not designed to hold up to hard cross-loading. Exposing biners to hard edges while under load risks focusing compounded and concentrated forces onto the weakest axis. Carabiners cross-loaded in this way are extremely prone to damage and failure. Cross loading often occurs when riggers underestimate stretch in the software as the load is applied to the system. The rope or webbing stretches just enough to allow a biner to reach a transitional edge or other obstacle. Design rigging in a way that positions carabiners well away from cross-loading problems.

When a carabiner is used to connect a climber to the rope system, there is strong potential for that connection to be exposed to abrasive cross-load forces. Optimally, a Type-4 auto-locking carabiner is best for this application to prevent accidental unlocking and opening. However, even Type 4 biners are weakest at the gate. For this kind of application, position the carabiner for the highest tolerance to scraping, lateral forces. When a carabiner used as a harness connection is oriented with the gate in (toward the Climber's abdomen) and the screw lock down (oriented to gravity) it will tolerate scraping lateral forces better and will be more likely to stay locked, undamaged, and closed.

Avoid linking carabiners like a chain to extend a connection. Doing so creates dangerous torsion that can bend the carabiner gate open and cause complete failure. Often the result of well-meaning but inexperienced riggers faced with extending a connection, biner chains do show their face from time to time. If a connection needs to be extended to make the rigging functional, use a software link to create the needed length instead of a carabiner. Chaining biners is not an example of clean rigging and should only be done as a last resort, as might be the case with a software shortage. If chaining is ever used, some means of relieving torsion must be integrated into the rigging and close monitoring is imperative. Modern pulleys are sometimes equipped with swiveling eyes that may help overcome this problem. But again, *avoid linking carabiners together in a chain*.

Carabiners - *Lateral & Torsional Strain*

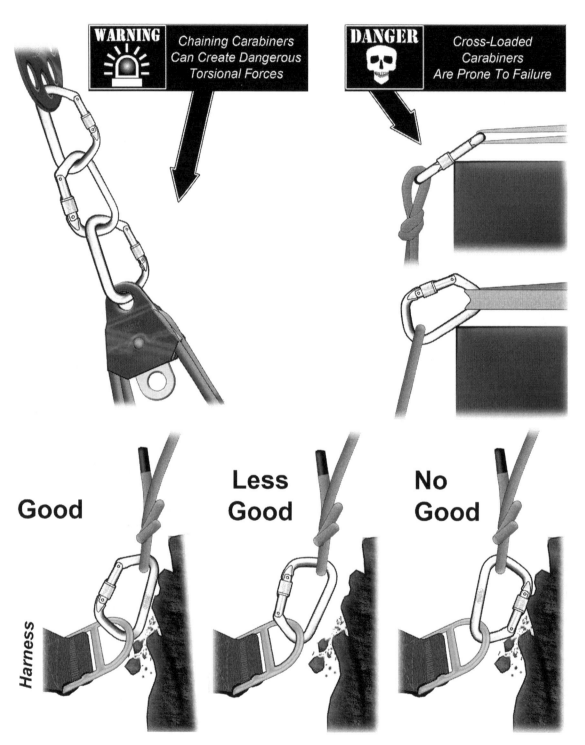

WARNING Chaining Carabiners Can Create Dangerous Torsional Forces

DANGER Cross-Loaded Carabiners Are Prone To Failure

Good

Less Good

No Good

Harness

Webbing, Rigging Slings, End-To-End Straps, & Multiple Configuration Straps
The rope in your cache can be used to fashion anchor attachments and other kinds of rigging, but flat stock software and pre-rigged straps and slings expand design and safety options in the field. Webbing and straps are generally less expensive to replace than rope and may be a better choice when connecting to abrasive anchors. Using webbing, straps, or slings for anchor attachments can free up more rope length that can be used for vertical travel or hauling. Pre-sewn anchor straps and rigging slings can save time and may be a good choice for organizations with limited expertise.

Be careful. There are many varieties of flat stock software available on the market. It can be difficult to distinguish utility grade materials from those suitable for vertical rescue. Make sure you know what's going into your cache. Study manufacturer information and compare the capacities of the stock to the standards you've chosen to follow. Recreation grade slings and straps may fall short of what you need.

Webbing: One-inch military spec webbing stock cut into different lengths is commonly found in fire service rescue caches. Look for shuttle loom tubular construction for the best durability and strength. Tensile strengths of one-inch webbing suitable for vertical rescue range from 4000 to 6000 pounds. Hot-cut webbing into uniform lengths with the ends on a sharp bias. A pointed end makes knot tying and rigging much easier. Mark each piece to indicate when the stock was placed in service. Some organizations create serial numbers for each length of webbing in the cache. Coordinating color with length can streamline field operations. Sorting through a pile of random colors and reading the markings to find the piece you need eats up valuable time.

Index Length & Color

Cut Webbing Ends On A Bias

12' 5-15-10

Mark In-Service Date (If Unlabeled)
Ends Not Load Bearing & Safe To Mark

Refer to manufacturer guidelines for service life limits to webbing stock. Decommission criteria for webbing is like that for rope. Remove webbing from service if it has sustained visible physical damage such as cuts or fraying or if it has been contaminated or exposed to excessive heat, excessive UV light, or impact.

An advantage to webbing is that it can be fashioned in many ways to support your rigging. Pre-fabricated slings and anchor straps are specialized for a focused range of applications. In anchor attachment situations, webbing may actually provide for better load transfer to carabiners. You're more likely to make attachments that are perfectly suited to the diameter, angle, or configuration of any given anchor by using webbing. A prefabricated anchor strap will interface with connections in different ways, depending on its length and the circumference of the anchor itself. Soft slings and prefab anchor straps with hard connection points that are just long enough to wrap an anchor may place undesirable stresses if connected directly to carabiners. Webbing can be tied at the perfect length around anchors to create optimal angles and orientation that properly focuses stress onto the major axis of carabiners. This can reduce the need for rigging plates and multiple connectors at the anchor attachment.

Webbing vs. Slings & Straps

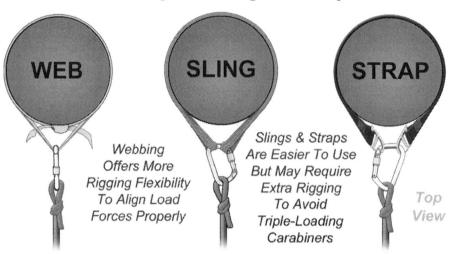

WEB

Webbing Offers More Rigging Flexibility To Align Load Forces Properly

SLING

Slings & Straps Are Easier To Use But May Require Extra Rigging To Avoid Triple-Loading Carabiners

STRAP

Top View

End to End & Multiple Configuration Straps: Also known as loops or runners, simple slings are good to have aboard for making quick anchor attachments, running anchors, or lanyard extensions. Less commonly found in fire/rescue caches, slings require little rigging expertise to use. It's simple to direct a firefighter without much experience to sling an anchor. But be careful. Most prefabricated slings are suited for single-person use and should be doubled up for heavier loads. Make sure the sling you use on your anchor choice will not triple-load connectors. This usually means rigging a longer, sharper departure angle with the sling. Slings are a great choice for running anchors (runners) used in lead climbing. In some cases, the weave of the fabric used for prefab slings is tougher and less prone to cutting and unraveling than those tied with tubular or flat webbing.

Anchor Strap Variations

Sling Used As A Runner

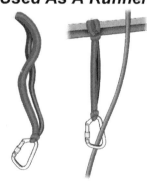

Rigging straps are heavy-duty lengths of flat webbing configured with the means to connect to parts of your vertical rescue system. Anchor straps are designed to be used as anchor attachments. Prefab anchor attachments are usually equipped with hard rings, while other types of rigging straps have soft end loops as connection points. Some are fitted with adjustment buckles. There are a variety of designs for many applications, such as lanyards, rescue basket bridles, guy lines, personal connection, lashing, and anchor attachments. Many are constructed for cut and abrasion resistance. Do not confuse utility strap equipment with life safety straps. Utility straps used for towing or heavy rigging are strong, but may not match up well with the dimensions of connectors designed for fire service rescue caches. This can result in poorly aligned load forces on connectors. Strap equipment that has been tested to meet NFPA standards must be fitted with an approved label that includes use information. NFPA establishes minimum breaking strengths and other performance standards for strap equipment (*see chart*). Life safety rigging and anchor straps are also tested and certified by other standards agencies such as ANSI. OSHA regulations require anchor attachments to hold a 5000lbs load. NFPA specifically identifies rigging straps that are used for pick-off maneuvers and establishes separate performance standards for them. Strength standards established by NFPA for straps are higher than those for ropes.

Choose strap equipment that has been sewn at critical points using thread that is a contrasting color. This makes inspecting and spotting damage to critical sewn connections easier.

NFPA STRAP PERFORMANCE STANDARDS				
Intended Use	Tech Strength	General Strength	Adjustment Slippage	Heat
Rigging	32kN - 7194 lbf	45kN - 10,120 lbf	Max. 2 inches	Min. 400° F
Anchor	32kN - 7194 lbf	45kN - 10,120 lbf	Max. 2 inches	Min. 400° F
Pick-Off	27kN - 6070 lbf	N/A	Max. 2 inches	Min. 400° F

Pick-off Straps: These pre-rigged straps are generally used as a means of tensioning the connections to a rescue subject prior to transferring that load onto the rope system. This prevents the shock that can occur when a rescue subject is pulled off of a ledge and onto your rope system. Using the pick-off strap to fully tighten all connections between the rescue subject and the anchor makes for a gentle transfer of the load onto rope rigging. While there are many ways to accomplish this kind of smooth transfer, pick-off straps are easy to clip on, very intuitive to use, and are comfortably sized to make gripping and pulling easy on the hands. The adjustability of pick-off straps makes them good for a quick initial connection to the rescue subject that is bomber strong. Once they're connected, you can easily adjust the tension on the strap, in or out, as needed, while you maneuver to set up and complete your rigging. When everything is rigged up and ready to go, use the strap to tighten everything up as much as possible to minimize sudden rope stretch and unwanted drop-down.

Pick-Off Strap - Rigging Options

✱ *Alternatives For Various Conditions*

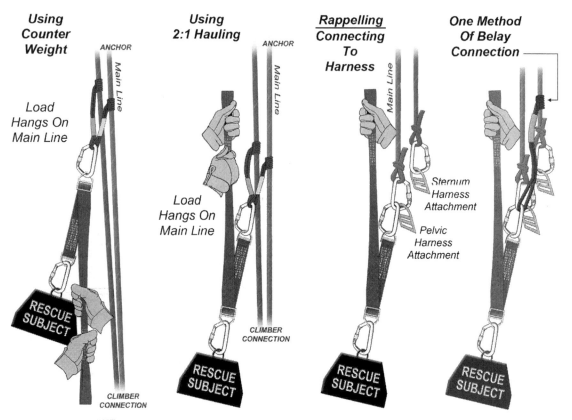

Using Counter Weight — ANCHOR — Main Line — Load Hangs On Main Line — RESCUE SUBJECT — CLIMBER CONNECTION — Longest Prusik Loop To The Belay Line

Using 2:1 Hauling — ANCHOR — Main Line — Load Hangs On Main Line — CLIMBER CONNECTION — RESCUE SUBJECT

Rappelling Connecting To Harness — Main Line — Sternum Harness Attachment — Pelvic Harness Attachment — RESCUE SUBJECT

One Method Of Belay Connection — RESCUE SUBJECT

The pick-off strap works great for connecting to and retrieving subjects positioned below the Climber, as might be the case in a tight, confined space rescue. When a Climber has to work upside down to reach a subject positioned below, pick-off straps provide a good means of reaching, connecting, and then removing slack and rope stretch prior to hauling. Using a pick-off strap this way serves to keep the Climber and rescue subject closer together when the entire load is hanging dependant on the rope system. This can be very important to keep within clearance limitations created by a portable overhead anchor such as a tripod. Whatever the situation, the Climber should always consider practical advantage when rigging up a pick-off strap. Depending on the position of the connections, the pick-off strap can create a theoretical 2 to 1 mechanical advantage. This can be a tremendous help when attempting to pull stretch out of the ropes or lifting a rescue subject off of his or her existing support. However, the position of the Climber and subject can make it ergonomically difficult to pull with mechanical advantage. In these situations connecting the directional hard point of the strap up high to create the practical advantage of pulling down with the Climber's own body weight works very well. Personal-sized accessory mechanical advantage blocks (sometimes referred to as "jiggers") are very useful when used in conjunction with a pick-off strap. Using a jigger to haul the load up or pull stretch out of the rope before setting the pick-off strap is easy to do from just about any ergonomic position.

Tying Off - *Pick-off Strap*
Cinch Half-Hitches Against The Directional Hard Point

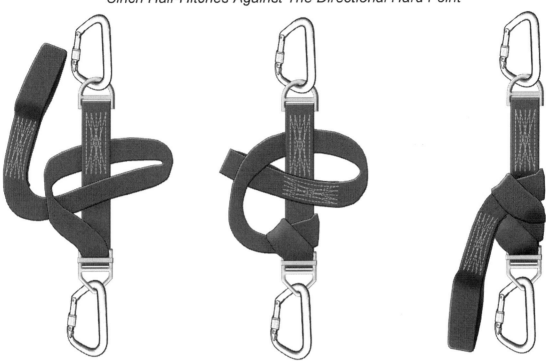

A general operating premise when connecting rescue subject loads to the rope system is to attach them independent of the Climber. In other words, whenever it's possible, rig the rescue subject in a way that he or she doesn't hang and pull on the Climber. Attach pick-off rigging directly to the main and belay lines instead of a harness connection whenever you can. Attaching the rescue load independently on the rope system enables the Climber to maneuver freely and handle the subject much more easily compared to linking directly to a harness connector. Never connect a rescue subject load to a harness hard point that is not directly connected to the main line of the hauling system. Doing so will create heavy opposing forces on the harness material and over-strain sewn connections, while adding heavy weight directly onto the Climber. Attach the pick-off rigging at the harness by clipping into the main line rope bite at the carabiner or onto the main line carabiner itself.

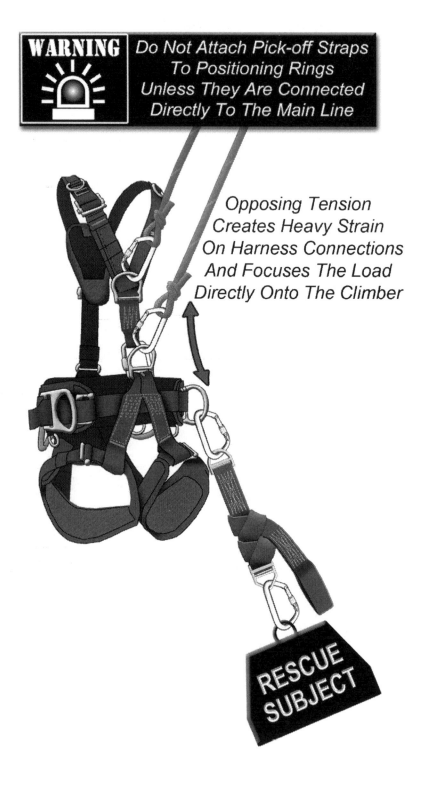

WARNING Do Not Attach Pick-off Straps To Positioning Rings Unless They Are Connected Directly To The Main Line

Opposing Tension Creates Heavy Strain On Harness Connections And Focuses The Load Directly Onto The Climber

RESCUE SUBJECT

Vertical Pick-Off - Lowering/Raising
✱ *Using Manufactured Pick-Off Strap & Improvised Subject Harness*

- *Stradle The Subject*

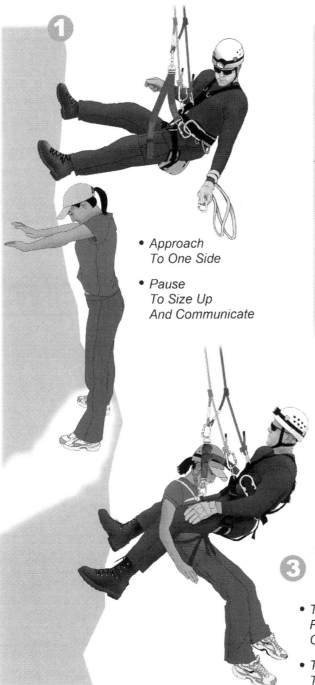

- *Approach
  To One Side*

- *Pause
  To Size Up
  And Communicate*

- *Place Chest Harness*

- *Attach Pick-Off Strap*

- *Integrate Seat Harness*

- *Adjust Prusiks & Strap*

- *Remove Slack
  And Rope Stretch*

- *Tie Off Pick-Off Strap*

- *Topside: Adjust Rigging
  For Additional Weight
  Or Convert To Raising System*

- *Transfer Subject Weight
  To The Rope System*

79

Rappelling - *Pick-Off Rigging*   Belayed From Above

✳ *Option For Attaching Rescue Subject While In Rappel Mode*

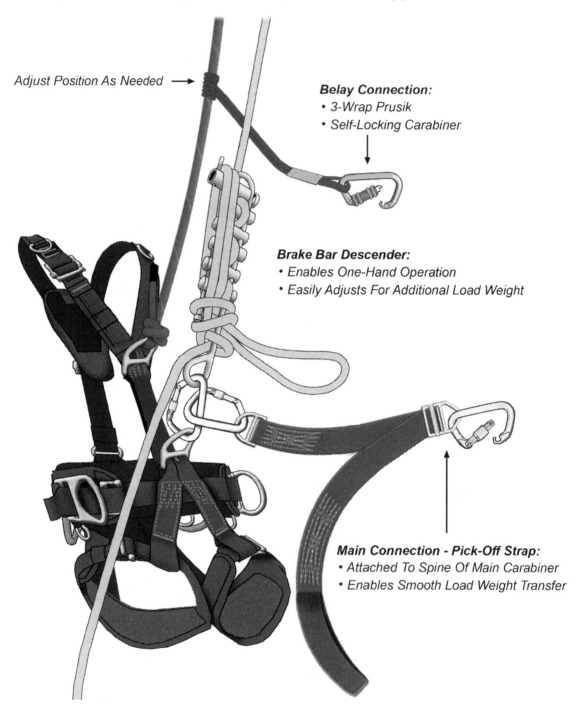

Adjust Position As Needed ➔

Belay Connection:
• *3-Wrap Prusik*
• *Self-Locking Carabiner*

Brake Bar Descender:
• *Enables One-Hand Operation*
• *Easily Adjusts For Additional Load Weight*

Main Connection - Pick-Off Strap:
• *Attached To Spine Of Main Carabiner*
• *Enables Smooth Load Weight Transfer*

Pulleys

There are many varieties of pulleys for every application imaginable, from extremely basic ones to complex systems equipped with brakes, swivels, and opening side plates. You name it. There are a few considerations common to all pulleys that will influence how you rig them into your system.

Pulley Capacity: Choose pulleys that can hold the loads you work with. Arborists use pulleys and blocks capable of dealing with loads in excess of 25,000 lbs., while recreational climbers routinely use light-duty pulleys. Make sure the pulleys you put into your cache are designed for rescue loads and match the rope diameters that you use. Compare the specification standards you've chosen to the pulleys you put into your cache. NFPA labeled pulleys are tested for a capacity of 22kN (4,946 lbf) tech use and 36kN (8,093 lbf) general use.

NFPA STANDARDS - PULLEY STRENGTH		
General Use	36kN (8093lbf)	**Becket** – 19.5kN (4383lbf)
Tech Use	22kN (4946lbf)	**Becket** – 12kN (2698lbf)

Basic Pulley Features

Single Sheave Pulley **Double Sheaved Pulley** **Prusik-Minding Pulley**

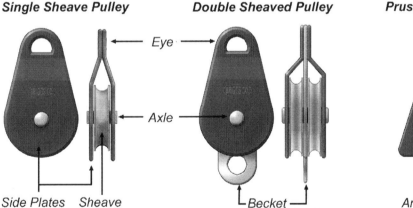

Side Plates   Sheave   Becket   Angular Side Plates

Eye
Axle

Pulley Size: There are size-related considerations when choosing pulleys. Sheave and rope diameter determine whether a pulley is appropriate for any particular application. Sheave diameter will influence how large and heavy the overall pulley is and may affect how practical it is for a given application. Larger diameter pulleys are generally more efficient and roll more smoothly. The diameter of the sheave also affects the strength of the rope that runs over it. Larger pulley sheaves distribute load forces over a larger area and reduce strain on the rope where it bends. A good rule of thumb is to use pulleys with sheaves that are at least 4 times the rope diameter to maintain full rope strength. It makes good sense to place your largest pulleys in the haul rigging on the rope leg that leads directly to the load. This can slightly increase efficiency and reduce rope strain at the sheave. Smaller, less bulky pulleys work better for the traveling positions in haul rigging and generally support smaller portions of the load.

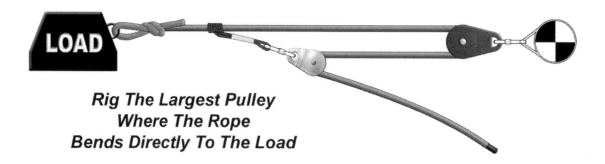

Rig The Largest Pulley Where The Rope Bends Directly To The Load

Rescue pulley sheaves are also designed to match rope diameters. A pulley with a sheave designed for a 3/8-inch rope will not work well for a ½-inch rope. A pulley made for ½-inch rope will work for a 9mm line, but the line will tend to flatten out and possibly weaken as it bends around the sheave. Pulleys with oversized sheave channeling accept the downside of rope flattening for the benefit of knot passing without re-rigging.

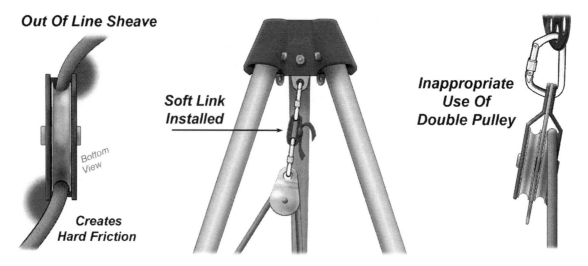

Out Of Line Sheave

Bottom View

Creates Hard Friction

Soft Link Installed

Inappropriate Use Of Double Pulley

Pulley Alignment: Whether a pulley is being used as a simple direction change or mechanical advantage, aligning the sheave with the route of the rope is important for smooth operation. If a pulley is connected in a way that holds it out of alignment, the rope entering and exiting the pulley will rub on the side plates and create friction and unwanted drag on the entire system. In some cases this can skew forces on directional anchors or cause tripods to tip. Pulleys rigged out of alignment will also have less contact where the sheave supports the rope, causing more strain. Rigging without the ability to swivel or rock is a common reason for pulleys to be out of line with the rope direction. This sometimes occurs when a carabiner and pulley are connected directly to the head of a tripod. The hard point connections on some artificial high directionals, such as tripods, do not line up well with the typical rope systems with which they are used. In these cases, a swivel or soft link can be rigged to the hard point to allow suspended pulleys to rotate or tilt freely. Adding this link will decrease overhead clearance and may require raising the height of the high directional.

Misalignment can also result from loading a single line onto a double-sheaved pulley. In this situation the load forces are offset slightly to the side, forcing the pulley to tilt sideways relative to the rope direction and causing the misaligned side plates to rub on the rope. The axle and sheave also take on unfavorable lateral strain, increasing friction and wear while reducing operational efficiency. Make sure pulleys have the ability to line up properly when they are loaded and always use double pulleys for double rope applications.

Prusik Minding: Pulleys with side plates designed to accomodate prusik brakes are referred to as "Prusik Minding Pulleys" (PMPs). These pulleys are designed with tolerances that allow appropriately-sized ropes to run through them, but they cleanly block the passage of a prusik hitch. Prusiks rigged with a PMP create reliable, hands-free progress capture mechanisms capable of holding 1,000 to 2,500lbs. before slipping, depending on the rope and cord used. PMPs usually have side plates that present a flat obstacle to the prusik hitch that is perpendicular to the rope direction. They must be rigged and operated properly for safe, smooth operation.

Prusiks integrated with PMPs for the purpose of capturing the hauling progress of a pulley system will completely support the load when the haulers stop pulling, and engage if an accidental shock occurs. For this reason, riggers must make sure that the prusik of a self-tending PMP brake is in line with the axis of the carabiner it is connected to. The pulley will rock out of the way when the prusik brake engages.

Gravity has an effect on self-tending prusik brakes that are rigged horizontally. The prusik loop will, of course, tighten and slack as the operation proceeds. In the slack state, there is potential for the cord to foul in the rigging and suck into the pulley. This problem can be minimized by orienting the self-tending rig so that the prusik loop droops down and clear of the pulley when slack. The prusik hitch itself tends to stay snug and intact better when rigged this way as well.

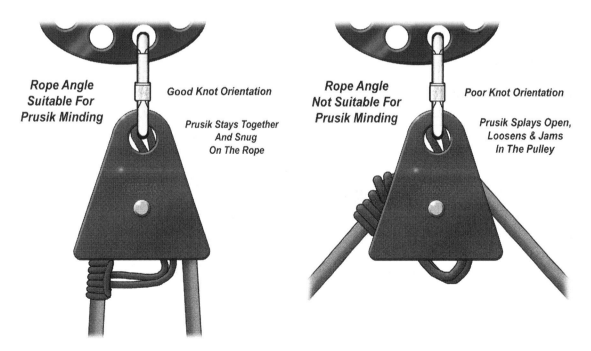

Rope Angle Suitable For Prusik Minding

Good Knot Orientation

Prusik Stays Together And Snug On The Rope

Rope Angle Not Suitable For Prusik Minding

Poor Knot Orientation

Prusik Splays Open, Loosens & Jams In The Pulley

Riggers must ensure that the pulley is appropriate for the rope used, and that the rope enters and exits the pulley properly. The prusik hitch must stay intact and snug when the rope is moving while hauling the load up. When the hauling rope incorrectly enters and exits the PMP at a wide angle, the prusik hitch sideswipes the side plates instead of contacting them flat and clean. This often results in the prusik getting partially sucked inside the pulley and loosening it enough to make it ineffective. This situation also increases friction and wear enough to damage the prusik cord and make hauling difficult. Self-tending prusik brakes work best when the rope is parallel with itself as it winds in and out of the PMP. Some PMPs are designed to tolerate wider angles, but they're not foolproof. Monitor the rigging and make sure your self-tending brakes are well set up and working properly.

Self Tending Prusik Brake - Rigged Horizontally

Position Prusik Against The Carabiner Spine

Prevents Prusik Loop Sucking Into The Pulley

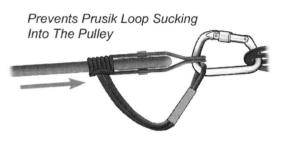

Position Rigging With Prusik Below The Pulley

Rope Grabs

8mm 3-Wrap Prusik On 1/2" Rope Holds A Static Load Of 1000 to 2500lbs

Hardware and software used to attach to ropes mid-length are generally referred to as "rope grabs." Rope grabs usually have the ability to adjust and change position along the length of the line they're attached to. Many grabs only hold a load in one direction and will slide freely along the line if loaded in the opposite direction. Prusik hitches and mechanical ascenders are examples of rope grabs. Rope grabs come in many styles for a wide variety of applications. Safety and efficiency depend on an operational understanding of the limitations of the particular rope grabs you choose. It's important to know how well a rope grab performs in a shock load situation and whether it needs to relieve shock forces where it is connected.

Open and Closed Grabs: Hardware or software that completely surrounds the rope when it's attached, requiring disassembling or untying for removal, describes "closed rope grabs." Hardware that captures and keeps rope in place via a spring-loaded cam or idler are considered "open rope grabs." Closed grabs will not accidentally detach from the rope when they are properly connected, even when they are used improperly. When closed grabs lose grip on the rope, they can fall along the length of the rope; however, they stay connected. Open grabs that are correctly rigged may completely detach from the rope if used improperly. Prusiks and mechanical ascenders that retain the rope with a pin or axle are examples of closed rope grabs. Handled ascenders that use thumb-controlled cams to hold the rope in correct position are examples of open rope grabs. It's more common to see closed rope grabs in fire service rescue caches. Open grabs usually connect and disconnect easily using one hand and are favored by arborists, industrial rope access, and recreational climbers.

Prusik Hitches

Usually tied with cord, prusik hitches grab onto the the rope and hold fast until manipulated or overloaded. The capacity for a prusik hitch to hold its position primarily depends on the diameters of the rope and cord used. Other performance factors include construction and material makeup of the rope and cord, along with conditions such as wear, cleanliness, and dryness. Prusik loops used for rescue work can be tied or presewn by the manufacturer. Either way, make sure the prusik loops in your cache are suitable for use with the ropes you use. An easy way to make sure prusiks perform as needed is to purchase ropes, cords and presewn loops from the same manufacturer, and study the specification information they provide.

Prusik hitches can be fashioned in ways that control gripping performance. The number of wraps, position of wraps, and cord choices all affect the gripping attributes of prusik hitches. Prusik rope grabs can be used for ascending, hauling cams, anchors, load limiters, and brakes. Each of these rope grab applications have differing performance needs that can be built into prusiks depending on how you fashion them.

It's currently common to use 8mm static kernmantle cord with 12.5mm (1/2-inch) kernmantle rope for prusik rope grabs. With this rope and cord combination, a 3-wrap prusik hitch has the capacity to hold a load force of about 1,000 to 2,500lbs. Cord with a smaller diameter on the same rope would slip less, and cord with a larger diameter would slip more. When prusik holding power is exceeded, the grab will begin to slip instead of catastrophically failing. This a favorable performance characteristic in the event of an accidental shock or overloading. If the hitch does slip, most damage is done to the prusik cord instead of the rope. If a 2-rope rescue system is operated correctly, the prusik should only slip a short distance and suffer tolerable damage before additional support is gained from the backup system. Imagine a 500lb dirt clod cleaving off the face and falling into the resuce basket. A brake fashioned from a prusik would slip enough to absorb some of the shock and allow the load to move downhill until the backup system tightens. Many mechanical rope grabs do not absorb shock in this way and damage the rope severely when a hard shock load occurs.

Prusik Hitch

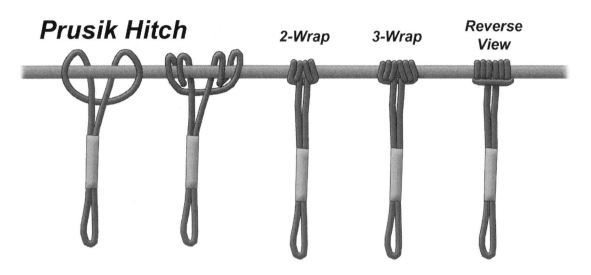

2-Wrap *3-Wrap* *Reverse View*

Systems that require less rope grab grip and more slip can be rigged using 2-wrap prusiks. An example of this kind of application is the adjustable bridle rigging described in this book for use on vertical rescue baskets. Two-wrap hitches have enough holding power for this use and are much easier for the Climber to manipulate while hanging vertical in akward positions. *Two-wrap prusik hitches are not appropriate for use as main line brakes or belay brakes.*

There is a technique to manipulating a prusik rope grab that makes setting and releasing easy and practical. It's common to see inexperienced riggers struggling to ascend a fixed line or reset a hauling system because they don't manipulate the prusik rope grab correctly. In normal conditions prusiks used as brakes or hauling cams can become very tightly set. Simply grabbing the knot and forcing it to slide to a different position on the rope is hard to do. It slows down the operation and can damage the prusik cord. It's better to slightly loosen and then reposition and retighten the knot. This can be done with little effort by backing off on the load and manipulating the bight that crosses the body of the knot (sometimes referred to as the "trigger"). Simply push back on the bight until the wraps loosen. Then move the knot into position, and snug it back up.

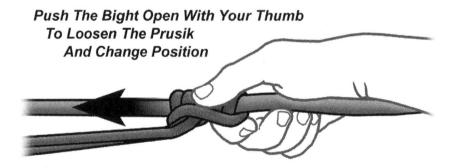

*Push The Bight Open With Your Thumb
To Loosen The Prusik
And Change Position*

Shock loading and jams can result in rigging with prusik hitches that are so tightly fixed on the rope, they're nearly impossible to release by hand. This usually occurs when prusik rope grabs are used for brakes on hauling systems. But it can also happen in other areas of the rigging. If a Climber gets a limb or piece of equipment jammed onto the cliff face, the hauling operation can accidentally continue long enough to stretch the rope and result in a fully-tensioned pulley system with the prusik brake set tightly. In situations like these, it's not possible to raise the climber to relieve tension on the prusik and release the brake.

LRH's Can Provide Useful Options For Dealing With Jams And Over Tightened Prusik Brakes

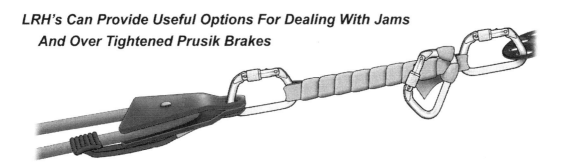

For this reason many rescue organizations connect load releasing hitches (LRHs) to hauling system prusik brakes and prusik belay systems. LRHs can also make changing a fully-loaded hauling system to a lowering system easy and smooth. Depending on the type, LRHs absorb small amounts of shock and reduce some of the prusik cord damage that can occur with a shock load. Diagrams in this book will depict vertical rescue systems that include LRHs to show how they are integrated with prusiks.

Prusik rope grabs can be installed "in-line" to provide redundancy and increased grip. Rigging multiple prusik hitches enlarges the cord to rope contact area, resulting in slightly more gripping strength and reduced strain and damage in the event of a sudden shock or overload. Double and triple prusik grabs are sometimes used to form anchor connections that overcome weakening of the rope created by knots, a good solution for high-strain operations like highlines. Most often used as a belay brake, double prusiks allow one knot to engage and catch, then slip enough to make the second knot tighten and provide additional support. The intended result is a strong, but relatively low-impact, belay system that can catch accidental falls and overloads. Handling double prusik belays requires proper rigging and good technique. It can take some practice to become proficient. Refer to Chapter 12 "Belaying" for detailed descriptions of belay system rigging and operation.

Double Prusiks

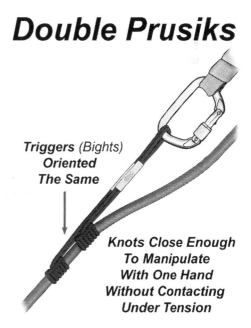

Triggers (Bights) Oriented The Same

Knots Close Enough To Manipulate With One Hand Without Contacting Under Tension

Handling prusik rope grabs for progress capture applications is easy, but demands attention to a few important details. In general, you capture haul progress with a prusik by holding the wraps stationary with one hand while pulling slack rope through with the other hand. Do this in 6 to 12-inch segments. A good way to position the hand holding the prusik is to capture the outside wraps with the heel of the thumb and forefinger. Keep thumbs clear of trap hazards to avoid injury if the rope snaps tight from a fall. In long-haul situations, one can fatigue and develop a major case of arm pump. In these cases, it makes good sense to pull the wraps and the slack line up together and then slide the wraps back toward the load to capture progress. Do this in 6 to 12-inch intervals as well. Prusiks that are too loose or that are exposed to capturing long falls will not work as needed and can result in disaster. A properly applied prusik should be snug on the rope to create "crisp friction noise" when slack line is pulled through. Something like, *"zzzZZZIP."* This measure of adjustment will enable the prusik to instantly cinch down and arrest an unexpected fall or shock. As an operation progresses, prusik wraps may loosen. Tighten the wraps as needed to maintain prusik performance. It's also very important to manage a prusik, or any other progress capture device, so that it will not be exposed to catching a long drop. Manipulate the progress capture device or brake to maintain proper amounts of slack and tension. This allows for operation without the possibility of an accidental drop of more than a foot. If the rope is short, as it would be when a Climber is close to topside in a raising operation, keep slack to an absolute minimum. Excessive slack in the line will allow more time for the load to pick up speed if the Climber loses his or her footing. More acceleration means more shock when the rope snaps tight. Drops exceeding 12 inches risk overwhelming or damaging the progress capture prusik and injuring the Climber. Drooping slack sometimes occurs during over-the-side operations with long lines because the weight of the rope is mistaken for downward movement of the Climber. Team members should be alert to spotting and quickly eliminating excessive slack between the progress capture mechanism and the load. Managing prusik belay systems for raising operations is more in-depth and requires more technique. Refer to Chapter 12 "Belaying" for detailed descriptions of double prusiks for fall protection.

Progress capture prusiks must be released and managed when a hauling line is used to lower the load. Simply use your forefinger and thumb to prevent the wraps from moving with the rope, just as the side plates of a prusik minding pulley would do. Keep fingers and thumbs clear from snags and injuries if the rope suddenly snaps tight. Managing prusik belay systems for lowering

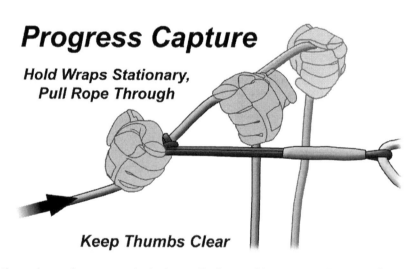

Progress Capture

Hold Wraps Stationary, Pull Rope Through

Keep Thumbs Clear

operations is more in-depth and requires more technique. Refer to Chapter 12 "Belaying" for detailed descriptions of double prusiks fall protection.

Mechanical Ascenders: There are lots of choices when it comes to mechanical ascenders. Every gear company out there has their own version of the utlimate ascender or progress capturing rope grab. The best choice for fire/rescue applications are closed ascenders that are simple and rugged in construction. Current NFPA standards address rope damage and deformation damage to the descender itself when loaded to 5kN (1,124 lbf) for tech use and 11kN (2,500 lbf) for general use without damaging ropes. At the time of this writing, ascender manufacturers have not marketed mechanical ascender rope grabs with NFPA compliance labels. However, mechanical ascenders are engineered and marketed for use with vertical rescue systems. They're generally engineered to support heavier loads than recreational versions. Many carry a CE marking denoting that the product has met at least one of three European consumer performance standards.

Closed ascenders that use a rocking cam to squeeze the rope against a casing may not slip favorably if a shock or overload occurs. These devices direct and concentrate force to a very small portion of the rope. Heavy shock loading often results in severe rope damage and/or dangerous fouling and jamming inside the device. Often the rope is damaged in a way that it will not run through the descender or other equipment, even though it may maintain enough strength to support the load. Hard shock loading can also cause these types of ascenders to warp or bend enough to lose grip on the rope.

Closed Mechanical Rope Grabs - Ascenders

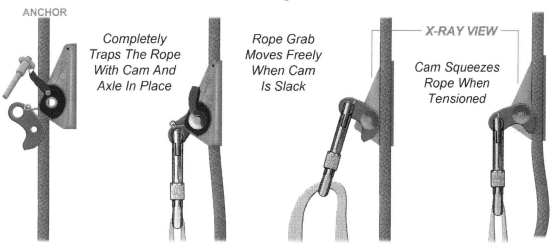

ANCHOR

Completely Traps The Rope With Cam And Axle In Place

Rope Grab Moves Freely When Cam Is Slack

X-RAY VIEW

Cam Squeezes Rope When Tensioned

Camming mechanical rope grabs should not be used for belays or main brakes that are directly placed on rescue raising systems. You may see advanced riggers and teams using mechanical ascenders as indirectly placed hauling system brakes. This is a very advanced application and should only be used by those with high levels of technical expertise. The best use for mechanical rope grabs is climbing up fixed ropes. Mechanical ascenders make rigging and climbing fixed ropes quick and easy compared to using prusik loops. An application described in this book uses closed mechanial ascenders to provide positioning flexibility for Climbers using rescue baskets. Closed mechanical ascenders can be cautiously used as hauling rope grabs in mechanical advantage pulley systems with loads of 600lbs or less.

CAUTIONS
1. Use closed mechanical rope grabs for 2-person rescue applications. Ascenders that completely trap the rope and require the removal of an axle or pin to disconnect are closed rope grabs.

2. Do not use ascenders as main brakes or belay control devices. Most ascenders do not slip in a way needed for brake or belay applications. Heavy shock forces can result in severe rope damage and/or damage to the ascender.

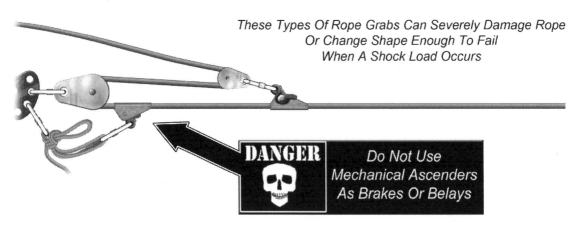

*These Types Of Rope Grabs Can Severely Damage Rope
Or Change Shape Enough To Fail
When A Shock Load Occurs*

DANGER
Do Not Use
Mechanical Ascenders
As Brakes Or Belays

CAUTION
Use Mechanical Ascenders
As Hauling Rope Grabs
With Extreme Caution

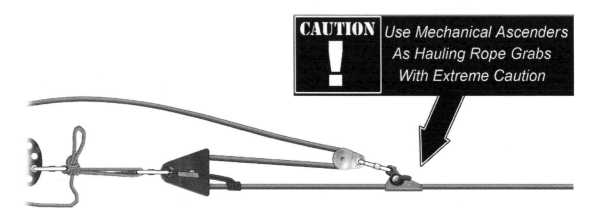

Descent Control Devices

Appliances used to control downward rope movement against gravity are referred to as "descent control devices" (DCDs). Some are designed specifically for the purpose of descent control, while others are tools that adapt well for the purpose of controlling lowering. DCDs can be connected to an anchor to lower a load or directly to a Climber for rappelling.

Brake Racks

Also called brake bar racks, brake racks were developed within the caving discipline by rigging multiple carabiners together. They work by creating friction on the rope as it serpentines through and across the bars. The more bars in contact with the rope, the more friction. The tighter (closer together) the bars, the more friction. The device has evolved over the years to better address rescue system needs. Not all racks are the same. Racks come in many shapes and sizes for differing needs and rope diameters.

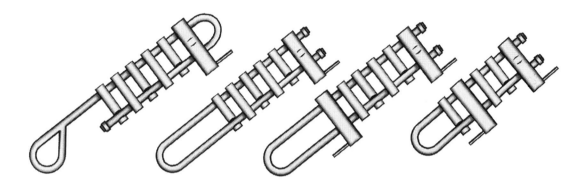

J-shaped racks are common. Look for racks that are built to support a 2-person load and include "hyperbars" for better rigging adaptability. It's good to know that racks with aluminum alloy bars provide slightly more friction than those with bars made of steel. Racks are great for rescue operations because the amount of friction provided by the device can easily be adjusted, even while the load is still on the system. Long rappels require less friction near topside and more friction toward the bottom. More important during rescues, friction can be added to a rack to accommodate the additional weight of plucking a person off the side of a cliff midway through an operation. Brake racks control descent without twisting and tangling the rope. Racks are easy and intuitive to use and can be locked and tied off with very little effort. However, brake racks only work in one direction, meaning that taking up unwanted slack is a little difficult. It's best to pull out all slack in the line before threading the rope onto the rack. Slack can then be extended by lowering the rope.

The top bar usually looks a bit different from the others on the rack. Referred to as the "training bar," the first bar is larger and normally has a small indent where it is intended to be in contact with the rope. This indent is a visual cue to help riggers lay the rope correctly and avoid threading it backwards onto the rack. The training bar is often fixed onto the rack and unable to pivot as the other bars do.

Brake Bar Rack - *'J-Bar' Type*

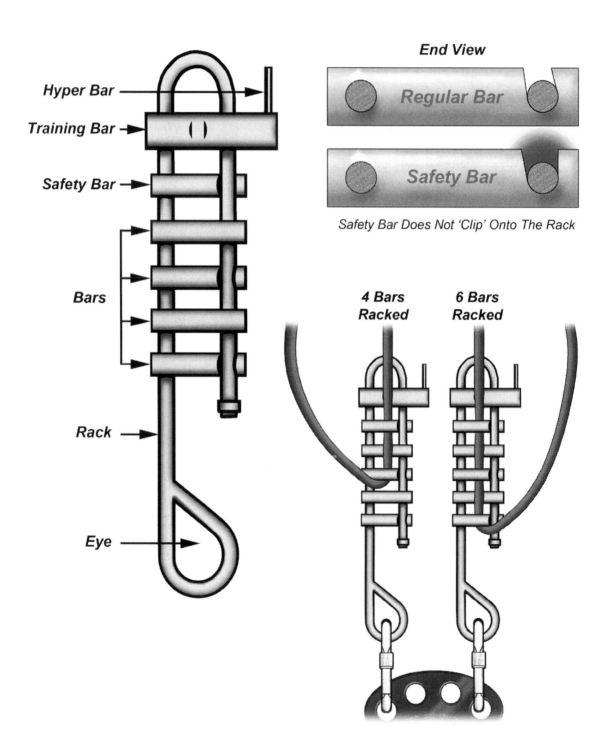

Hyper Bar

Training Bar

Safety Bar

Bars

Rack

Eye

End View

Regular Bar

Safety Bar

Safety Bar Does Not 'Clip' Onto The Rack

4 Bars Racked

6 Bars Racked

The small horn mounted on the training bar of some racks provides a means to quickly add more friction, and it also makes locking off easy. This horn is mounted to an extended training bar referred to as the "hyper bar." The horn acts as a retainer that holds the rope in place when it's wrapped over the extended training bar outside of the rack. More specialized racks have top and bottom hyper bars.

The next bar in line is the "safety bar." The safety bar pivots like a gate on the rack to enable looping a bend of rope around it. Sometimes referred to as the "idiot bar" in the field, it usually looks like the other bars with one important exception. Other bars on the rack pivot open to thread the rope and have notches milled to "snap" and lightly hold in the closed position for rigging convenience. The safety bar has a notch that is milled straight so that it will not snap and hold closed. This design feature is an additional measure to prevent loading the rack backwards. If the rack is loaded backwards, the pivoting bars will pop open and release the rope as soon as a heavy load is applied. Because the safety bar doesn't hold closed on its own, it's difficult to incorrectly wrap the remaining bars. The safety bar flops open and releases the rope if it's wrapped backwards. Some bars are constructed of folded sheet steel, making the correct rope route very obvious.

The remaining bars act as simple friction points. As mentioned above, modern racks usually have bars that snap to lightly hold in the closed position to make rigging easier. Squeezing the rack with one hand makes opening and closing bars easier. Wrap the number of bars you need for the job at hand. In general, it's best to start an operation with enough friction to hold the load with no effort or adjustment. If less friction is requested after things get started, spread out or unwrap the bars. A good default rule is to start every operation that uses ½-inch rope with four bars wrapped for a single person load (1 to 299lbs), and 6 bars wrapped for a two-person load (300 to 600lbs). Closing any unused bars makes adding friction clean and simple and decreases flexing of the rack under load.

Operating a brake rack is the same whether attached to the Climber or an anchor. When connected to an anchor for a lowering operation, it's best if the operator positions close enough to cradle the rack in one hand and grip (brake) the rope with the other. Once threaded, the rack controls lowering by spreading the bars for less friction and compressing the bars together for more friction. The primary method of spreading or compressing the bars is to change the position of the hand that grips and controls slippage of the rope, also known as the braking hand. To spread the bars on the rack, move the braking hand back, away from the load. To compress the bars and increase friction, move the braking hand forward toward the load. To stop lowering, fully compress the bars by pulling hard on the rope toward the load. Spreading and compressing the bars can be aided by using the cradling hand to manipulate the bars further apart or closer together. The cradling hand usually comes into play when a Climber moves to the edge just before loading the system.

Brake Bar Rack - *Handling*

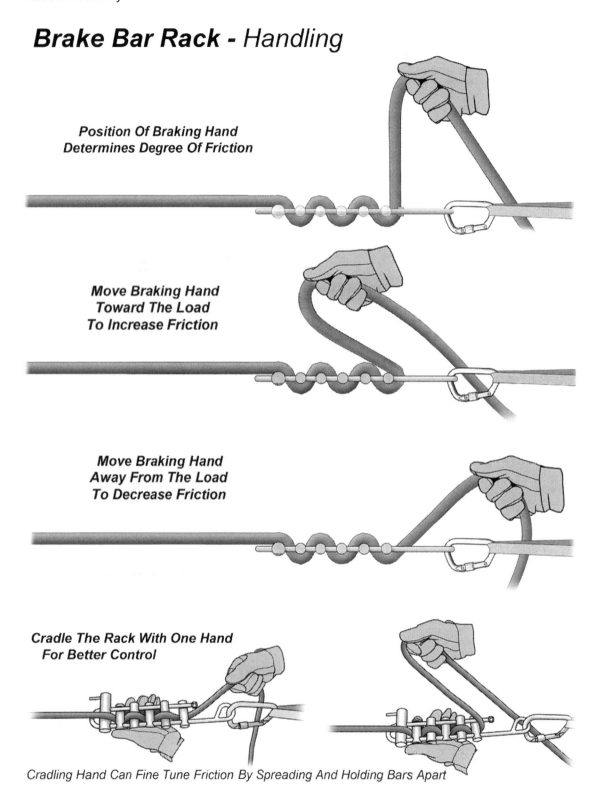

**Position Of Braking Hand
Determines Degree Of Friction**

**Move Braking Hand
Toward The Load
To Increase Friction**

**Move Braking Hand
Away From The Load
To Decrease Friction**

**Cradle The Rack With One Hand
For Better Control**

Cradling Hand Can Fine Tune Friction By Spreading And Holding Bars Apart

Brake Bar Rack - *Add Friction - Lock Off - Tie Off*

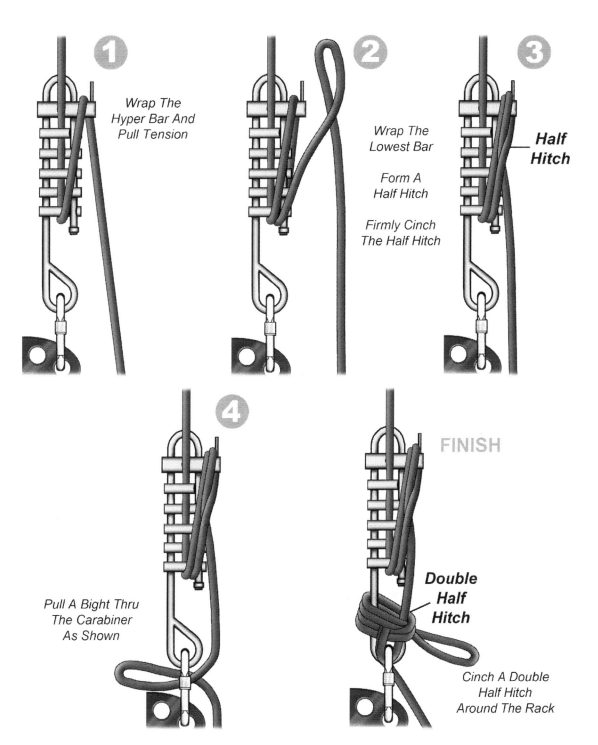

1 Wrap The Hyper Bar And Pull Tension

2 Wrap The Lowest Bar

Form A Half Hitch

Firmly Cinch The Half Hitch

3 *Half Hitch*

4 Pull A Bight Thru The Carabiner As Shown

FINISH *Double Half Hitch*

Cinch A Double Half Hitch Around The Rack

To quickly add another layer of friction without stopping, or to stop and hold lowering movement, fully compress the bars, and then drape a bight of rope around the top hyper bar. This adds enough friction to hold the load with the brake hand without having to thread additional bars. To further secure the brake rack to stop, hold, and lock off, wrap an additional bight of the rope around the bottom bar and then half-hitch it over the hyper bar. If a closed U-shaped rack is used, thread the second bight through the eye of the rack or the connected biner, and simply drape it over the hyper bar. Either way, racks rigged in this way allow operators to remove their cradling hand for adjusting other rigging or to assume a more restful position. To work hands free, operators must further secure the rack by tying it off. Simply thread a long bight of the loose (standing) rope through the connected biner and fashion a double half-hitch (mule hitch) in a way that it holds the rigging tightly in place.

To wrap or unwrap bars while the system is hot, compress the bars to stop lowering movement, and use the cradling hand to open or close the bars needed to adjust the friction. Next, position the thumb or fingers of the cradling hand to hold the rope in the stopped position. While holding the rope tension with the cradling hand, use the gripping hand to loosely wrap or unwrap bars as needed with the slack standing rope. Pull quickly and firmly with the braking hand, and let go with the cradling hand to snug up the wraps. Close any bars that are not in use with the cradling hand. Continue lowering as needed. NOTE: U-shaped racks can be manipulated similarly but require slightly different technique. Some racks rely solely on hyper bars to add or reduce friction and cannot be manipulated in this way.

Cautions: Brake racks are very safe and easy to use. But be aware of situations that can wad up an operation or even injure workers.

1. As the rope moves through a rack during normal operation, it can act like a conveyer belt to drag loose hair, clothing, straps, etc. in between the bars. You can end up with a tightly-tangled bird's nest that can be very difficult to clean up. This is not good for anyone over the side. A longhaired Climber can be forced into very awkward and uncomfortable positions if his or her locks are sucked into the rack. Operations will come to a dead stop, and recovering can be very difficult if a rack becomes packed with hair or clothing. Bind long hair back and up to avoid an emergency trimming. Tuck in loose clothing and straps before going over. You'll be glad you did.

2. Be careful about pulling excess tension on the standing section of a rope that has been threaded into a rack. This kind of rigging focuses force on the bottom bar of the rack. Heavy tension on the bottom bar sometimes occurs when advanced teams change from a raising operation to a lowering operation while the system is still hot. Advanced users sometimes make this maneuver without the use of a load-releasing hitch by locking off the rack and using the standing section of rope to haul on a traveling pulley that is attached to the running section. This can be done successfully, but it's easy to overstress and damage the rack. This can and does happen, resulting in a badly bent rack and popped out bars.

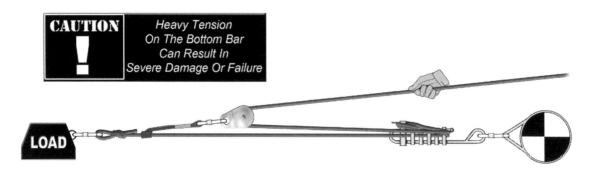

8-Plates

The descent controller most familiar to firefighters is the 8-plate, or Rescue 8. With no moving parts and straightforward operation, firefighters tend to gravitate to the 8-plates and shy away from brake racks. Eights are good tools but have several limitations that make them less desirable for rescue work. In days of old, fire rescue teams used 8s to lower 2-person loads, for belay control, and as rigging plates. Since those times, manufacturers and rescue organizations have determined that typical 8s are not suitable for these applications. It was learned, sometimes the hard way, that 8s do not reliably hold the rope when a shock occurs, especially with 2-person loads. Eight plates are now mainly used for rappelling by Climbers weighing under 300lbs. Using 8s as rigging plates tends to damage the smooth surface where ropes run through them during descent control operations. This is not a good thing. Nicks and burrs on these surfaces will act like a rasp on the rope sheath when they're used for descent control. Feel for problems on the working surfaces every time an 8 is installed. Always provide for back-up protection when rappelling or lowering with an 8-plate in rescue

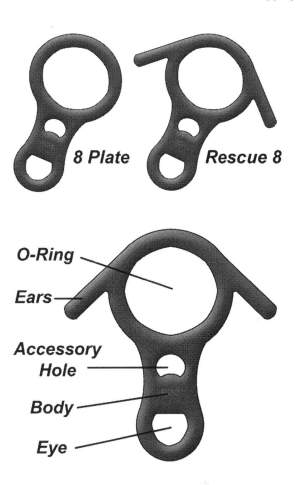

operations. Do not use 8s to control belay ropes. Don't use 8s as substitutes for rigging plates or rings. It's good to know that aluminum plates provide slightly more friction than those made from steel. Plates vary in size to accommodate different rope diameters. In general, plates with larger O-rings provide less friction than smaller versions. Rescue 8s have horns that extend from the O-ring that are referred to as "ears." The ears prevent a lark's foot hitch accidentally setting at the top of the O-ring, which happens when ropes slip up and off of the body on regular 8-plates. Ears can also aid in locking off. Some plates are equipped with accessory holes that can be used for prusik minding or as a Sticht plate.

Typical 8-plates are compact, lightweight, and easy to use. They can be threaded to adjust friction but require extra rigging to make these adjustments once the load has been applied. Specialized 8-plates with accessory spurs, horns, or hooks improve adjustability while under load. But all these devices control descent by creating friction as the rope snakes through and around the hardware. This causes the rope to twist enough to create tight curls that can cause fouling or a Climber to spin when hanging free.

Rescue 8 - *Threading & Working*

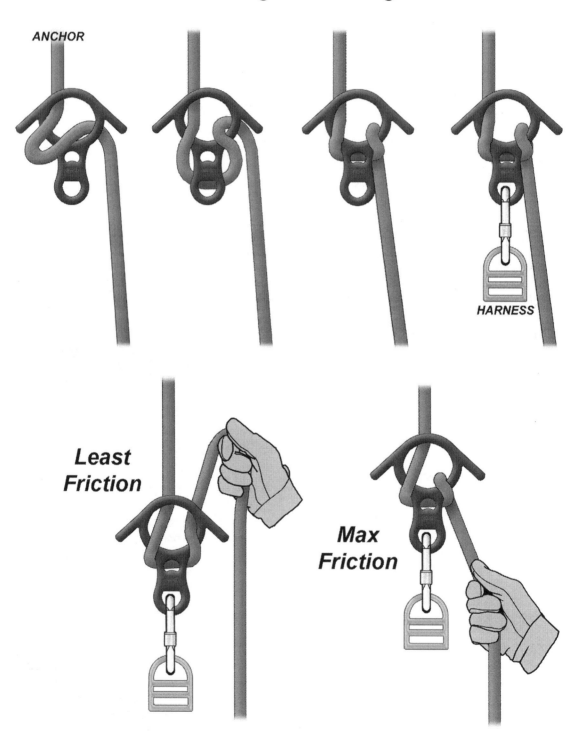

ANCHOR

HARNESS

Least
Friction

Max
Friction

Descent/Lowering Control: The position of the standing rope and grip of the braking (controlling) hand determines downward movement speed. Smoothly loosen the grip of the controlling hand to allow rope to move through the 8. If an 8 is connected to a Climber's harness in a rappelling maneuver, you increase friction and slow descent by moving the controlling hand back toward the Climber. Holding the standing rope tightly in the five o'clock position develops maximum friction. Positioning the controlling hand behind the Climber's butt, causing the standing rope to round and rub against the hip area, increases friction even more. Friction decreases and descent speed

THREADING VARIATIONS

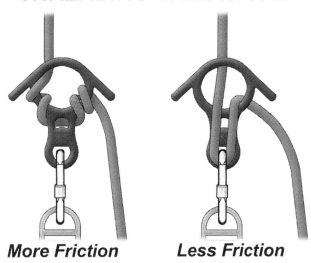

More Friction   **Less Friction**

increases as the controlling hand moves toward the twelve o'clock position. Friction variations can be rigged into the 8-plateeight depending on how the rope is threaded. More advanced means of adding friction include installing carabiners or Münter hitches onto the standing section of rope.

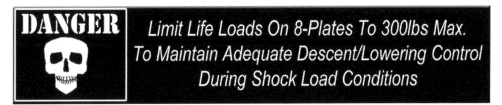

DANGER Limit Life Loads On 8-Plates To 300lbs Max. To Maintain Adequate Descent/Lowering Control During Shock Load Conditions

Locking Off: There are several methods for locking off and tying off for the purpose of working hands free. Some hold better than others but require some practice to execute smoothly. Some are easy to carry out but are not as secure as other methods. Either way, the basic means of locking off with an 8 is to jam the standing section of rope between the hardware and the tensioned working section. Achieving this without initially wrapping the ears provides the best purchase because the standing rope seats deeper and tighter between the 8 and the tensioned working section. This can be a real white-knuckled affair for less experienced Climbers locking off during a rappel. But with a little practice, it's easy to lock off without first wrapping the ears. One pitfall that gets some people in trouble is the natural tendency to begin the lock off maneuver too quickly while the control hand is gripping the rope too far from the 8. Another pitfall is when the 8 rotates during the maneuver because the Climber didn't stabilize its position with the free hand. Grab the carabiner and the body of the 8 to stabilize them, and allow the control hand to get close (about 10 inches) to the hardware before making the motion to lock in. With the hands in the proper position, place the standing line up and over the top of the O-ring using one smooth motion. It's important to maintain tight contact with the standing line and the back of the O-ring when making this move to minimize unwanted downward movement. Once the rope is in this position, it should be much easier to hold fast and prevent downward movement. With the standing line in place atop the 8 and snug against the working line, pull down hard on the standing section so that it slips below the top of the O-ring. A solid "thunk" sound indicates that the rope has moved and is seated tightly between the 8 and the working line. This partially locks the descender and makes it almost effortless to hold position. To lock off fully, bring the slack standing line around the front of the 8 and catch it under the opposite ear. Now repeat the steps for the first locking maneuver to create a second purchase between the hardware and the working line.

Rescue 8 - Lock & Tie Off

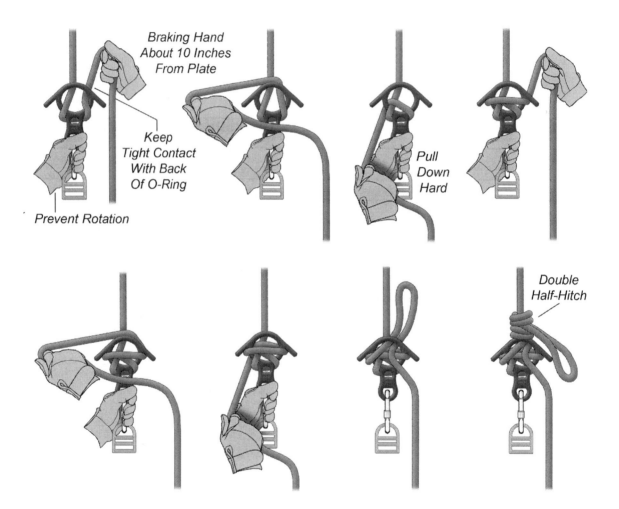

Using the ears to stop downward movement before locking off is much easier to execute, but is slightly less secure because the standing rope doesn't seat as deeply between the 8 and the tensioned working section. With either method, safety requires tying off the standing rope before working hands-free. A good way to do this is to form a long bight in the standing rope, thread it through the O-ring, and then tie a snug double half-hitch around the working line.

Rescue 8 - *Lock & Tie Off - Using Ears*

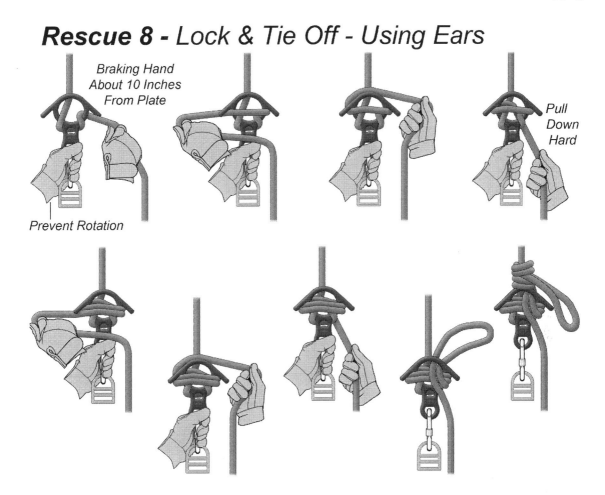

Braking Hand About 10 Inches From Plate

Prevent Rotation

Pull Down Hard

Unlocking to continue rappelling or lowering requires a small amount of setup and technique. Ergonomic considerations for hand placement are important for unlocking to hold position and maintain control. Pulling the standing rope that is tightly jammed between the 8 and the running section can be tough and often requires a good yank with both hands. Start by draping the loose rope over the top of and behind the O-ring, and grab it with both hands. Then pull down hard and pop the standing rope out from behind the 8. Before making the last pull that fully unlocks the 8, be sure to place your controlling hand on the standing section of rope, so that it instantly ends up in the position of maximum friction when it pops out from behind the O-ring. During a rappel, this usually means the control hand needs to instantly end up behind the butt with the standing rope rounding the hip area.

Rescue 8 - Unlocking Progression

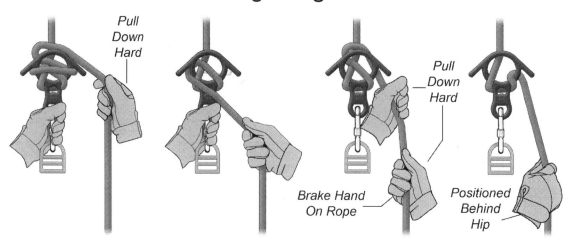

Pull Down Hard

Pull Down Hard

Brake Hand On Rope

Positioned Behind Hip

CAUTIONS

1. 8-Plates and Rescue 8s are currently considered to be suitable for single-person use. 8-plates and Rescue 8s cannot safely control the descent of a life-load exceeding 300lbs.

2. Confirm that 8-plate friction surfaces that contact the rope during descent control are smooth and free of burrs, cracks, or excessive wear prior to each installation.

3. As the rope runs through an 8-plate, friction creates heat that stores and builds up in the metal. Long or fast rappels and lowering operations can cause the 8 to become very hot. It is possible to develop enough heat to damage rope and software or burn skin. Rescue ops usually progress at a pace that doesn't require rapid raps or lowering as might be the case with military or law enforcement missions. Use 8s at a slow enough speed to allow heat to dissipate away from the hardware. Pay attention to the warmth of the descender throughout the operation. One reason why many Climbers reserve the option to work without gloves whenever they are on the rope is so they can better feel if hardware is hot or cool.

4. Eights used to support life-loads should not be used as gathering plates.

5. Do not use 8-plates or Rescue 8s to control belay ropes.

Self-Braking Descenders

Industrial workers routinely use self-braking descenders to access difficult job sites. Rope access professionals need a safe means to maneuver freely using rappelling, ascending, and traversing techniques without the benefit of a 7-person team. Self-braking descenders have evolved to meet these needs, and many more applications have been adapted for these versatile tools. Relative newcomers to the fire/rescue service in the United States, manufacturers are beginning to offer self-braking descenders that fit on ½-inch ropes and meet NFPA standards for tech and general use. Many rescue operations can be significantly streamlined by using these multi-functional descenders. Engineered to favorably slip when overloaded, self-braking descenders often eliminate the need for additional shock absorbing and load releasing rigging. Other safety features include wear indicators and a toothed flipper that prevents movement if the descender is threaded incorrectly. Various rescue applications require strict adherence to manufacturer instructions and may even require that the descender be permanently installed onto a rope as a kit. Manufacturer instructions and warnings must be studied carefully. While not difficult to use, self-braking descenders require practice to develop confidence and smooth handling.

Self-braking descenders control friction on the rope with a cam contained inside a housing that is made up of fixed and moveable side plates. Inside the housing, the rope follows a path around a directional pin before it is squeezed between the spring-loaded cam and a friction plate. Beyond the friction plate, the rope exits the housing and curls over a rolled surface with a smooth edge that provides additional friction as it is directed to the gripping (braking) hand. When the descender is threaded and weight is added to tighten the rope, the spring-loaded cam acts to grip and hold the load. The handle allows the operator to change the position of the cam to adjust the grip and allow movement. There are 5 rotary handle settings for controlling the cam. Each has a range of movement that can vary slightly, depending on rope diameter and weight of the load. You can feel "bump" markers and hear clicks as the handle rotates to various dial positions. Sometimes referred to as bobbin appliances, these descenders are capable of moving up or down on the rope and stopping movement if the Climber lets go of the handle. They require the use of two hands when used for rappelling or lowering. With the braking hand in place holding the rope, the handle is manipulated with the other hand. Think of using the throttle and clutch pedals together when driving a standard transmission vehicle. Coordinated grip pressure of the braking hand and handle adjustment with the other hand controls speed and smooth movement along the rope. Always have a hand on the braking section of the rope before manipulating the handle. Using the handle without firmly holding the rope will result in very choppy downward movement with dangerous bursts of near freefall speed and sudden stops. The horizontal movement button on the handle helps with cam control in situations where loads are very light (below 110lbs), as would be the case whenever a climber moves on flat or low angle ground.

Self-Braking Descenders - *Details*

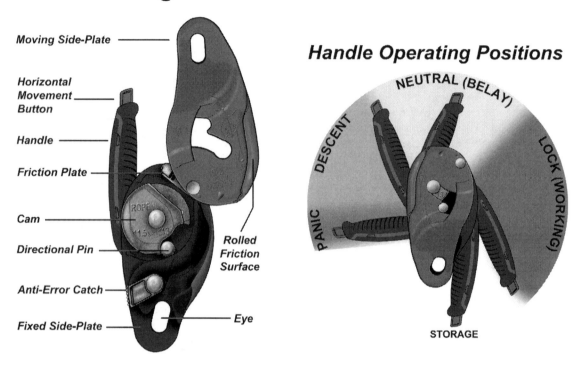

Moving Side-Plate

Horizontal Movement Button

Handle

Friction Plate

Cam

Directional Pin

Anti-Error Catch

Fixed Side-Plate

Rolled Friction Surface

Eye

Handle Operating Positions

DESCENT

NEUTRAL (BELAY)

PANIC

LOCK (WORKING)

STORAGE

Self-Braking Descenders - *Installing*

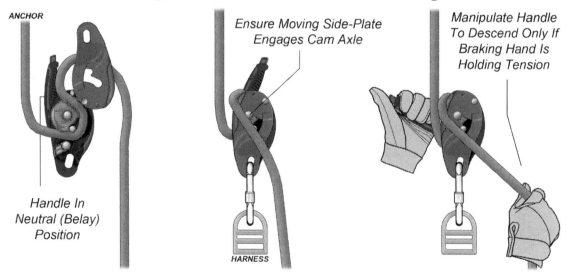

ANCHOR

Handle In Neutral (Belay) Position

Ensure Moving Side-Plate Engages Cam Axle

HARNESS

Manipulate Handle To Descend Only If Braking Hand Is Holding Tension

Self-Braking Descenders - Handle & Hand Positions

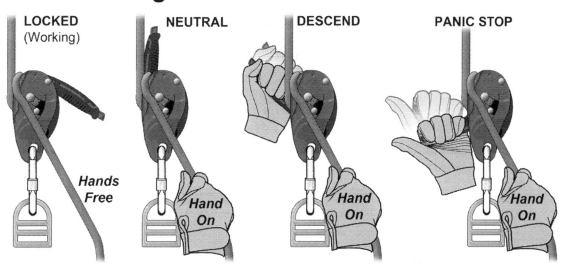

Locked/Working Handle Position: To hold position on the rope and work hands free, rotate the handle toward the five o'clock position. Depending on rope thickness and load weight, the handle will begin to encounter increasing resistance somewhere within the locked/working range on the dial. The handle will come to a point where it stops. Continue rotating the handle with adequate force until it feels like it has clamped down and nested on the rope. Depending on the application, movement can be further locked out by tying off the descender. Be careful not to defeat the shock absorbing ability of the descender if it is needed for the operation.

Neutral Position: When the handle is within the neutral range of rotation, the load will hang on the rope without movement until tension is equal on the input and output sides of the descender. Keep the braking hand in place and leave the handle in neutral position until you need to descend or lock and work hands free. The handle will bounce to the neutral position if the Climber lets go while descending. If the Climber were to move the braking section of rope to the twelve o'clock position and pull up with enough force to lift the load, the descender would move up on the rope and capture progress. This working feature allows self-braking descenders to be used for ascending and belaying. Rope access workers ascend in this way without changing to rope grabs when they need to move short distances up the rope.

Descend Position: To move down, start by pulling adequate tension on the braking section of rope with the gripping hand, and move the handle out of the locked/working range to the neutral position with the other hand. Slowly pull the handle down into the descend range on the dial. As resistance increases on the handle, the cam begins to release the rope. Begin allowing rope to slip through the braking hand to move down the rope. Balancing handle and braking control is intuitive and easy to "get." You will quickly find that the handle releases the rope while the braking hand manages speed.

Panic Position: The panic position is a safety feature that prevents the operator from losing speed control while descending or lowering. If the operator pulls down too quickly or too far within the descending range, the handle will "break over" into the panic position and stop movement. This places a stop feature on either side of the descent range of operation on the dial. Errors by an overwhelmed or frightened Climber will result in the handle ending up in either the panic or neutral position. Either way, movement stops. To resume descending, rotate the handle to neutral to disengage the panic feature, and then back into the descend range.

The handle can break into the panic position high or low in the range depending on the weight of the load. Lighter loads tend to cause the handle to slip into the panic position more easily and closer to the top of the range. If a Climber is descending on a very low-angle surface, the panic feature can become a nuisance and prevent safe movement. Depressing the horizontal movement button and tilting the housing to two o'clock can make descending easier when the load force is light.

Storage Position: Rotate the handle to the six o'clock position on the dial for transportation and storage. The descender is more compact, and the handle will not swing freely in this position.

2-Person Loads and Lowering: Additional rigging is required for handling 2-person loads or when using self-braking descenders for lowering. Rappelling or lowering with heavier loads requires added friction and constant, firm rope contact with the rolled friction surface on the outside of the housing. Whenever the descender is rigged horizontally or upside down for a lowering operation, the braking section of the standing line will fall out of position, making it very difficult to manage. To keep the rope properly oriented, redirect the braking section of rope through an additional carabiner that is securely clipped below the descender (toward the eye). Doing so will keep the rope where you want it and add needed friction and control. Advanced teams sometimes rig a Münter hitch onto the redirect biner for even more braking control when dealing with very heavy loads.

Self Braking Descenders - *2-Person Load Rigging*

HARNESS

HARNESS

Reversing Direction: Unlike brake racks, self-braking descenders can be moved up or down on the rope as needed. This flexibility allows for easy removal of unwanted slack, ascending, or belaying, and for a progress capture directional with pulley systems.

Tension created by the load tightens the rope, causing friction to move the cam and clamp down to stop movement. The rope can be moved through the device in either direction if the rope is slack or if tension on the input and output sides of the cam are equal. If a Climber intending to rappel down is standing at the cliff edge with too much loose line between the anchor and the descender, slack can be easily taken up. Start by removing all tension on the descender to make the rope completely slack. Rotate the handle to neutral, and lightly push the rope into the device while gently pulling rope out with the braking hand. Cocking the descender to about two o'clock can help keep the anti-error cam from accidentally engaging. Always keep the braking hand on the rope and ready to support the load.

Adjusting slack is similar when rigged as a fixed descent control device in a lowering operation. Since the descender is anchored off, simply pull the working line toward the anchor to remove all load force. Then ease rope through the descender as needed. This maneuver can be used to belay a Climber as well. Keep the braking hand on the rope and ready to support the load.

To ascend short distances, rotate the handle to the locked/working position, and attach a rope grab and foot loop above the descender. When able to grip the braking section of rope, rotate the handle to the neutral position. This rigging will enable the Climber to stand up and unload the descender. When the Climber stands, there is no weight on the descender, and the rope can move through the device in reverse when pulled to twelve o'clock. To capture ascending progress, confidently sit down. Sitting down too slowly or squeamishly will not engage the cam and grip the rope as needed. A common pitfall for this skill is pulling up on the braking line too soon. The rope will not move in reverse until the Climber is fully standing and the rope entering the device is completely slack.

Self-braking descenders used as directionals with a progress capture function within a pulley system work by adjusting tension on either side of the cam. If the descender is anchored and supporting a load as part of a pulley system for hauling, the cam will grip the rope unless the braking section of rope is pulled on with a force equal to or greater than the load. This can be accomplished by rigging the braking section of rope as an in-line pulley system or by ganging a separate pulley system onto the line. Either way, riggers can move the rope up or down as needed by creating or relieving adequate tension on the braking section of rope. To capture progress, confidently allow the system to lower the load and make the cam grip. Don't let go of the rope unless the handle is in the locked position.

Self Braking DCD's - Progress Capturing Directionals

- *Converts To Lowering Without Changing Equipment*
- *Provides Load-Releasing Capability*

3:1 Z-Rig Shown

Self Braking Descenders - *Slacking & Ascending*

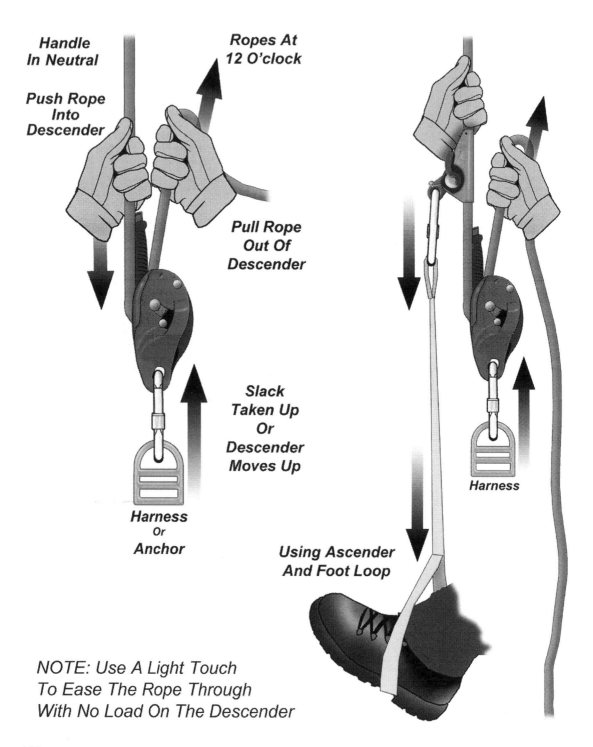

**Handle
In Neutral**

**Push Rope
Into
Descender**

**Ropes At
12 O'clock**

**Pull Rope
Out Of
Descender**

**Slack
Taken Up
Or
Descender
Moves Up**

**Harness
Or
Anchor**

Harness

**Using Ascender
And Foot Loop**

*NOTE: Use A Light Touch
To Ease The Rope Through
With No Load On The Descender*

Hot Change-Over Maneuvers Using Self-Braking Descenders: Covering hot change-overs (converting rope rescue systems while supporting a life-load) in this section is a good way to show how adaptable and useful self-braking descenders are in the rescue setting. Integrating self-braking descenders into hauling and lowering systems used to support life-loads reduces rigging changes and simplifies operations. The working features of descending, ascending, and locking allow changes from lowering to hauling and back to lowering without the use of load-releasing hitches and prusiks, or without having to haul the load up to release a brake, even when the system is hot. Rotating the handle to the locked position and applying or removing rope grabs and pulleys are all that's needed. These descenders also remove the need for load-releasing hitches as a means of dealing with jams or other problems that freeze up raising systems in full tension. A downside is that self-braking descenders that are currently available are far less efficient than pulleys when used as directionals within a hauling system. Pulley systems that provide high amounts of mechanical advantage may be needed to smoothly manage common rescue loads when self-braking descenders are used as directionals.

Changing a lowering system to a raising system is very common in top-down vertical rescue operations. To convert a rescue lowering system to a hauling (raising) system, rotate the handle to the locked position to allow the operator to work hands free. Remove the carabiner that is redirecting the braking section of rope. Place a rope grab and pulley onto the main line, and install the braking section of rope for hauling. To begin hauling up on the system, grab and hold slight tension on the rope to remove slack, and then rotate the handle to neutral. As the load moves up, the descender will capture progress. To reset the pulley system when it fully contracts, rotate the handle to the locked position to allow the operator to work hands-free, and then move the rope grab and hauling pulley. With hands back on the rope, rotate the handle back to neutral to continue hauling.

To convert a pulley hauling system to a lowering system while hot, rotate the handle to the locked position to work hands-free. Remove or loosen the haul rope grab and pulley. Orient the braking section of rope for descent. Be sure to redirect the rope through an additional carabiner to maintain proper orientation and to add friction. Now grip and brake the rope as you rotate the handle to the descend range to lower the load.

Converting Lowering System To Hauling
Self-Braking Descender

Converts To Raising Under Full Load

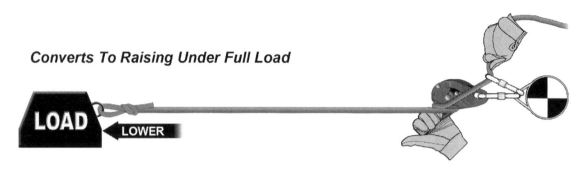

Lock Descender - Remove Redirecting Carabiner - Rig Rope Grab & Pulley

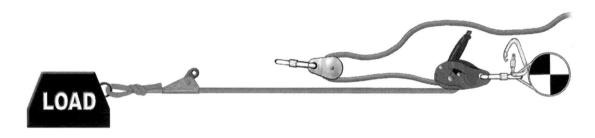

Grab Rope - Rotate Handle To Neutral

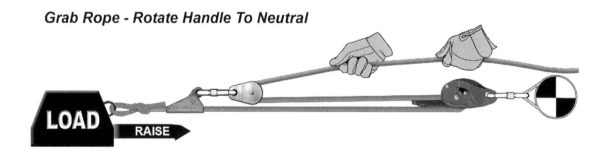

Converting Hauling System To Lowering
Self-Braking Descender

Provides Load-Releasing Capability

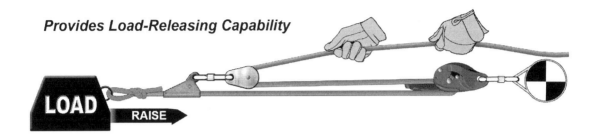

Lock Descender - Remove Rope Grab & Haul Pulley - Redirect Braking Rope

Converts To Lowering Without Changing Equipment

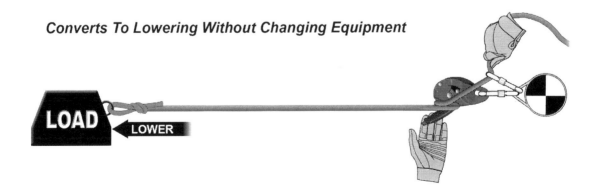

Self Braking DCD's - Lock & Tie Off

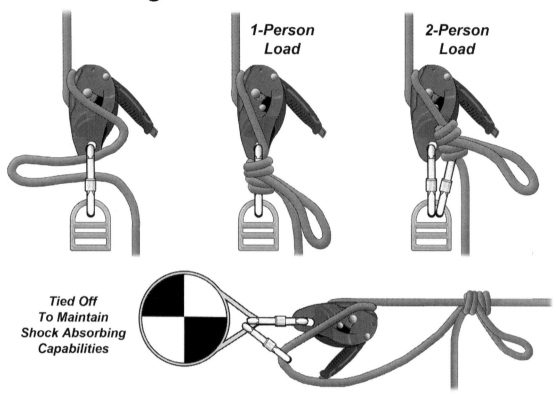

1-Person Load

2-Person Load

Tied Off To Maintain Shock Absorbing Capabilities

Tying-Off: In situations with a high risk of accidental, unwanted handle movement, or if the rigging has to be left unattended, it may be necessary to further secure self-braking descenders by tying them off. One method is to form a long bight of rope with the braking section and tie a double half-hitch on the connecting or redirecting carabiner. Ensure the rope is properly oriented and in contact with the rolled friction edge. When using as a belay with a need to decelerate impact force, provide adequate slack in the braking section and then tie off on the supporting line.

CAUTIONS

1. Make sure the self-braking descender you use is made to accept the rope you are rigging. It is possible to install ropes with the wrong diameter size. The descender will not work properly or safely when the rope diameter doesn't match the cam size.

2. Always keep a grip on the braking section of rope unless the handle is in the locked position.

3. Always redirect the rope through an additional carabiner for 2-person loads. The curled friction edge alone will not provide adequate friction for braking 2-person loads.

4. Always redirect the braking section of rope through an additional carabiner when the descender is anchored for lowering. If the redirect carabiner is not added, the rigging will be very difficult to manage and the anti-error cam may not engage if the rope is accidentally installed backward.

5. Carry out a function test every time a self-braking descender is installed. Simply pull on the anchored rope to determine if the rope is threaded correctly, and see if the descender is functioning properly. With a back-up safety line connected and staffed, add weight to the descender prior to committing a life-load over the side or overhead. This is usually done by sitting down or leaning back on the rope.

6. Contact with the edge or other obstacles can cause the descender to change orientation with the rope and unload the cam. This can result in loss of grip on the rope, causing, in turn, the load to free-fall. Do not allow the descender to jam against hard obstacles during rappels, and maintain working clearance when the descender is anchored for lowering.

NFPA: It's hard to fully interpret the descent control devices performance standards in 1983-2012. Durability and functionality tests are specified, but the standards only cite breaking strength minimums for general use controllers. Technical use descent controllers are tested for deformation, but not breaking strength. Technical use durability and functionality is tested as described in Standard 1983-2012 Chapter 8 (8.6 Procedure A). It appears that NFPA falls back on ISO industrial standards for other performance specifications for descent controllers that are not clearly general use. This may be because of the wide variety of controllers available today.

If descent controllers are engineered to slip as part of their functionality, NFPA specifies that they must hold at 9kN (2,023 lbf).

Rigging Plates and Rings

Also known as gathering plates, rigging plates are used to collect and focus multidirectional load forces. They also arrange components in an orderly manner to keep rigging clean and free of unwanted cross-loading. Rigging plates come in a huge variety of styles, from very basic to extremely exotic. Plates made from thick stock with rounded edges allow riggers to hitch ropes, cords, and straps directly onto them without other connectors. The plates in your cache should have at least one hole through which several carabiners can be clipped. NFPA standards for rigging plates and rings specify a capacity of 36kN (8,093 lbf) without deformation. Plates and rings are most commonly used for rigging anchors and basket bridles.

Safely Link Multidirectional Loads

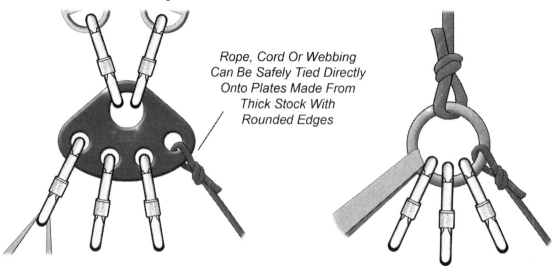

Rope, Cord Or Webbing Can Be Safely Tied Directly Onto Plates Made From Thick Stock With Rounded Edges

Be mindful not to overuse rigging plates. It's easy to fly on autopilot and clip a plate into the rigging only because you usually do. Leave plates out of the rigging if there is no need to support multidirectional loads. As is true with any component, a plate is just one more opportunity for failure or to make a rigging mistake. It's a reasonable practice to place plates for the purpose of providing easy adaptability for rigging adjustments, even though you may not start out supporting multidirectional loads.

Harnesses

Personal harnesses suitable for rescue work come in many designs, all of which address functionality, comfort, and safety. NFPA establishes rigorous performance standards for harnesses and classifies them into three function categories. Each class has its own testing protocol consistent with its intended use.

NFPA STANDARDS - LIFE SAFETY HARNESSES				
Class	Intended Use	Configuration	Design Load	Heat
Class 2	Rescue	Fastens Around Waist, Thighs and/or Buttock	2.67 kN (600lbf)	min 400^{0}F
Class 3	Rescue	Fastens Around Waist, Thighs/Buttock & Shoulders	2.67 kN (600lbf)	min 400^{0}F

Performance testing determines the ability of each class of harness to contain the wearer in positions pertinent to the intended use as well as supporting rescue loads. Overall testing includes strength and drop testing of the entire harness, and component parts and materials are subject to specific testing as well. NFPA also establishes some design and construction specifications for life safety harnesses including webbing woven of virgin continuous filament fibers, sewing patterns and methods, attachment point placement, etc.

Choose harnesses that are right for the job. Some harnesses are specialized to a single function while others are outfitted for multiple applications. Though a fall-arrest harness is suitable for life safety, it may not work well for rescuing people from cliff faces. Some harnesses are more comfortable than others and may be easier to put on. Try to anticipate how a harness will perform not only during rescue operations, but also during an accidental fall or other shock. Consider the connection points a Climber will need for your hazards.

NFPA standards allow life safety harnesses to be adjustable for sizing purposes. NFPA compliant harnesses are fixed with use labels that include detailed sizing information for waist, chest, and height dimensions. The waistband should fit snugly at the top of the hips and below the kidneys and ribs. Chest harnessing should be adjusted to fit firmly, while stilling allowing free movement so as not to restrict breathing. Leg loops should be adjusted close to mid-thigh with enough slack to allow repositioning while working. Some Class 3 harnesses are comprised of a Class 2 seat harness with a removable chest harness. Two-piece harnesses may be a good choice for hard-to-fit team members.

A single front waist or sternum load-bearing attachment point is all that is required for NFPA compliant rescue and escape harnesses. However, few harnesses marketed to the fire service are outfitted with a single connection ring. Manufacturers have come a long way in designing ergonomic safety and functionality into rescue harnesses. Make sure your team knows which rings are load-bearing attachment points, positioning rings, travel restriction connections, accessory rings, etc. Choose harnesses for your cache that have a minimum of three load-bearing attachments in the following positions:

1. Pelvic (Ventral): Load-bearing connection on the front of the waist belt.
2. Sternum (Chest): Load-bearing connection on the front chest.
3. Dorsal (Back): Load-bearing connection on the back, between the shoulder blades (Climber should be able to reach the dorsal ring with both hands).

Additional load-bearing attachment points are available on some harnesses that include rear waist and shoulder connections. The rear waist ring is handy for connecting to a travel-restricting lanyard to prevent falls, but it is too low on the back to be used for suspension. Shoulder lift connections are designed for use with a spreader bar for working in confined spaces with tight, vertical entrances.

Fall arrest attachment points are the load-bearing connections on the harness that are ergonomically placed for a more favorable outcome in the event of a fall over the side. In other words, fall arrest attachments are less likely to create a situation where the body will be forced to bend or twist at impact as the rope fully tightens when a fall occurs. If a worker falls over the side while wearing fall arrest rigging connected to the dorsal ring of the harness, his or her body will elongate in a more ergonomically favorable position upon impact. Fall arrest rigging incorrectly connected to the pelvic ring on a harness could result in the Climber violently and severely bending backwards at the waist upon impact. Fall arrest attachment points are not restricted to fall arrest use alone and are okay to use for suspension on the vertical rescue system. Whenever it's possible, connect the main line and the belay line of a 2-rope system to separate load-bearing attachment points on the harness. This practice is not only prudent for safe redundancy, but it is also required by most OSHA jurisdictions. Most often the main line connects to the pelvic attachment, and the belay connects to the sternum or dorsal attachments.

Work-positioning attachment points on harnesses differ from load-bearing attachment points. While NFPA requires load-bearing connections to support full fall arrest and design loads, positioning attachments are only required to support the weight of the wearer for maneuvering purposes. Think of a belayed Climber on a structural tower slinging a flip-line around a crossbar and clipping it to side "D" rings on his or her harness for additional stability to work hands free. The flip line isn't the Climber's main rescue load support, but it is providing position stability. Many harnesses are equipped with positioning rings that are just as strong as load-bearing attachments. Usually, the location of the attachment point on the harness determines whether a ring should be used for full support or for work positioning only. Side "D" rings should be used together for work positioning with a flip line. Attaching to a single side "D" ring will usually force the Climber out of a comfortable position and tension the ring and harness at a weak angle.

Equipment loops and accessory rings are for carrying gear conveniently. Never support a life-load or rig for work positioning using the equipment loops or accessory rings on a harness. Tools or other equipment clipped onto a harness should weigh less than 10lbs. Any gear weighing over 10lbs. should be rigged in a way that it is supported either by the rope system or by a rope system anchored separately from the Climber. Heavy objects should only be clipped to positioning or load-bearing attachments that connect directly to the main line. Non-emergency, work-at-height professional associations including SPRAT and IRATA use similar safe practices.

Life Safety Harnesses - Attachment Points

STERNUM
Best For Belay
Good For Fall Arrest
Full Design Load*

PELVIC
Full Design Load
Best For Main Support
OK For Positioning

DORSAL
Best For Fall Arrest
Good For Belay
Full Design Load*

REAR WAIST
Best - Travel Restriction
Full Design Load*

EQUIPMENT LOOPS
10 Pound Max

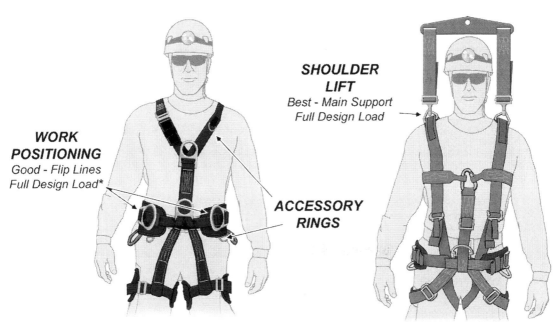

WORK POSITIONING
Good - Flip Lines
Full Design Load*

ACCESSORY RINGS

SHOULDER LIFT
Best - Main Support
Full Design Load

* Check Manufacturer Specifications To Confirm Full Design Load Capacity Of 2.67kN - 600lbf

Victim Harnesses (Victim Extrication Devices): There are many choices of manufactured harnesses designed for placement on rescue subjects. NFPA establishes construction and performance standards for harnesses used to connect rescue subjects to the rope system. Some comply with NFPA rescue harness standards. Victim seat and chest harnesses are usually made with clip-on functionality for quick and easy application. Some have color-coordinated connection points that simplify installation. Most manufactured victim harnesses adjust to fit a very wide range of sizes. Large fabric triangle or diaper types of victim harnesses cradle the rescue subject much like reclining in a hammock. Seat harnesses may be a better choice for operations with ambulatory rescue subjects expected to keep their footing during movement. Manufactured victim harnesses may be very difficult to place on rescue subjects that are lying down or are in awkward or cramped positions. Choose a victim harness that can be placed on the rescue subject without disconnecting it from the rope system.

Load Releasing Hitches

Used as a means of releasing tension on the fixed components of a rope system, Load Releasing Hitches (LRHs) provide riggers with options for dealing with a variety of situations. LRHs are commonly integrated into rope systems to relieve  tension on brakes for knot passing or when changing from raising to lowering operations. Many teams install LRHs whenever prusik rope grabs are anchored and attached to main or belay lines. Doing so ensures the ability to release tension and remove even the tightest prusik hitch. For this reason LRHs are sometimes added to overcome accidental lock-ups caused by snagged equipment or Climbers that get jammed. In some cases LRHs can add favorable shock cushioning to rope systems.

Functionality: Some release hitches are assembled using webbing or strapping, while others use cord or rope. The basic premise of most release hitches is based on some kind of non-working mechanical ad-vantage block and tackle. Some tie in a Münter hitch for additional friction and control. The non-working mechanical advantage and/or Münter hitch remains static and supports the load until the need to release tension arises. Then, whatever the mechanism is used to hold the hitch together is untied or unwrapped to allow controlled extension. The hitch is extended (lowered) to release tension. Generally speaking, hitches tied using long cords are easier to extend a longer distances than those made from short sections of webbing. Hitches tied with cord generally fare better when drop tested.

Fail-safe integrity of Load Releasing Hitches depends on proper use. Always connect the load to a tied-off part of the system before unlocking an LRH. This usually means establishing the connection to whatever device or rope to which you intend to transfer the load. Example: when changing a rope system from raising to lowering mode, thread and tie off the descent control device before unlocking the LRH to release the brake. If an operator suddenly loses the grip on the LRH, the load will be caught by the separate connection. Never unlock an LRH without making and safety-checking this secondary connection first.

Controversy: Depending on the region or realm of operation, LRHs are either used heavily or ignored by Rescue Teams. Rigging paradigms that rely on personnel with high levels of technical expertise carrying personal rope systems tend to ignore load-releasing hitches. These groups can quickly attach a personal mechanical advantage rig, use advanced methods to deal with a locked brake, or change a loaded raising system to lowering. Teams made up of personnel with operational levels of expertise who rely on a central cache of equipment tend to favor using LRHs. And why not? Routinely adding an LRH to a rope system can make very good sense when you're trying to standardize the operations of a large organization or region made up of personnel with varying levels of expertise. The inclination to eliminate LRHs from a playbook often stems from the difficulty in maintaining user competency. For all but the most interested, LRHs are complex and can be hard to understand and use. Because they support a life-load, it's absolutely critical that LRHs are tied and rigged correctly. The average firefighter with operational levels of training and expertise may have trouble remembering how to correctly use load-releasing hitches without frequent, repetitive, and detailed practice. Teams sometimes come to the realization that the risk of clipping on a poorly tied LRH greatly outweighs the downside of dealing with Climber jams and equipment snags or the occasional unexpected changeover. These problems are sometimes addressed by using mechanical belay devices that have the ability to release tension when needed or by using commercially available pre-sewn hitches that are easier to remember how to use.

Another controversy has to do with the actual performance of LRHs. There are commercially available prefabricated versions and many improvised LRHs that are widely used. Which type to use is often determined by regional preference and traditional familiarity. Some LRHs were regional favorites for a time but were partially phased out or improved upon after testing revealed performance problems. Testing that evaluates operational integrity following severe shock loads identifies problems such as melting and fusing of webbing and strapping used in some LRHs. This kind of damage may render an LRH useless for releasing tension after sustaining a severe impact. Even so, a variety of LRHs are routinely used world-wide, including types that are difficult to use or that sustain damage during testing. Some endure impact forces better than others. If an LRH is rendered useless because of fusing after a severe shock, it puts riggers in a situation similar to using a system that didn't have an LRH to begin with. Some say that's a risk worth taking. Those who favor using LRHs sometimes claim that the worst-case impact testing protocols used to evaluate performance are unrealistic and impractical.

Some of the most widely-respected data used to evaluate release hitches was compiled in an exhaustive comparative analysis administered by Kirk and Katie Mauthner using the Belay Competence Drop Test Method (BCDTM) established by the British Columbia Council of Technical Rescue (BCCTR). The core format of this test drops a 200kg load the distance of 1 vertical meter while connected to 3 meters of 11mm low-stretch life safety rope. The LRHs tested were anchored and tied directly to the rope without a descender, pulley, or belay mechanism. Acceptable performance required that LRHs endure the fall without elongating more than 20cm, develop a maximum peak force less than 15kN, and function properly after the impact. Additional performance criteria that was measured includes complexity, ease of use, extendibility, and grip strength needed to control the load. Static failure tests were also conducted, but in all cases the 3-meter rope failed before the LRH. The study categorized ten different LRHs assembled using different sizes and types of materials as "Recommended," "Acceptable," "Caution Against," or "Not Recommended."

Critics point out that testing an LRH without the benefit of a load-limiting rope connection, such as a prusik or tandem prusik brake, unrealistically exposes the device to too much shock. An LRH connected to the rope system via a directly-placed prusik or tandem prusik brake will be less exposed to shock energy because of the slipping characteristics of the prusik(s). Makers of prefabricated versions advise users to rig in ways that protect release devices from excessive shock and even suggest using shock-absorbing links.

Recommendation: Obtain and study the release device comparative analysis by Kirk and Katie Mauthner ©1999/2000 to determine which LRH best suits the needs of your organization.

Radium 3 to 1 Hitch: (BCDTM rating for version similar to diagram = "Recommended") Developed as a better alternative when the Mariner's Hitch was more widely used, the Radium 3 to 1 uses 8mm or 9mm cord to fashion a 3:1CD reinforced by a Münter at the change of direction. Use pear shaped or offset "D" shaped carabiners. Half-hitches and overhands hold the Radium tight until released. Remaining standing cord can be chained or bagged. An operational advantage of using this hitch is that it can be tied to any length needed without degrading strength or functionality and be extended as far as the cord allows.

To release a load, begin by untying the overhand knot. Then hold the standing cord with both hands and pull until the half-hitched bight comes undone. Your hands should be in position to securely hold tension on the Münter and control movement. Allow the MA to extend until slacked to release the load. The hitch can then be removed or reassembled in place. Simply tighten the MA sufficiently, and hold position by replacing the half-hitch and overhand.

BC-Load Releasing Hitch: (BCDTM rating for version similar to diagram = "Acceptable") The BC-LRH uses 8mm or 9mm cord and relies on a doubled Münter hitch for control. Use pear shaped or offset "D" shaped carabiners. This load releaser performs fairly well in BCDTM impact tests, can be assembled to any length needed without reducing strength, and can extend as far as the cord allows.

To release a load, begin by untying the overhand knot. Then hold the standing cords with both hands, and pull until the half-hitched bight comes undone. Your hands should be in position to securely hold tension and control movement. Unwind the doubled cord until three wraps remain. Be careful not to allow the hitch to twist and unwrap on its own. Two people may be needed to safely control tension. Allow the wraps and Münter to slip until slacked to release the load. The hitch can then be removed or reassembled in place. Simply tighten the cord sufficiently and hold position by rewinding the cord and replacing the half-hitch and overhand.

Mariner's Hitch: (BCDTM rating for version similar to diagram = "Not Recommended"). This type of release hitch was adapted from the maritime and naval salvage fields. It can be tied using 1 inch webbing, cord, or rope. Versions using heavier strapping fitted with appropriately matched hard points are commercially available. *Be careful not to assemble this hitch with webbing or strapping wider than 1 inch when using carabiners as attachment points.* The basic Mariner's Hitch uses a non-working mechanical advantage block and tackle that stays fixed by wrapping the standing section of rope or webbing around its body (legs of the MA). The Naval version simply tucks in the standing end while common rescue versions use several methods to finish and tie off the hitch. If the standing end is long, it can be chained or bagged and kept close to the rigging. The hitch is attached so that the block can be used as a 3:1 MA to release the load. When tied with webbing, this hitch suffers software damage such as sticking, glazing, hardening, fusing, and welding when drop tested. Never use this LRH without a load-limiting connection such as prusik or tandem prusik rope grab.

To use the hitch and release a load, begin by unclipping the carabiner that secures the standing end. Follow the steps used to assemble the hitch in exact reverse order, including unclipping from the double bight first. The biner should remain connected to the standing end of the loop. Pull the carabiner to unthread the double bight. Now unwind the standing loop until three wraps remain on the body of the hitch. Use one hand to manipulate the remaining wraps as the other hand slacks the hitch to release tension. If you run out of webbing before the load is sufficiently released, attach another loop of webbing to extend the throw of the hitch. Once the load has been released, the hitch can either be removed or reassembled while still connected. Simply tension and shorten the MA, and replace the wraps. Rethread the double bight, and secure it with the third carabiner.

Anecdotal Observations: FEMA USAR Task Forces and fire organizations in California used the improvised version of the Mariner's for many years. Belay training and personnel competency testing was carried out using rigging fitted with Mariner's Hitches assembled with webbing for over ten years. The LRHs were anchored and connected to tandem prusik brakes. The hitches never failed or sustained meaningful damage after catching hundreds of "realistic" training falls, some quite severe, with loads ranging from 75 to 275kg (165-600lbs).

Pre-Sewn LRHs: Several reputable companies manufacture release devices, including pre-sewn straps that function as a Mariner's Hitch. Because they are permanently fixed to their own attachment hardware, these devices are straightforward to tie. For this reason manufactured pre-sewn LRHs are popular within the fire service. As with other Mariner's Hitches, pre-sewn release straps should never be directly attached to a rope system supporting a life-load. Always attach these devices with a load-limiting connection like a prusik or tandem prusik brake.

Load Releasing Hitches - Typical Placement

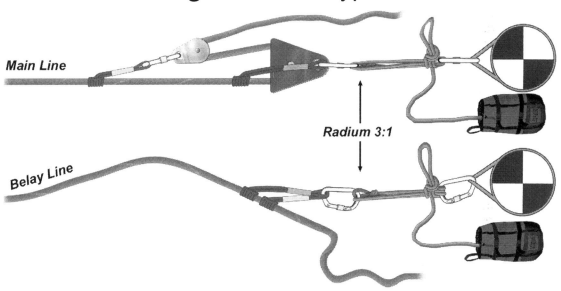

Main Line

Radium 3:1

Belay Line

Hokie Hitch (not pictured): It's worth mentioning the Hokie because it may still be used in some areas. The Hokie hitch uses cord tied into a large loop and relies on a double Münter for control. The hitch is secured by making several winds through connecting carabiners and is finished with half-hitches and overhands. Once rigged, the cord is bulky and may cause harmful strain on carabiners. As of this writing, the Hokie is less favored across the United States.

Load Releasing Hitches - *Tying A Radium 3 to 1*

Tied Using 8mm or 9mm Kern Mantle Cord

Similar Versions BCDTM Tested
"Recommended"

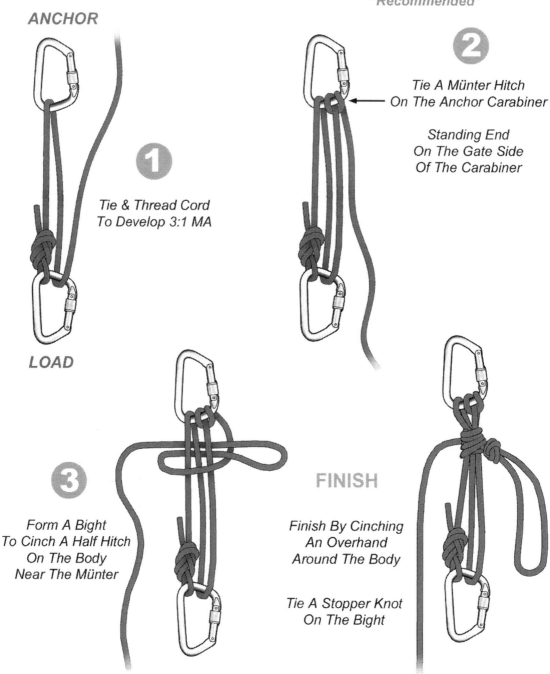

ANCHOR

1

Tie & Thread Cord
To Develop 3:1 MA

LOAD

2

Tie A Münter Hitch
On The Anchor Carabiner

Standing End
On The Gate Side
Of The Carabiner

3

Form A Bight
To Cinch A Half Hitch
On The Body
Near The Münter

FINISH

Finish By Cinching
An Overhand
Around The Body

Tie A Stopper Knot
On The Bight

Load Releasing Hitches - *Tying A BC-LRH*

Tied Using 8mm or 9mm Kern Mantle Cord

ANCHOR

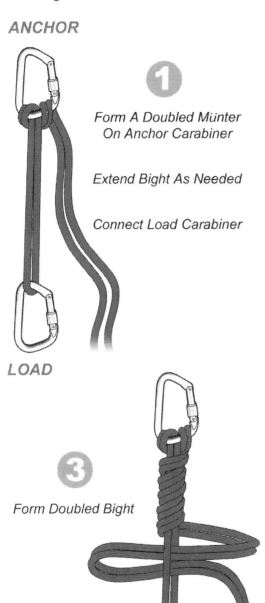

① Form A Doubled Münter
On Anchor Carabiner

Extend Bight As Needed

Connect Load Carabiner

LOAD

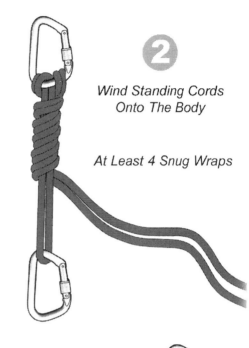

② Wind Standing Cords
Onto The Body

At Least 4 Snug Wraps

③ Form Doubled Bight

Thread Strands
Of The Body

FINISH

Secure With Half Hitch
And Overhand

Tie A Stopper Knot
On The Bight

Load Releasing Hitches - *Tying A Mariner's*

Tied Using 1 Inch Webbing

1

Use A 6 Foot Loop
To Form 3:1 MA

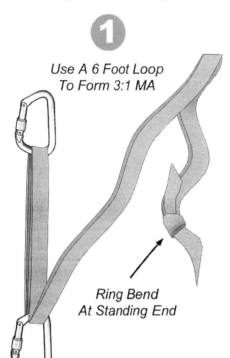

Ring Bend
At Standing End

2

Tightly Wrap Body
With Standing Line

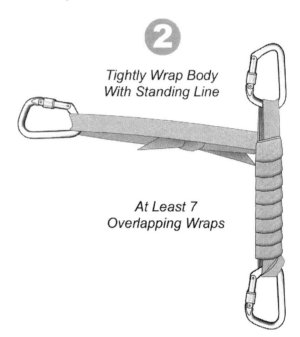

At Least 7
Overlapping Wraps

3

Thread A Double Bight
Of Standing Loop
Between MA Legs

Be Sure To
Thread Both Layers
Of The Standing Loop

Do Not Allow Knot
To Pass Through

ANCHOR   FINISH

Clip Carabiner Onto
The Doubled Bight

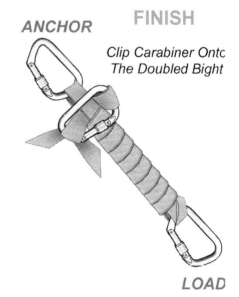

LOAD

Load Releasing Hitches - *Transferring The Load*

*Transfer From Hauling System Brake To Descender
* Radium 3:1 LRH
*Excessive Slack Shown For Clarity

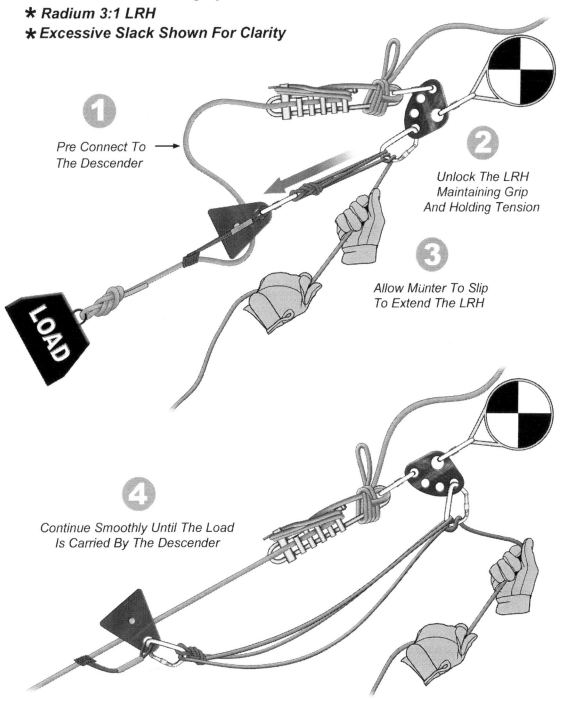

1

Pre Connect To
The Descender →

2

Unlock The LRH
Maintaining Grip
And Holding Tension

3

Allow Münter To Slip
To Extend The LRH

LOAD

4

Continue Smoothly Until The Load
Is Carried By The Descender

Pre-Rigged Equipment Clusters

Block & Tackles: Pre-rigged block and tackles in the cache provide riggers with additional setup options and, in some cases, reduce staffing needs and set-up time. Using a pre-rigged block and tackle as a lowering/raising system, or clipping a pre-rigged 5 to 1 onto a lowering system to raise the load, is quick and easy to do. These applications are easily understood by teams that may not have technician levels of expertise. Block and tackle systems are commercially available but are easily assembled with typical cache equipment. A good version is to thread ½-inch life safety rope into 2 double pulleys with 3-inch sheaves to form 4:1CD/5:1 MA, depending on which end is anchored. If one of the pulleys is fitted with a becket, the rope can terminate at that connection point with a screw link. A prusik brake can be installed whenever it's needed.

Smaller block and tackles outfitted with brakes are sometimes referred to as "jiggers." These systems can also be purchased or self-assembled. Pre-rigged jiggers are usually assembled with 8mm or 9mm cord, small double-sheaved pulleys with beckets and 6mm or 7mm 3-wrap prusik brakes. Some teams use jiggers with mechanical brakes or no brakes at all. Jiggers can be used wherever someone needs more horsepower to lift loads, as would be the case with a Climber working over the side moving an unconscious subject into a rescue basket. Jiggers can also be used as adjustable connections, ganged on mechanical advantage, or even raising/lowering systems.

Lowering/Raising Cluster: Keeping hardware used for lowering/raising systems together can help shave minutes off of setup time. Many teams anchor the descent controllers and stationary pulleys of their systems onto rigging plates as part of their normal operations. Using the same rigging plate to neatly package and store this combination allows riggers to easily grab the complete cluster of lowering/raising equipment out of the cache and go anchor it off. This grouping of equipment can be used to lower a Climber over the side and easily change to a raising system. It can also be used to create a double prusik belay station. Connect the following equipment to a rigging plate so that it's sensibly arranged to set up and convert a two-person lowering and raising system:

- Descent controller of choice.
- Prusik Loop–Short: used as main brake or to form double prusik brake.
- Prusik Loop–Long: used as hauling rope grab or to form double prusik brake.
- Pulley: 3-inch prusik-minding.
- Pulley: 2-inch (used as traveling pulley).
- Load Releasing Hitch (optional).
- Carabiners: 4 for anchor attachment and connecting equipment. *(5 five if using LRH)*

Belay Systems: Dedicating equipment to a pre-assembled belay system not only makes set-up quick and easy, but also it also keeps the equipment used for belays more pristine. Belay systems normally function without bearing a load. Using the same equipment for the belay system every time means the component parts will be less worn and perform optimally when impacted. Simply assemble the belay system you normally use, and bag it up.

Backup System: A standard action plan to assist Climbers that become injured or exhausted is essential whether a team is working a real emergency call or just practicing. Pre-rigging a standard system that enables a Backup Climber to quickly anchor off and rappel down makes backup operations routine. A pre-made rappel rig helps make backup rappelling procedures common knowledge among team members. A good method for rappelling down is to anchor off a separate line for a brake rack and connect to a traveling prusik brake that is attached to any of the existing lines already over the side (preferably the belay line). Using a brake rack as the descent controller allows the backup Climber a free hand to manipulate the traveling prusik belay as he or she rappels down. A second prusik loop may be needed to pass knots and hardware. This system can be assembled using the rappel rope itself to create its own non-directional anchor attachment.

Pre-Rigged Equipment Kits

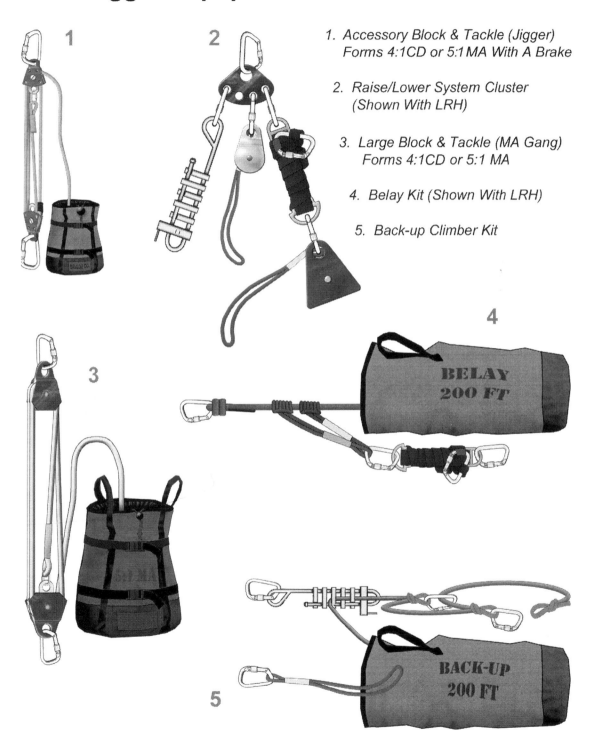

1. *Accessory Block & Tackle (Jigger)*
   Forms 4:1CD or 5:1 MA With A Brake

2. *Raise/Lower System Cluster*
   (Shown With LRH)

3. *Large Block & Tackle (MA Gang)*
   Forms 4:1CD or 5:1 MA

4. *Belay Kit (Shown With LRH)*

5. *Back-up Climber Kit*

7 Pulleys & Mechanical Advantage

Mechanical Advantage & Pulleys

Setting up pulley systems to raise a rescue package is pretty simple. Memorizing or pre-rigging a few pulley systems is an approach many departments take to prepare for hazards. But an operational understanding of how pulleys and pulley systems work to create mechanical advantage helps workers remember how to set up and strengthens their ability to solve problems or design new solutions. Knowing when pulleys create advantage and when they create disadvantage will prevent some common mistakes.

Mechanical Advantage

Arranging equipment to form simple machines that reduce the effort needed to do work is a basic definition for mechanical advantage (MA) as it relates to rope rescue. Simple machines—like levers, pulleys, and pulley systems—are force multipliers. But how do they do it? Why is it easier?

Picture two hikers standing at the bottom of a mountain with plans to get to the summit and take in the view of the valley below. They see that there are two paths to choose from. Both lead all the way to the top of the mountain. One route is named "Mountain Goat Trail" and the other is the "Leisure Time Trail." Mountain Goat is a straight line directly to the top and very steep. Leisure Time is more scenic with many switchbacks and an easy slope angle. With the same summit goal in mind, one hiker takes Mountain Goat and the other takes Leisure Time. They walk at about the same pace.

Eventually both hikers make it to the top. The Mountain Goat hiker arrived first and waited for the Leisure hiker, but in the end the same amount of elevation was climbed by both. The same work was accomplished. But as you might expect, the hiker that walked on Mountain Goat Trail is winded and dripping with sweat. He needs to sit down and take a break. The Leisure Time hiker feels much less tired and focuses on the beautiful view. The interesting thing about the hikers is that they each applied the same amount of energy to reach the summit. They each burned roughly the same number of calories. So why is one exhausted and the other fresh?

Your intuition and experience tells you that the Leisure trail was better suited for the human body because it wasn't steep. But because it wasn't as steep, it was a longer distance to the summit. Essentially, the same amount of energy was needed no matter which route was taken, but the effort needed to summit was spread over a longer distance and time on the Leisure trail. The reverse perspective is that the effort was more concentrated on the steep trail.

The same time and distance factors apply to levers, pulleys, and pulley systems. These simple machines can be set up so that manual effort to haul or raise a load is spread out over a greater distance and time. The greater the distance and time, the easier it feels to do a given amount of work.

Levers Explained

We've all used simple levers to get work done when human power falls short or the job is ergonomically impractical. But how do levers create mechanical advantage and make work feel easier on the human body? A few simple physical principles that relate to the hiker story above enable levers to concentrate human power and focus it where it's needed. When it comes to levers, it helps to think in terms of input force and output force. Input force describes the human power applied to the handle of the lever. Output force is the moving power of the lever where it is in contact with the load. With any given input force, the intensity of the output force depends on the position of the lever fulcrum and the load.

Type-1 Levers: Two examples of type-1 levers are teeter-totters and pry-bars. Both are configured with the fulcrum somewhere between the load and the handle. The handle is where the input force is applied, and the output force is focused where the load is positioned at the opposite end. If the fulcrum is positioned half way between the input handle and the end where the load is located, the lever is balanced like a teeter-totter. There may be ergonomic or practical advantages for using a balanced lever, but there is no mechanical advantage. The handle must have an input force that is at least equal to the load and must move the same distance the load moves. Input force energy is transferred equally on both sides of the fulcrum. Because the sections on both sides of the fulcrum are equal, the lever swings the same distance on either side when it moves.

If the fulcrum of the teeter-totter is positioned closer to the load, like a pry-bar, mechanical advantage is created. Energy contained in the lever when input force is applied is still the same on either side of the fulcrum. But now the energy is more concentrated into the short section between the fulcrum and the load. Because the lever is solid and theoretically does not bend, the output force remains equal to the input force but is deployed to move the load over a proportionally shorter distance, depending on the position of the fulcrum. You have to move the handle more, but it feels easier.

The amount of mechanical advantage (the ratio) is proportionate to the lever lengths on either side of the fulcrum. If the lever is 3 feet long between the handle and the fulcrum and 1 foot long between the load and the fulcrum, the mechanical advantage ratio is said to be 3 to 1. The output force is theoretically 3 times stronger than the input force but only moves 1/3 of the distance.

Levers - *Type 1*

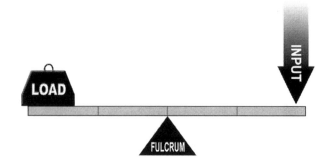

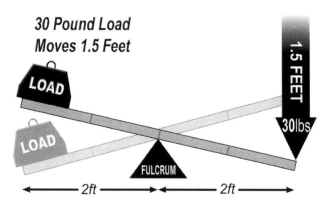

30 Pound Load Moves 1.5 Feet

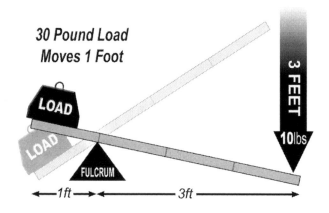

30 Pound Load Moves 1 Foot

Type-2 Levers: A good example of a type-2 lever is a wheelbarrow. The wheel and axle of the wheelbarrow act as the fulcrum. The handles are levers. The barrel (the load) is positioned between the fulcrum and the lever handle.

The amount of mechanical advantage that a type-2 lever creates depends precisely on where the load is positioned relative to the fulcrum. If the load is moved closer to the fulcrum, MA increases. If the load is moved closer to the handle, MA decreases. If the load is positioned exactly mid-way between the fulcrum and the handle, the MA will be 2 to 1. This is because the distance between the fulcrum and the handle is twice as long as the distance between the fulcrum and the load. If the handle is lifted 2 feet, it feels lighter, but the load will only move 1 foot.

Levers - *Type 2*

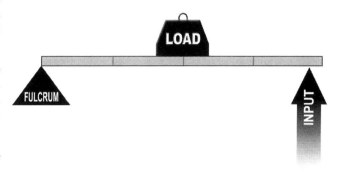

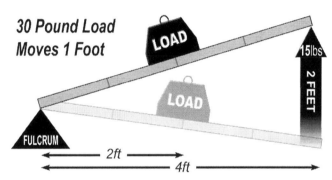

30 Pound Load Moves 1 Foot

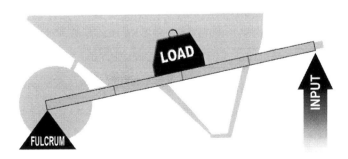

Type-3 Levers: Type-3 levers have their fulcrum positioned on one end and the load on the other. Lifting force is applied to the lever between the fulcrum and load. Think of how a shovel works when lifting dirt out of a hole. Your left hand placed on the end of the handle is the fulcrum. The spade full of dirt is the load. Your right hand positioned mid-handle is the lifting force as your left hand remains stationary. In this case a mechanical disadvantage is created in the interest of practicality.

If input is applied exactly mid-lever, the mechanical disadvantage ratio is 1/2 to 1. It feels harder, but the load moves twice the input distance at a faster rate of speed.

Levers - *Type 3*

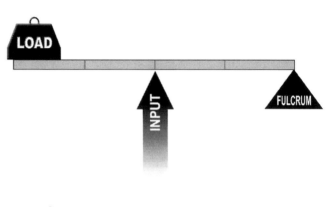

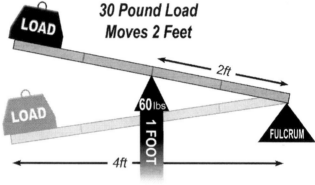

30 Pound Load
Moves 2 Feet

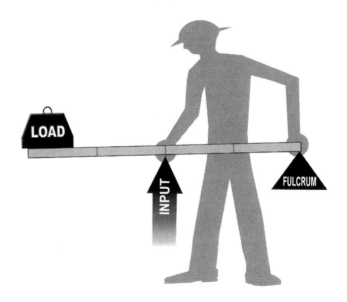

Vector Force Mechanical Advantage

Input force directed to the perpendicular plane of a tensioned rope can concentrate that force on each end of the rope. You've probably experienced this principle when you destroyed your mom's clothesline by pulling down on it mid-span. Imagine a rope strung horizontally and anchored on both ends. Now, grasp the rope mid-way between the anchor points and pull or push in a perpendicular direction. The same angle principles that apply to load-sharing anchors now act to create MA focused to tension the rope. Rope angles where the input force is directed that are between 180° and 120° will create MA. The amount of MA depends on the actual rope angle. Your intuition tells you that it feels easier to push sideways on the rope at first, but it feels harder as you push further. When the rope is pushed far enough to achieve a 120° angle, MA is no longer created. Angles less than 120° result in mechanical disadvantage.

Some practical applications for vector MA include the need for a short, quick raise during lowering operations, when the belay system brakes accidentally or during overhead rescues to raise the rescue subject enough to disconnect his or her personal equipment.

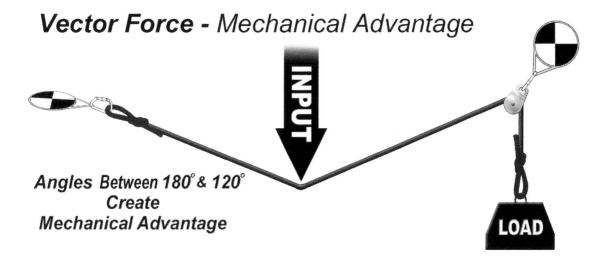

Vector Force - Mechanical Advantage

Angles Between 180° & 120°
Create
Mechanical Advantage

INPUT

LOAD

Pulleys

Pulleys have many uses but are basically for altering rope or cable direction while creating as little friction as possible. There are many types to choose from and a wide variety of applications. Pulleys can be used in specialized ways to fashion anchor attachments or to make brakes self-tending. Some are engineered to work well in wet and dirty conditions, while others emphasize friction efficiency.

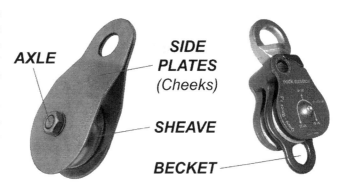

AXLE

SIDE PLATES *(Cheeks)*

SHEAVE

BECKET

Rescue pulleys are designed to be rugged, compact, and lightweight. NFPA-rated pulleys meet tough capacity standards but are generally low on the efficiency scale. Most rescue pulleys are constructed in similar fashion and share common component parts. Other varieties of pulleys feature exotic designs that add flexibility or solve specialized problems.

Pulley Applications

There are three broad categories that describe how pulleys are used and how you should expect them to perform in each application.

Stationary Pulleys: Pulleys that are connected in such a way that they hold their position as rope is rolled through are described as stationary. Generally, pulleys rigged in this fashion provide a low-friction direction change for the rope. Though stationary pulleys make the work easier, they do not usually provide mechanical advantage (MA). Using an overhead pulley to haul down and counterbalance your weight to lift a load describes a "practical advantage" application for a stationary pulley. The work is easier for ergonomic reasons, but there is no mechanical advantage added by the pulley.

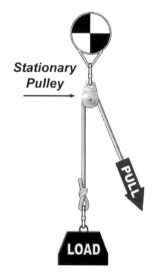

Stationary Pulley

Stationary pulleys can be used to change rope direction, to provide practical improvement, to create edge protection, as stress reducing anchor attachments, or to add rope length to mechanical advantage systems.

Force Amplification by Stationary Pulleys: Stationary pulleys can amplify the load forces they support and direct them to the anchor to which they are attached. When the angle created by the rope entering and exiting a stationary pulley is

CAUTION ! *Stationary Pulleys Amplify Forces Where They Are Anchored*

between 0° and 120°, input forces applied to the pulley are amplified where they are anchored. As the angle sharpens toward 0°, the force increases. If the rope entering and exiting the pulley are perfectly parallel, the forces transferred to the anchor double. As the angle widens toward 180°, the force on the anchor decreases. When this angle is exactly 120°, the load on the anchor is identical to the input force on the pulley. Riggers refer to this 120° angle property as **"The Golden Angle."** As the angle widens, the force on the anchor continues to decrease. When the angle reaches 180°, there is no force on the pulley or the anchor. Angle amplification occurs with any stationary pulley, whether it's placed vertically or horizontally. Use caution and consider force amplification when rigging stationary pulleys. This angle phenomenon applies to other kinds of rigging and is covered further in the anchoring chapter. Committing several angles to memory is an important rigging competency. Knowing amplification factors for 0°, 60°, 90°, and 120° angles will greatly improve a rigger's ability to safely engineer or check systems.

Stationary Pulleys - Force Amplification

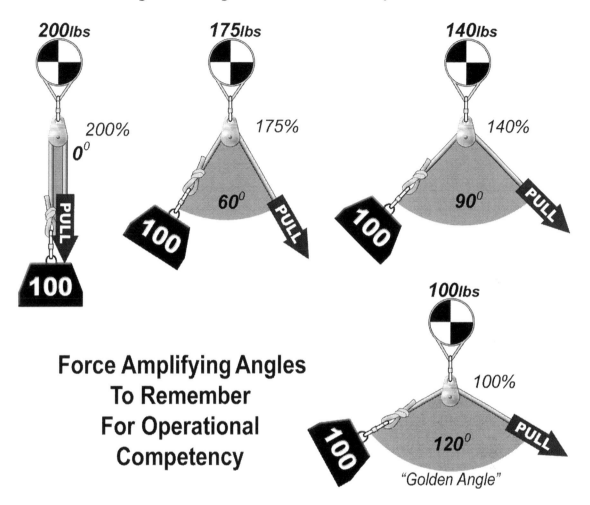

**Force Amplifying Angles
To Remember
For Operational
Competency**

"Golden Angle"

Traveling Pulleys: Pulleys rigged so that they move what they are connected to as the rope rolls through are described as traveling. In most rescue applications, pulleys rigged in this fashion theoretically provide 2 to 1 mechanical advantage, depending on the angle the rope enters and departs. If the sections of the rope that enter and exit the pulley are parallel, the theoretical MA is 2:1. As that angle widens, the MA decreases.

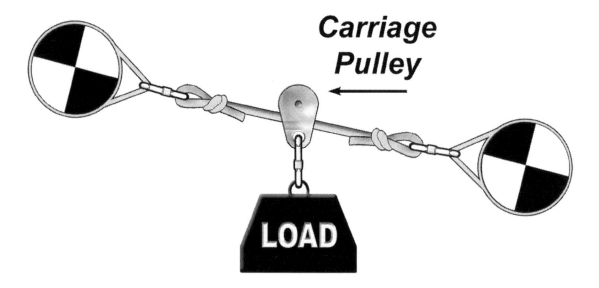

Carriage Pulley

Carriage Pulleys: Pulleys that roll on a fixed line that is horizontal or sloped while supporting a load below, as with a tram or a high line, are described as carriage pulleys. Carriage pulleys provide a low-friction means of tracking a load below a fixed line. No mechanical advantage is created with the use of a carriage pulley.

Pulleys as Levers

It may not seem like it, but pulleys are simply rolling levers. Factors that make more familiar levers work affect pulleys in the same way. Generally speaking, pulleys with large diameter sheaves are more efficient and smooth running than pulleys with small sheaves, just as long-handled levers are. You'll never see a 2-inch pulley on a heavy crane rig. Pulley leverage variations are the same types as other levers.

Type-1 Pulleys: Stationary pulleys work exactly the same way as a type-1 lever. When a pulley is rigged to an anchor in a way that it stays put as rope rolls through, it works as a balanced type-1 lever. There is no mechanical advantage because the fulcrum is positioned mid-lever. Think of the teeter-totter. Stationary pulleys have a fulcrum that is fixed mid-lever. The axle is the fulcrum. The distance from the fulcrum (the axle) to each end of the lever (the sheave) is the same (balanced). The output to input force ratio is 1:1. There is no mechanical advantage here.

The only difference between the teeter-totter and the stationary pulley is friction. The arm of the teeter-totter rocks up and down but

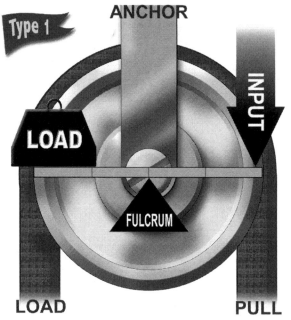

does not slide on the fulcrum surface. There is no friction worth measuring. The pulley, on the other hand, produces friction as the sheave rubs on the surface of the axle as it turns. Most rescue pulleys reduce this friction with a bushing. More efficient pulleys use bearings to lower friction.

Type-1 stationary pulleys are usually used to route rope in ways that add rope length in mechanical advantage systems, to improve ergonomics, or to optimally arrange the work area.

Type-2 Pulleys: Most of the time traveling pulleys work the same way as type-2 levers. When a pulley is rigged to move as rope rolls through, it works as a type-2 lever with the load positioned for 2:1 MA. In this case the fulcrum is positioned at one end and the load is placed 1/2 the length of the lever from it. Think of the wheelbarrow. A traveling pulley works just like a wheelbarrow with its load positioned right in the middle.

As with the type 1 pulley, traveling pulleys create friction. No significant friction is created with a regular type 2 when the lever is moved to lift the load. When a traveling rescue pulley hauls a load, the sheave rubs on the axle and bushing to develop some friction.

Type-3 Pulleys: Pulleys that are rigged as idlers work the same way as any type-3 lever. Even though type-3 pulleys can be rigged to move, don't confuse them with type-2 traveling pulleys. Because they are pulled on where they attach to the system, they do not create mechanical advantage like type-2 pulleys. Type-3 pulleys more closely resemble type-1 pulleys that are attached to a movable anchor. Type-3 pulleys are often found in industry to manage speeds. Cable elevators are rigged with type-3 pulleys. Loads connected to type-3 pulleys will move twice as fast as the hauling input. In the rope rescue setting, type-3 pulleys are used to rig offsets or dynamic directionals. Type-3 pulleys will not be emphasized in this book, but you should be able to recognize them when you see them.

Pulley Friction: Efficiency lost because of friction between the mechanical parts of a pulley is usually of little concern for most vertical rescue field applications. The rotation speeds and durations to which pulleys are exposed during vertical rescue operations usually make friction calculations unnecessary in the field. However, it is important to understand how friction degrades efficiency and how over-rigging with pulleys can bog down functionality. Striving to rig for the most mechanical advantage using the least number of pulleys is a good means to manage friction in the field. Pulley friction and hauling efficiency is covered more in depth in Chapter 8.

Pulley Types (Classes) - *Examples*

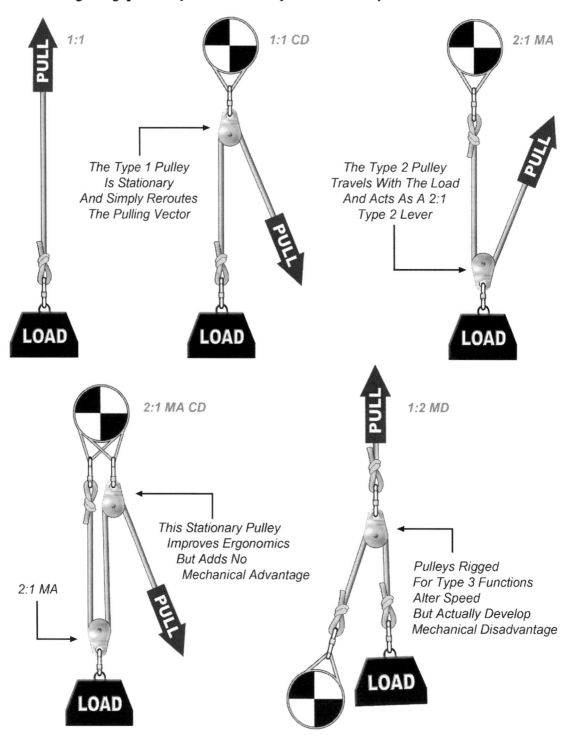

1:1

The Type 1 Pulley
Is Stationary
And Simply Reroutes
The Pulling Vector

1:1 CD

2:1 MA

The Type 2 Pulley
Travels With The Load
And Acts As A 2:1
Type 2 Lever

2:1 MA CD

This Stationary Pulley
Improves Ergonomics
But Adds No
Mechanical Advantage

2:1 MA

1:2 MD

Pulleys Rigged
For Type 3 Functions
Alter Speed
But Actually Develop
Mechanical Disadvantage

8 Pulley Systems

Pulley Systems and Hauling

Configuring ropes and pulleys in the field in order to move a load is as much an art form as it is a science. Operational expertise in vertical rescue requires a good understanding of how to choose, assemble, and operate an appropriate hauling system for the job. The ability to calculate the power, speed, and footprint of any pulley system is essential. Equally important is the ability to recognize how much strain hauling systems direct to anchors and brakes. This section focuses on pulley system mechanics as a means of developing an operational understanding of hauling systems used for vertical rescue.

Basic Rigging and Hauling Considerations

Several real-life factors are important to building and operating vertical rescue hauling systems. Understanding how to properly pull on a hauling system will help determine how systems are placed, assembled, and staffed.

- **People Power:** In testing done by CMC, it has been determined that 3 averaged-sized people pulling on a ½-inch rope with gloved hands while standing on a paved surface wearing steel-toed boots can haul 500 to 550lbs.

- **Clear, Level Haul Field:** Whenever possible, locate hauling systems in a way that allows the operators to haul down or level in a clear area. Avoid hauling uphill.

- **Pull In Line:** As much as possible, haul parallel on pulley systems. Pulling in line keeps mechanical advantage working in your favor. Pulling toward the perpendicular plane of a hauling system reduces mechanical advantage. If the hauling area is less than desirable, connect a pulley in a way that changes the direction of the hauling rope while keeping the pulling force parallel on the system.

- **Build In Enough Power:** Assemble hauling systems with enough power so that the people you have on hand do not strain or rhythmically jerk to move the load. Jerky movement on the system caused by struggling haulers creates bouncing on the load and anchors.

Non-Mechanical Advantage Hauling Systems

Simple Hoisting & Hauling: Placing a stationary pulley to raise or haul a load with a rope is a common way to increase ergonomic favorability. Your intuition and experience help you recognize the obvious practical advantage of counterbalancing your weight as you pull down or lean back on the rope. With enough weight to counter balance, the load will raise by simply hanging on the rope. Fashioning a progress capture device (brake) onto the rope changes this rig from a plain old pulley system to a hauling system.

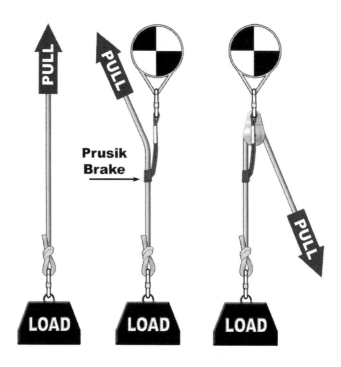

Prusik Brake

Mechanical Advantage Pulley Systems for Hauling

Pulley systems used for hauling a rescue load can be set up in many ways, but generally they will be rigged **"in line"** or **"ganged"** onto the main rope. In line describes rigging where the main hauling rope is used to create the pulley system. A pulley system made from a separate section of rope that is then attached to the main line with a rope grab is said to be ganged on.

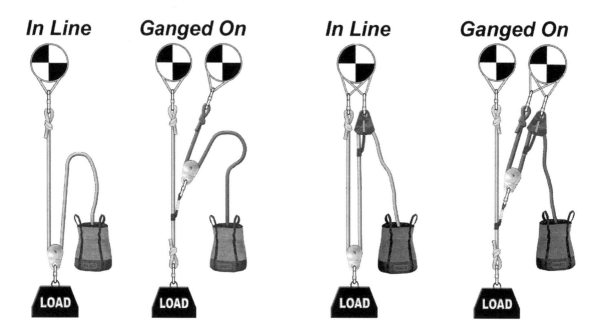

In Line   *Ganged On*   *In Line*   *Ganged On*

Mechanical Adavantage Pulley Systems Types

Vertical rescue mechanical advantage pulley systems fall into three types depending on how they are rigged and connected. Each type has its own set of advantages and disadvantages.

- **Simple Mechanical Advantage**
- **Compound Mechanical Advantage**
- **Complex Mechanical Advantage**

Simple Mechanical Advantage

Systems with pulleys connected directly to either the anchor or the load create simple mechanical advantage. Common block and tackle systems usually fall into the simple MA category. These systems create mechanical advantage primarily by adding length to the hauling rope and routing it through stationary pulleys attached to the anchor and traveling pulleys connected to the load.

Calculating Simple MA: There are several methods for determing the output to input ratios of pulley systems depending on the type. Mechanical advantage of simple pulley systems can be calculated by:

- **Comparative Measurement**
- **Counting Or Measuring Lines That Support The Load**
- **Locating Connection Of Rope Termination**
- **Tracing Tension**

Comparative Measurement: Get out your tape and measure how much the load moves when you haul on the pulley system. If pulling 5 feet of rope through the pulley system moves the load 1 foot, the MA is 5:1. A more practical method for field use is to compare the length of rope that is threaded between the anchor and the load to the actual distance between the anchor and the load (the stroke). If 9 feet of rope makes up the system between the achor and the load when the stroke is only 3 feet, the system calculates to 3:1 MA. These calculating methods do not account for pulley friction, therefore the results are regarded as theoretical MA (TMA).

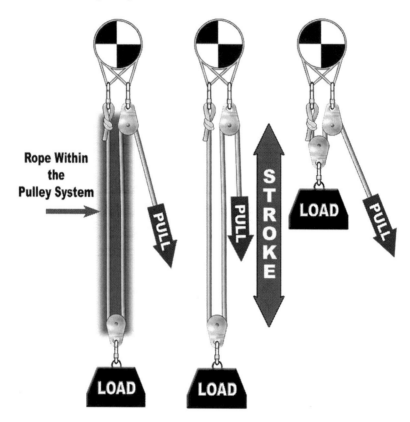

Counting Supporting Lines: Look at the pulley system as if it were vertical and determine which segments of the rope would overcome gravity and hold up the load. Add up the segments, and use the sum as the figure against 1 for the MA ratio. If the load would hang on 2 segments, the MA is 2:1. Segments of the rope routed away from the pulley system with a change of direction pulley do not count in these calculations. This calculating method only determines TMA.

Rope Sections Supporting The Load

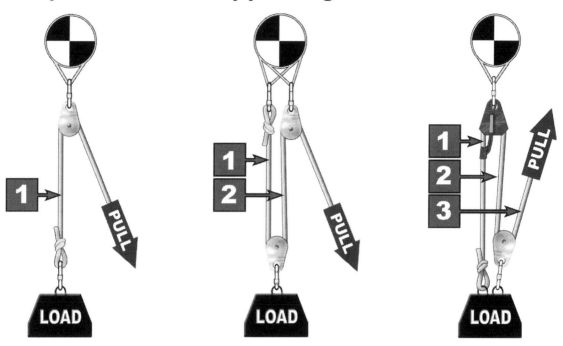

Connection of Rope Termination: Where the end of the rope is tied off in a pulley system determines whether the MA calculates to either even or odd numbers. If the rope terminates at the load, the MA will be an odd number. If the rope terminates at the anchor, the MA will be an even number. Remember: *Odd Load, Even Anchor (OLEA)*. This method does not result in the final MA figure, but it can help confirm other calculations and indicates whether there is a fixed line within the pulley system. This method does not calculate friction in the system.

Rope Termination - *Odd or Even Advantage*

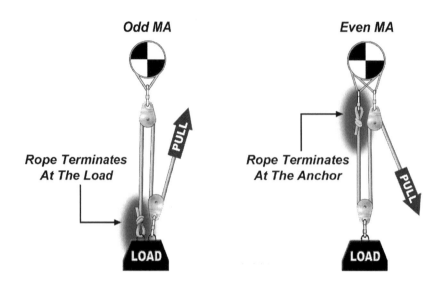

Odd MA

Even MA

Rope Terminates
At The Load

Rope Terminates
At The Anchor

Simple M/A - *Field Calculation*

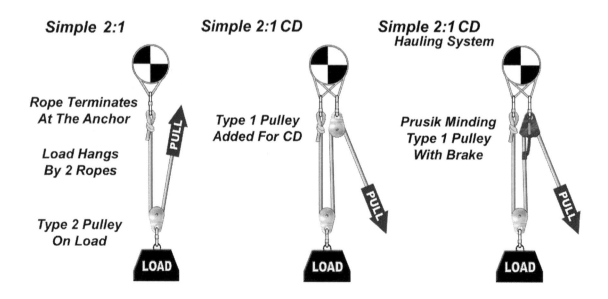

Simple 2:1

Simple 2:1 CD

Simple 2:1 CD
Hauling System

**Rope Terminates
At The Anchor**

**Load Hangs
By 2 Ropes**

**Type 2 Pulley
On Load**

**Type 1 Pulley
Added For CD**

**Prusik Minding
Type 1 Pulley
With Brake**

Tracing Tension: Following the reverse path of the input force as it winds through the pulley system is an accurate means of determining MA because pulley friction can be factored into the calculation. Regardless of what the actual measurement is, start by identifying the input force as 1 unit of tension. As the force is traced along the path of the rope, calculate changes created by the pulleys. Theoretically, force exiting a pulley is the same as the force entering, which creates a situation that doubles the force where the pulley is connected. This is true whether the pulley is traveling or stationary. This method also identifies the stress on each segment of rope, each anchor attachment, and the brakes. Forces above and below the pulley system always balance. For theoretical results, disregard pulley efficiency.

Tracing Tension - Stationary Pulleys

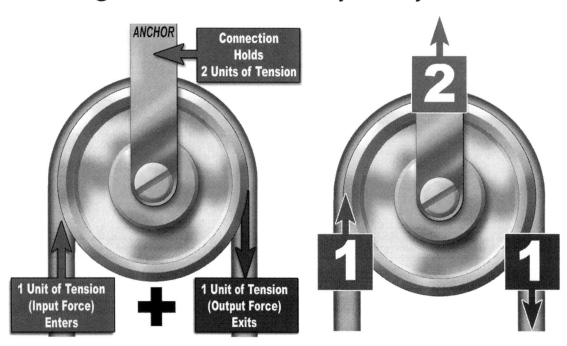

Tracing Tension - Traveling Pulleys

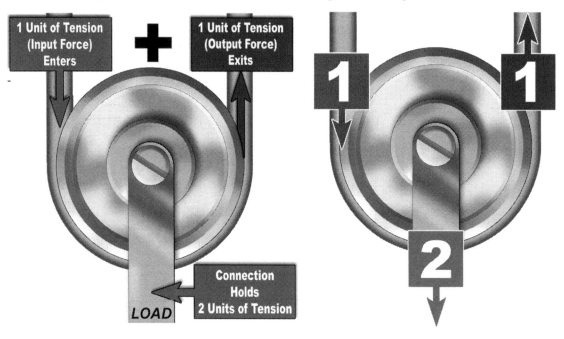

Tracing Tension - Pulley Systems (Basic)

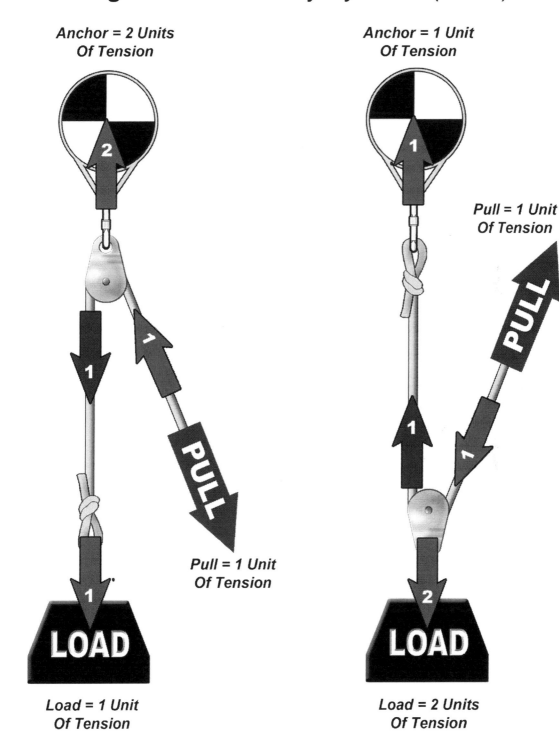

Anchor = 2 Units Of Tension

Anchor = 1 Unit Of Tension

Pull = 1 Unit Of Tension

Pull = 1 Unit Of Tension

Load = 1 Unit Of Tension

Load = 2 Units Of Tension

Tracing Tension - *Pulley Systems*

* Added Strain From Change Of Direction Pulleys

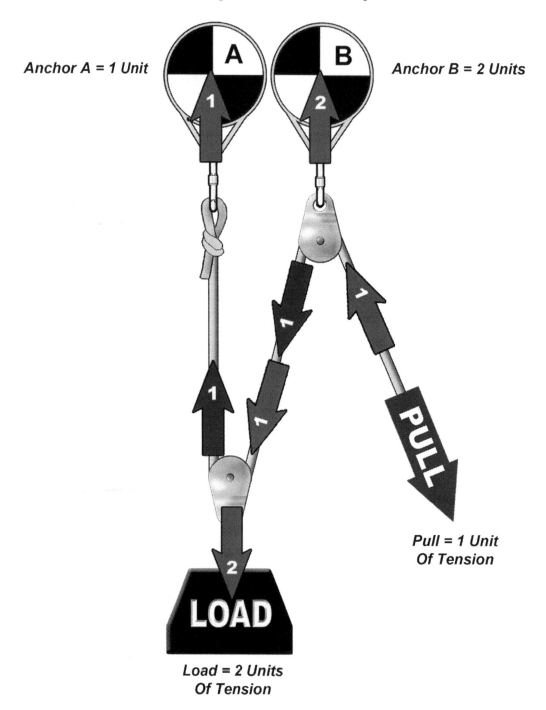

Anchor A = 1 Unit

Anchor B = 2 Units

Pull = 1 Unit
Of Tension

Load = 2 Units
Of Tension

Actual Mechanical Advantage: To calculate the actual MA created by a pulley system, factor in efficiency figures as each pulley is encountered. As the input force turns the pulley, some of the energy is directed away from the rope in the form of heat and vibration because of friction. If the pulley is 90% efficient, energy on the output side of the pulley will be reduced by 10%. With one unit of tension entering the pulley, 0.9 units of tension will continue through the rope on the output side of the pulley. With our formula, the force transferred to the point where the pulley is connected will add up to 1.90. If the unit of tension on the input side of the pulley is equal to 100lbs, 10lbs of pulling power will be lost to friction. The rope on the output side will retain 90 pounds of force, and the connection will hold 190lbs. However, in real life, most of the pulling force lost to friction actually transfers to the anchor connection. So the anchor will bear that difference in pulling force because of the energy displaced by friction. These attributes affect rigging choices as more pulleys are added to hauling systems. Friction figures differ between pulley models.

NOTE: To simplify the concepts, the following diagrams will not calculate for friction energy transferred from stationary pulleys to anchor connections. Trace pulling energy to the load for actual mechanical advantage, and use the anchor tension figures as a means of gauging how pulling forces differ among multiple pulleys. Anchor tension figures are actually higher in real life.

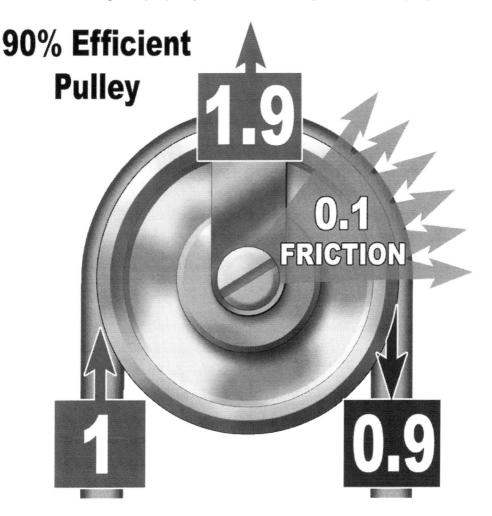

90% Efficient Pulley

Tracing Tension - *Pulley Systems & Friction*

★ Pulley Friction Degrades Actual Mechanical Advantage

Anchor = 1.9 Units Of Tension

Anchor = 0.9 Units Of Tension

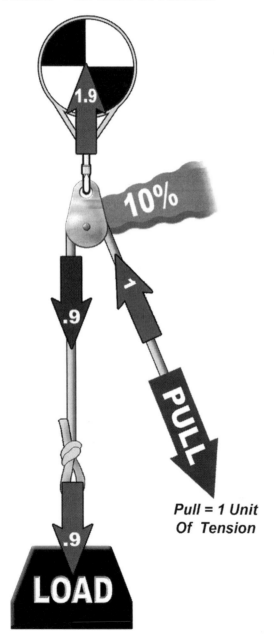

Pull = 1 Unit Of Tension

Pull = 1 Unit Of Tension

Load = 0.9 Units Of Tension

Load = 1.9 Units Of Tension

Tracing Tension - *Pulley Systems & Friction*

* Change Of Direction Friction Further Degrades Overall Advantage

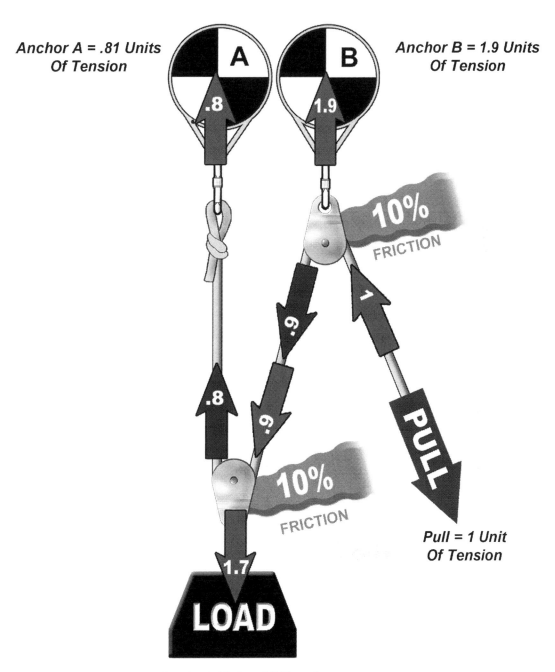

Anchor A = .81 Units
Of Tension

Anchor B = 1.9 Units
Of Tension

.8

1.9

10% FRICTION

.9

1

.8

.9

PULL

10% FRICTION

1.7

LOAD

Pull = 1 Unit
Of Tension

Load = 1.71 Units Of Tension

Tracing Tension - *Practice*

* Practice Calculating Advantage For Each Pulley System Assuming That All Pulleys Are 90 Percent Efficient

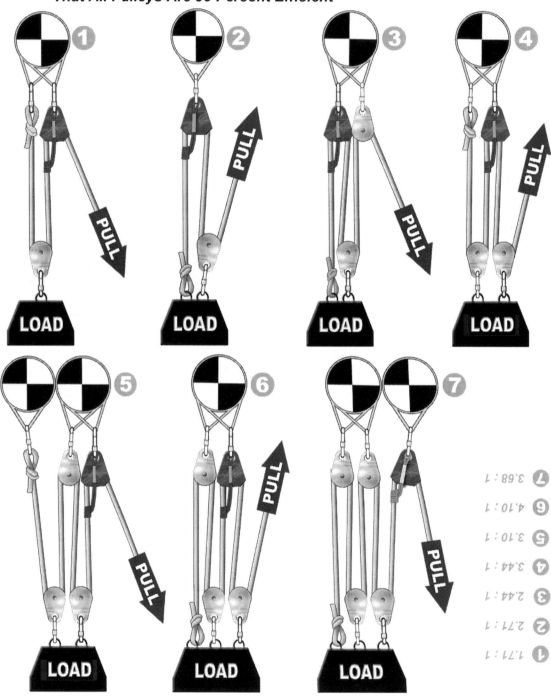

Calculate the theoretical and actual MA for each of the above simple hauling systems as if the pulleys are 90% efficient. Consider how pulling forces act on each pulley and anchor attachment in each system as the load is hauled up.

Orientation: Disregarding the placement of the brakes, inverting the rigging in these types of pulley systems results in changes in MA. When the rigging for a 2:1 is flipped vertically, the MA changes to 1:1. When a 2:1 CD is flipped vertically, it creates 3:1MA. When a 3:1 CD is flipped, it turns into a 4:1, etc.

Fixed Leg Hazard: Simple hauling systems with the rope termination tied to the anchor result in even numbers of MA and have a section of rope that remains stationary (fixed). Simple systems with fixed sections of rope create an increased risk of rope damage from abrasion wherever it contacts an edge, another rope, or any solid object. Consider this disadvantage when choosing simple MA hauling systems. Many times a hauling system with a fixed section of rope can be easily replaced with a system that creates uneven MA without fixed sections.

CAUTION ! *Simple Systems With Even Number MA Have A Fixed Section Of Rope*

Simple M/A Fixed Leg Hazard

2:1 CD

Stationary Leg Of Even MA Hauling Systems Create Potential For Severe Abrasion Hazards

EDGE

Provide Adequate Clearance Or Pad EdgesTo Protect Stationary Sections From Abrasion

Shared Attachments and Multi-Sheaved Pulleys: For more clarity, the simple hauling systems in the diagrams above are shown with separate attachments for each pulley. Simple block and tackle style hauling systems are usually assembled using shared attachments and multi-sheaved pulleys. All the calculation principles are the same, but the rigging is much cleaner and more compact when attachments are shared or when multi-sheaved pulleys are built in.

It's important to rig systems in a way that is clean, without letting pulleys pry and cam on each other, and to ensure rope sections run freely without rubbing. Allowing pulleys to clank together can put them out of line with the rope course, causing significant friction and dangerous torque. Pulley systems with ropes rubbing together because of twists can compound friction and be surprisingly hard to haul. Taking the safety step of preloading a hauling system with false tension to reveal twisting pays off in tremendous dividends. Working through with a hauling system that has twists can foul up an otherwise good operation.

Prerigged hauling system bundles with integrated mechanical brakes and cams are abundantly available and good to use, but can limit application adaptability needed for a variety of hazards. Mechanical hauling systems are well-suited for industrial rescue applications where overhead anchors are always handy and staffing and expertise is limited. Be careful to evaluate the shock absorbing capability of any

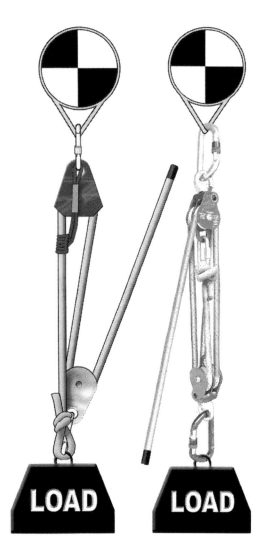

mechanical, pre-rigged hauling system. Some use brakes that do not allow rope to adequately slip when shocked. Filling your cache with prerigged hauling systems for every application can be a real budget-buster, especially if you're looking to keep in step with NFPA standards.

Z-Rig Hauling System: Rearranging the rigging of a simple 3:1 hauling system to configure a "Z-Rig" greatly increases hauling practicality for most over-the-edge raising operations. Indirectly connecting the traveling type-2 pulley to the load using a suitable rope grab retains the 3:1 pulling power of the simple system without having to lower the traveling pulley over the edge. This keeps the components of the actual hauling system topside even though the load may be hundreds of feet below. Block and tackle style rigs work well for short runout hauling needs where anchors are positioned directly above or close to the load. Situations like confined space and trench operations require short lowering and raising maneuvers. Generally in those circumstances the hauling system is used for both raising and lowering. The Z-Rig configuration makes converting from lowering systems to raising systems, and vice versa, quick and easy in long runout situations. Block and tackle systems rigged using the main line can make changeovers cumbersome and very slow.

NOTE: Do not use rope grabs with aggressive, toothed camming mechanisms. The rope grab used to connect the traveling pulley in a Z-Rig does not function as a brake, so it is marginally acceptable to use mechanical ascenders for this rigging. However, the amplified forces directed to this connection point make toothed ascenders very rough on the rope and less safe for rescue work using Z-rig hauling systems.

The Z-Rig is still a simple MA hauling system so calculation methods work the same way as for the previous block and tackle style systems. The load hangs on 3 sections of rope; the rope in the system is approximately 3 times longer than the distance between anchor and the load (the prusik); and the rope terminates at the load. You can also trace tension to determine TMA or factor in pulley efficiency for actual mechanical advantage.

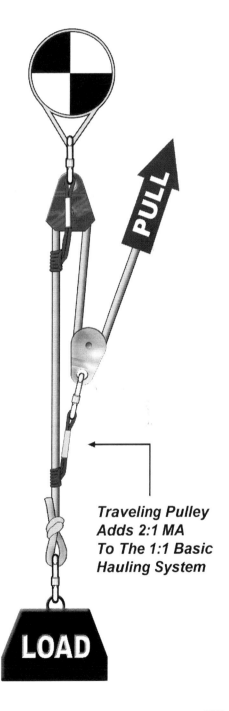

3:1 Z-Rig

Traveling Pulley Adds 2:1 MA To The 1:1 Basic Hauling System

Tracing Tension - *3:1 Z-Rig*

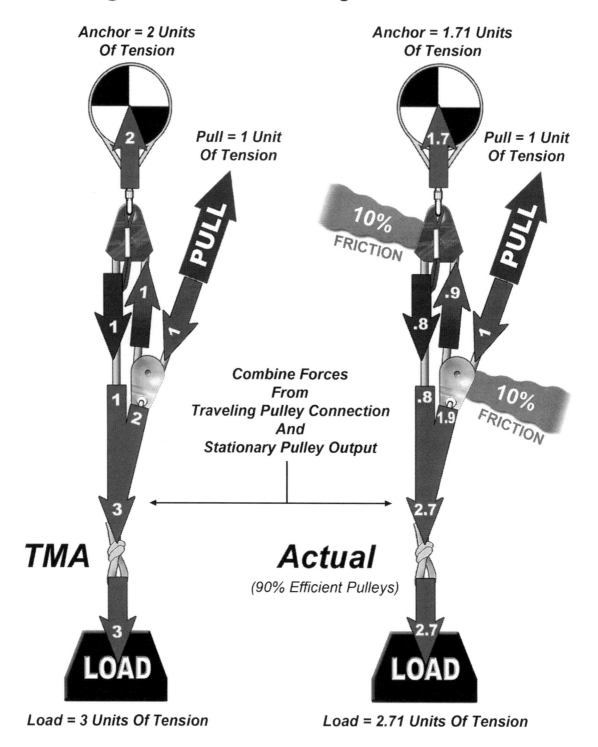

Anchor = 2 Units Of Tension

Pull = 1 Unit Of Tension

Anchor = 1.71 Units Of Tension

Pull = 1 Unit Of Tension

10% FRICTION

10% FRICTION

Combine Forces From Traveling Pulley Connection And Stationary Pulley Output

TMA

Actual
(90% Efficient Pulleys)

LOAD

LOAD

Load = 3 Units Of Tension

Load = 2.71 Units Of Tension

Compound Mechanical Advantage

Any configuration where a mechanical advantage system is being hauled on by another mechanical advantage system results in compound MA. These arrangements result in force multiplication. Compounding pulley systems often results in more MA with fewer pulleys and therefore less friction.

Calculating Compound MA: Mechanical advantage of compound pulley systems can be calculated by:

- **Comparative Measurement**
- **Multiplying Component Systems**
- **Tracing Tension**

Comparative Measurement: Measuring the difference in hauling rope length and the stroke is the most empirical method to calculate MA for any pulley system. But the field methods of comparative measurement used for simple MA will not work for compound pulley systems. Compound MA rigging does not add up in the same way, so comparing rope length to the stroke will fall short.

Multiply Component Systems: The best field method to calculate compound MA is to multiply the power of the pulley systems acting on each other. Example: If a 2:1 simple system is pulling on the hauling end of a 3:1 pulley system, the total compound MA is 6:1. The method works no matter how many pulley systems are acting on each other. Calculating compound MA in this way does not take friction into account, and thus the results are theoretical.

Tracing Tension: Tracing tension by following the reverse path of the pulling force works very well to calculate compound MA. Using this method has the advantage of identifying how forces are distributed throughout the system and can also factor in pulley friction. Use this method to calculate actual MA.

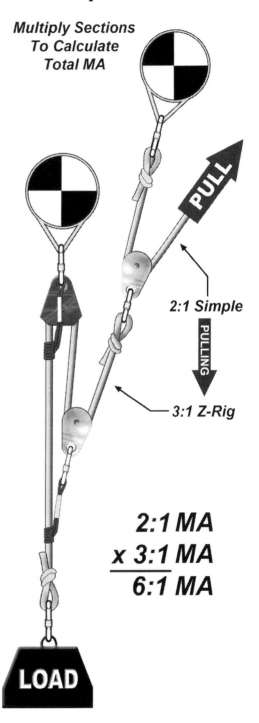

Compound M/A

*Multiply Sections
To Calculate
Total MA*

2:1 Simple

3:1 Z-Rig

$$\frac{2{:}1\ MA}{x\ 3{:}1\ MA}$$
$$6{:}1\ MA$$

Tracing Tension - *Compound M/A*

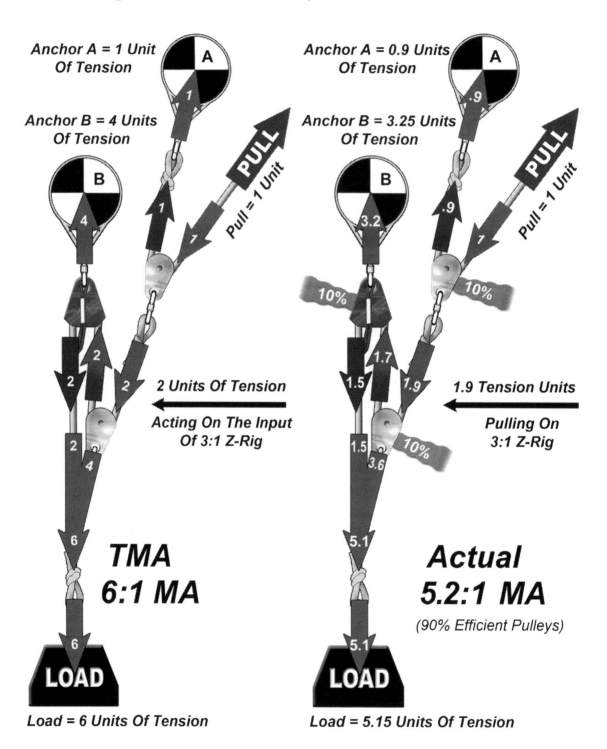

Anchor A = 1 Unit Of Tension

Anchor A = 0.9 Units Of Tension

Anchor B = 4 Units Of Tension

Anchor B = 3.25 Units Of Tension

PULL — Pull = 1 Unit

PULL — Pull = 1 Unit

2 Units Of Tension

Acting On The Input Of 3:1 Z-Rig

1.9 Tension Units

Pulling On 3:1 Z-Rig

TMA 6:1 MA

Actual 5.2:1 MA

(90% Efficient Pulleys)

LOAD

LOAD

Load = 6 Units Of Tension

Load = 5.15 Units Of Tension

Tracing Tension - Compound M/A - Practice

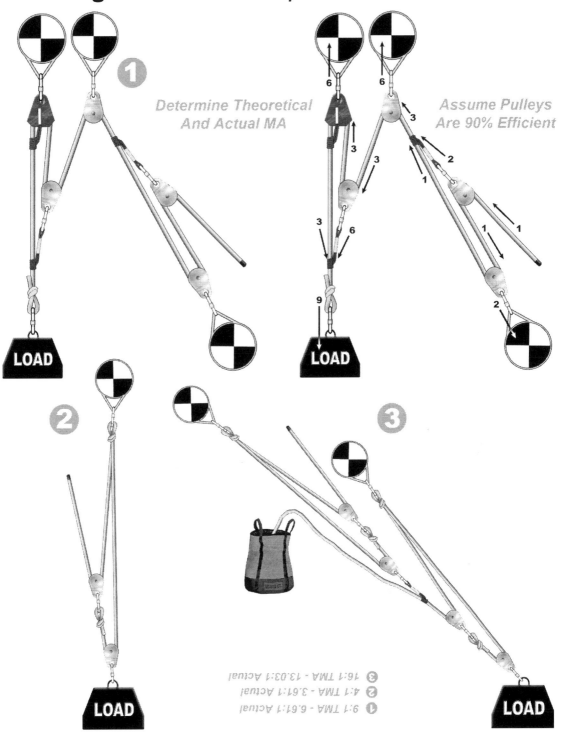

Determine Theoretical
And Actual MA

Assume Pulleys
Are 90% Efficient

① 9:1 TMA - 6.61:1 Actual
② 4:1 TMA - 3.61:1 Actual
③ 16:1 TMA - 13.03:1 Actual

Tracing Tension - Compound M/A - Practice

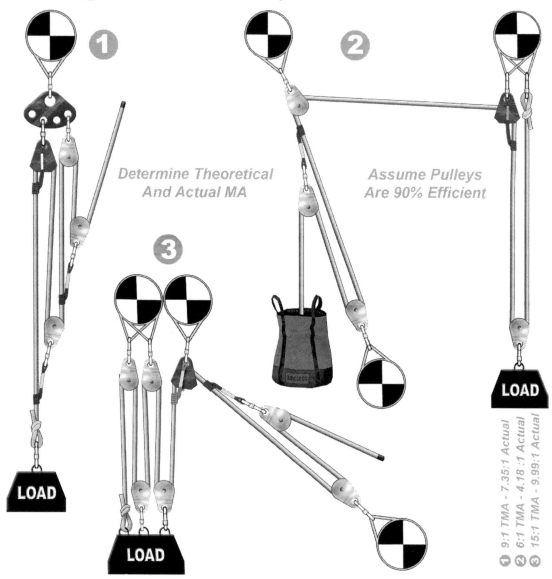

Determine Theoretical
And Actual MA

Assume Pulleys
Are 90% Efficient

① 9:1 TMA - 7.35:1 Actual
② 6:1 TMA - 4.18 :1 Actual
③ 15:1 TMA - 9.99:1 Actual

Use the compound hauling system diagrams shown above to calculate theoretical and actual mechanical advantage as if the pulleys are 90% efficient. Consider the forces on each anchor attachment and pulley. Assign varying weight figures to the loads to dermine the actual input force needed for hauling.

Rigging and Operating Considerations for Compound Hauling Systems: Using compound hauling systems can add more power to your cache, but there are a few tricks to trimming the rigging for increased cfficiency.

- **Synchronize compounded systems:** Because adding length to the rope that hauls the load spreads effort over a longer distance, component pulley systems will contract at different rates. If component pulley systems within a compound hauling rig have the same stroke length, the initial system will fully contract (reach 2-blocks) well before the secondary system. It is better to have the initial pulley system fully contract at the same time as the remaining compounded systems. The second best scenario is to have the secondary system fully collapse before the initial system. This can be accomplished by adjusting the stroke length of each system relative to the rope length contained in the system it acts upon. If a 3:1 Z-Rig is pulling on another 3:1 Z-Rig, adjust the stroke length of the initial system to match or slightly exceed the length of rope contained within the secondary system. This principle can work no matter how many pulley systems are compounded. Be sure to factor in inevitable rope stretch by making the initial stroke slightly longer than needed.

Synchronized Compound Hauling System

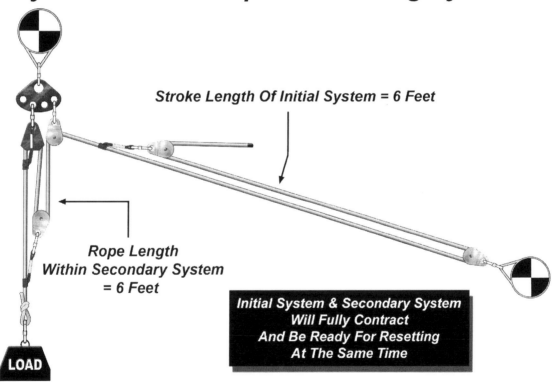

Stroke Length Of Initial System = 6 Feet

Rope Length Within Secondary System = 6 Feet

Initial System & Secondary System Will Fully Contract And Be Ready For Resetting At The Same Time

LOAD

- **Unsynchronized compounded systems:** Many times anchor availability is less than desirable. It's not always possible to synchronize compound pulley systems. Sometimes component pulley systems are close to the same length. When this is the case, it makes sense to employ resetting methods that maximize efficiency to save time and smooth operations. It seems natural and intuitive to reset all parts of the compound hauing system whenever the initial system reaches 2-blocks. However, your resets and overall hauling operation will be quicker and smoother if you resist resetting the entire system every time the initial system bottoms out. Instead, reset the inital system, and then continue hauling. Continue resetting in this way until the secondary system achieves 2-blocks. When the second system bottoms out, reset the entire system. Use the same principle when hauling systems contain more than two components. Haul and reset on the initial system until the secondary system 2-blocks, then reset systems one and two. Continue until the tertiary system bottoms out, and then reset the entire hauling system.

Complex Mechanical Advantage

Any system that is neither simple nor compound is called complex. Complex MA usually appears in situations where more power is needed for an existing hauling system. Clipping a rope grab and a traveling pulley onto a Z-Rig is an easy way to add hauling power when the system is still supporting a load. A disadvantage to using this type of complex pulley system is the short stroke length. Because the traveling pulleys converge toward each other as the load is hauled, the stroke length is shortened considerably. This type of complex hauling system is best used in situations that allow for very long stroke lengths.

Calculating Complex MA: Mechanical advantage of complex pulley systems can be calculated by:

- **Comparative Measurement**
- **Tracing Tension**

Comparative Measurement: Measure how much the load moves when you haul on the pulley system. As is true with any pulley system, if pulling 5 feet of rope moves the load 1 foot the MA is 5 to 1. Field methods of measurement used for simple MA will not work for complex systems. Empirical measurement during practice sessions is best.

Tracing Tension: Follow the reverse path of the input force as you would with other types of MA pulley systems. Combine forces where traveling pulleys haul on rope grabs regardless of direction. Factor in pulley friction for actual MA.

Complex Mechanical Advantage

Shown: Converting 3:1 Z-Rig To Complex 5:1 MA

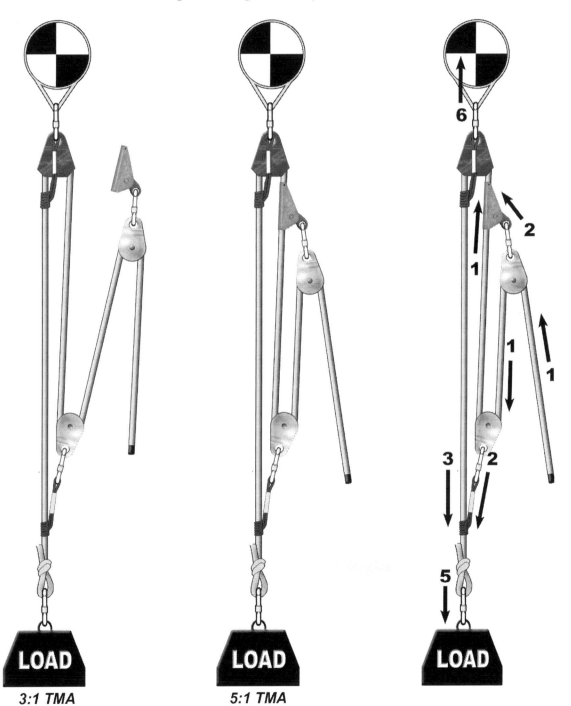

3:1 TMA

5:1 TMA

Brake Placement

Where the progress capture feature (the brake) is placed determines how a hauling system functions. Location also determines the amount of strain on a brake. Rigging configuration variations of the brake can make a hauling system self-tending, suitable for lowering, good for long hauls, or able to support very heavy loads. There are many ways to capture progress, but we'll focus on a few practical variations. Position the brake of your hauling system where it makes the most sense.

Direct Placement: Positioning an appropriate brake on the section of rope in a pulley system in a way that it supports the entire weight of the load is described as direct placement. In most cases, direct placement of the brake allows for resetting of the pulley system once it has reached 2-blocks. Systems with direct brake placement are well suited for long distance hauls where attaching a traveling pulley to the load is impractical, such as over-the-side cliff operations.

An important consideration with direct placement is that the brake will endure maximum strain from the load or any shock that occurs. An 8mm 3-wrap prusik that has been placed directly on a ½-inch haul line can be expected to slip if the load reaches a weight of around 1000lbs or a shock load of about 4.5kN occurs. This can be a positive or a negative depending on the situation. Generally speaking, 1000lbs of braking capacity is adequate for rescue applications, discounting freak events like a 2000lb dirt clod falling into the litter. That's what the 2-rope system approach is all about. In a well-rigged and well-run operation, the main brake would slip a short distance before the belay system, with its double prusik brake, begins to help support the load. You can consider the 1000lb prusik brake to be a built in relief valve for the rest of the system, like a circuit breaker that will trip before the anchors are pulled out or other rigging snaps. If the main brake begins to slip during an operation, it's a clear indicator that safe working load limits have been exceeded and rigging changes are needed.

Another advantage of direct brake placement is that the rigging upstream of the brake can be less bomber. In other words, if you gang an MA system made from a clothes line onto your main haul line, the brake will catch if the clothesline snaps. The bolted-on system never really supports the live load. Mechanical rope grabs that do not slip to absorb shock or excessive loading can sometimes be used upstream in pulley systems for this reason.

Indirect Placement: Rigging the brake in a way that it holds less than the entire weight of the load describes indirect placement. Positioning the brake on a section of rope within the pulley system that is behind other sections will distribute some of the weight of the load among the other sections whenever the brake is engaged. The hauling system will support more weight or shock before the brake begins to slip. Indirectly placed brakes usually make resetting the pulley system impossible under load. Whenever an indirect brake is set and holding the load, some or all of the rope sections within the pulley system remain under tension. This can be an advantage for hauling loads connected to several traveling pulleys or if the raising system is also used for short lowering operations, as in confined space rescues. Indirect brake placement also makes hauling systems more responsive. The recovery time of taking up the slack in a system with direct brake placement is not needed with a system rigged with an indirect brake. This may be a very important attribute for some rescue situations, such as those over water or moving traffic.

Direct Brake Placement

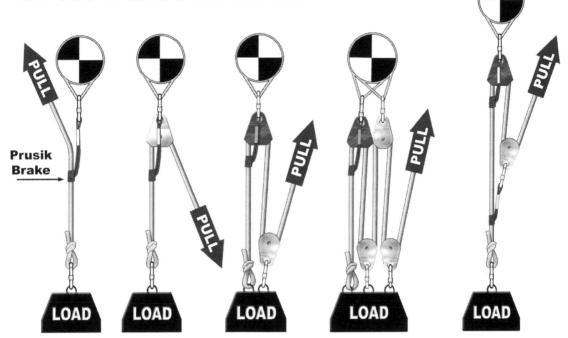

Indirect Brake Placement

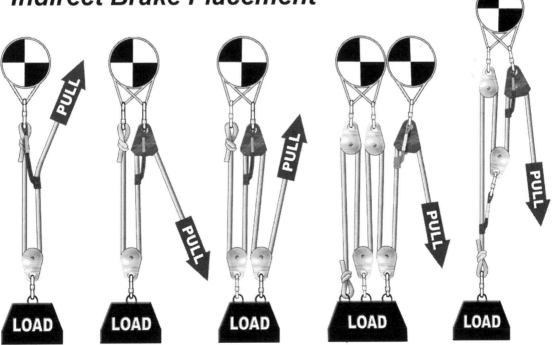

Indirect brakes are much less effective as relief mechanisms for excessive loads. Because they are upstream in the pulley system rigging, brakes will be exposed to less force. Much more force on the system is required for the brake to slip and transfer weight to the belay line. This can be an important factor for shock load tolerance considerations.

Load Placement: Hauling systems rigged with load-placed brakes allow the climber to apply the brake and stop motion, or to prevent motion until the brake is released. Load placement brakes are usually rigged onto the traveling pulley. Load-placed brakes are sometimes used in technical level high-line or short runout lowering and raising operations.

Load Placement

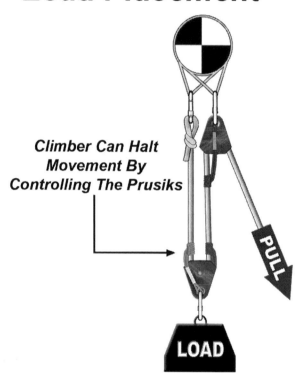

Climber Can Halt Movement By Controlling The Prusiks

LOAD

Lock-out Placement: Lock-out brakes are used to prevent pulley system movement in any direction until the brake is manually released. Lock-out brakes make sense in situations where rigging may have to be left unattended or when public access is a possibility, as might be the case in a wide-spread disaster with rescue crews in hit-and-run mode.

Lock-Out Brake Placement

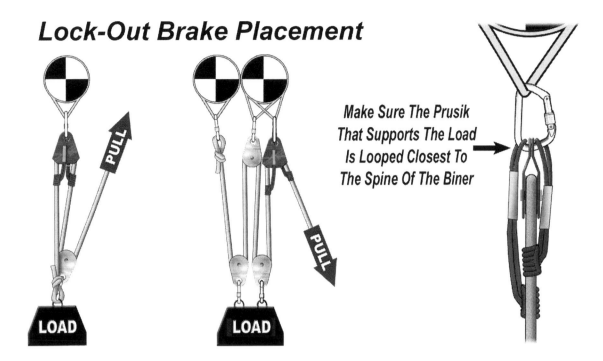

Make Sure The Prusik
That Supports The Load
Is Looped Closest To
The Spine Of The Biner

Working vs. Non-Working Mechanical Advantage Systems

Any mechanical advantage system rigged with the intention of pulling tension for the purpose of moving a load is described as a working system. Anchored at one end, the load moves as the rope is pulled through the pulley systems. In most rescue applications, working systems are rigged with pulleys to reduce friction and improve efficiency. Ropes can be rigged to create MA without pulleys, but its not very practical for extended or repeated hauling because of the high amount of friction involved. Working MA systems without pulleys are often used by rafters and kayakers to peel boats off of rocks.

Non-working MA systems are primarily used to create a strong, high-tension link between two points. It's not always the case, but non-working MA systems do not move a load. In these kinds of situations, using pulleys to improve efficiency may not be practical. Sometimes adding friction to the direction changes in the rope of a non-working MA system improves the practicality of the overall operation. In some cases an MA system can be used to move a load a short distance and then hold it in place, with no intention to move it again. Think of a fire company bending a partially fallen tree away from a house until the arborist arrives several days later.

Non-working MA systems are often used by rescue companies to strengthen or backup anchors and connections. Connecting several anchor choices together with strong and tightly-set non-working MA rigs to improve strength or positioning is very common. In these cases, it's important to place brakes indirectly so that all legs of the MA system stay tensioned and share the load. This greatly reduces unwanted rope stretch and maintains tightness.

Non-Working Mechanical Advantage

These Rope Systems Are Used To Pull And Hold Hard Tension Between Two Points. Pulleys Can Be Used, But Basic Pulley-Free Versions Employ The Increased Friction As Added Holding Power. The Diagrams Show Indirectly Placed Prusik Brakes, But Theses Systems Can Be Pulled Tight And Tied Off Using Double Half Hitches. Non-Working MA Systems Are Commonly Used For Back-Tying Or Focusing Anchor Rigging.

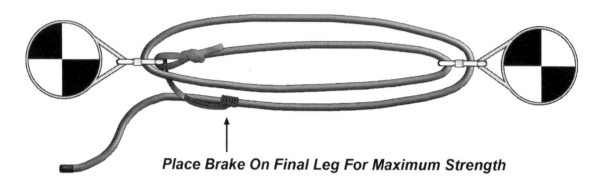

Place Brake On Final Leg For Maximum Strength

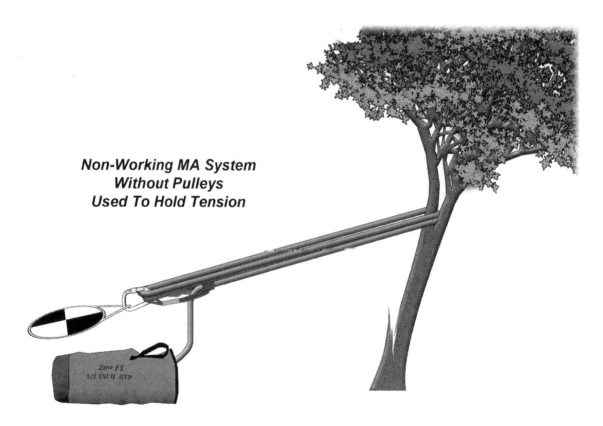

Non-Working MA System Without Pulleys Used To Hold Tension

170

9 Personal Competencies

Personal Competencies

Individual Members must possess core abilities that enable assignment to any of the seven operational positions that make up the Vertical Rescue Team. Optimally, each team member should be equally comfortable leading the team, safety-checking, going over the side, or rigging and operating in any of the tactical positions. There is a tendency for individuals to gravitate toward positions in which they feel most competent. This can impair the team's ability if one or more members who have specialized in a specific competency take time off or get reassigned. All members must be able to safely navigate the scene, understand tactics and strategies, understand commands, and communicate adequately. Knot craft and rigging skills are essential and should be considered prerequisites for all team positions, including the Leader and Safety Officer. Initial training followed by regular, meaningful, and realistic practice sessions that rotate personnel into all seven of the tactical and leadership positions are key. Realistic practice sessions carried out even when unskilled personnel are temporarily assigned are also beneficial for operating adequately whenever the team is short of expertise. The ability to adjust personnel assignments is vital to functionality in the real world. This kind of flexibility absolutely depends on the competency of individual team members. Team performance depends on personal competency. This section of the book will identify elements of personal competency that make up operational levels of expertise to achieve top team performance.

Knot Craft

Most of the following group of basic knots, hitches, and harnesses are common to the fire service and can be used to assemble all the rigging examples in this book. Others are knots used by arborists, rope access workers, cavers, and climbers. Of course, the more knot crafting depth a firefighter possesses, the better.

In general, knots should be well dressed (laid snug and neat) and adjusted appropriately for a given application. Knots that are tied well will be stronger and hold better than those that are loose and sloppily tied. For safety and functionality, the gain (size or length) of tied loops should be only as long as necessary. Excessively long loops allow knots to flail around when the rope moves and frequently contribute to clearance problems. Tail (rope end) lengths should be at least 6 times the diameter of the rope used to tie the knot. Example: a figure-8 bight tied using a ½-inch rope should have a tail that is 3 inches or longer. Adequate tail length is important because rope ends 'suck in' and shorten under tension, especially when shock loaded.

Knot Form Terms: Tying knots and hitches requires manipulation to contort, wrap, and thread the rope to create friction and binding. Identifying the simple form elements a rope takes as a knot or hitch is tied establishes a vocabulary for teaching, learning, and managing. This language of rope shapes enables team members to picture knot-building progress in their minds whenever it is described verbally.

- **Knots:** Tucking and tying a rope, cord, or string to create a functional form such as a loop or lump. True knots do not rely on other objects to retain their form.

- **Hitches:** The term hitch refers to rope formations that rely on solid objects for proper functionality. In other words, hitches are tied onto other objects, including other ropes. The combination of rope tension and friction on a solid object makes a hitch grip or slip as needed.

- **Bends:** Any knot form that joins ropes together, end-to-end, is called a "bend."

- **Standing Line:** Picture a rope with one end connected to a load weight and half of its length stuffed into a bag. If you grab the rope and pull it to move the load, the section between the point where you grab the rope and the bag would be considered the "standing" section or standing part. If a free-floating knot is tied at the mid-point of the exposed section between the load and the bag, the rope between the knot and the bag is considered the standing line relative to the free-floating knot. If the free-floating knot were replaced by a knot or hitch that ties onto a tree trunk, the section between the tree and the bag would be considered the standing line. If the knot is removed and the rope threaded into a brake rack that is anchored to the tree, the section between the rack and the bag would be considered the standing line. Standing line describes the part of the overall length that is unused but available for whatever system it connects to. Think of the part of the rope you hold stationary as you tie most knots. That part is usually the standing part of the rope. The hauling end of rope on a pulley system (the part you grab) is also a standing section of the rope. In some regions, the unused rope that is in either a bag or pile is referred to as the "running" part and running end.

- These interpretations are relative. A rope rescue system may have multiple standing sections depending on your focus at any given time. In our example, the section of rope between the load weight and the brake-rack can be a standing section if you focus on the knot that connects to the load weight as it is being tied. If a figure-8 bight was used to connect to the load weight, the standing section for that knot is between the 8 bight and the brake-rack. Each individual knot or piece of hardware has its own standing section, but when you pull back your focus and look at an overall system, it will have its own relative standing section as well. You would identify the standing line for each point if you were teaching a rookie how to tie the knots while you build up a larger rope rescue system that has its own overall standing section. Get it? It can be confusing. Imagine a Climber carrying the bag of rope as he or she rappels down a cliff. To the Climber, the standing section is the part between the descent control device on their harness and the bag they're carrying. The topside team would consider the standing section of the same rope to be any part lying slack up at the anchor.

- **Working Line:** Again, picture a rope connected to a load weight with half of its length stuffed into a bag. If you grab the rope and pull it to move the load, the section between the point where you grab the rope and the load would be considered the 'Working' section, working part or working line. Now picture yourself tying an overhand knot at the end of a rope. You would grasp the rope a couple of feet from the end with one hand to hold it stationary as you use the other hand to bend and thread the end of the rope into a knot. The part of the rope you bent and threaded would also be considered the working line while you tie that knot. If rope is tied onto a tree trunk, the part of the rope that wraps around the tree and makes up the knot is considered a working part. In a hauling system, the working section would be the length of the rope that threads through the pulleys and extends down to the load.

- **Bight:** Grabbing the rope to form a tight U-turn or "hairpin" shape describes a "bight" of rope. The bight form is elemental to many rescue service knots and rigging.

- **Loop:** Forming a circle mid-point in a rope describes a "loop."

- **Round Turn:** Adding an inverted loop to the top of a bight of rope is a way to describe the "round turn" form. A round turn is usually created when the rope is wrapped around an object and directed back toward a single point.

- **Turn:** Any change in direction that does not form a bight or round turn could be described as a turn.

- **Knot Body:** The actual bulk or knob of the rope that makes up a knot describes the "knot body."

- **Tail:** The short end of rope that results from tying a knot is called the "tail." Tails can actually be any length, and usually refers to a "working end." But most often, tails are shorter. For rescue purposes, the general best practice for adjusting tail length is to make them at least 6 times the rope diameter. Remember, that's the minimum. Excessive tail length can cause operating difficulty within some rigging.

- **Gain:** The finished size of a loop is referred to as the "gain." It's best to pay attention to gain whenever loop-forming knots are tied. Gain can make-or-break a smooth running operation. Excessive loop gain can interfere with many aspects of vertical rescue rigging and operations. Adjust loop gain only as large as necessary for whatever you're rigging.

- **Twist:** Forming a loop mid-rope and rotating it describes a "twist."

- **Elbow:** A nice-to-know term for referencing the bent parts of rope on the knot body is the "elbow." Elbows are a consideration when deciding on knots used for rigging that must be very streamlined to reduce friction, snagging, or rope damage.

Basic Knots, Bends & Hitches
Rope Forms, Shapes & Identifiers

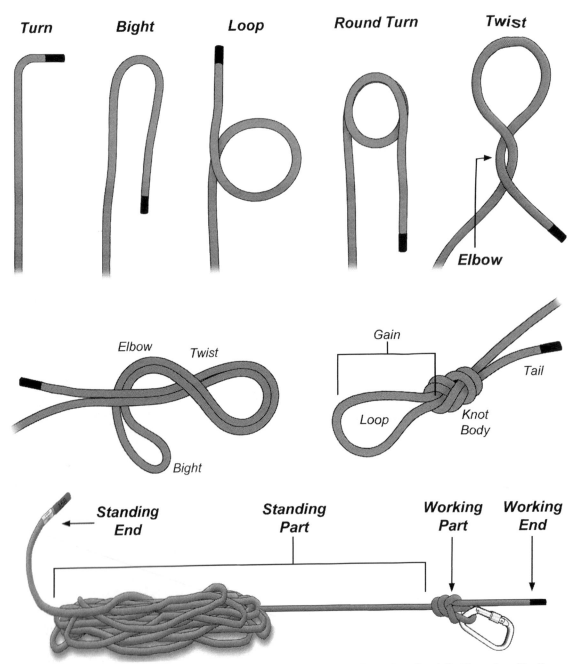

Turn **Bight** **Loop** **Round Turn** **Twist**

Elbow

Elbow *Twist*

Bight

Gain *Tail*

Loop *Knot Body*

Standing End **Standing Part** **Working Part** **Working End**

✱ Rope In The Bag/Pile Sometimes Referred To As The 'Running Part Or Running End'

Figure-8 Knots: The figure eight family of knots is very familiar to firefighters. People are quick to understand, retain, and apply the figure-8 method making teaching and learning easy. Figure-8 knots are also easy to recognize and inspect during safety checks. They look something like the number eight when tied correctly. Figure-8 knots are quite strong compared to other core knot-tying methods. Depending on the application, "8" knots can retain as much as 75% of the rope's strength. On the down side, some applications can cinch figure-8 knots down hard enough to make untying nearly impossible.

Overhand Knots: Knots tied using overhand methods are easy to teach and learn. The overhand method is the instinctive natural motion that presets itself whenever an unskilled person needs to tie a knot. You may have heard the fire service jest, *"forgot your knot, tie a lot."* This usually refers to tying multiple overhand knots together, one atop the other. However, overhands can be used to assemble knots that are well suited for rescue applications. Depending on how they're used, overhands can sometimes create unfavorable strain on ropes. Safety checking various overhand knots can be challenging because they are sometimes difficult to recognize, especially when they are poorly tied. The knots themselves can cinch down rock-hard, making untying impossible. Overhands are commonly used in the fire service to create stoppers, bends, loops, and nooses.

Bowlines: Widely-used, bowline knots are familiar to everyone from Boy Scouts to sailors to heavy riggers. If you ever need to rescue a tree worker, you'll probably have to deal with whatever bowline knots they've used in their own rigging. Bowlines provide a lot of application flexibility with adequate strength for rescue work. Used for everything from anchor attachments to mid-rope loops, the bowline is the "Transformer" of the knot world. Advanced riggers tend to favor bowline methods because of this adaptability and adjustability. Bowline methods generally result in knots that are more easily untied after heavy loading, one reason they're favored by arborists. The bowline style is easy to recognize during safety checks. Some bowline forms can be tied using only one hand. A few simple bowline applications will be shown in this book.

Half-Hitches: Usually used in conjunction with other hitches or knots, "half-hitches" are about as basic as it gets. A simple wind around the object with the standing and working sections of the rope binding against each other in opposite directions, half-hitches can clean up rigging by aligning vectors or securing loose ends. Half-hitches can be stacked to create a "double half-hitch" for a more secure hitching choice that's quick and easy to tie onto ropes that are under tension. Half-hitches and double half-hitches are generally not considered to be suitable for supporting a life-load.

Clove Hitch: Familiar to firefighters, the "clove hitch" is a very secure way of tying off a rope end or creating an attachment point mid-rope. The clove can tie off ropes that are under tension. After it's been tied, the clove can also be loosened up to adjust rope tension and/or position. Consisting of two opposing half-hitches, the clove is easy to tie, easy to adjust, and holds very well. There are several ways to tie this hitch depending on the application, and it can even be tied using one hand while lead climbing. The clove should be considered directional in functionality as it must be loaded properly to maintain the shape and integrity of the hitch.

Münter Hitch: The "Münter" is a dynamic hitch used for adjusting the length of ropes that are under tension or completely slack. A Münter is capable of supporting a single-person load when handled properly. This makes it a good choice for applications such as lead-climbing belays, emergency lowering, and emergency rappels. The Münter can be hitched onto a fixed structural element or, more commonly, onto a Münter-suitable carabiner. "D"-shaped carabiners can choke and bind Münter hitches, severely degrading functionality. Pear-shaped (HMS style) carabiners are engineered to support Münter hitch functionality. With a little practice, Münters are easy to tie and can even be installed using one hand in lead climbing situations. Münters must be handled properly to safely support a life-load. Teaching and learning proper manipulation should only be done in clinical settings with simulated rescue loads until apprentices demonstrate consistent proficiency.

When hitching onto a carabiner, it's important to consider how rope movement will affect the gate mechanism as the Münter is used. Friction from rope winding through the bends of a Münter can cause screw-lock carabiner gates to open. Aligning the loaded strand of rope along the spine of any carabiner is usually the best practice. However, doing so with Münter hitches increases the likelihood of normal rope action unlocking and opening a screw-lock carabiner. Hitching a Münter onto a carabiner with the standing (braking) part opposite the gate can reduce undesirable rope contact with the lock. If you're using a compatible auto-locking carabiner, hitch the Münter with the working (loaded) strand opposite the gate to optimize strength and to provide better clearance for the standing part. D-Shaped carabiners can choke and pinch off the standing part of the rope as the Münter is used. It's best to use pear-shaped biners for Münters, but its better to orient the standing part of the rope on the gate side if a "D" is your only option. Make sure you rotate the hitch to determine how the Münter will be oriented when the rope is loaded. These details may be a matter of regional practice, and you will likely encounter alternative preferences.

Mule Hitch: Used to tie off or finish the end of a rope in a system, the "mule hitch" can be used to secure such things as non-working MAs for back-ties or unstaffed pulley systems. Mules are an easy way to tie off ropes under heavy tension and can also be easily untied while maintaining control of the rope tension. Some organizations use the mule hitch as the default method for tying off any locked-off pulley system. The mule not only provides backup security, but is also a clearly recognizable signal that the system has been tied off even from a distance.

Lark's Foot: You've probably been tying the "lark's foot" hitch since you were a Cub Scout; it's intuitive and easy to use. Usually used with loops, a lark's foot simply wraps a bight of rope around an object and threads the opposite end through the bight. When tensioned, the hitch will cinch down tight onto the object that it is hitched on. The lark's foot will remain stable and hold tight as long as both legs of the rope (or loop) are tensioned equally. Unequal tension may cause the hitch to spin or even unravel.

For situations where cinching would be detrimental (as with an improvised chest harness), the hitch can be modified to a "doubled lark's foot." The doubled lark's foot simply rethreads the bight through the opposite end of the loop to create a binding, non-slip intersection.

Butterfly Knot: Although not in the figure-8 or bowline families, the butterfly is very well suited for rescue applications nonetheless. Used to create non-directional loops mid-rope, butterflies are easy to tie and easy to untie after heavy loading. Unlike the directional figure-8, the loop of a butterfly can be strained from any direction without splaying the body of the knot apart. A favorite of recreational climbers, the butterfly is great for quickly creating a secure clip-off point anywhere along the length of a rope.

Water Knot: Also called the ring bend, the "water knot" joins two ends of webbing together with an overhand knot that is retraced in reverse. This is the knot used to create webbing loops or to join lengths of webbing together. This "retrace" method of creating the water knot results in a very reliable connection because of the flat configuration of the webbing. Water knot bends can cinch down very tightly and can be difficult to untie. Water knots tied using 1-inch webbing should have tails that are at least 2 inches long.

Backing Up: Most knots and hitches do not require the addition of a back-up knot as long as tails are adjusted properly. Back-up knots can be added to just about any knot, hitch, or bend if it is deemed necessary. However, backing up all knots, bends, and hitches as a default may only serve to reduce efficiency and bog down operations.

Because of the potential for failure caused by human error, the figure-8 follow-through knot should be secured with a double overhand back-up whenever it supports a life-load. Climbers have been distracted enough while tying this knot to skip the final thread of the working end, resulting in complete knot failures and severe falls. Simply adjust the tail long enough to tie a double overhand knot onto the standing part.

Many bowline knots can be shaken loose or completely apart. Bowlines used in rescue rigging should be backed up whenever they support a life-load. Bowlines with tails on the outside ("outside bowlines") can be secured with a double overhand back-up. Inside bowlines can be secured by retracing the working end back into the knot body (see diagram). Long-tailed bowline knots do not require backing up.

Basic Knots, Bends & Hitches - *Half Hitch*

✱ Simple Half Hitch

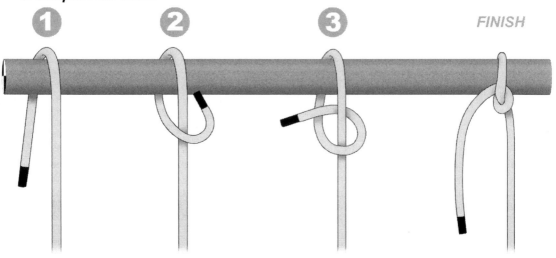

①   **②**   **③**   *FINISH*

✱ Double Half Hitch

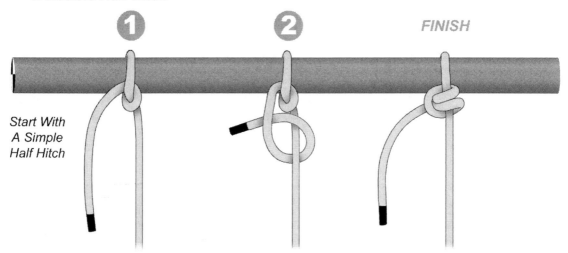

①   **②**   *FINISH*

Start With
A Simple
Half Hitch

✱ Mid-Line Half Hitch

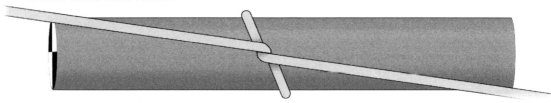

Basic Knots, Bends & Hitches - *Overhands*

Overhand

Overhand Bight

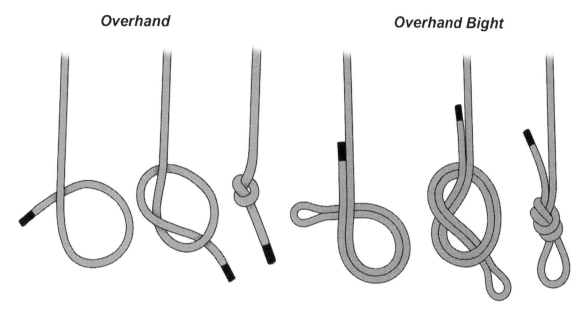

Double Overhand *(Stopper)*

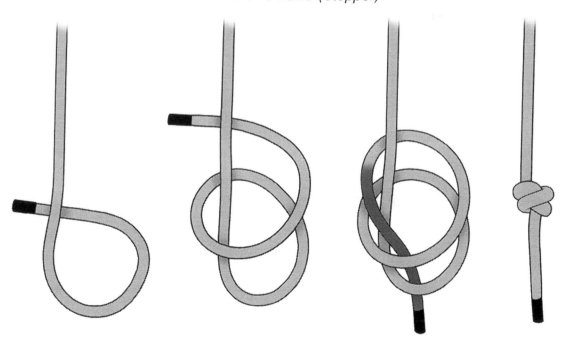

Basic Knots, Bends & Hitches - Overhands

Double Overhand Noose

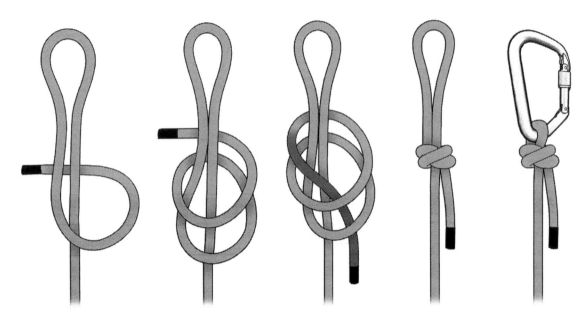

Double Overhand Bend

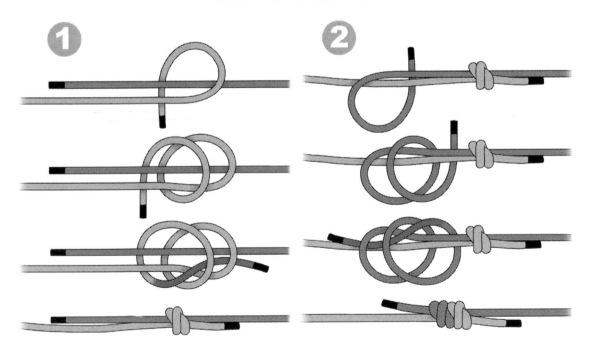

Basic Knots, Bends & Hitches - *Water Knot*

∗ Used To Join Webbing Ends

*Start With A
Neatly Tied Overhand*

*Neatly Thread
2nd End In Reverse*

*Nest 2nd End
Neatly Along The Path
Of The Overhand*

*Ensure
Adequate Tail Length*

*Snug Up
Neat And Compact*

Basic Knots, Bends & Hitches - Figure 8

Figure 8 Stopper

Figure 8 Bight

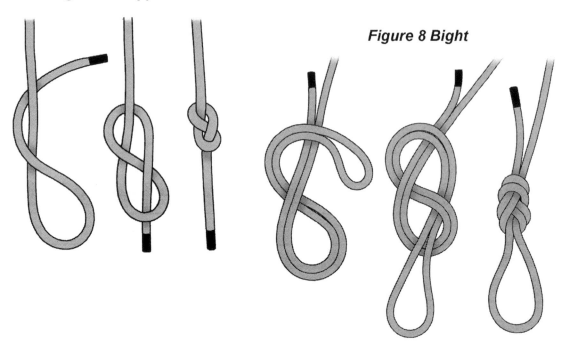

Figure 8 Follow-Through

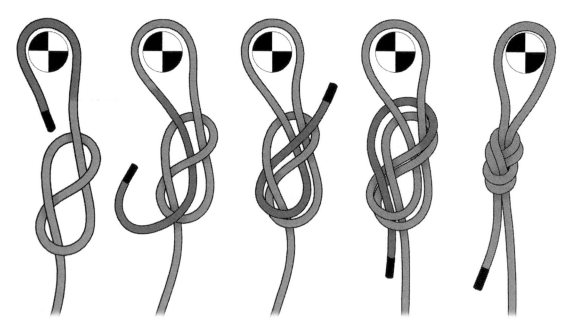

Basic Knots, Bends & Hitches - Figure 8

Figure 8 Bend

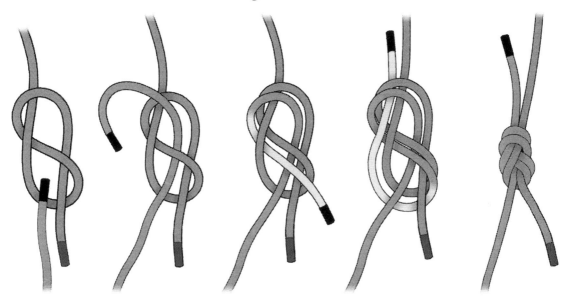

Directional Figure 8 *(In-Line 8)*

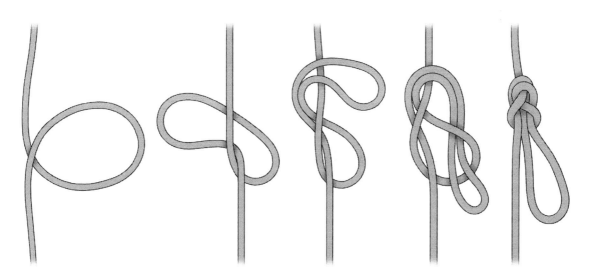

Basic Knots, Bends & Hitches - *Bowlines*

＊*Working End Positioned 'Inside' And 'Outside'*

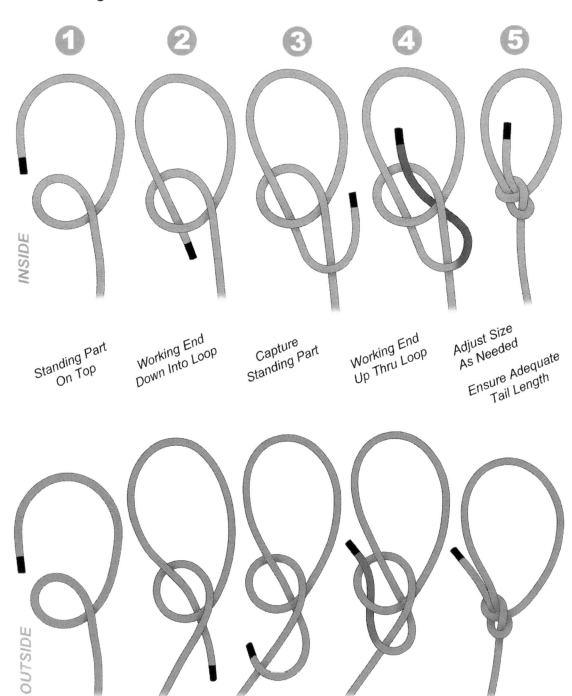

INSIDE

① ② ③ ④ ⑤

Standing Part
On Top

Working End
Down Into Loop

Capture
Standing Part

Working End
Up Thru Loop

Adjust Size
As Needed

Ensure Adequate
Tail Length

OUTSIDE

Basic Knots, Bends & Hitches - *Clove Hitch*

✱ *End Of Rope Placement*

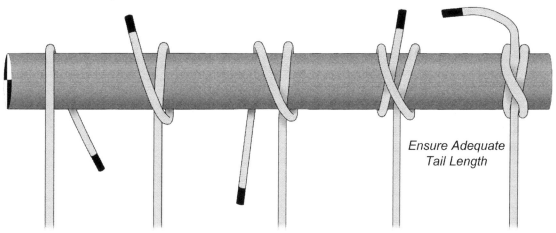

Ensure Adequate Tail Length

✱ *Mid-Rope Placement*

1 *Form 2 Identical Loops*

2 *Orient & Overlap Loops*

3 *Form Doubled Loop*

4 *Place Hitch Onto Object*

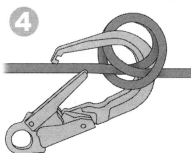

5

Snug & Dress

Load Must Strain The Hitch As Shown

Basic Knots, Bends & Hitches - *Clove Hitch*

✱ *Mid-Rope Placement - One Hand Technique - Lead Climbing*

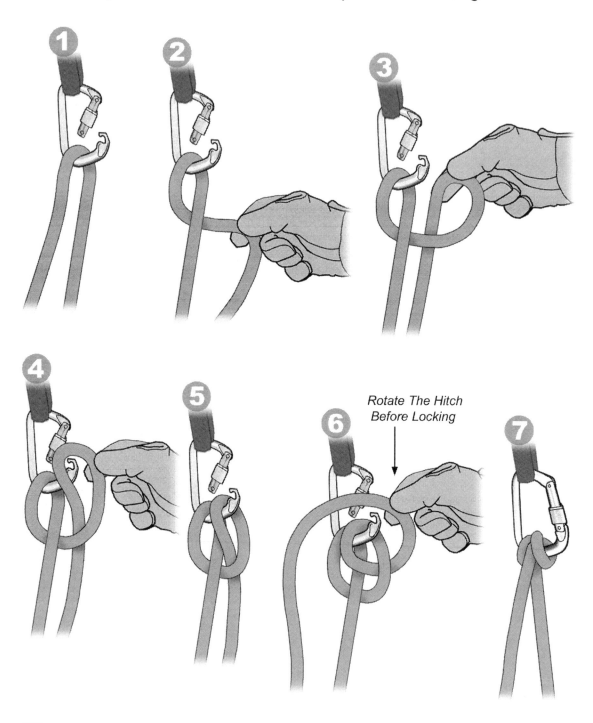

Rotate The Hitch
Before Locking

Basic Knots, Bends & Hitches - *3-Wrap Prusik*

✱ *Loop Tied With A Double Overhand Bend*

*Same Technique
For 2-Wrap Prusik*

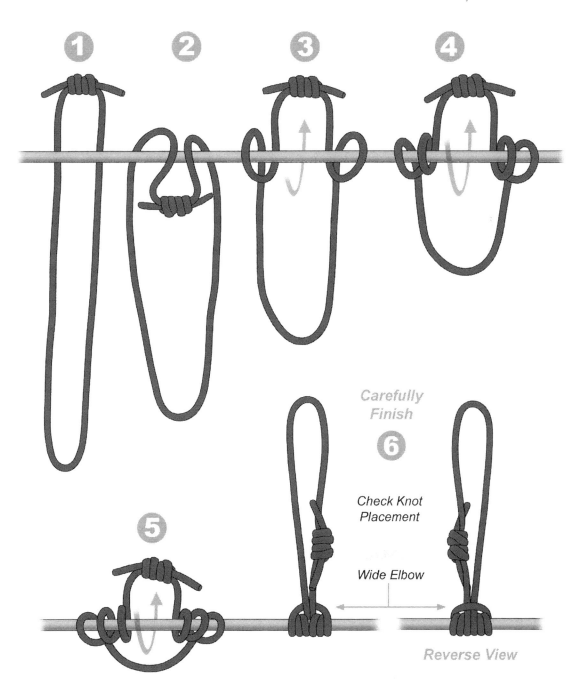

*Carefully
Finish*

Check Knot
Placement

Wide Elbow

Reverse View

189

Basic Knots, Bends & Hitches - *Butterfly*

★ Standard Technique

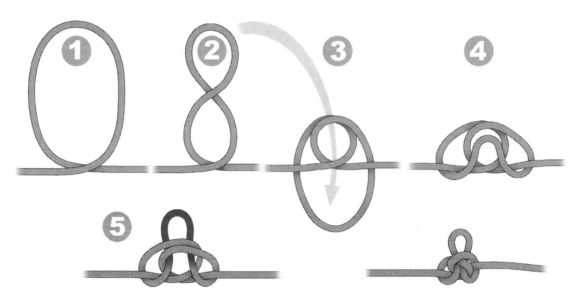

★ Palm Technique

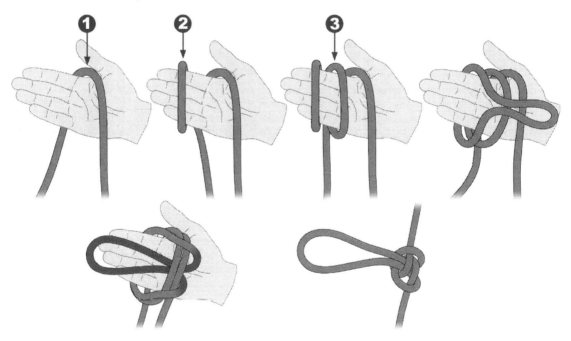

Basic Knots, Bends & Hitches - Münter

✳ *Installed Onto Compatible Carabiner*

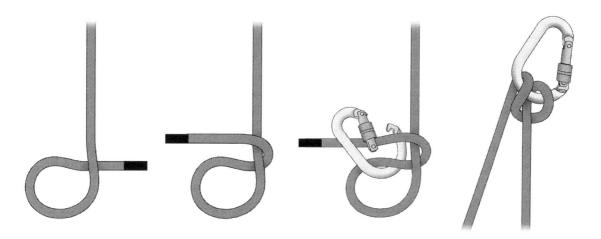

- *Pear-Shaped Carabiners Designed For Münter Functionality Perform Best.*

- *'D' Shaped Carabiners Pinch The Rope To Degrade Münter Performance*

- *Running Rope Can Unlock Screw Gate Carabiners*

- *Pay Close Attention To Position Of Standing And Working Sections*

✳ *Hitched Onto Fixed Object Such As A Handrail*

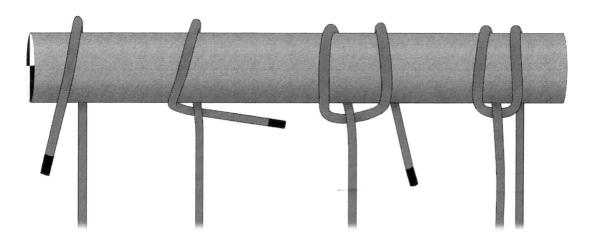

Basic Knots, Bends & Hitches - *Mule Hitch*

✱ *Shown Tying Off A Non-Working M/A System*

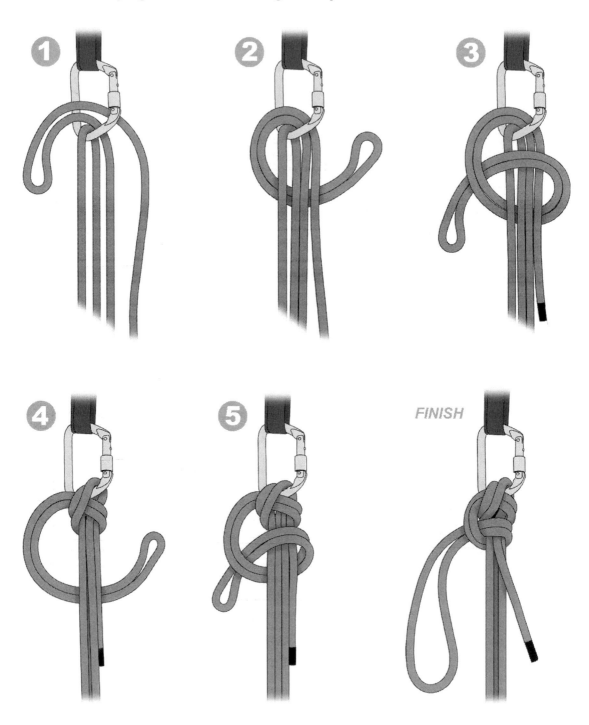

Basic Knots, Bends & Hitches - *Lark's Foot*

✱ *Referred To As A 'Girth Hitch' On Large Objects*

SIMPLE LARK'S FOOT

FINISH

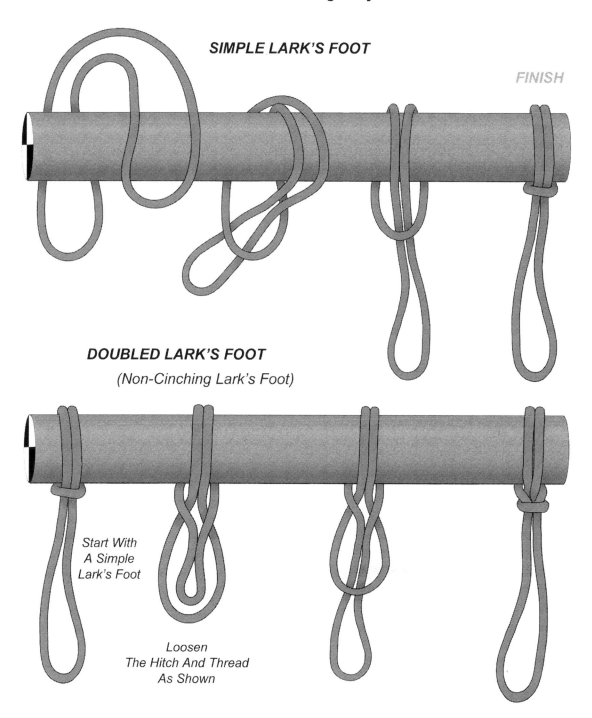

DOUBLED LARK'S FOOT

(Non-Cinching Lark's Foot)

*Start With
A Simple
Lark's Foot*

*Loosen
The Hitch And Thread
As Shown*

Basic Knots, Bends & Hitches - Backing Up

✱ Any Knot Can Be Backed Up When Needed

✱ Knots Shown Below Must Be Backed Up When Supporting A Life Load

✱ Use A Double Overhand Knot Or Tail Retrace

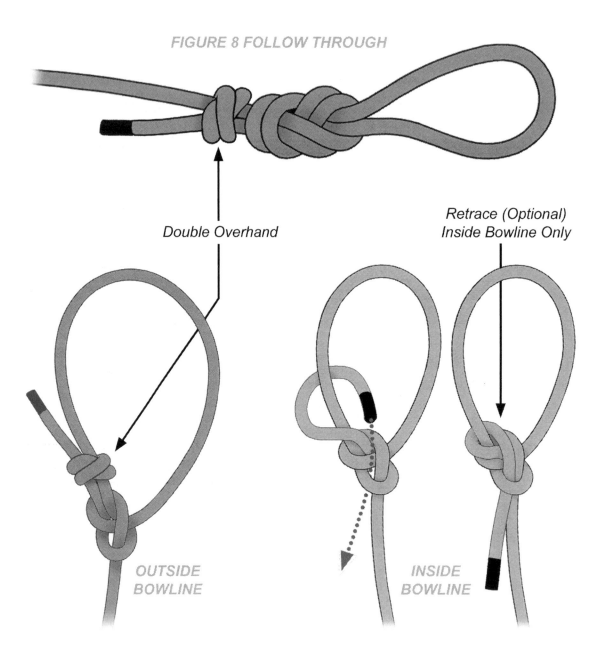

FIGURE 8 FOLLOW THROUGH

Double Overhand

Retrace (Optional)
Inside Bowline Only

OUTSIDE BOWLINE

INSIDE BOWLINE

Improvised Victim Extrication Harnesses: Usually used to capture and secure rescue subjects, harnesses improvised from webbing slings or straps install quickly, easily, and securely. Improvising seat and chest harnesses to fit any size person

CAUTION
!

Improvised Harnesses Used For Full Suspension May Hasten Harness Induced Pathology

requires only 2 lengths of webbing or strapping and a carabiner. Be careful. Harnesses made up of 1-inch webbing or 2-inch strapping should be worn briefly for suspension and not worn by a Climber as a rescue harness. Harness induced pathology (HIP, injury or illness caused by prolonged suspension) can be exacerbated by harnesses without integrated padding and support banding.

There are several methods of improvising harnesses using webbing or straps. The methods shown have been proven to work well for a variety of applications including freestanding, sitting, supine, prone, or tightly clinging rescue subjects. Begin by making 2 slings with the ends connected by water knots that have 2 to 3-inch tails, one from a 12-foot length and the other from a 15-foot length of web or strap. Slings of this size will fit a large man and anyone smaller. Very large people may require larger lengths of flat stock. The 12-foot sling will be used for the chest harness. The 15-foot sling is for the seat harness. The chest harness will use a <u>doubled lark's foot</u> method to wrap and secure the subject. The seat will use a simple "Hasty Seat" method.

Chest:

- Beginning with the chest harness, drape the 12-foot sling on one shoulder of the subject as if it were a woman's handbag.

- Position the knot of the sling at the back just below the armpit.

- Wrap the hanging bight of the sling around the back under the opposite armpit all the way to the front of the subject. Try to do this in a way that the knot on the sling remains at the back.

- A wrap should now be formed around the shoulder you started with.

- Without allowing the knot to change position, thread the loose bight of the sling under the snug wrap on the shoulder as if you were tying a lark's foot hitch.

- Without allowing the knot to move, adjust the position of the lark's foot intersection close to the subject's sternum.

- You now should have a single strap over one shoulder, a single strap under one arm, and doubled straps running under the opposite arm with the loose bight hanging down in front.

- Now form a doubled lark's foot without allowing the knot to move from the back. Do this by using one finger between the two legs of the loose bight to hook the portion of webbing that was wrapped around the shoulder, and pull it out until the loose bight portion is snug against the chest.

- Adjust the lark's foot and straps of the harness so that they are firmly in place high on the chest and tight in the armpits.

- You should have a loose bight that is knot-free hanging down in front.

- Wrap the loose bight under the single-side strap and shoulder strap and form a tight half-hitch. Continue tying half-hitches in this way until the loose bight is only about 1 to 2 inches long at the most. You need at least 2 half-hitches to secure the harness.

- The remaining loose bight is the attachment point of the chest harness. Clip a carabiner onto this attachment point.
- It's **very important** that this loop is small. A chest attachment made from a loop larger than two inches will cause the rescue subject to suspend in a bad position, with the head down.

An alternative method of improvising this chest harness is to form the doubled lark's foot without capturing the shoulder. Do this by forming a bight and running it around the back under both armpits. This is a good method for subjects in cramped or awkward positions, or for those who will not let go of whatever they're holding onto. For a subject who is facing away and refusing to let go, you can place this kind of simple doubled lark's foot with the loop on the back and then rotate the harness until the attachment point is at the sternum.

Seat:
- Standing in front of the subject, wrap the 15-foot sling around the back so that the knot is positioned snuggly in the lumbar region while one leg of the sling is drooping down at the back of the knees.
- Cinch the upper leg of the sling with one hand, as if it were the rescue subject's belt.
- Reach the other hand through one of the lateral loops in the front and go between the subject's legs to grab the section of webbing that is drooping in the back.
- Without allowing the knot to slip to the front, pull the drooping section up between the legs and all the way out of a front lateral loop.
- Use the other hand to grab one of the straps coming up from between the legs and pull a second bight up though the other lateral loop until it is all the way out.
- You should now have a bight of the sling in each hand with double straps running through lateral loops on each side of the subject.
- Adjust this arrangement by pulling up on the 2 bights until there is a tight belt around the waist with leg loops that are high and tight in the crotch.
- Now use the 2 bights in your hands to tightly tie the harness in place using overhand knots.
- Continue tying overhand knots until you end up with 2 loops that are just large enough to pass a fist through them. These loops are the attachment points of the seat harness.
- It is **very important** that these attachment points are the appropriate length. If it is impossible to fashion the harness with attachment points that are long enough, you may have to use a larger sling.

Connect the carabiner on the chest harness to both attachment loops of the improvised seat harness. If the chest harness is already connected to the rescue rope system, then do not open the carabiner to connect to the seat. Clip a separate carabiner onto both loops of the seat harness and then connect it to the attachment point on the chest. If the chest and seat harnesses were fashioned correctly, the connection between the chest and seat should be very tight and may be difficult clip together. This is okay. Once the subject is fully suspended, the harness will be perfectly adjusted and will maintain proper heads-up orientation.

Climbers should be practiced enough to fashion seat and chest harnesses while standing in front of or behind the rescue subject. With regular practice, this harness system goes on very quickly and holds very well. Climbers should also practice placing these harnesses without removing the slings from a pick-off strap that is connected to the hauling system and belay to reduce the possibility of dropping equipment while over the side. It's easy to do. Just use separate carabiners to connect each sling to the pick-off strap.

Improvised Harness - *Chest*

Sling Tied With 12 Foot Web

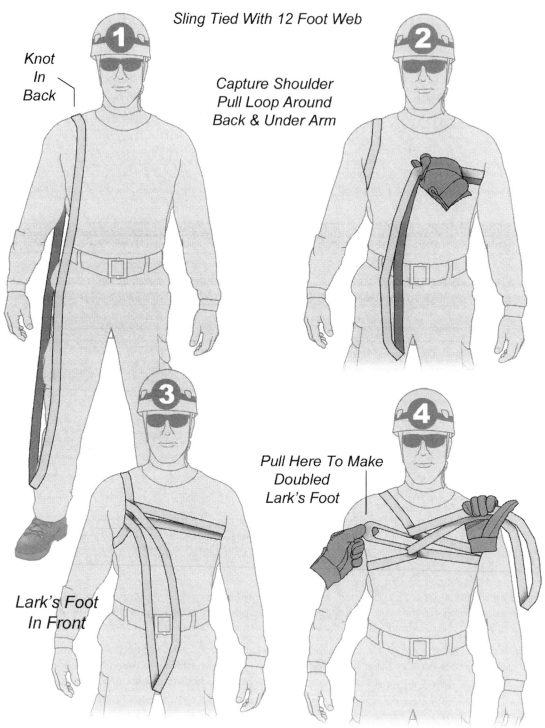

Knot
In
Back

Capture Shoulder
Pull Loop Around
Back & Under Arm

Pull Here To Make
Doubled
Lark's Foot

Lark's Foot
In Front

Improvised Harness - *Chest (continued)*

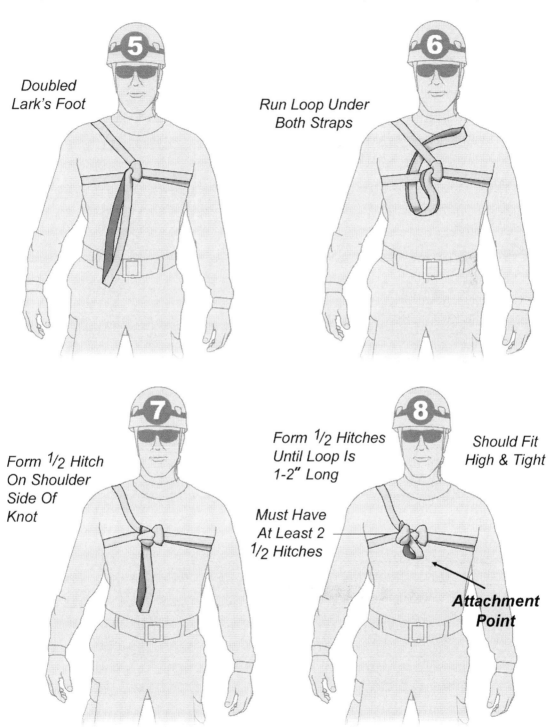

Doubled Lark's Foot

Run Loop Under Both Straps

Form 1/2 Hitch On Shoulder Side Of Knot

Form 1/2 Hitches Until Loop Is 1-2" Long

Should Fit High & Tight

Must Have At Least 2 1/2 Hitches

Attachment Point

Improvised Harness - *Seat*

Sling Tied With 15 Foot Web

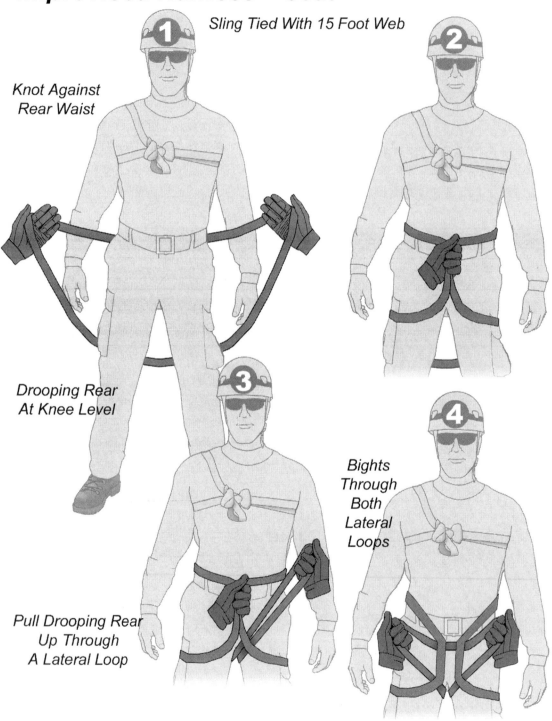

Knot Against
Rear Waist

Drooping Rear
At Knee Level

Pull Drooping Rear
Up Through
A Lateral Loop

Bights
Through
Both
Lateral
Loops

Improvised Harness - *Seat* *(continued)*

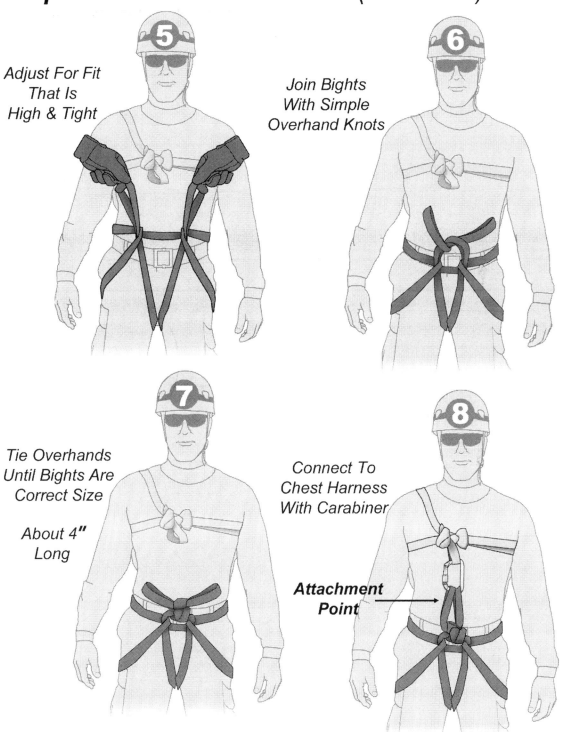

Adjust For Fit
That Is
High & Tight

Join Bights
With Simple
Overhand Knots

Tie Overhands
Until Bights Are
Correct Size

About 4"
Long

Connect To
Chest Harness
With Carabiner

**Attachment
Point**

Rear View

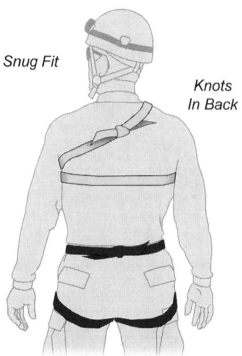

Snug Fit

*Knots
In Back*

Climbing Basics

Safe and effective maneuvering and work positioning while supported by ropes greatly depends on the application of a few basic practices related to speed and stance. You have to use your body a little differently when the surface you're standing on is parallel with the vector of planetary gravity. It seems obvious, but proper positioning while hanging on a rope does not come naturally and requires some instruction and a little practice.

Speed: Rates of travel while over the side should be slow and steady. Maneuver at a pace that enables good belay management. Moving at a rapid pace or in a jerky manner dislodges more soil, rocks, and debris that can fall and hit Climbers, rescue subjects, and ropes. Go slow. Unlike military or law enforcement workers, firefighters usually don't have people shooting at them. The occasion for high-speed rescue rappels or lowers is extremely rare. Hauling ass and making large, sweeping jumps while rappelling is definitely fun, but save those maneuvers for your Hollywood stuntman career.

Foot Purchase: Solid foot purchase requires friction between the soles of your boots and the climbing surface. Friction increases as the area of touching surfaces increases in size. Maximizing footprint contact with the climbing surface increases stabilizing friction. Generally speaking, flat-footed contact with the climbing surface is best for good foot purchase. Keeping feet flat on the surface also reduces fatigue and prevents foot soreness. Surfaces that do not allow absolutely flat foot contact may require balancing on the foot arch or jamming the boot toe into a hole or crack.

Improper body positioning can cause Climbers to stand tiptoe against the climbing surfaces as they move, resulting in poor foot purchase and sketchy stability. Climbers should understand the importance of keeping the body positioned for good foot contact with the climbing surface.

Anatomical Axis and Personal Gravity: Standing up requires friction between the soles of your feet and the surface with which they're in contact. A relatively low amount of friction is required to stand straight up plumb with gravity on a flat surface. Even standing upright on a low-friction surface like an ice skating rink is easy enough to do as long as you stand plumb with gravity. It's a different story if the flat surface gets tilted. Standing on a sloped surface requires some means of adding friction or counteracting the gravitational pull of the earth. Adding boot soles made from friction-adding materials will help stabilize foot purchase. As the surface tilts more, it may get to enough of an angle that it causes an upright standing Climber to become fearful and lean away from the downhill side and toward the uphill side. Although this feeling is instinctive, it is counterproductive. Foot purchase degrades when a Climber leans toward the uphill side of his or her stance. When a Climber leans uphill in this way it directs forces to the feet at a sideways angle that works to break them free and slip. We'll call that "skate force." Foot purchase is much better when a Climber stands plumb with planetary gravity while working on a slope without ropes.

As our imaginary surface tilts more and more, it reaches a point where gravity overcomes friction, making it impossible to stand up. That's when you need ropes to counteract gravity. Whenever you're hanging against an angled or vertical surface, you need to rethink how gravity-counteracting ropes affect your contact with the climbing surface. As the rope counteracts the force of gravity, it seeks a plumb orientation to hold the load stationary. This creates a force vector that is perpendicular to the supporting rope. In the case of a Climber over the side of a vertical cliff, this force vector will drive him or her toward the cliff surface. Climbers should align their bodies with the perpendicular force vector that drives them toward the cliff face to maintain stable foot purchase and work positioning. Climbers can consider this perpendicular force vector to be the "personal gravity" that keeps their feet in contact with the surface. Just like standing up on flat ground, Climbers should stand straight against the climbing surface for the most stable foot purchase. When over-the-side Climbers improperly align their anatomical axis with planetary gravity instead of their personal gravity, they will have a very difficult time maintaining stable foot purchase and their feet will repeatedly skate out from under them. They will use a tiptoe action to fend off the cliff face. Practice helps nervous Climbers overcome their fear of leaning back on the ropes to stand up against their own personal gravity. Leaning back on the rope system aligns a Climber's anatomical axis with their personal gravity, making their feet "stick" to the surface better and reducing skate forces that cause slipping.

Climbers sometimes need to realign their anatomical axis away from the perpendicular force vector as surface topography changes. Moving smoothly past cornices, outcroppings, windows, etc. may require a Climber to lean back dramatically with their feet above helmet level. This maneuver allows the rope to orient plumb with planetary gravity to prevent abrupt and risky pendulum swings. When the supporting rope is plumb with gravity, the Climber can step off of an overhang without swinging past the vertical plane.

Hand Purchase: There are a few simple techniques that can improve hand purchase for a variety of climbing situations. In most cases, it helps to apply your hands as either "hooks" or "wallpaper" instead of the more instinctive grabbing style. Think about combining the strength of your fingers to improve hand purchase by squeezing them tightly together in a "karate chop" manner. Doing so adds staying power and comfort when holding onto small or rough climbing features. The technique of using hands as hooks is especially helpful for overhead climbing situations. Applying as much hand surface onto a climbing surface adds friction. Friction is good for hand purchase. Whether hooking or planting a hand like a foot, careful attention to applying maximum surface area to a climbing feature improves comfort and stamina and adds favorable friction.

In some cases, gloves can degrade hand purchase. Personnel with recreational rock climbing experience may be accustomed to climbing on natural surfaces with bare hands. It can make sense to climb barehanded in some cases.

Climbing Up: In general, it's best to climb up with your legs doing most of the work. To endure a long climb, it's important to stand up to support and lift your body weight with your legs. Hands and arms should be used mainly for balancing and work positioning. Inexperienced or fearful Climbers will often use their arms to pull themselves up as they maneuver. This is a very ineffective practice and will cause arms to tire quickly. Muscles will quickly fatigue when arms are holding or pulling a load while flexed. Arms will fatigue less when they are extended straight. Use hands to "hook" a feature, and use extended arms like ropes to hold your body in a position that optimizes foot purchase.

Lead climbing (climbing up) belays should not be used as a means of Climber support. Belay rigging for Climbers working their way up a cliff or structure should serve as a means of fall protection only. The main gravity defying support for a Lead Climber is the cliff or structure. The main support connection to the Climber is his or her own legs, hands, and arms. Though there is only one rope, it's similar to a 2-rope system strategy. If the Climber loses his or her footing and falls from the main support, the rope will catch the fall. Hanging from or leaning back on the belay line is a single-rope technique that is not suitable for rescue work.

To work hands free, use a "flip line" the same way you would use your arms. A flip line, in combination with leg support (standing up on your legs), enables workers to lean back and let go. Tree workers and linemen routinely use an adjustable short length of rope or strap to wrap climbing features for the purpose of working hands free. A simple version of a flip line uses a carabiner tied onto one end and an ascender. Attach the ascender to a work-positioning harness ring, and thread the rope through it. Wrap the flip line around a climbing feature, such as a branch or cross arm, and then connect the end carabiner to another work positioning harness ring. Use the ascender to adjust rope length and tightness. Attach flip lines to lateral rings at hip level to optimize ergonomics and comfort. Flip lines are easy to rig, carry, and use. Pre-rigged flip lines are commercially available. REMEMBER: Do not use flip lines that are connected to work positioning harness rings as the main support for a Climber. Flip lines rigged with appropriate components can be attached to full load harness rings for Climber support in some cases.

Edge Transitions: Making the initial move from the topside surface to the vertical workspace involves a few principles of physics that Climbers can feel as the transition occurs. The old-fashioned technique of leaning back while standing with stiff legs spread like an A-frame to go over the edge of a drop develops a very powerful and undesirable force vector against the Climber. Anyone who's done it knows it. This is especially true when the main climbing rope is not rigged with a high directional over the edge. Teaching demonstrations using dynamometers have shown that Climbers can end up having to pull against more than 1000 pounds of force with their legs and back just to remain standing when using the old stiff-legged technique. 1000 pounds is more than enough to cause an earthen edge to crumble, to cause a windowsill to break, or to cause a back injury.

Kneeling down and straddling the vertical edge to get off the topside surface keeps vector forces low and makes transitioning easy. Getting low this way also keeps belay attachments on the Climber safely close to the topside surface. The maneuver is easy to do, even if the Climber is taking a rescue basket down. Simply kneel down, lean back against the main line rope, and straddle the edge. It's easy to get legs in position and stand up as the Climber continues slowly down below the edge. It's kind of like getting off of a horse. The technique works when maneuvering up or down over an edge. To get up and over an edge, simply kneel on the vertical surface just below the edge, and hike a leg up topside as if you are getting on a horse. Using this technique, Climbers make transitions without experiencing a severe load pulling down on their pelvic attachment.

Climbing Basics - *Anatomical Axis*

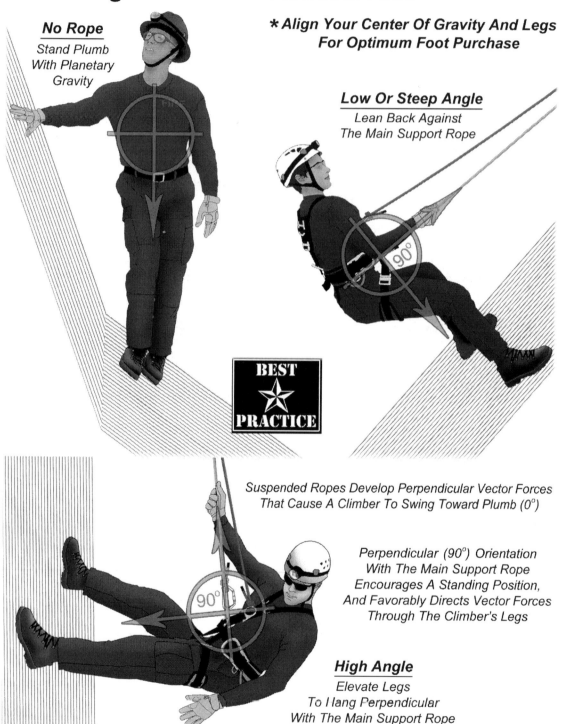

No Rope
Stand Plumb
With Planetary
Gravity

*** Align Your Center Of Gravity And Legs
For Optimum Foot Purchase**

Low Or Steep Angle
Lean Back Against
The Main Support Rope

90°

**BEST
★
PRACTICE**

Suspended Ropes Develop Perpendicular Vector Forces
That Cause A Climber To Swing Toward Plumb (0°)

Perpendicular (90°) Orientation
With The Main Support Rope
Encourages A Standing Position,
And Favorably Directs Vector Forces
Through The Climber's Legs

90°

High Angle
Elevate Legs
To Hang Perpendicular
With The Main Support Rope

Climbing Basics - *Anatomical Axis - Bad Form*

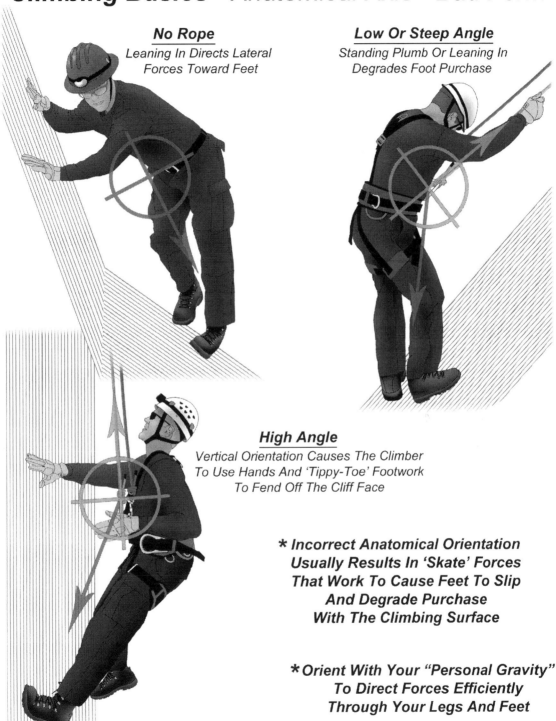

No Rope
*Leaning In Directs Lateral
Forces Toward Feet*

Low Or Steep Angle
*Standing Plumb Or Leaning In
Degrades Foot Purchase*

High Angle
*Vertical Orientation Causes The Climber
To Use Hands And 'Tippy-Toe' Footwork
To Fend Off The Cliff Face*

*** Incorrect Anatomical Orientation
Usually Results In 'Skate' Forces
That Work To Cause Feet To Slip
And Degrade Purchase
With The Climbing Surface**

*** Orient With Your "Personal Gravity"
To Direct Forces Efficiently
Through Your Legs And Feet**

Climbing Basics - *Edge Transitions*

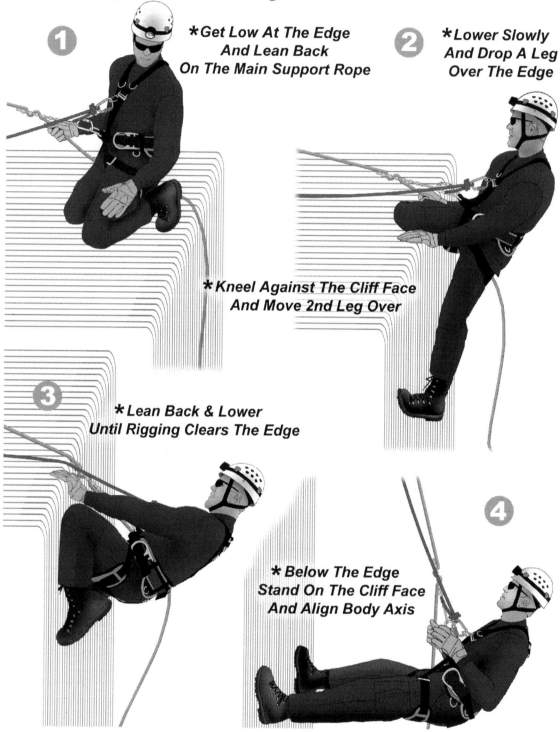

1 *Get Low At The Edge And Lean Back On The Main Support Rope*

2 *Lower Slowly And Drop A Leg Over The Edge*

Kneel Against The Cliff Face And Move 2nd Leg Over

3 *Lean Back & Lower Until Rigging Clears The Edge*

4 *Below The Edge Stand On The Cliff Face And Align Body Axis*

Climbing Basics - *Flip Lines* **✱ 2nd Point Of Connection While Climbing Up**

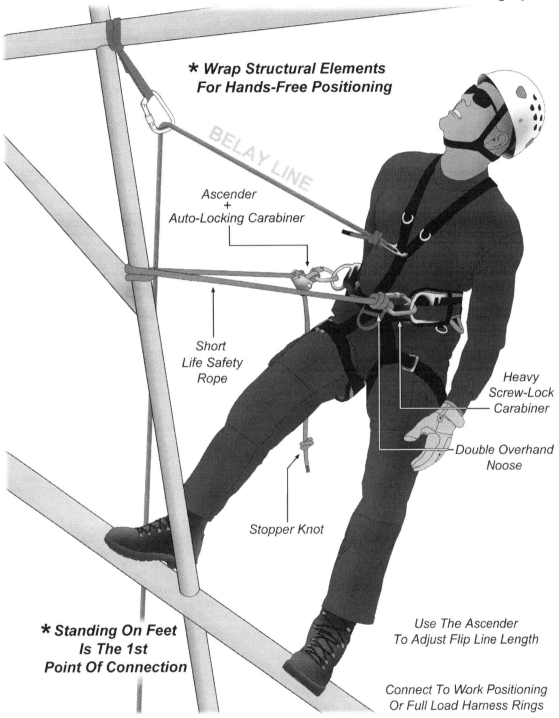

✱ Wrap Structural Elements For Hands-Free Positioning

BELAY LINE

Ascender
+
Auto-Locking Carabiner

Short
Life Safety
Rope

Heavy
Screw-Lock
Carabiner

Double Overhand
Noose

Stopper Knot

✱ Standing On Feet Is The 1st Point Of Connection

Use The Ascender To Adjust Flip Line Length

Connect To Work Positioning Or Full Load Harness Rings

Rappelling

Sending Climbers over the side with the means to control their own descent can be an important option for rapidly accessing rescue subjects. Rappelling is often the first over-the-side competency Climbers develop during their apprenticeship training. Learning to rappel in a clinical setting builds confidence and develops comfort with vertical worksites. It's easy to imagine how a competent Climber can quickly get set up and rappel over the side to access a person in distress.

Most of the basic techniques and considerations for working in the vertical environment are the same when the descent control device (DCD) is connected to and controlled by the Climber. But it is important to remember that rappelling requires Climbers to use their hands to control descent. Both hands are required to control some descenders; some are controlled with one hand. The availability of free hands can influence the strategy and/or tactic used for accessing a rescue subject. Ease of locking off a DCD can also be an important consideration. Some DCDs lock with a simple swing of a lever to enable Climbers to work hands-free. Most require rope manipulation to lock off and then must be tied off to safely work hands-free. Working with traveling self-belays, for example, can be difficult and slow while using an industrial DCD that requires the use of both hands. Brake bar racks are a good choice for rescue applications because they are a 'one-handed' descender that adjusts easily to add or reduce friction as needed.

Descent control device performance changes as a Climber rappels down the length of a rope, especially when hanging vertically. The full weight of the hanging rope will pull on the braking function of a DCD when the Climber is at the highest point of the rappel. The weight of the rope alone can brake and stop a Climber when rappel ropes are several hundred feet long. It will sometimes be necessary for a Climber to lift the standing part enough to allow rope to reeve through a descender. As a rappel operation progresses, there will be less rope weight acting on the braking function of the descender. Longer rappels may require a Climber to make adjustments that add friction as he or she descends. Descent control devices adapt and adjust differently in these situations. Some add or reduce friction more easily. Rope weight affects braking function and can influence equipment choices for any given situation.

Combining climbing basics information in this chapter with DCD handling information in Chapter 6 will provide all the necessary guidelines for safe rappelling. Good form when making the transition over the edge and attention to good body positioning make rappelling maneuvers safer and easier. It's important to remember that the majority of climbing injuries occur while rappelling. This may be because rappelling seems uncomplicated and natural-feeling enough to cause some Climbers to drop their guard. Jumping out to clear obstacles and high-speed descending worsens the hazard of falling rocks, soil, and debris. As with lowering ops, jerky, high-speed rappelling maneuvers make belaying very difficult. Remaining focused and moving at a sensible pace is the professional approach to rappelling safety and effectiveness.

Rappelling Rescues: Plucking a rescue subject from the face of a cliff while on rappel is difficult. Pick-off methods while on rappel are similar to those used when a Climber is on a lowering system. The primary difference is where and how the rescue subject load is connected on the system. When a Climber is lowered down by the topside team to capture and pick off a subject, the additional load is most often connected directly to the main support rope. Obviously, this cannot work with a rappelling operation. Any additional loads, including the rescue subject, must be connected directly to the descent control device. Do this by clipping the rescue subject load onto the carabiner that connects the DCD onto the harness or onto the harness ring where the DCD is connected. The choice can depend on the type of carabiner that connects the DCD onto the harness. Offset "D" carabiners work well for this application. In some cases, it may be necessary to hitch a cord loop onto the spine of the DCD carabiner to support the rescue load properly.

Never connect the rescue subject, or any additional heavy load, onto a free ring on your harness while rappelling. Doing so will create a severe spreading force between the DCD and the harness. Connect directly to the DCD or the same carabiner where the DCD is connected.

It's critical for the Climber to make any necessary adjustments to the descent control device prior to clipping on the additional weight of a rescue load. Increasing load capacity by routing rope through an additional biner or adding bars on a brake rack will almost certainly be necessary to support the additional weight.

Teaching and Learning Rappelling: Competent Climbers should possess the abilities to assemble and connect to their own rappelling rigging, safely maneuver over the edge, and remain in complete control as they descend and work over the side. Complete control means Climbers must be able to descend, stop, lock off, tie off, and connect to a rescue subject as needed.

Rappelling principles and methods should be introduced and described in detail and then demonstrated by technically competent persons. Apprentices should first practice rigging for rappelling and handling descent control devices in a clinical setting on a level surface. With enough competence demonstrated, set up and practice on a low angle surface. Always include belay protections that would be used during normal operations. Emphasize smooth edge transitions, stance, and proper working pace. Allow apprentice Climbers to practice working fully suspended when they can demonstrate rappelling competence on a low angle surface. Practice vertical maneuvers with the Climber rappelling against a wall and while hanging in free space. It's also important to provide apprentice Climbers with the experience of rappelling on long (150 feet or more), vertical ropes whenever possible.

Wes Schultz

Rappelling - *Basic Considerations*

* Practices Appropriate For Rescue Operations

*Descent Controller Should Be Suitable
For 2-Person Loads*

*Use A Descent Control Device
That Is Easily Operated With One Hand*

*Lean Back To Orient Body Axis
For Good Foot Purchase*

*Descend Smoothly At A Pace
That Allows Proper Belay Function*

*Move Slowly & Avoid Jumping
To Minimize
Dislodging Of Rocks & Debris*

Always Carry Back-Up Rigging
(3 Prusik Loops + Carabiner)

*Keep Slack Rope Below
Clear Of Snags & Obstacles*

Rappelling - *Pick-Off Rigging*   Belayed From Above

★ *Option For Attaching Rescue Subject While In Rappel Mode*

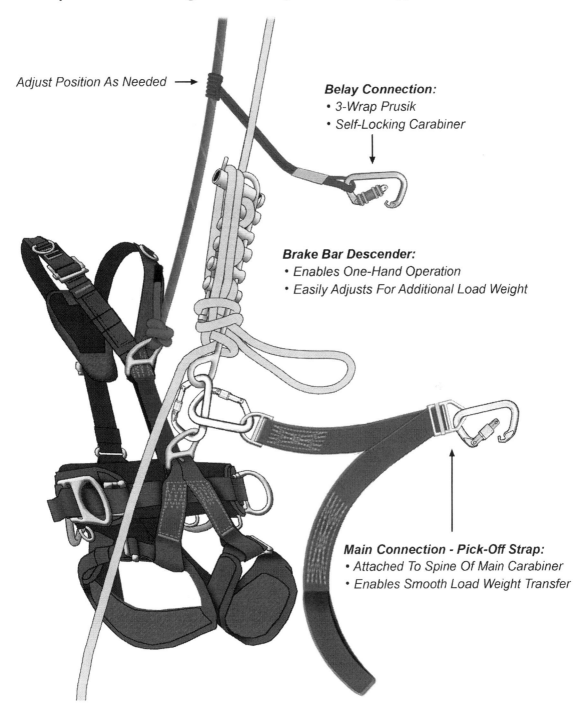

Adjust Position As Needed ➞

Belay Connection:
- *3-Wrap Prusik*
- *Self-Locking Carabiner*

Brake Bar Descender:
- *Enables One-Hand Operation*
- *Easily Adjusts For Additional Load Weight*

Main Connection - Pick-Off Strap:
- *Attached To Spine Of Main Carabiner*
- *Enables Smooth Load Weight Transfer*

Basic Ascending

The ability to securely ascend a rope enables Climbers to get out of trouble without help from the rest of the team. Conditions that disable the raising or lowering functions of a rope rescue system can leave a Climber stranded and exposed. Climbers that possess competent ascending skills can climb up seized ropes to release snags or continue up to topside. Ascending skills also add depth and dimension for work positioning. Time and effort can be economized when a Climber can quickly and easily move him or herself up the rope a few feet without assistance from the topside team.

Methods and tools for ascending ropes vary, but all use a basic "inchworm" action of one form or another. Two rope-grabs connect the Climber to the main support line. The grabs are often rigged so that one is slack while the Climber sits in the harness, and the other is slack whenever the Climber stands up on a foot strap, also known as an etrier. Then it's a matter of moving one connection point up while the other supports the weight of the Climber. The Climber alternates between sitting and standing in the rigging to progressively move the rope-grabs and ascend. Depending on the situation and the work to be done, ascending rigs can be assembled in many ways, basic to complex. Anything from mechanical advantage assisted to rope-walking designs are used. *Vertical Academy* will focus on methods familiar to rope access workers using very basic equipment carried in most fire service caches.

Ascending for Access and Work Positioning: Climbing up rope as a rescue maneuver is rare in the fire service. Rescue basket rigging and handling is one case where ascending can be routinely used. Good basket handling often requires lowering or raising adjustments of less than a foot or two. When a Climber can move up and down on their own to make these adjustments, the operation goes much smoother and faster. Other work positioning situations can benefit from ascending capabilities. Climbers can sometimes ascend short distances to recover tools, release fouled lines, or assist coworkers. Often it's just a matter of taking a few steps up to fix something that is out of reach.

Start by establishing a belay connection. In the case of rescue basket rigging, establish a traveling self-belay.

To rig for basic rescue ascending, clip ascenders onto each end of a lanyard with carabiners. The lanyard should match the length from your armpit to your wrist. Use closed ascenders designed for rescue work. Connect both ascenders on the lanyard to the main climbing rope. Ensure they are both oriented to grip and hold a downward-pulling load. *Two ascenders combined with a lanyard establish a complete connection to the main support rope. A single ascender is not a sufficient connection by itself.* Clip a foot strap (etrier) into the carabiner holding the top ascender. Now attach the carabiner on the lower ascender to the pelvic ring on your harness. Move the top ascender up to helmet level or until the lanyard is straight. Orient the climbing rope between your legs, and place one foot into the foot strap. Use the foot strap to pull tension and remove stretch in the climbing rope. As you do this, pull rope through the bottom ascender. Make as many pulls as necessary to tighten the climbing rope enough to sit down in your harness. You should be sitting in your harness with one foot resting in the foot strap. Your leg should be bent, as if you're reclining in a comfortable chair, whenever the top ascender is pushed up and the lanyard is straight. Adjust the foot strap length for easy standing. Now is the time for a safety check.

To climb up, grab the top ascender with both hands, and orient your standing leg below your body weight. Now stand up on the foot strap. Use your free leg for balance and stabilization. While you're standing, release one hand, and pull rope through the lower ascender until tight. Sit down firmly in your harness. Push the top ascender up until the lanyard is straight again, and repeat the action to continue climbing. Be sure to monitor and adjust the traveling self-belay if you're using one. Go slow and steady in short increments for best results and to preserve strength. Try placing both feet in the foot strap for free-hanging ascents where there is no need to fend off the cliff face.

Practice moving up and down the rope while rigged for ascending. To move down, stand up on the foot strap and use one hand to release the cam of the lower ascender. Squat about 6 inches to move rope through the lower ascender. Be careful not to fully load the lanyard with the pelvic attachment. In other words, don't squat down too far. Doing so will only cause you to have to stand up again to release the top ascender. Go slow and steady and move in short increments.

In some cases rappelling Climbers can ascend using their descent control device. A rappelling Climber using a self-braking descender attached to a pelvic harness ring can capture upward progress just like an ascender. Simply add an upper rope grab of some kind with a foot strap and use the self-braking descender like an ascender. A lanyard is optional in this case because the self-braking descender is a complete connection to the main climbing rope.

Using an etrier that has multiple foot loops can reduce the need for adjusting length. Mountaineering etriers often combine multiple foot loops with a lanyard or daisy chain pre-sewn onto the foot strap. Rope access workers usually use a slender foot strap with a length-adjusting buckle. It's easy to improvise a foot strap rig from webbing or cord.

Avoiding Ascending Pitfalls: Good form is essential for ascending success. You don't have to be big and strong. It is much more about technique. Adjust ascending rigging so that you can stand up straight in the foot strap. When Climbers find themselves contorted and hunched to keep their weight on the foot strap they will have to repeatedly use bicep curls to pull up and hold a standing position. Avoid this pitfall by taking the time to properly adjust the foot strap length before you start out. With both feet still on the ground, position the top ascender (or rope grab) at helmet level on the climbing rope. Now adjust the foot strap length so that it is six to twelve inches from the ground while a foot is resting in it. Proper adjustment will compel the Climber to take shorter advances to climb up while making standing and letting go with one hand much easier. More experienced Climbers will usually shorten the foot strap length a bit for more ascending speed.

Poor standing technique is another pitfall that causes Climbers to become exhausted very quickly. It is very important to orient your body weight over the standing foot before making the move to stand up straight. Novice Climbers often try to stand up while they recline in their harness with their feet out in front of them. This just doesn't work. Move your body close to the rope, as if you are sliding on a fire pole, and get your weight over your foot (feet) before you stand up. When your body weight is properly situated before making the standing motion, less effort is needed to stand comfortably and move the ascenders efficiently.

Passing Knots and Routine Ascending: Knots and rigging in the main support rope are obstacles for ascending maneuvers. It's easy to move past knots and rigging. The trick is to remain fully connected to the main support rope as you do it. Two attached mechanical ascenders are necessary to establish a complete connection to the support rope. Moving past an obstacle requires removing and reconnecting the ascenders. To do this, an additional connection to the main support rope must be established first. This can be a matter of simply connecting a cord loop onto the support rope with a prusik hitch and attaching it to the pelvic ring on your harness. The loop can be hitched above or below the obstacle, but because it is difficult to advance a prusik rope grab with one hand on a slack rope, it may be better to attach the loop above the obstacle. If a Climber is carrying a descender, it can be threaded onto the support rope below the obstacle and then locked off to establish a hands-free complete connection. With the locked-off descender in place, ascenders can be disconnected and moved past the obstacle. Because a descender constitutes a complete connection to the support rope, both ascenders can be disconnected if necessary. Of course, a third descender can be used as well. Because closed rescue ascenders can be very difficult to disconnect and reconnect using one hand, *Vertical Academy* recommends hitching a cord loop with a 3-wrap prusik to establish the third complete connection.

To pass an obstacle while moving up, continue until the ascenders are as high as they can go. Establish a third connection to the rope by hitching on a cord loop just above the obstacle using a 3-wrap prusik. Disconnect the top ascender, and then reconnect it above the knot and prusik hitch. Continue climbing up until the lower ascender is as high as it will go. Now continue climbing up using the cord loop to support your weight when you sit in the harness. Do this until there is sufficient slack and clearance to disconnect, and move the lower ascender above the obstacle. Usually, it's easiest to reconnect the lower ascender below the prusik hitch. Adjust the lower ascender close to the prusik. Stand up to disconnect the cord loop, and sit down on the lower ascender.

To pass an obstacle while climbing down with ascending rigging, continue moving down until the lower ascender reaches the obstacle. Connect a cord loop to the rope between the ascenders. Using the cord loop to support your weight, ascend up enough to create sufficient slack to remove the lower ascender. Reconnect the lower ascender below the obstacle. Now climb down until the lower ascender supports your weight, and the cord loop is slack. Disconnect the cord loop, and reconnect it below the obstacle. Continue climbing down using the lower ascender to support your weight until there is enough clearance to disconnect and move the top ascender below the obstacle. Remove the cord loop, and continue climbing down on the original ascending rigging.

Basic Ascending - *Routine Rigging*

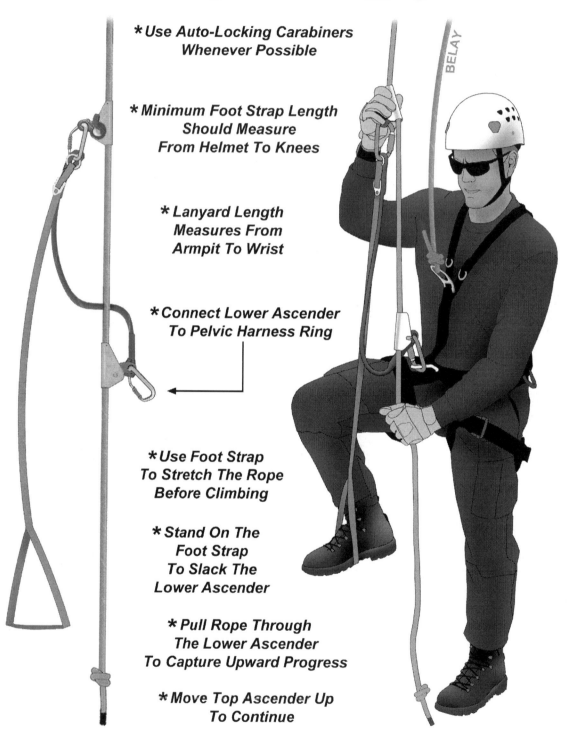

* **Use Auto-Locking Carabiners Whenever Possible**

* **Minimum Foot Strap Length Should Measure From Helmet To Knees**

* **Lanyard Length Measures From Armpit To Wrist**

* **Connect Lower Ascender To Pelvic Harness Ring**

* **Use Foot Strap To Stretch The Rope Before Climbing**

* **Stand On The Foot Strap To Slack The Lower Ascender**

* **Pull Rope Through The Lower Ascender To Capture Upward Progress**

* **Move Top Ascender Up To Continue**

BELAY

Basic Ascending - *Standing Action*

* Grab Top Ascender With Both Hands

* Align Body Weight Directly Over Foot

* Orient Torso Close To The Rope

* Use Leg Muscles To Stand Straight Up

* Use Arm Muscles To Keep Body Aligned

* Use Free Leg For Balance

* Hold Torso Close To The Rope To Remain Standing

Basic Ascending - *Routine Rigging*

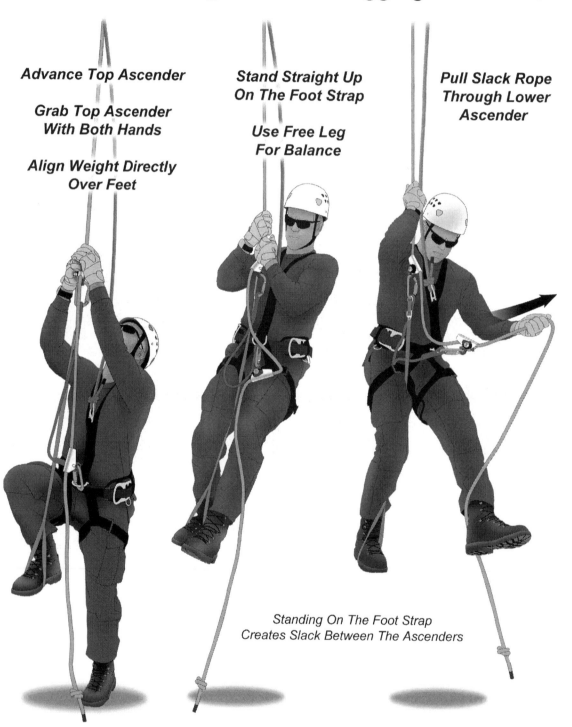

Advance Top Ascender

*Grab Top Ascender
With Both Hands*

*Align Weight Directly
Over Feet*

*Stand Straight Up
On The Foot Strap*

*Use Free Leg
For Balance*

*Pull Slack Rope
Through Lower
Ascender*

*Standing On The Foot Strap
Creates Slack Between The Ascenders*

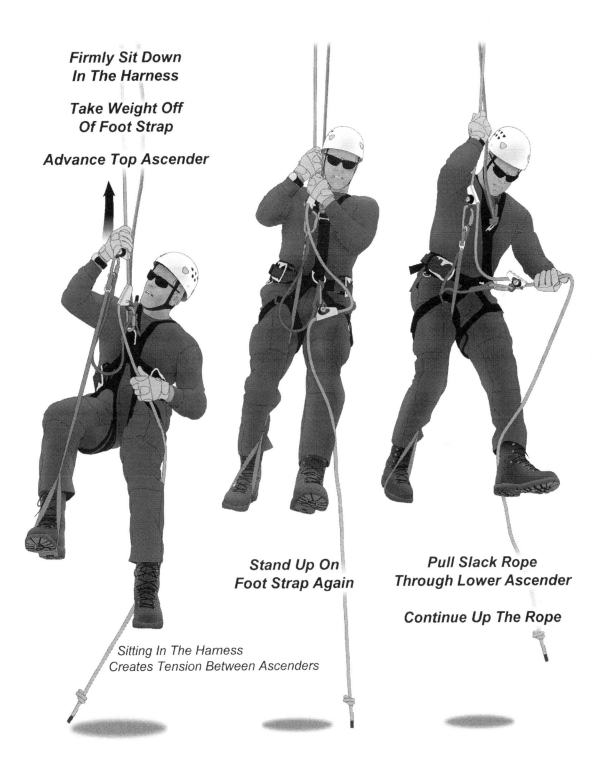

*Firmly Sit Down
In The Harness*

*Take Weight Off
Of Foot Strap*

Advance Top Ascender

Sitting In The Harness
Creates Tension Between Ascenders

*Stand Up On
Foot Strap Again*

*Pull Slack Rope
Through Lower Ascender*

Continue Up The Rope

Basic Ascending - *Passing Knots*

* Using Backup Prusik Loop
Foot Strap Not Shown For Clarity

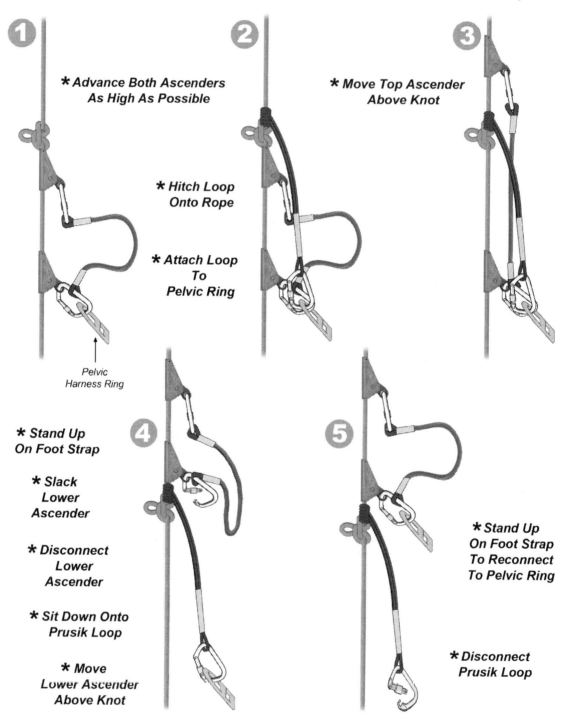

1

* Advance Both Ascenders
As High As Possible

* Hitch Loop
Onto Rope

* Attach Loop
To
Pelvic Ring

Pelvic
Harness Ring

2

3

* Move Top Ascender
Above Knot

* Stand Up
On Foot Strap

* Slack
Lower
Ascender

* Disconnect
Lower
Ascender

* Sit Down Onto
Prusik Loop

* Move
Lower Ascender
Above Knot

4

5

* Stand Up
On Foot Strap
To Reconnect
To Pelvic Ring

* Disconnect
Prusik Loop

Escape Ascending: Emergency ascending is an important skill for the professional Rescue Climber. Ascending up and out of trouble on disabled lowering or raising lines should always be in the back of a Climber's mind. Competency with rudimentary ascending practices adds a level of independence that contributes to greater personal safety. Every Climber should carry what they need to ascend back up to topside anytime they go over the side. Fortunately, they don't need to carry very much. In some bare bones situations, a single prusik loop and a carabiner can work.

Three 22-inch prusik loops and a couple of carabiners can form a bare bones but decent emergency ascending mechanism for escaping from a lowering/raising system. Longer loops can make ascending a bit less strenuous. Start by connecting loop #1 onto the main support rope using a 3-wrap prusik hitch, and attach it to the pelvic ring on your harness with a carabiner. Push the prusik wraps up as high is you can reach. Below the 3-wrap prusik, hitch loop #2 onto the main line using a 3-wrap prusik. This loop will act as a foot strap (etrier). Tie loop #3 onto loop #2 using a lark's foot to temporarily extend the etrier. Position the etrier low on the main line. Orient the etrier between your legs, and place one or both feet into the loop. Adjust the lower prusik position at least several inches above the original lowering/raising connection and so that your knee is slightly bent when your foot is resting in the etrier. Now is the time to carry out a remote safety check.

Reach up with both hands and grab the main line rope. Stand up slowly on the etrier until loop #1 and the original lowering/raising connection are slack. While standing up on the etrier, push the top prusik hitch up to remove slack in loop #1. Set the prusik hitch tight, and sit down in your harness. You should now be sitting in your harness supported by loop #1 with your foot "resting" in the etrier. Disconnect from the original lowering/raising system. Loosen and slide the lower prusik six inches to a foot higher on the rope. Do not move the etrier up more than about a foot. Stand up on the etrier and push the 3-wrap prusik up again to continue ascending.

Once you've moved up a couple of feet, remove loop #3 from the etrier, and connect it to the belay rope using a 3-wrap prusik hitch. Attach this loop to the sternum ring on your harness with a carabiner (use the biner taken from the lowering/raising connection). Use this connection as a traveling self-belay as you ascend. Disconnect the original lowering/raising belay connection. Place your foot back into the shorter etrier, and alternate standing and sitting to move the prusik hitches and move up the rope. Remember to closely monitor and properly adjust the traveling self-belay as you ascend. You'll quickly develop a working rhythm and begin to move more and more efficiently.

You will immediately notice that your ability to stand up and handle the prusik wraps efficiently depends on the length and position of the loops. Move slowly in short intervals. Moving the main supporting loop (loop #1) and the etrier in small increments works best and lessens fatigue. Making big steps is harder and increases the risk of stumbling and causing a shock load. Adjust and position the etrier so that you can stand up easily to create slack in the main support connection.

BE CAREFUL: This ascending rigging connects the Climber to the main support rope using a single attachment. This ascending method should be reserved for emergency escape situations only. Move slowly and deliberately. Be aware that grasping the main support rope above loop #1 risks disabling the top prusik should the Climber stumble and grab the hitch. For this reason, it is preferable to grab the main line rope below the top prusik before standing up on the etrier whenever possible. Doubling up on main line connection loops works fine and may reduce hazards related to disabling. Another method of backing up a single hitch connection is to knot the climbing rope below the prusiks as ascending progresses. This is a good option when forced to climb on a single rope.

BE CAREFUL: Do not climb too high without establishing a belay connection. The connection to the original lowering/raising system makes it necessary to extend the etrier to initiate these emergency maneuvers. Establish a traveling self-belay as soon as there is enough clearance to use a single loop as an etrier.

Passing Knots and Escape Ascending: Passing obstacles while using an improvised ascending mechanism can be done simply and easily. Ascend until the top prusik reaches the obstacle. While sitting in the harness, remove the foot loop and hitch it to the supporting rope above the obstacle using a 3-wrap prusik. Clip a carabiner onto the new loop. Tie a foot loop into the main support rope itself below the obstacle. Form this foot loop so you can stand up easily and connect to the cord loop above the obstacle. Stand up and attach the top loop to the pelvic ring on your harness. Push the top prusik hitch up until your weight is supported by the new attachment. Now use the lower cord loop as a foot strap to continue climbing up. To pass obstacles while climbing down with improvised ascending rigging, use the same method in an upside-down orientation.

Basic Ascending - *Escape Rigging*

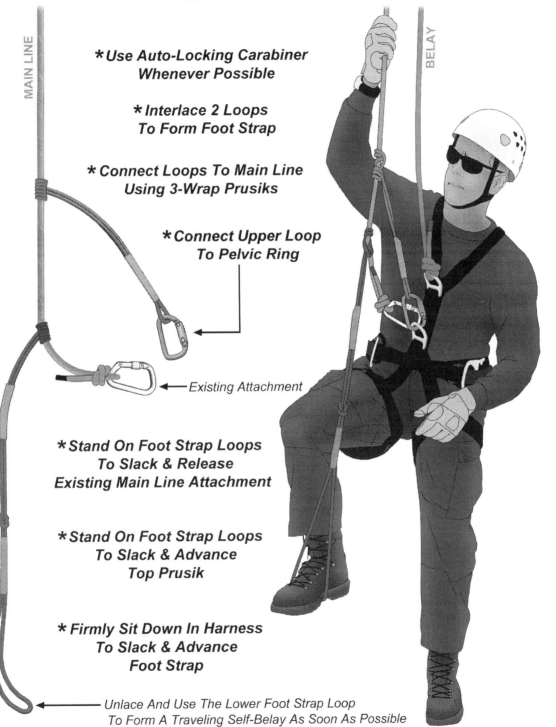

MAIN LINE

BELAY

***Use Auto-Locking Carabiner
Whenever Possible***

***Interlace 2 Loops
To Form Foot Strap***

***Connect Loops To Main Line
Using 3-Wrap Prusiks***

***Connect Upper Loop
To Pelvic Ring***

Existing Attachment

***Stand On Foot Strap Loops
To Slack & Release
Existing Main Line Attachment***

***Stand On Foot Strap Loops
To Slack & Advance
Top Prusik***

***Firmly Sit Down In Harness
To Slack & Advance
Foot Strap***

*Unlace And Use The Lower Foot Strap Loop
To Form A Traveling Self-Belay As Soon As Possible*

Basic Ascending - *Escape Rigging*

★Transition From Suspended On Main Line To Escape Rigging

MAIN

BELAY

Original Main Line Attachment

Lower Foot Strap Loop

Sit Down In Harness

**Disconnect
Original Main Line
Attachment**

**Assemble
Traveling Self-Belay
Using Lower Foot Strap
Loop**

**Original Main Line
Attachment Goes Slack**

Belay Line Goes Slack

Advance Top Prusik

**Ascend To Develop 18 Inches
Of Slack In Original Main Line
Attachment**

**Alternate
Standing & Sitting
To Advance Prusiks
And Ascend**

★

**Hitch Prusik Loops
To Main Line**

**Attach Top Loop
To Pelvic Ring**

Stand Up On Foot Strap

Form Stopper Knots On Rope Ends

Teaching And Learning Ascending: Ascending principles and methods should be introduced and described in detail before demonstrations by technically competent persons. Apprentices should then be allowed to practice ascending methods under close training supervision in a clinical setting. Always protect apprentice-level training participants with an independent belay system, even when practicing with self-belays.

Initially, ascending ropes should be rigged and handled in a way that keeps novice Climbers close to the ground. Thread the climbing rope onto a descent control device, and anchor it at ground level. Use an overhead directional to form the vertical climbing (working) section of the rope. Rigging the climbing rope this way enables trainers to lower the learning Climber as he or she ascends. This technique keeps learning Climbers at a safer elevation should a problem arise. More advanced Climbers who've ascended up high can be lowered to safety on this kind of rigging if they are in distress. Lock off and tie off the descender as the Climber moves up. Untie and unlock the descender to lower the Climber if a problem arises, or if the training session does not include down-climbing.

Anchor and orient ropes so learning Climbers can ascend fully suspended against a vertical face and while hanging free. Ascending against a vertical face makes positioning and standing easier. For best results, learning Climbers should demonstrate competency ascending against a wall before attempting to climb up a free-hanging rope.

TEACHING & LEARNING ASCENDING SKILLS - INSTRUCTIONAL ORDER

Instructor	Introduction	Introduction of ascending concepts and technical information using enhanced lecture techniques
Instructor	Demonstration	Dry demonstrations of ascending rigging and practices performed by technically competent people
Student	Application	Practice rigging and dry handling ascending systems under close training supervision
Instructor	Demonstration	Demonstrate ascending techniques
Student	Application	Practice ascending methods while fully suspended and on belay
Student	Evaluation	Demonstrate proficiency with routine ascending and emergency escape ascending techniques
Student	Competent	Ready to ascend in the field

Basic Ascending - Clinical Exercise

* Simple Rigging For Use With All Ascending Methods

* Enables Precise Positioning Of The Climber

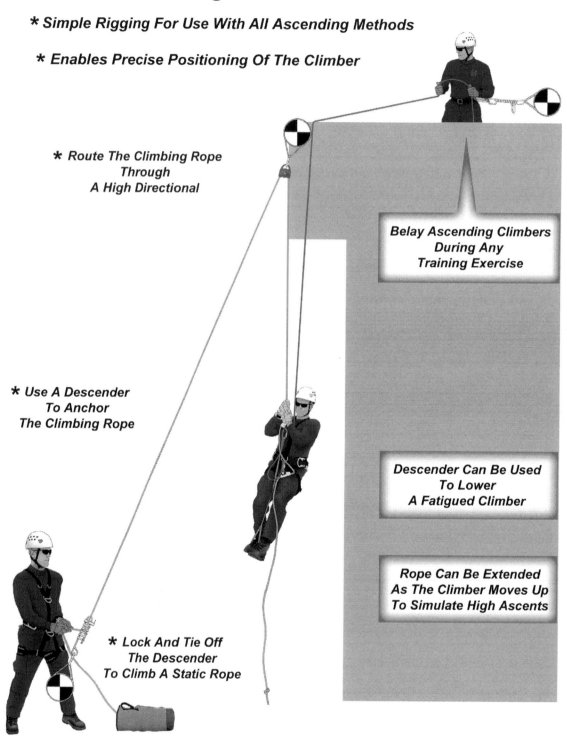

** Route The Climbing Rope
Through
A High Directional*

**Belay Ascending Climbers
During Any
Training Exercise**

** Use A Descender
To Anchor
The Climbing Rope*

**Descender Can Be Used
To Lower
A Fatigued Climber**

**Rope Can Be Extended
As The Climber Moves Up
To Simulate High Ascents**

** Lock And Tie Off
The Descender
To Climb A Static Rope*

10 Anchoring

Anchoring

All rigging systems must at some point connect to a mass that is stationary relative to the load. For most teams that means connecting to the earth. For some, it may mean connecting to a hovering helicopter. Any rope system used to lower, haul up, or belay a Climber and/or a rescue subject must be solidly fixed to an anchor that is not only strong enough to support the rescue package, but also able to hold up under shock load conditions. Anchors must also be selected and rigged in ways that prevent abrasion, cutting, and contamination of software attachments. Selecting anchors and anchoring off rope rescue systems is a skill in itself. Many anchor choices are obvious and make attachment selection intuitive and easy. A concrete overpass pillar with smooth surfaces is immediately recognizable as a *bomber* anchor choice. OSHA regulations and related professional standards organizations such as SPRAT or IRATA regard anchors that are able to support 5000lbs as minimally safe. It starts to get tricky when anchor choices on scene are not obviously rescue system worthy or are not located right where you need them.

This section of the book will examine anchor choices and explain simple rigging methods that create safe, strong connections to the earth using both bomb proof and not so bomb proof objects.

Anchors

Objects used to establish a solid, stationary foundation for rope rescue systems or fall protection systems come in many forms. Anchors can be classified by their basic type and level of integrity. For the most part, anchors are either naturally made or man-made in type. Both natural and man-made anchors are considered to be either bomb proof ("bomber") or less than bomber when it comes to describing holding integrity. Other sub-classifications identify holding characteristics and the quality of connection points that prevent attachments from moving or slipping completely off.

Natural Anchors: Objects like rocks and trees are termed natural anchors. Rocks and trees do not come with NFPA labels or engineering spec sheets to help determine suitability for your application. Judgment based on life experience and instinctive intuition plays a huge role in determining the integrity of natural anchors. For those who may need more assurance, there are engineering and materials testing reports available that provide strength assessment information for various materials found in natural settings. In general, natural anchors should be sufficiently sunk into good soil or otherwise be firmly attached to the surrounding terrain. Even very large boulders can be rolled or slid out of place by the forces rope systems create. Riggers must evaluate factors such as grade and slipperiness of the terrain that an anchor choice is resting on; the presence of gravel or sand that may act like ball bearings; cracks that may forecast disintegration of the base; erosion vulnerability caused by rainfall or rising river levels; etc. Living anchors such as trees, shrubs, and vines that appear to be strong must be inspected and determined healthy with well-planted root systems that are not weakened by insect infestation, rot, or dubious soil conditions. Natural anchors often require the placement of abrasion protections that prevent damage to rope, straps, and webbing.

In most cases, natural anchors are strongest when attachments are placed close to the ground. Life experience and intuition tells you that tying off close to the roots is obviously the strongest way to make a simple attachment to a tree. Rigging methods that reinforce weaker points higher up on the tree can be used to position anchor attachments more favorably for use. Methods that cinch around and tighten as the load increases is often a good way to maintain attachment placement for anchors that are narrowest at the bottom, as would be the case with a stout shrub or a round boulder resting on flat ground. But be careful. Natural anchors like rock horns that are wide at the bottom and narrower near the top will cause cinching attachments to migrate up and eventually slip off. Any cone-shaped object like a typical rock horn, whether natural or man-made, should use a simple (non-cinching) loop as an anchor attachment.

Man-made Anchors: Objects and systems such as pickets, vehicles, tripods, and structures are examples of man-made anchors. Some are designed for the specific purpose of supporting rope rescue systems. Most are simply structural elements that are adaptable as rope rescue or fall protection anchors. There is a wide range of equipment designed specifically for attaching onto a variety of structures for the purpose of anchoring off personal fall protections or rope systems. Double lanyards used for climbing vertical ladders and towers are an example of this.

It's important to understand how man-made objects are constructed before assigning them anchor status. Always check out the object to which you're connecting to determine where and how it gets its anchoring strength. Most handrails encountered in everyday life are not suitable as life safety anchors. Rooftop HVAC units may appear large and heavy, but they are commonly much lighter than they appear and are often held together and held down with very small fasteners. Many metal features on vehicles are too weak to be used as anchors. Most personal vehicles are not heavy enough in themselves to comply with common anchor capacity standards. Vehicles also have wheels that make movement easy. Vehicles may have to be tied off and always require lock-out-tag-out measures. Walkways and catwalks are often very strong in only one direction as would be necessary for supporting the load of people walking only on the top surface. Tying off to and pulling up on the same catwalk flooring may cause structural failure. Tripods, multi-pods, and picket systems are also strong only when rigged correctly and stressed from the proper direction. Steel building materials are notorious for exposing software to unforgiving sharp edges and burrs and frequently require software protection measures. Structural trusses are only strong where they are designed to bear a load. Connecting to the cord or web elements of a truss, including truss-structured aerial ladders, can cause catastrophic failure. The best-case scenario is to size up man-made anchor choices available to you at your hazard sites during training exercises before actual incidents occur and to develop proficiency using tripods, multi-pods, picket systems, and aerial ladders with regular practice.

Bomber Anchors: Slang for "bomb proof," the term "bomber" describes an anchor choice that is easily recognized as being impossible to move using any rope or fall protection systems that your team may attach to it. The term bomber can also be used to describe an engineered anchor that has been tested and rated as having holding strength that exceeds any stresses you might apply to it. Remember, anchor choices must be able to support any accidental shock load as well as the entire rescue package. Fixed rooftop window washer anchors, large healthy trees, or the headache ball on a large construction crane are examples of anchor choices that may be considered bomber for typical fall protection or rope rescue systems. A practical measure for deciding if an object is bomber is to assess the need, or lack thereof, for load sharing among multiple anchors. If an object does not require back-tying or connections to other objects for adequate strength it can be considered

bomber. In some regions, anchors must be so strong that they can obviously support the raising/lowering rope rescue system and the belay with no possibility of failure before they can be deemed bomber.

Directional vs. Non-Directional: Anchors that are only strong enough when loaded from one direction are termed "directional." Anchors that are strong when loaded from any direction are referred to as "non-directional." A picket holdfast system is an example of a directional anchor because it must be loaded along the correct linear axis. A concrete freeway overpass pillar would be considered a non-directional anchor choice for rope rescue purposes. Some rigging methods allow anchors to be safely pulled from a limited range of directions and are also considered non-directional or partially non-directional.

Open vs. Closed Anchors: Anchors with a profile that limits movement and completely eliminates the possibility for attachments to slip off are known as "closed anchors." Examples of closed anchors are things like metal eyes, railing systems that are made of welded tubing, or the trunk of a tree that has a large canopy. Open anchor choices may be very strong, or even bomber, but are not able to guarantee that anchor attachments will not slip off. Examples of open anchors are things like freestanding posts and bollards, trailer hitches on vehicles, or tree stumps with no canopy. Hazards associated with attaching to open anchors that are unusually shaped may require special rigging considerations.

Open vs. Closed Anchors

OPEN

*Attachment Depends On Gravity
Or System Tension To Stay In Place*

CLOSED

*Anchor Object Completely Traps
The Attachment*

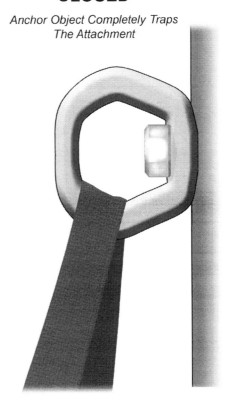

Load-Sharing Anchors: Less than bomber anchors can be fortified by connecting with other anchor objects. If an anchor is in a good location but not strong enough by itself, it may be possible to fortify it sufficiently by connecting with other nearby objects or objects that you plant. There are several load-sharing approaches to fortifying weak anchors. All have important rigging limitations. It can be as easy as placing webbing loops on 2 nearby tree trunks and clipping them together. But there are some engineering principles that must be considered when joining anchors together. Angles created by the attachment software can either relieve or amplify stresses on individual anchor objects that support load-sharing rigging. In general, angles created by legs of the software that joins weak anchor objects together should be sharper than 90º. Angles flatter than 90° should be considered past the point of effective load sharing. Riggers sometimes refer to the 90° angle as the *'Critical Angle,'* as it is considered the limit of safety. Angles between 45° and 60° are best for efficient load sharing and for keeping attachment rigging compact for clearance purposes. It's also important to forecast whether a load-sharing anchor will be used to support a load that is directionally stationary or dynamic.

Load Sharing - *Vector Forces*

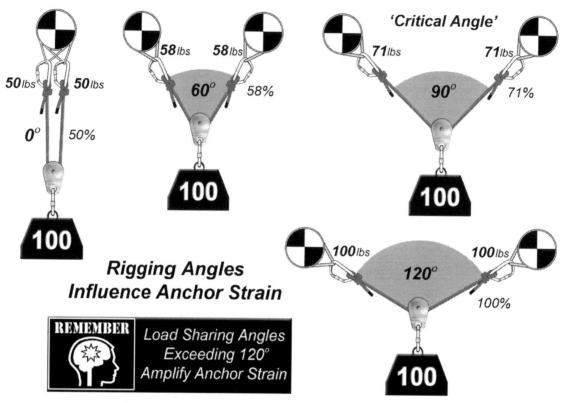

50 lbs   50 lbs

0°   50%

100

58 lbs   58 lbs

60°   58%

100

'Critical Angle'

71 lbs   71 lbs

90°   71%

100

100 lbs   100 lbs

120°   100%

100

Rigging Angles
Influence Anchor Strain

REMEMBER
*Load Sharing Angles
Exceeding 120°
Amplify Anchor Strain*

Anchor Attachments

There are many ways to attach rope systems with anchor objects. Depending on the discipline, everything from pitons, chains, and glue to rope, webbing, and strapping have been used to connect rope systems with a solid foundation. This section will shed light on attaching to anchor objects using software components commonly found in fire service rescue caches. There are several basic attachment principles and methods that are easy to learn and that adapt well for just about any situation.

Direct vs. Indirect Attachment: If the line that forms the rope system is tied onto an anchor object the method is described as a "direct" anchor attachment. If the rope system clips onto separate rigging attached to an anchor object the method is described as "indirect." Direct and indirect are both valid means of making anchor connections. The rationale for making direct attachments might be simplicity, equipment conservation, strength factors, speed, or skill levels. The reasons for making indirect attachments might be conservation of rope, protection of rope, anchor object strength, and levels of skill. It may be necessary to make a full strength attachment with very little equipment on hand. It may make better sense to attach to pitch-covered utility poles using inexpensive webbing instead of expensive life-safety rope. Even things like division of labor during setup can affect whether attachments are direct or indirect.

Direct Attachment To A Natural Anchor

Indirect Attachment To A Natural Anchor

Direct Attachments: Using the system rope to wrap an anchor object can speed things up when time is short or serve as a matter of convenience or a tactic for maintaining full rope strength. Direct anchor attachments usually require a bit more knot crafting skill and rigging savvy than indirect methods. For typical rope systems, a simple loop tied around the anchor choice using the end of the rope is easy and intuitive for anyone with basic knot skills. It gets a little tricky in situations where a non-directional or full-strength attachment is needed. A simple loop in the rope that wraps around an abrasive anchor object will not work well under non-directional conditions. The same simple loop method may create a weak point in the rope where it is knotted, making it unsuitable for heavily-loaded systems such as high-lines. More advanced complex methods of direct attachment can be fashioned with non-directional and/or full-strength functionality.

- **Direct Simple Loop:** Form a loop on the end of the system rope, and drop it over an open anchor object to establish a "direct simple loop" attachment. The loop will have to be tied onto closed anchor choices using a figure-8 follow-through or bowline. Keep the loop small for compactness, but reserve strength by rigging the yoke angle 90° or sharper. Direct simple loop attachments should be considered directional in functionality unless the anchor object is polished very smooth. The overall strength of this attachment depends on the rope and knot used. Because it does not cinch on the object, the simple loop attachment may not be suitable for some open or horizontal anchors.

- **Direct Multi-Loop:** Wrapping the system rope 2 or more times around an anchor object before knotting describes a "direct multi-loop" attachment. Different from the simple loop, the multiple wraps cinch tightly to better hold position and reduce crushing or kinking strain on the anchor object. One application might be where cinching is needed to keep the attachment low on a shrub without weakening the anchor by damaging small branches. Direct multi-loops are directional attachments and require some fine adjustment before loading. Strength of the software depends on the rope and knot used. Do not use this attachment method on open anchors that are wide at the base and narrow at the top. Doing so will cause the software to migrate up and off of the anchor object.

- **Tensionless Hitch:** A "tensionless hitch" uses the system rope to wrap enough loops around an anchor object to develop sufficient friction for supporting the load. Principles of belt and drum friction maintain full rope strength as the rope winds around the anchor object. This attachment also reserves all the rope strength that would be degraded by tying a knot, making it a good choice for high-tension rigging. Choose anchors that are rounded and at least 10 times the diameter of the rope for best performance. Your default should be at least 4 wraps, but consider realistic conditions to determine the need for additional wraps on any anchor object. The texture of the anchor object affects holding ability. Use caution when dealing with coatings or tree bark that may de-glove or rotate under strain. The tensionless hitch can be slacked under full load by slipping the wraps as needed and can even be used as a descent controller. By doing the reverse, this attachment can be used to capture hauling progress. No hardware or knot tying skills are needed. These favorable attributes make the tensionless hitch a favorite with swift water rescue teams. It's important to understand that the rope must be wrapped neatly onto the anchor to maintain functionality. Overlapping wraps cancel the ability to adjust the attachment and can make releasing tension impossible. In general, the tensionless hitch performs best and holds together better when the standing line is wrapped downward on the anchor object. Winding the standing line upward holds the load just fine, but gravity will cause the wraps to loosen and fall. To secure the tensionless hitch, simply drape enough standing line over the working section so that gravity holds it in place. If that makes you uncomfortable, tie or clip the standing line to the tensioned working section. When rigged correctly, tensionless hitch attachments can be used for non-directional applications.

Direct Attachments - Basic Methods

Simple Loop

To Capture The Anchor Object

*Strength Varies Depending On
Diameter And Knot Choice*

*Attachment Is Directional
Unless Object Is Very Smooth*

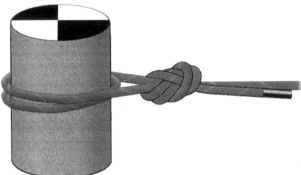

Multi-Loop

*Sling Or Tie 2 Or More Wraps
To Capture The Anchor Object*

*Strength Depends On
Diameter And Knot Choice*

Attachment Cinches Tight Onto Object

Attachment Is Directional

FULL STRENGTH

Tensionless Hitch

*Minimum Object Diameter 10 Times
Rope Diameter*

Wind Rope Onto Anchor Object

Minimum Of 4 Full Wraps

Neatness Is Important For Functionality

*Drape Or Tie Standing Line
Onto The Working Section*

Attachment Is Non-Directional

Indirect Attachments: Using straps or webbing to wrap anchor objects can provide for a lot of rigging flexibility without the need for advanced rigging skills. Separate ropes can also be used to make indirect attachments. Manufactured straps and pre-tied or sewn loops can be used to wrap anchor objects for non-directional functionality without tying a single knot.

- **Indirect Simple Loop:** Sling or tie an ordinary loop around an anchor object using webbing to create a "simple loop" anchor attachment. A simple loop attachment can also be fashioned from an anchor strap or a hank of rope. Tie loops that achieve a good compromise between compactness and strength. Resulting angles in the software should not be flatter than 90° to optimize strength. If the anchor object is large, knot placement is not a critical issue. If the anchor object is smaller than 4 inches in diameter, it's best to arrange loops so that the knot is suspended free of the object and carabiner. This will ensure the bend knot is not subject to lateral strain and splaying. Simple loop attachments are non-directional because the carabiner that holds the load can slide freely without affecting strength. Indirect simple loop attachments fashioned by tying 1-inch webbing can support loads up to about 7,000lbs. Stronger simple loop attachments can be fashioned using multiple wraps that capture the anchor object.

- **Indirect Multi-Loop:** Commonly called a "wrap-3-pull-2." Wind webbing or rope 3 or more times around an anchor object. Connect the ends of the software, and pull the knot-free wraps snug. The remaining knotted strand will then girdle and cinch onto the anchor object. Position the bend knot against the anchor object and inside the software yoke. Doing so significantly reduces knot strain. If the anchor object is smaller than 4 inches in diameter, arrange the attachment to position the knot on one of the suspended legs of the yoke. Rig to achieve a good compromise between compactness and strength. For optimum strength, resulting angles in the software should not be flatter than 90°. Multi-loop attachments are non-directional in function because the carabiner can slide freely on the yoke. Multi-loops have the added benefit of staying in place by cinching tightly onto an anchor object. Multi-loop attachments fashioned from 1-inch webbing can support loads upwards of 15,000lbs. Superior strength and cinching characteristics of multi-loops make them a top attachment choice for most anchors. Exceptions are open anchors that taper away from the base as many rock horns do. The cinching action can actually cause the software to migrate toward the narrow, open end of that type of anchor.

- **Basket Hitch:** Connecting bights formed on each end of a pre-tied or sewn loop with a carabiner creates a basket hitch attachment. Simply run one of the bights around or over the anchor object and close the hitch by clipping both ends of the loop together with a carabiner. Adjust the hitch so that the bend knot is free-floating. Anchor straps can be used in the same way. The rope system is then connected to the same biner used to close the hitch. Unless the anchor object is polished smooth, basket hitch attachments are usually directional. Non-directional capability can be achieved by connecting the load to the software instead of the carabiner that closes the hitch. In other words, allow the carabiner holding the basket hitch together to float freely, and use a separate biner to clip the rope system directly onto the webbing. The rope system connection will slide on the webbing as the load direction changes. Try to hit that sweet spot between compactness and strength. Keep the hitch short, but do not allow angles in the software to flatten out beyond 90° to reserve software strength. Basket hitch attachments made from 1-inch webbing can hold as much as 14,000lbs. Because they do not cinch, basket hitch attachments may not hold position and may not be suitable for some open or horizontal anchors.

- **Lark's Foot:** Rigging a simple snare around an anchor using a pre-tied or pre-sewn loop describes a "lark's foot" attachment. Grab a bight in the pre-formed loop, and run it around or over the object. Then thread the bight through the remaining opening in the loop on the other side of the anchor. Adjust so the bend knot floats free, and pull the bight snug. Some regions refer to this type of attachment as a "girth hitch" when used on larger anchor objects. Some anchor straps can be rigged in this way by threading through larger end rings instead of loops. It's possible to enhance stationary holding power on horizontal or open objects by positioning the bight in a way that makes the hitch crank down hard, similar to a strap wrench. Generally considered to be the weakest attachment choice, the lark's foot may be best for single person lead climbing situations on structures. This is because it's easy to rig using one hand, and it holds tight on horizontal or open anchor objects. When snug on the anchor object, the lark's foot functions as a non-directional attachment. Do not use lark's foot attachments on tapered, open anchors.

Tapered Anchors - Be Careful !

Attachments That Cinch Down Under Tension Are Not Appropriate For Open Anchors That Are Wide At The Base And Narrow At The Top. Cinching Attachments, Like The Multi-Loop And Lark's Foot, Can 'Squeeze' Up And Over The Top Of Round Or 'Cone-Shaped' Anchor Choices.

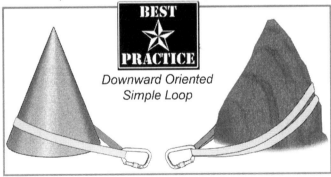

Indirect Anchor Attachments - *Basic Methods*

** Using 1" Webbing Loops Tied With Ring Bend* ** Strength Values For Field Comparison Only*

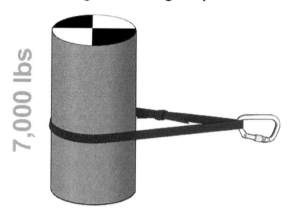

7,000 lbs

Simple Loop

Sling Or Tie Ordinary Loop(s) To Capture The Anchor Object

Clip Carabiner Onto The Loop

Attachment Is Non-Directional

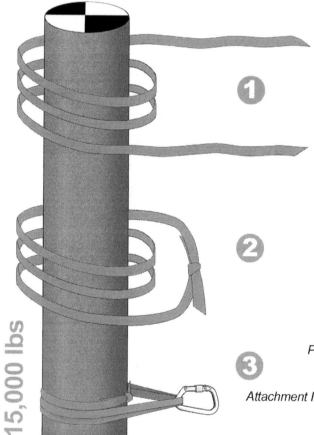

15,000 lbs

Multi-Loop

BEST PRACTICE

**1**
Make 3 Wraps Around The Anchor Object

2
Join Ends Of Webbing Using A Ring Bend

Clip Carabiner Onto The Knot-Free Wraps

3
Draw Wraps Snug Around Anchor Object

Position Knot Against The Object And Inside The Yoke

Attachment Is Non-Directional & Cinches Onto Object

Indirect Anchor Attachments - Basic Methods
* *Using 1" Webbing Loops Tied With Ring Bend*   * *Strength Values*
For Field Comparison Only

Basket Hitch

Flatten Large Loop
And Capture The Anchor Object

Connect Loop Ends With Carabiner

Draw Carabiner To Snug Wraps

Knot Should Float Free

Attachment Is Directional

Alternative:
Clip Second Biner Onto Wraps
For Non-Directional Function

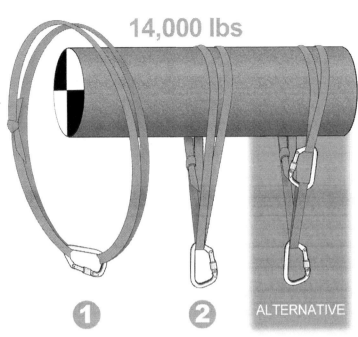

14,000 lbs

1 **2** ALTERNATIVE

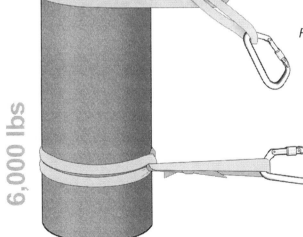

6,000 lbs

Lark's Foot

Flatten A Loop And Capture The Anchor Object

Thread One Loop End Through The Other

Connect A Carabiner And Draw Snug

Attachment Is Non-Directional

243

Backing Up Anchor Attachments: Some organizations and regions routinely back up any improvised anchor attachments made from webbing or rope. Unlike manufactured anchor attachments, improvised attachments provide an additional opening for human error because of the need to tie knots. Manufactured attachments usually involve capturing an anchor object and then simply clipping hardware connectors together. Knotted attachments are good, but they represent just one more opportunity for a mistake. Some bend knots look right even when they're improperly tied. Safety checks may not recognize a bad knot. Redundant attachments can be a means to help rule out attachment failure.

If anchor objects are somewhat suspect, backing up rigging for improvised or manufactured attachments can make sense. Attachment rigging can be fashioned to connect the rope system to a separate secondary anchor point for the purpose of taking over if the primary anchor object fails.

Backing up can be as simple as capturing a bomber anchor object with two separate webbing loops. The trick is to rig up so there will be no shock load when the backup takes over after primary attachment or anchor failure.

Back-tying: Fortifying a forward anchor by using non-working mechanical advantage block and tackle rigging to establish strong, tight connections with other anchors located to the rear is a load-sharing method known as tying back, or "back-tying." Back-ties are best made using life safety ropes. The rope can sometimes be wound directly around the anchor objects to form the MA, but more often anchor attachments are made for each object used. It's important that back-tie rigging meshes within the attachment that connects the ropes system. Doing so establishes a continuous link from the back anchor all the way to the rope system. If magic termites suddenly eat a back-tied tree used as a forward anchor, the non-working MA should still be connected to (meshed with) the rope system and the load should remain supported.

Back-ties are best assembled using non-working MA systems that minimize problematic stretching that occurs more readily with single strands of rope. The objective is to establish a tight, rigid link between the forward anchor and the backup object. Non-working 3:1CD MAs make tightening and adjusting back-ties easy, and enable riggers to manipulate the stretch out of the rope. The back-tie should be locked and/or tied off so that all legs of the MA are tight and supporting the load.

Objects used for back-tying should reasonably line up with the direction of force affecting the forward anchor. To reinforce a forward anchor using a single back-tie, any anchor object to the rear is fair game if it lies within a 15° margin on either side of the rope system axis ("fall line") behind the forward anchor. Fix load-sharing multiple back-ties to forward anchors whenever objects to the rear do not line up within 15°. Multiple back-ties should capture rearward objects that are on both sides of the fall line axis. Multiple back-ties can also be used as a tactic for optimizing anchor position, increasing overall stability, adding strength, and adding non-directional functionality.

Focused Attachments: Rigging methods that collect and direct the strength of two or more anchor objects forward to a single stationary point are known as "focused anchors." Depending on regional preference, rigging methods of this type are sometimes referred to as "multi-point anchors." Focusing is a method of load sharing. Focused anchoring methods generally form directional anchors (anchors that are strong in only one direction) or partially non-directional anchors with a limited range of lateral load movement.

Focusing can be used to form strong anchors from multiple weak objects, to create redundancy for back-up purposes, or to optimize anchor placement. There are many ways to form load-sharing focused anchors for rescue systems.

- Capturing two or more anchor objects within a single loop of webbing and then gathering the loop and knotting it in a way that forms separate, sling-like strands for each object is a common method of creating a focused load-sharing attachment. This method is directional in nature and can be a quick solution for fortifying or backing up anchor objects.

- Extending back-ties from two bomber anchor objects to a single forward gathering plate or ring is a method of load-sharing for the purpose of improving anchor position. The exact placement of a gathering plate can be easily adjusted by lengthening or shortening the individual back-ties as needed. The rigging can be held rigid using a tether that links the gathering plate to a forward tie-off point. When the back-ties are tightened hard against the tether, the gathering plate remains stationary, and the entire assembly stays rigid, even when the rope system is slacked. This kind of focusing rigging is often used to create anchors that conveniently float above the ground for improved ergonomics.

Distributing (Equalizing) Attachments: Attachments that adjust to divide the load evenly among multiple anchor objects as the axis of the rope system moves are referred to as "distributing." In some regions, distributing anchor attachments are called "self-adjusting" or "self-equalizing." Distributing attachments make strong anchors from multiple weak objects and, therefore, also fall under the category of load-sharing. Distributing anchor rigging should only be necessary when available individual anchor objects are weak, and the rope system axis will be expected to move about. There are good reasons to be conservative with the use of distributing attachments for load-sharing. Distributing methods generally complicate rigging. One notorious characteristic is that if any of the individual anchor objects in a distributing rig fails, there is potential for creating enough shock to pull out the remaining anchor object(s) that share the load. Using distributing attachments as a default in standard operations may not be the wisest approach.

BE CAREFUL: Distributing attachments should be compact and must respect angle influences on anchor objects. Outermost angles should be no flatter than 90° for efficient load sharing. Strands of the distributing rigging should be no longer than 12 inches and should be as symmetrical as possible. It should look like a "V" or a "W," not a hockey stick or lightning bolt. Bend knots should be positioned on interior strands and close to stronger anchor objects. Rapid, jerky movements can overwhelm the self-equalizing functionality of distributing rigging and cause the load to be directed onto a single weak anchor object. Excessively long distributing attachment rigging can create severe shock loads if one anchor object blows out. Poor knot placement can snag and bind up smooth operation and lead to dangerous, uneven load distribution.

Understand that some regions, especially in the recreational climbing community, refer to any focused load-sharing attachment rigging as distributing. Using webbing to form focused attachments that gather the strength of multiple anchoring points does indeed "distribute" load forces.

Floating Anchors: Usually a method used in conjunction with focused or back-tied anchors, rigging that elevates and steadies the connection point of an anchor system for the purpose of ergonomic or operational favorability is referred to as "floating." Crouching or kneeling to the ground for the duration of an extended over-the-side operation can be very difficult and fatiguing. Working at ground level can be impossible if terrain is rugged. Simple techniques that raise anchor rigging from the ground and enable workers to stand comfortably improve workability, reduce abrasion hazards, and smoothes out operations. Floated anchors enable rope systems to operate smoothly above rough terrain with less need for other edge protection measures.

All that is needed to float an anchor connecting point is a rigging component that holds anchor attachments in tension while the rope system is slack. This is usually done by using a static rope or webbing section to link the anchor connection (usually a rigging plate) with a tie-off point toward the front. More than one forward link may be needed in some cases. The link(s) and the tie-off point(s) do not have to be of life-safety strength; rather, they only need to be tough enough to keep the anchor connection and its rigging under tension. Doing this will cause the anchor connection to remain suspended, even when the main rope system is slack. Stability can be further improved by placing a solid object such as a box or bag of rope underneath the attachment rigging. Anchor connection points can be elevated by simply placing a solid object under the rigging. However, this floating method allows the attachment rigging to go limp when the rope system is slacked.

Back-Tying Anchors

*To Reinforce A Well-Placed Forward Anchor That Is Too Weak

Shown With Optional Prusik Brake

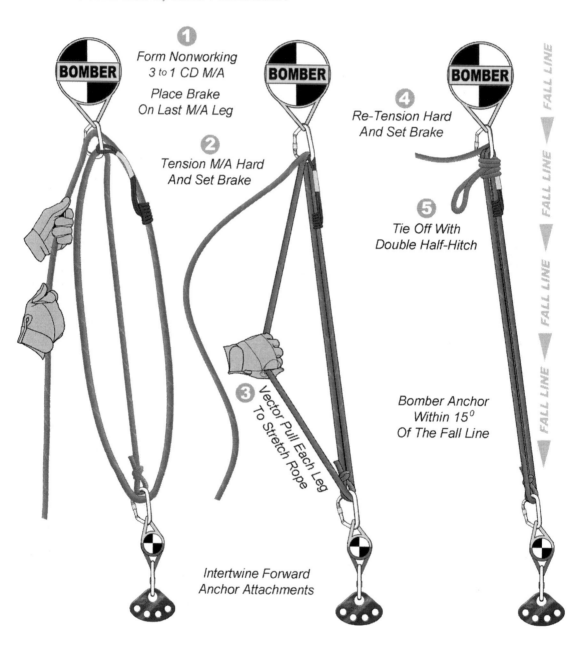

1 Form Nonworking 3 to 1 CD M/A

Place Brake On Last M/A Leg

2 Tension M/A Hard And Set Brake

3 Vector Pull Each Leg To Stretch Rope

Intertwine Forward Anchor Attachments

4 Re-Tension Hard And Set Brake

5 Tie Off With Double Half-Hitch

Bomber Anchor Within 15⁰ Of The Fall Line

FALL LINE

Back-Tying Anchors

Intertwine Back-Tie Attachments With Forward Attachment To Establish Direct Connection

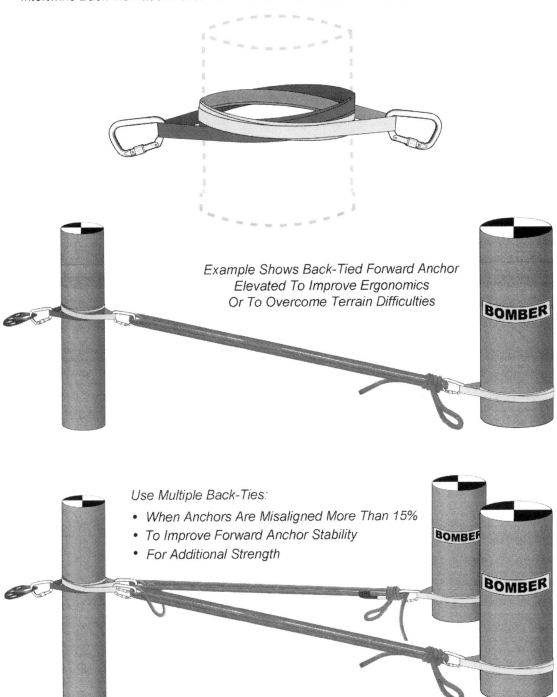

*Example Shows Back-Tied Forward Anchor
Elevated To Improve Ergonomics
Or To Overcome Terrain Difficulties*

BOMBER

Use Multiple Back-Ties:

- *When Anchors Are Misaligned More Than 15%*
- *To Improve Forward Anchor Stability*
- *For Additional Strength*

BOMBER

BOMBER

Focusing Anchors - *Load Sharing*

* Using 1" Webbing Loop To Capture Multiple Weak Anchor Objects

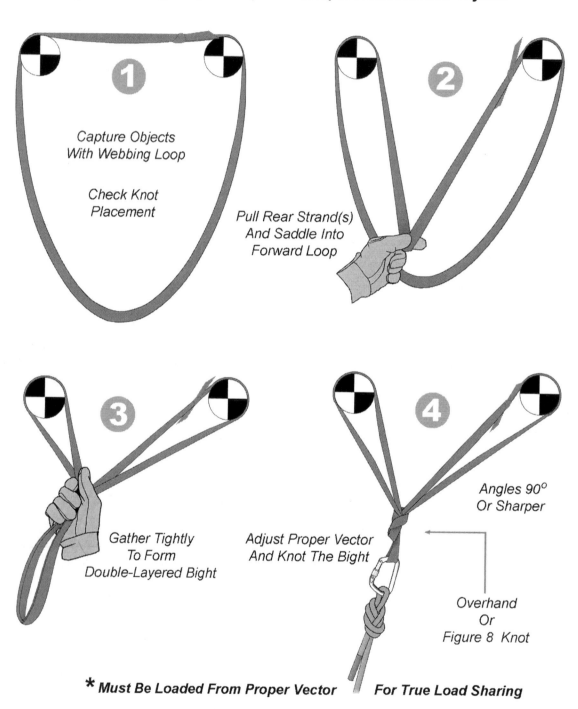

1 Capture Objects
With Webbing Loop

Check Knot
Placement

2 Pull Rear Strand(s)
And Saddle Into
Forward Loop

3 Gather Tightly
To Form
Double-Layered Bight

4 Adjust Proper Vector
And Knot The Bight

Angles 90°
Or Sharper

Overhand
Or
Figure 8 Knot

* Must Be Loaded From Proper Vector   For True Load Sharing

Focusing Anchors - *Load Sharing*

* Some Regions Describe Any Focused Attachment As "Distributing"

* Directional Focused Attachments Distributing To Multiple Points

Focused Attachments Can Be Used To Distribute Load Forces Among Many Objects That Are Less Than Bomber To Establish A Strong Rescue-Worthy Anchor.

Load-Sharing Rigging Of This Type Combines The Strength Of Multiple Objects And Provides Shock Minimizing Back-Up Should Any Of The Anchor Objects Fail.

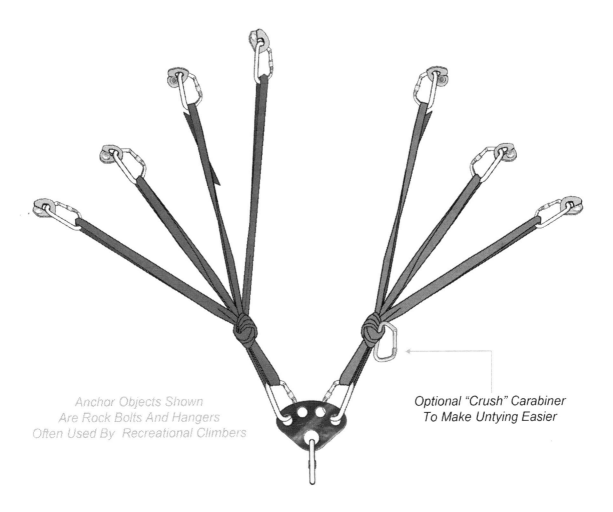

Anchor Objects Shown Are Rock Bolts And Hangers Often Used By Recreational Climbers

Optional "Crush" Carabiner To Make Untying Easier

Static Distributing Attachments Are Directional, And Must Be Loaded From The Proper Vector To Distribute Forces Evenly To All Points.

Focusing Anchors - For Optimum Positioning

✱ *Using 2 Nonworking MA Back-Ties With A Single Forward Tether*

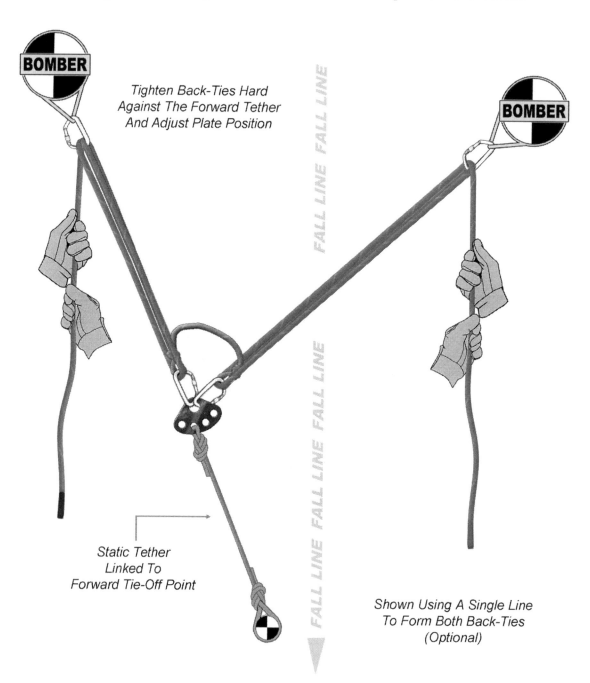

*Tighten Back-Ties Hard
Against The Forward Tether
And Adjust Plate Position*

*Static Tether
Linked To
Forward Tie-Off Point*

*Shown Using A Single Line
To Form Both Back-Ties
(Optional)*

250

Focusing Anchors - *For Optimum Positioning*

* Using 2 Nonworking MA Back-Ties With A Single Forward Tether

* (continued)

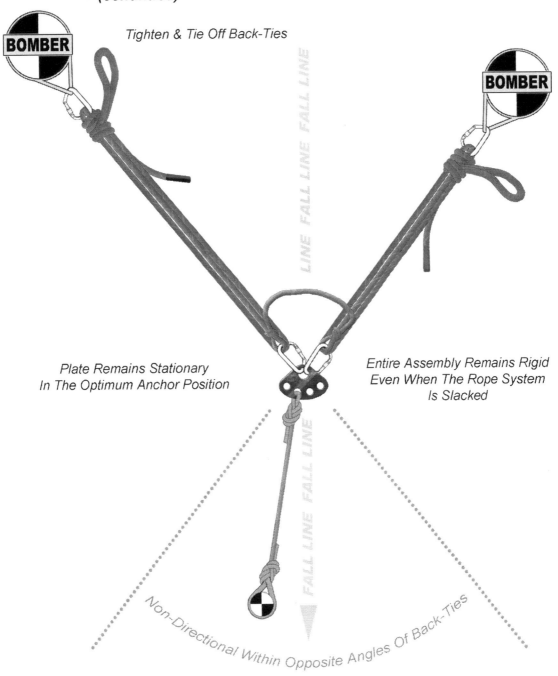

Tighten & Tie Off Back-Ties

Plate Remains Stationary
In The Optimum Anchor Position

Entire Assembly Remains Rigid
Even When The Rope System
Is Slacked

Non-Directional Within Opposite Angles Of Back-Ties

Distributing Attachments - Self-Equalizing

* Rigged To Back Up Failure Of One Anchor Object

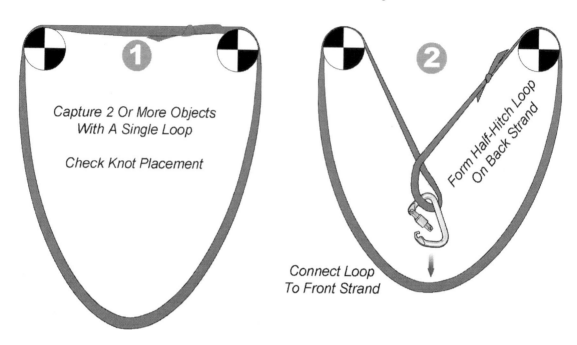

Capture 2 Or More Objects
With A Single Loop

Check Knot Placement

Form Half-Hitch Loop
On Back Strand

Connect Loop
To Front Strand

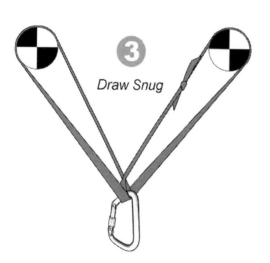

Draw Snug

*Rigging Slips To Distribute Forces Evenly
As The Load Vector Changes*

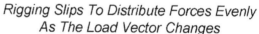

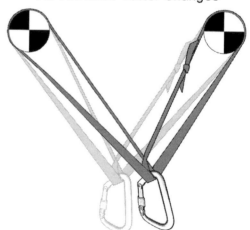

Practical Efficiency Limitations Allow Capturing Up To 4 Anchor Objects

Distributing Attachments - Self-Equalizing
- Potential Operating Shortfall

* Potential Hazards To Self-Equalizing Flimsy Anchor Objects

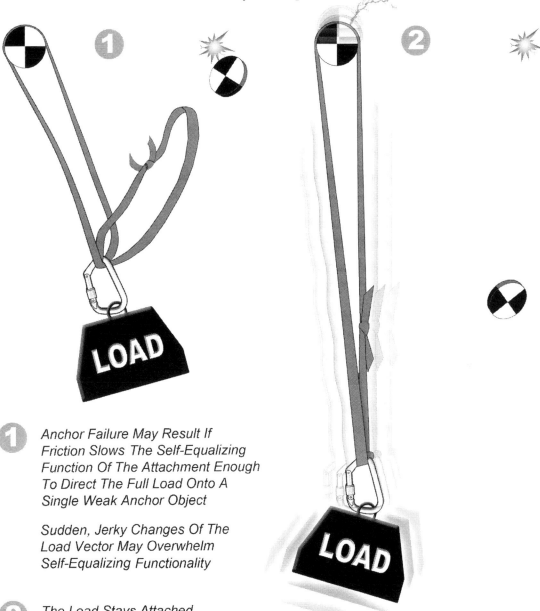

Anchor Failure May Result If Friction Slows The Self-Equalizing Function Of The Attachment Enough To Direct The Full Load Onto A Single Weak Anchor Object

Sudden, Jerky Changes Of The Load Vector May Overwhelm Self-Equalizing Functionality

The Load Stays Attached Via The Half-Hitch Loop, But The Shock Load That Occurs When The Attachment Reaches Full Extension May Cause Remaining Anchor Objects To Fail

Distributing Attachments - Critical Elements

* Optimizing Self-Equalizing Function & Minimizing Shock Generation

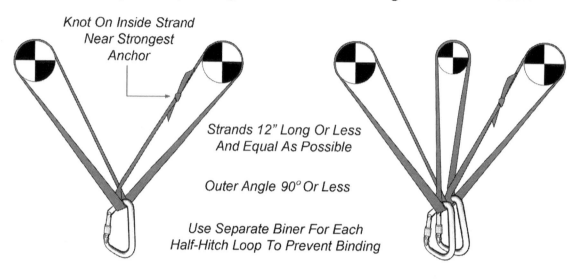

Knot On Inside Strand
Near Strongest
Anchor

Strands 12" Long Or Less
And Equal As Possible

Outer Angle 90° Or Less

Use Separate Biner For Each
Half-Hitch Loop To Prevent Binding

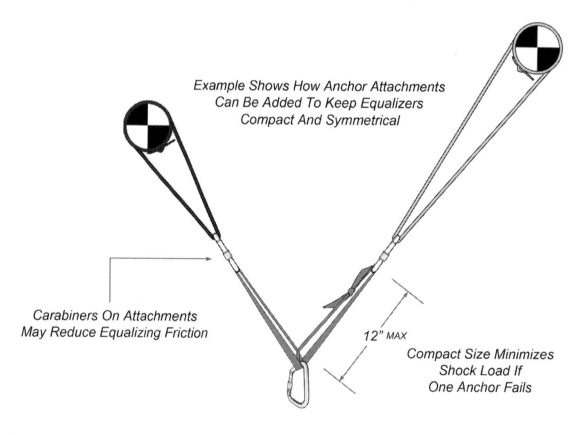

Example Shows How Anchor Attachments
Can Be Added To Keep Equalizers
Compact And Symmetrical

Carabiners On Attachments
May Reduce Equalizing Friction

12" MAX

Compact Size Minimizes
Shock Load If
One Anchor Fails

Floating Anchors

* *Suspending Anchor Connections For Ergonomics Or Obstacle Clearance*

Elevating The Point Where A Rope System Connects May Be As Simple As Placing A Solid Object Under The Rigging To Act As A Compression Strut.

Floating An Anchor This Way Will Allow The Attachment Rigging To Go Limp Whenever The Rope System Is Slacked.

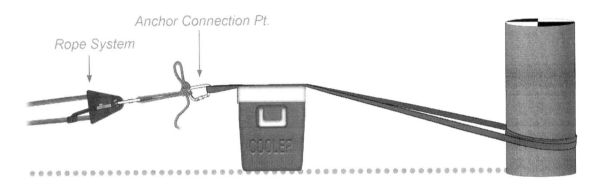

Position-Optimizing Focused Attachments Float The Anchor Connection Point Whether The Rope System Is Tensioned Or Completely Slacked.

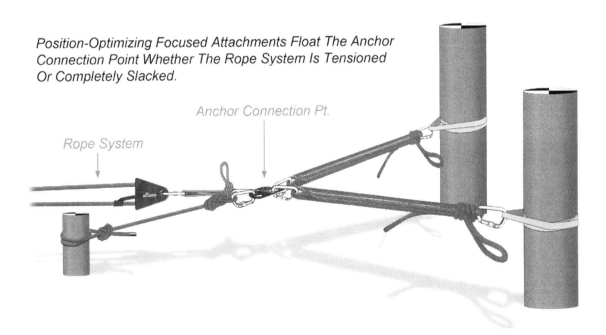

Backing Up Attachments - Redundancy

* *Single-Strand Webbing Attachments Are Not Favoured By Some Organizations*

* *Simple Redundancy Measures Provide An Added Layer Of Attachment Back-up*

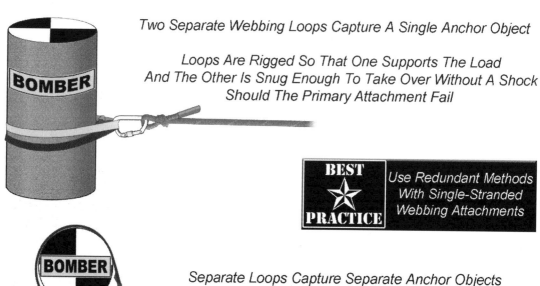

Two Separate Webbing Loops Capture A Single Anchor Object

*Loops Are Rigged So That One Supports The Load
And The Other Is Snug Enough To Take Over Without A Shock
Should The Primary Attachment Fail*

BEST ★ PRACTICE *Use Redundant Methods With Single-Stranded Webbing Attachments*

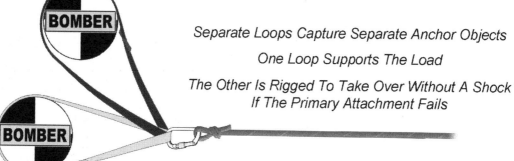

Separate Loops Capture Separate Anchor Objects

One Loop Supports The Load

*The Other Is Rigged To Take Over Without A Shock
If The Primary Attachment Fails*

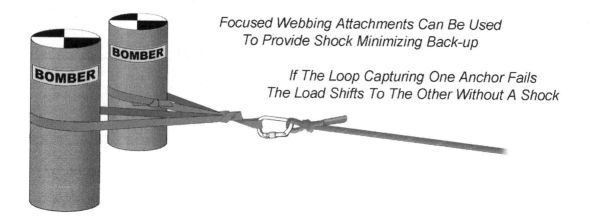

*Focused Webbing Attachments Can Be Used
To Provide Shock Minimizing Back-up*

*If The Loop Capturing One Anchor Fails
The Load Shifts To The Other Without A Shock*

Directionals: In many situations the best anchoring options require a bit of "reverse thinking." Instead of elaborate efforts to extend or construct anchors, it may make better sense to "steer" a rope system toward that big, fat, juicy anchor that is a little out of place. It may be possible to anchor "directional" pulleys in ways that create a path to direct the rope system from the fall line back to a bomber anchor, or in some cases the only anchor option on the site. Directionals can steer ropes vertically or horizontally. A pulley that is anchored to the head of a tripod is one example of a directional that guides a rope vertically. A pulley anchored to the base of a tree can reroute a rope vector horizontally.

Various directional attachment methods can add tremendous flexibility for fine-tuning the path that the rope follows back to the anchor. This usually involves lengthening or shortening the attachment rigging that anchors the directional pulley(s). Using non-working MA systems to connect directional pulleys can enable easy adjustment, even when the rope system is under tension.

Pickets

Used for establishing solid anchors at outdoor worksites, pickets provide a means of setting up rope systems exactly where they're needed. Most often, picket anchor systems are needed at locations without vehicle access. Basic pickets suitable for rope rescue work should be made from 1-inch cold-rolled steel rod and be at least 42 inches long with a sharp point on one end. Lightweight commercial versions are available that are made from titanium tubing fitted with replaceable hardened striking caps and points. Some integrate with strikers, similar to those used for installing fence posts that not only pound pickets into the ground but also pull them out. Picket plates that mechanically connect pickets together at the base can be made or purchased. A cache of 15 pickets is usually adequate. 15 or so windlass rods will also be needed as a means to firm up the software

that binds picket anchor systems together. These rods should be about 20 inches long and at least 3/8 of an inch thick. Steel concrete forming stakes can be used for windlass rods and are handy in the cache for utility purposes such as hobbling, securing edge protection, etc.

There are many variables that affect the ability of pickets and picket systems to anchor a load. Soil composition, moisture, vegetation cover, angle of attack, and depth are just some of the factors that contribute to the holding power of picket anchors. In general, soil profile schedules used for trench rescue size-up and construction purposes can be used in the field to help evaluate how solid a picket anchor system will be.

SOIL PROFILE TYPES			
Type A	Hard Clay	Uniform Cohesive Soils	UCS > 1.5 Tons / Sq. Ft.
Type B	Some Clay	Not Uniform – Some Cohesiveness	UCS < 1.5 Tons / Sq. Ft.
Type C	Gravel	Loamy Sand or Soft Clay	UCS < 0.5 Tons / Sq. Ft.
UCS = Unconfined Compressive Strength			

In general, a single picket should be sunk 2/3 to 4/5 of its length and angled 15° to 30° away from the load force it supports. Anchor attachments should be connected to the base of the exposed part of the picket. A single picket that is properly placed in Type-A soil can hold a static load of 600 to 800lbs. This figure can serve as a good baseline for making field estimates of the holding power of picket anchors systems. Individual pickets can be lashed together to increase anchoring strength. It may seem logical to assume that lashing pickets together in a line, one after another indefinitely, will result in adding about 700lbs of holding ability as each picket is added on. However, there is an element of diminishing returns whenever individual pickets are connected together for the purpose of increasing holding power. In other words, pickets closer to the back of the lineup receive less load force and contribute less holding power to the overall anchor system. Software stretch, picket flexibility, and load distribution physics can direct load forces out of line and away from pickets positioned toward the rear. Pickets 4th in line or farther back in the system may only be useful as redundancy for backup purposes.

Picket anchors and picket systems should be considered directional in nature. Because they are planted at an angle relative to the load force, picket anchors must be strained from the proper direction to be strong. It's important that the load pulls in a direction opposite to the tilt of the picket. The same is true when pickets are lashed together to form a picket anchor system ("picket holdfast"). Anchor attachments should be connected at the base near the ground and pulled parallel with the holdfast.

Holdfasts arrange and lash pickets together in ways that gather the combined strength of each individual piece. There are many ways of applying this concept that work very well. Most involve lashing the top of each picket to the base of another. This technique of bracing uses simple leverage to add rigidity to the exposed portion of the pickets and can actually transfer load-bearing strength. It can also serve to morph a picket anchor from an open-topped anchor choice to a closed anchor. It's important to stress the need for measuring the distance between the stakes before planting them. Stakes must be separated correctly to create a 90° angle between the pickets and the lashing. If the lashing does not depart a picket at a perpendicular angle, then the software will slip out of position and either weaken or collapse the anchor. Simply use another stake held at a perpendicular angle to determine how far back to plant the next trailing picket. Best practice is to lash no more than 3 pickets in line. Complex systems may combine 2 or more 3-piece picket holdfasts together to share a load. Lashing can also be used to essentially back-tie the bases of individual pickets together. This back-tying concept is how picket plates work to join individual stakes together to create strong anchors. Combining picket plates or software base connections with windlass lashing may increase overall anchoring strength.

Anecdotal Observations: Dozens of commercial rescue training classes with as many as 30 people pulling lines that were connected to 3-piece picket holdfasts planted in sandy riverbed soils demonstrated the holding power of these anchoring tools. In virtually every case, the picket holdfast or holdfast anchor system held strong. Failure only occurred several times when large groups rhythmically pulled perpendicular to the axis of the lashings in a heave-ho style.

Single Picket Anchor

Tilt 15⁰-30⁰ Away

Holds 600 to 800lbs

Attach At Base

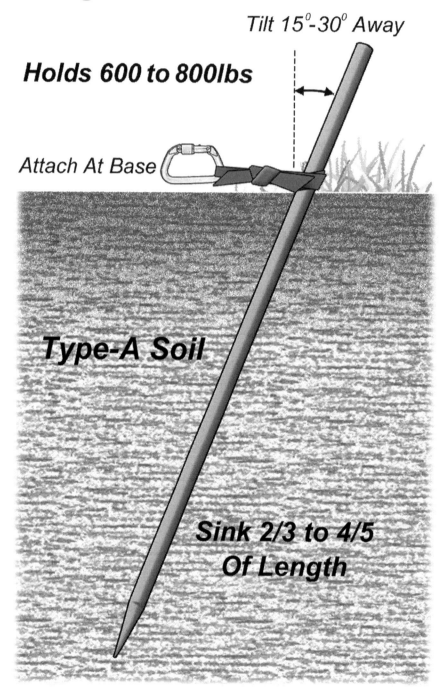

Type-A Soil

Sink 2/3 to 4/5 Of Length

Picket Systems - *Lashing Pickets Together*

✱ Can Be Lashed Using 1" Webbing Or 8mm/9mm Cord

- *Tie Ends Using Clove Hitches*
- *Wrap High And Low As Shown*
- *At Least 3 Strands Between Pickets*
- *2 Strands If Cord Is Used*

- *Distance Between Pickets Should Create 90° Angles With Software*
- *Insert Rod To Create Spanish Windlass*
- *Tighten Webbing Until Rigid Without Displacing The Pickets*

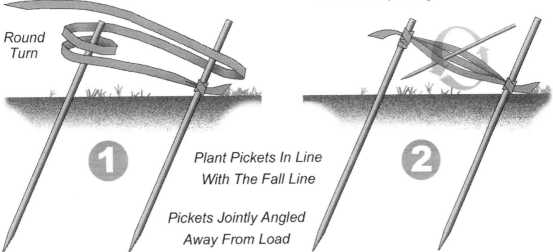

Round Turn

Plant Pickets In Line With The Fall Line

Pickets Jointly Angled Away From Load

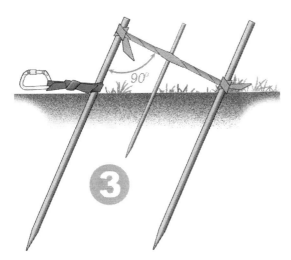

- *Plant Windlass Stakes into The Soil Whenever Possible*
- *2 Pickets Lashed In Line In Good Soil Can Hold Up To 1400lbs*
- *3 Pickets Lashed In Line In Good Soil Can Hold Up To 1800 lbs*
- *4th Picket In Line Does Not Add Meaningful Strength*

Picket Systems - Alternative Methods

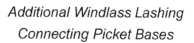

Additional Windlass Lashing
Connecting Picket Bases

Clove Hitches

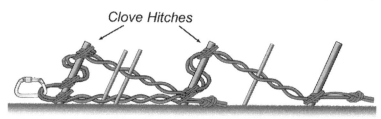

Windlass Lashing
Using 8-9mm Cord

Picket Bases Connected
With A Picket Plate

Picket Plate

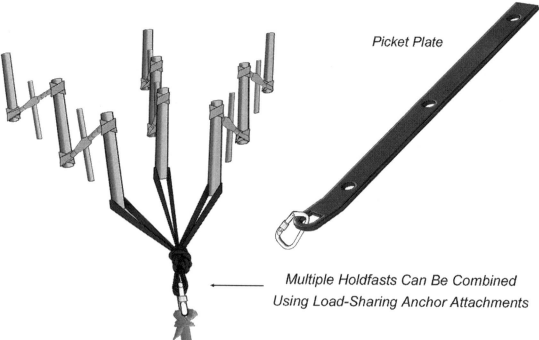

Multiple Holdfasts Can Be Combined
Using Load-Sharing Anchor Attachments

11 Portable Anchors

Portable Anchors

Tripods and Multi-pods

Rescue Teams responding to confined space, industrial, or over-the-side incidents have a great need for providing their own means of anchoring a directional pulley above or near a horizontal opening or edge. Bomber anchor choices for high directional pulleys are rarely located exactly where they are needed. Tripods are great for positioning a high directional pulley precisely over the top of vertical confined space openings. Multi-pods can be set up to do the same, but they are also great for positioning high directional pulleys above edges or anywhere there is a need to elevate rigging off the ground.

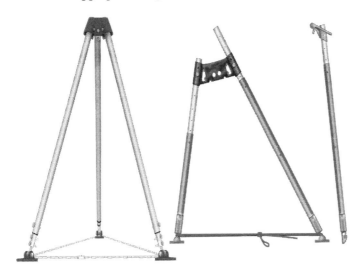

NFPA STANDARDS PORTABLE ANCHORS	
Intended Use	Minimum Breaking Strength
Tech	22 kN (4946 lbf)
General	36 kN (8093 lbf)

NFPA performance standards compliance requires third-party testing of rescue tripods and multi-pods for durability and breaking strength. Referred to in NFPA standards as "portable anchors," compliant tripods and multi-pods are categorized for both tech (single person) and general (2-person) use. Durability and breaking strength tests are conducted for each attachment point while the tripod or multi-pod is set up in its weakest configuration. The weakest configuration is usually the tallest setting. Compliant equipment will have a permanently affixed NFPA spec label. Many OSHA jurisdictions require all anchors to hold a minimum of 5000lbs. Most portable anchors are engineered to only comply with OSHA regulations.

It's important to study manufacturer instructions and practice using tripods and multi-pods in realistic practice sessions to determine the best way of safely establishing the artificial high anchors your team needs.

Tripods: Rescue tripods are usually comprised of three adjustable legs of telescoping steel or aluminum tubing that hinge on a single bulkhead where the anchor attachment points are located. Pads, treads, or points are fitted on the ends of the legs where they contact the ground. In some cases these feet are removable. In almost every case, an adjustable chain or cord connects the feet together to prevent the legs from spreading. Many tripods are able to mount cable winches that usually attach to one of the legs for lowering and raising. In most cases, these winches have a capacity of less than 600lbs, which is under capacity for an NFPA 2-person load. This can limit rescue operations to lowering and raising a single person at a time for those organizations concerned with NFPA compliance.

Tripods are best suited to lowering and raising Climbers along a plumb trajectory into and out of openings like manholes. Industrial settings have many of these types of situations. Tanks, hatches, ducting, and vertical pipes are other examples where tripods may work well. Some tripods may be limited to use on flat, level surfaces. Most portable tripods rely on the weight of the load to compress all three legs for vertical stability. You may occasionally see advanced teams using conventional tripods to elevate a directional pulley above an edge that is outside the footprint during over-the-side operations. Using a tripod this way can result in at least one leg bearing tension instead of compression. Conventional tripods can be used this way with additional advanced rigging not shown in this book.

Tripods can also be fashioned using lumber, timber, or metal materials. Improvised tripods that are properly lashed with ropes, webbing, or strapping can be very strong and suitable for rescue operations. Mountain and wilderness rescue teams who access worksites on foot favor high anchors made from materials they find on scene. Knowledge of using improvised high-directional anchors can be very useful to firefighters during widespread disaster operations. Materials needed to improvise tripods are abundant during collapse-inducing disasters such as earthquakes, tornados, or hurricanes.

Multi-pods: Equipment adaptable to constructing tripods, A-frames, and gin poles are known as multi-pods. Usually kits of component parts, multi-pods are excellent tools for establishing strong elevated anchors almost anywhere they're needed. In some cases, multi-pod components can be adapted for use as shoring in collapse situations, and some shoring equipment kits are adaptable for use as portable anchors similar to multi-pods. Multi-pods can be assembled to precisely conform to the natural or man-made surfaces by which they're supported. Whether the high anchor needs to be out over a rocky edge or directly over a railcar hatch, there is usually a way to erect a multi-pod to get it in place.

Multi-pod - Kit

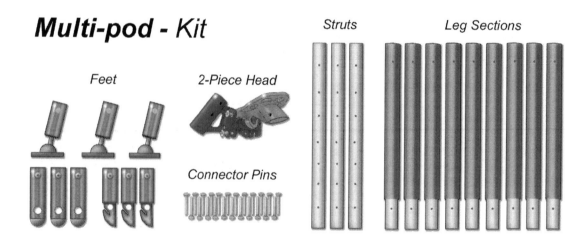

Struts   Leg Sections

Feet   2-Piece Head

Connector Pins

Popular multi-pods on the market today use a bulkhead that braces highly-adjustable legs into a rigid A-frame with a hinged third support leg. Bulkheads also provide a number of anchor attachments. Unlike most tripods, the legs are able to support either compressive or tensile forces to greatly improve functionality. In some cases, the bulkhead can be disassembled to form a stand-alone A-frame brace and a separate gin pole head. Some way of hobbling or anchoring the legs in place is necessary to prevent spreading and the splits. Feet are usually changeable with options suitable for various surfaces or attachments.

Multi-pod - 2-Piece Head

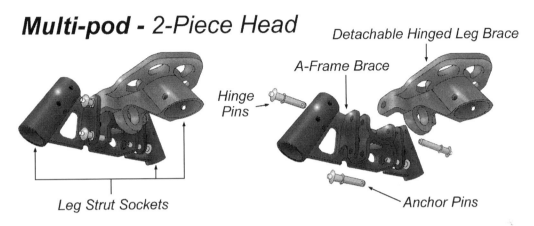

Detachable Hinged Leg Brace

A-Frame Brace

Hinge Pins

Leg Strut Sockets

Anchor Pins

A-frames and gin poles can also be fashioned using lumber, timber, or scavenged metal materials. Improvised A-frames that are properly lashed with ropes, webbing, or strapping can be very strong and suitable for rescue operations. Mountain and wilderness rescue teams who access worksites on foot favor gin poles and A-frames made from materials they find on scene. As with tripods, A-frames and gin poles assembled with scavenged materials can be very useful to firefighters during widespread disaster operations with multiple worksites.

Anchoring and Hobbling: While supporting heavy loads, compression forces against the ground will cause the legs and feet of tripods and multi-pods to "skate" outward and collapse unless they are rigged to hold position. Linking legs and feet together (hobbling) with rope, cord, cable, or chain can prevent legs that are under compression from skating out. It is not necessary to over-tighten when hobbling in this way. A snug, straight fit is all that is needed. Sometimes feet under compression can be firmly planted into cracks or divots in soil to prevent skating without hobbling or anchoring.

Anchoring feet and legs using a combination of lashing, pickets, expansion bolts, rock pro, or conventional anchor attachments can accomplish the same thing when topography makes hobbling difficult. It may be necessary to combine hobbling and anchoring, as would be the case when the hinged leg of a multi-pod bears tensile forces. The legs and feet of the A-frame portion of a multi-pod may be hobbled with cord while the hinged leg might need to be anchored to hold against tension. With proper hauling orientation and hobbling, the weight of the load is usually sufficient to keep feet in contact with the supporting flat surface for portable anchors erected as freestanding tripods with equilateral footprints. But when tripods and multi-pods are set up on uneven surfaces, or hauling orientation directs load forces laterally, the feet must be anchored to prevent unwanted lifting or shifting. You must always anticipate how slack and shock loads will affect the stability of portable anchors. If the portable anchor stability relies on the weight of the load to maintain compression on the legs, the feet may lift or change position if the Climber unexpectedly stands up on terra firma and slacks the rope system. Anchoring the feet or tying the portable anchor to the earth with non-working MA systems can keep legs compressed whether the rope system is taut or slack. Consider whether the sudden tightening of a belay system will maintain enough clearance to prevent feet from being swept out of position. Some portable anchor manufacturers disclaim any ability of their products to be used without anchoring the feet.

Anchoring Feet *- Prevent Skating Or Lifting*

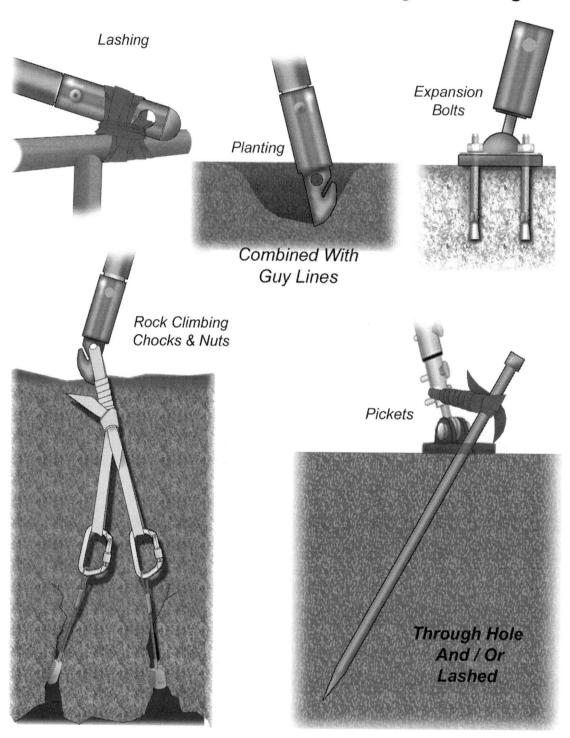

Lashing

Planting

Combined With Guy Lines

Expansion Bolts

Rock Climbing Chocks & Nuts

Pickets

Through Hole And / Or Lashed

Hobbling - Examples

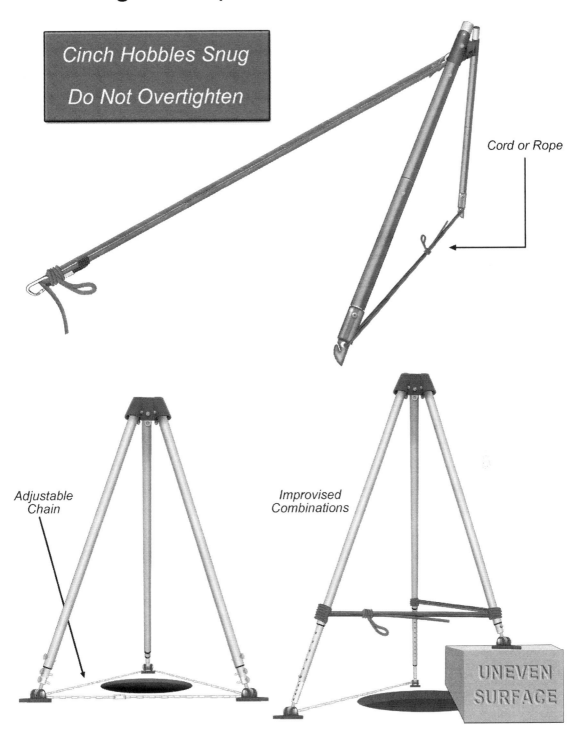

Cinch Hobbles Snug

Do Not Overtighten

Cord or Rope

Adjustable Chain

Improvised Combinations

UNEVEN SURFACE

Force Direction and Stability: There are many considerations for rigging tripods and multi-pods for use as high directionals. It's important to understand how loads act on this equipment as rope systems are tensioned, slacked, and shock loaded. When set up properly, tripods and multi-pods are a safe means of establishing a stable overhead anchor exactly where you need them to overcome the difficulties of running rope systems over an edge. Done improperly, these devices can violently tip and cause the Climber to suddenly drop and experience a severe shock impact. Stability of tripods and multi-pods is primarily influenced by the direction of the forces they are supporting. Usually created by loaded ropes running through directional pulleys, the resulting supported forces should always be directed in a way that keeps the tripod or multi-pod stable. The stability of a tripod or multi-pod can be reasonably predicted by identifying the direction of the forces created by the rope system. In the case of a directional pulley, you can simply imagine it or actually apply false tension on the rope system to see what direction the pulley indicates. The long axis of the pulley connected to the tripod or multi-pod will point out the direction of the forces affecting stability. The direction indicated by the pulley is known as the "resultant angle." Team members should understand this indicator and use it to forecast and monitor how forces act on tripods and multi-pods throughout any operation.

If a freestanding tripod is set up over a manhole with a directional pulley anchored at the head, you can look at the pulley to check the resultant angle and determine stability. In some cases, the resultant angle can change radically as the rope is tensioned and slackened depending on the hauling orientation. The approach and departure angles of the ropes affect the pulley and resultant angle. If everything is set up in a way that the resultant angle points to the area inside the feet (the "footprint"), the freestanding tripod will remain stable. If the rope system is set up in a way that the resultant angle points to the area outside the footprint, the freestanding tripod will tip. One or more legs will lift. To keep this tripod stabile, guy lines could be anchored to tie back the head and oppose the tipping force. However, it's always best to stabilize a freestanding tripod by rigging for resultant angles that are within the footprint area. Multi-pods, A-frames, and gin poles are much better options for establishing a high anchor point where the resultant forces of the rope system will be outside the footprint of a freestanding tripod. Combining guying ("guy line") techniques with multi-pods can provide riggers with an almost unlimited array of bomber high anchor choices.

Force Direction - *Resultant Angles*

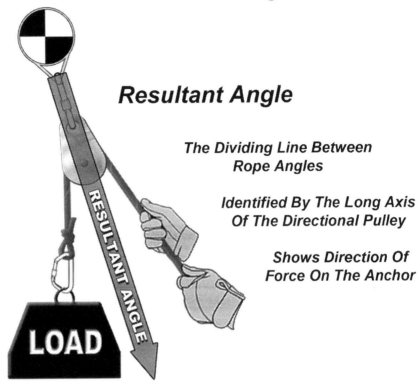

Resultant Angle

*The Dividing Line Between
Rope Angles*

*Identified By The Long Axis
Of The Directional Pulley*

*Shows Direction Of
Force On The Anchor*

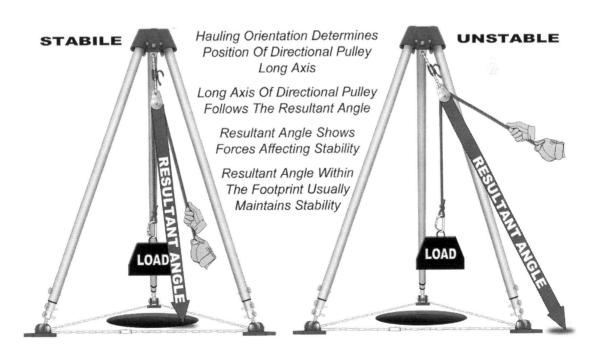

STABILE

UNSTABLE

*Hauling Orientation Determines
Position Of Directional Pulley
Long Axis*

*Long Axis Of Directional Pulley
Follows The Resultant Angle*

*Resultant Angle Shows
Forces Affecting Stability*

*Resultant Angle Within
The Footprint Usually
Maintains Stability*

Guying: Just like your old-school camping tent, guy lines are used to hold up the legs of your A-Frame or gin pole. Guy lines are sometimes used to stabilize tripods. The operating premise of guy line function is to hold the bulkhead and anchor attachments stationary and keep the legs of the apparatus compressed. To hold bulkheads and anchor attachments stationary, guy lines must be angled appropriately on the horizontal plane. Imagine a bird's eye view above the A-frame or gin pole. To keep legs compressed, guying systems must also have the correct vertical angle. Picture a side view of your A-frame or gin pole. Guy lines can be placed to prevent swaying by holding tension against any force that makes the bulkhead move out of position on the horizontal plane, such as gravity, resultant angle forces, wind, etc. To compress the legs, the guy line system must be under hard tension and arranged in a way that develops its own resultant force angle that pushes down where you need it. Resultant forces created by guying systems should also be directed to create stability in the A-frame or gin pole. Doing so can reduce the need for anchoring the feet.

Practical and effective guying systems enable riggers to easily adjust the length and tension of the individual guy lines. In most cases, a guying system is a two-part arrangement. One part is the line (or lines) that holds tension, while the other part is the line (or lines) used to create tension. In actuality, both lines will hold tension against each other, but one line is set up for quick length adjustment while the other is set up as a nonworking mechanical advantage system to pull hard tension. The line set up for adjustment will restrain the tensioning guy and determine the final position of the bulkhead. The arrangement could be one non-working MA system pulling against a single restraining line. Or it could be a single non-working MA pulling against two or more restraining lines. Or it might be two MAs pulling on two restraining lines. You get the idea. Sometimes guy lines are only used to pull tension on the vertical plain. Imagine a hobbled equilateral tripod set up over the top hatch of a cylindrical railcar with a single non-working MA pulling the bulkhead straight down to hold the feet fast. Any number of guy lines can be used in any arrangement to stabilize your portable anchor. But it's important to remember that we're thinking in terms of rescue and keeping systems simple, practical, and quick to set up.

It's important to understand how rope stretch and leverage can affect guying systems. Portable anchors supporting lateral forces can leverage enough strain onto guy lines to cause them to lengthen. Riggers must pay close attention to the angle between guy lines and the vertical plane  created by the A-frame or gin pole legs. Imagine the "arm pits" of the guy lines. If a taut guy line stretches enough under strain, the vertical angle (the arm pit) will become narrower and narrower until the A-frame or gin pole violently snaps over the apex of travel and down to the ground like a mousetrap. This is not good. Think of how the handle on a chain binder creates enough leverage to stretch the chain beyond the apex of travel to snap tight. This also applies to angles between any leg(s) and the plane aligned with any two guy lines. The solution for this hazard is to angle guy lines appropriately so that the rope cannot stretch enough to allow the portable anchor to snap over the apex and to aim the guy line resultant force angles to create the most stability. In situations where compression on the legs is not needed, the most bomber vertical angle for guy lines would be 90°. A 90° angle can sometimes be achieved when guy lines can be anchored on nearby hillsides, cliff faces, structures, etc. The most efficient vertical guying angle is 45°. A 45° angle keeps the portable anchor well away from the break-over point while providing solid compression on legs. **The minimum safe vertical guying angle is 30°.** It's also important to use static rope for guying applications. Guy lines fashioned with non-working MA systems will significantly reduce the risk of failure caused by rope stretch.

Guying - Angle Specifications

Angles Between Taut Guy Lines
And The Vertical Plane
Created By The Legs

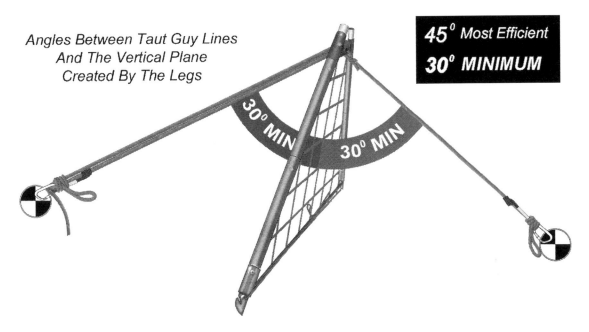

**45° Most Efficient
30° MINIMUM**

A few practical methods can be used to rig guying systems for any application. You can conserve equipment and use a single length of rope to fashion both the non-working MA guys and the restraining guys. Simple 2 to 1 or 3 to 1 MA guys are suitable. Guy lines can easily be hitched or wrapped directly onto the leg struts of many A-frames, gin poles, or tripods to conserve connectors and anchor attachments, as well as to speed up and simplify rigging.

The hinged leg of multi-pods can be used as a form of guy line. Placing the hinged leg where a guy line would be appropriate can significantly simplify rigging and cut setup time. Because the leg is rigid and able to carry compressive or tensile loads, it can sometimes be set up without opposing guy lines

Gin Poles: Gin poles can work well where other forms of portable anchors might not. Work areas that are very tight or hard to access may require the compact size and weight of a small gin pole. Some situations may require dividing up a multi-pod kit to assemble two elevated anchors. Fire companies may only have a ladder to use as an elevated anchor. Whatever the reason, a gin pole can provide a bomber means of elevating an anchor for a directional pulley. Except in the most advanced examples, gin poles require at least three guy lines for adequate horizontal stability and leg compression. It's usually best if a gin pole is rigged to angle the resultant force of the rope system forward of the foot.

Some fire training organizations use ladder gins assembled with only two single-strand guy lines that rely on the weight of the load for stability. Ladder gins of this type can be used, but watch out. Rigging like this is ideal for straining the single-strand guy lines enough that they will elongate to the point of breaking over the apex of travel. Close monitoring of the resultant force angle is important to minimize rope stretch and ensure ladder stability. Better to reduce rope stretch by using two non-working MA guy lines instead of single-strand guy lines. Even better if a restraining guy line can be added in front so the two MA guy lines can be cinched down hard before the load is applied. This will ultimately make it easier and better for optimizing the ladder angle and favorably aiming the resultant force and load direction.

A-frames: A-frames are often oriented parallel with the rope system to better position directional pulleys as close to the edge as possible. When positioned this way, an A-frame can be right on or even over the edge, while still maintaining a clear launching area for the Climber. A-frames positioned this way will be referred to as "parallel." Parallel orientation of an A-frame enables riggers to use anchors that are close to but not over the edge. Choosing anchors that are topside results in faster and simpler rigging. Scrambling or rappelling over the edge to set up and monitor guying anchors can be very time consuming and difficult to do. Parallel positioning is also a great adaptation for dealing with uneven topography. Parallel A-frames tend to strain guying systems less and may reduce the risk of lines overstretching and failing. With favorable angles of resultant forces, parallel A-frames usually require no more than two guy lines. If a multi-pod uses a hinged leg, a single MA guy line can work to stabilize a parallel A-frame.

Lateral Forces: Complex operations may lead to rigging with heavy lateral forces acting on portable anchors. With proper anchoring and guying, multi-pods can be set up to support a load from almost any direction. The hinged leg feature can sometimes provide support to an A-frame under lateral strain without using guy lines.

Guying - *Basic Elements*

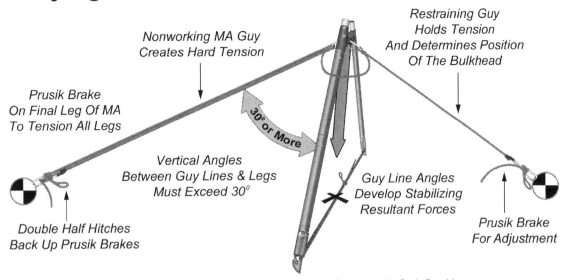

Nonworking MA Guy
Creates Hard Tension

Restraining Guy
Holds Tension
And Determines Position
Of The Bulkhead

Prusik Brake
On Final Leg Of MA
To Tension All Legs

30° or More

Vertical Angles
Between Guy Lines & Legs
Must Exceed 30°

Guy Line Angles
Develop Stabilizing
Resultant Forces

Double Half Hitches
Back Up Prusik Brakes

Prusik Brake
For Adjustment

*Above Shown Using A Single Length Of Rope To Assemble Both Guy Lines

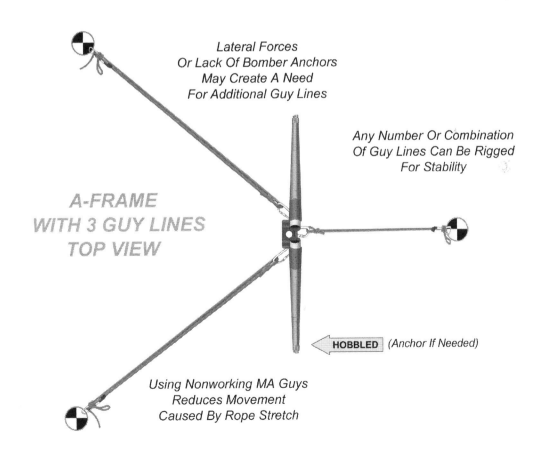

Lateral Forces
Or Lack Of Bomber Anchors
May Create A Need
For Additional Guy Lines

Any Number Or Combination
Of Guy Lines Can Be Rigged
For Stability

A-FRAME
WITH 3 GUY LINES
TOP VIEW

HOBBLED (Anchor If Needed)

Using Nonworking MA Guys
Reduces Movement
Caused By Rope Stretch

Guying - Rope System Resultant Force

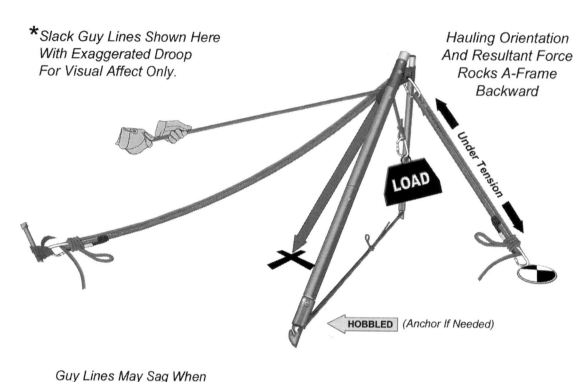

*Slack Guy Lines Shown Here With Exaggerated Droop For Visual Affect Only.

Hauling Orientation And Resultant Force Rocks A-Frame Backward

Under Tension

HOBBLED (Anchor If Needed)

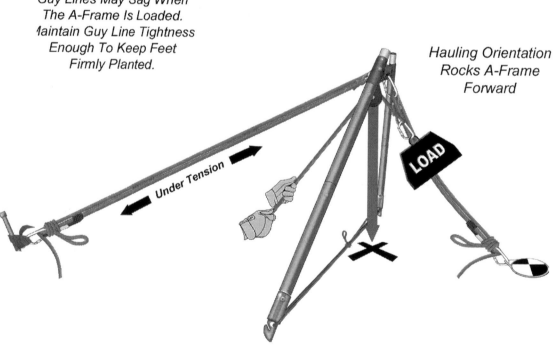

Guy Lines May Sag When The A-Frame Is Loaded. Maintain Guy Line Tightness Enough To Keep Feet Firmly Planted.

Hauling Orientation Rocks A-Frame Forward

Under Tension

Guying - Leg Positioning & Tension

IN THIS EXAMPLE: *Rope System Orientation And Resultant Force Stays The Same. The Position Of The Legs Are Changed.*

*Slack Guy Lines Shown Here With Exaggerated Droop For Visual Affect Only.

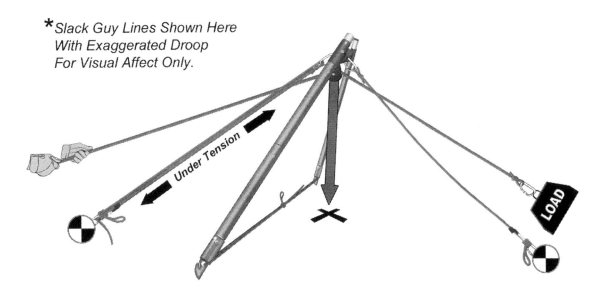

- *Consider Rope System Resultant Forces When Positioning Legs*
- *Place Beefier Guy Lines And Anchors Where They Are Needed Most*
- *Anchor Availability May Influence Guy Placement And Leg Positioning*

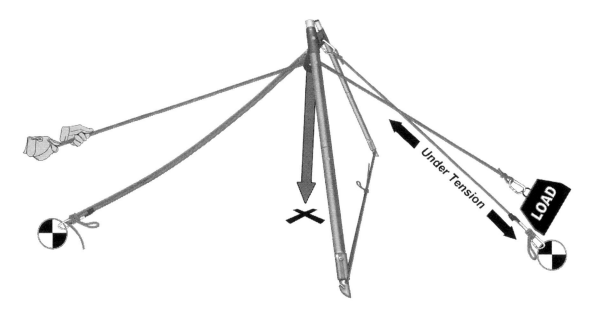

Multi-pod - *A-Frame Supported By Hinged Leg*

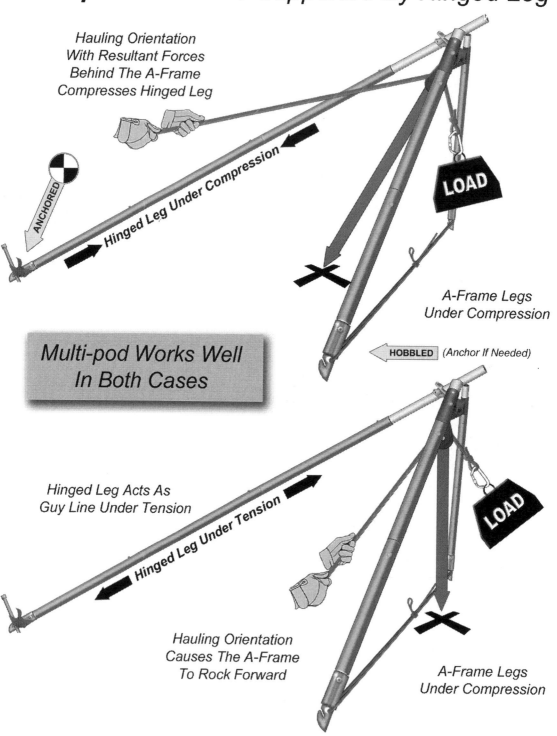

Hauling Orientation
With Resultant Forces
Behind The A-Frame
Compresses Hinged Leg

ANCHORED

Hinged Leg Under Compression

A-Frame Legs
Under Compression

*Multi-pod Works Well
In Both Cases*

HOBBLED (Anchor If Needed)

Hinged Leg Acts As
Guy Line Under Tension

Hinged Leg Under Tension

Hauling Orientation
Causes The A-Frame
To Rock Forward

A-Frame Legs
Under Compression

Multi-pod - Lateral Forces

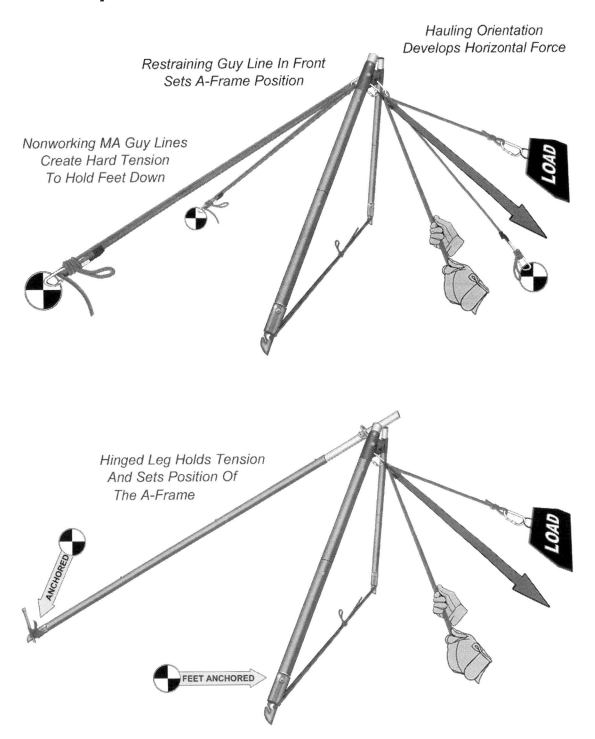

Hauling Orientation
Develops Horizontal Force

Restraining Guy Line In Front
Sets A-Frame Position

Nonworking MA Guy Lines
Create Hard Tension
To Hold Feet Down

LOAD

Hinged Leg Holds Tension
And Sets Position Of
The A-Frame

ANCHORED

FEET ANCHORED

LOAD

Multi-pod - Perpendicular A-Frame

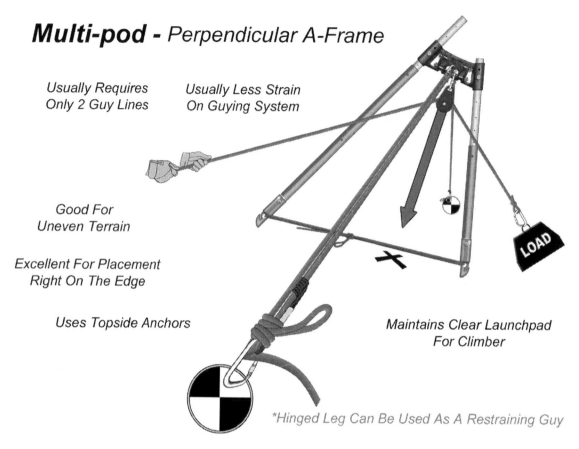

Usually Requires Only 2 Guy Lines

Usually Less Strain On Guying System

Good For Uneven Terrain

Excellent For Placement Right On The Edge

Uses Topside Anchors

Maintains Clear Launchpad For Climber

*Hinged Leg Can Be Used As A Restraining Guy

Multi-pod - Gin Pole (Mono-pod)

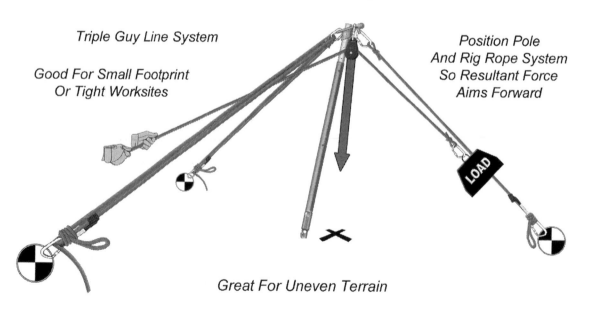

Triple Guy Line System

Good For Small Footprint Or Tight Worksites

Position Pole And Rig Rope System So Resultant Force Aims Forward

Great For Uneven Terrain

Multi-pod - Retrofitting

* Rigging A High Directional
Onto A Loaded Line

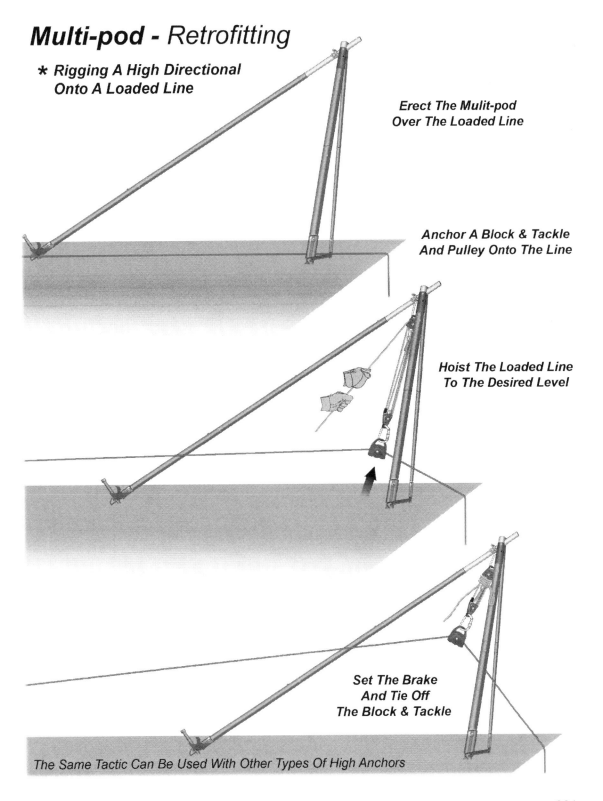

Erect The Mulit-pod
Over The Loaded Line

Anchor A Block & Tackle
And Pulley Onto The Line

Hoist The Loaded Line
To The Desired Level

Set The Brake
And Tie Off
The Block & Tackle

The Same Tactic Can Be Used With Other Types Of High Anchors

Multi-pod - Examples

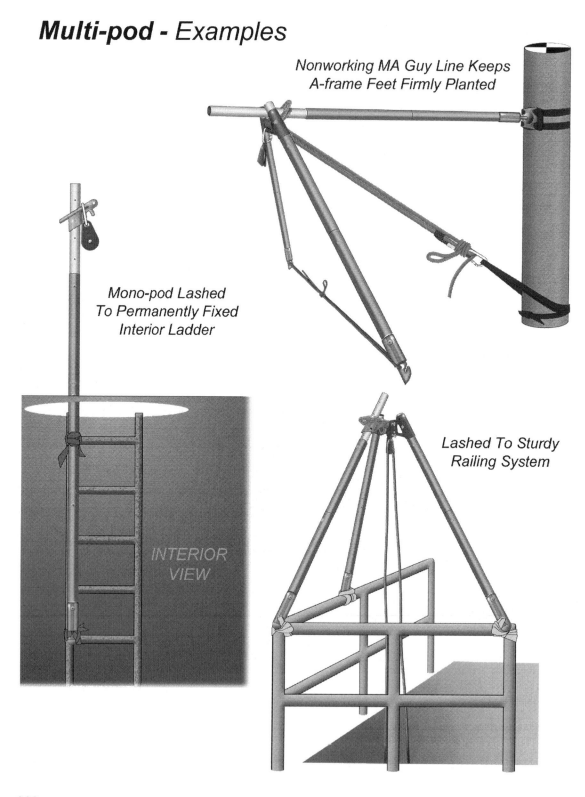

Nonworking MA Guy Line Keeps
A-frame Feet Firmly Planted

Mono-pod Lashed
To Permanently Fixed
Interior Ladder

INTERIOR
VIEW

Lashed To Sturdy
Railing System

12 Belaying

Belaying

Not to be confused with fall prevention measures like travel-restricting leashes, belay systems are used to back up main support systems and deal with accidental falls once they have occurred. Backing up climbing systems to rectify falls and any resulting harmful impact is an absolute necessity in the rescue profession. The "belay everything" mentality is the crux of an overall culture of safety that must be fostered by every professional rescue team. Belaying methods and systems are usually simple, but they require an in-depth level of understanding by every team member. Belaying is definitely one operational element that should not be taught or learned by rote. Very dangerous conditions can develop on a worksite when teams work with a superficial level of understanding of belay concepts. All team members must comprehend the attributes and limitations of belay systems and be able to recognize when belays are working well and when they're not. Full understanding of belay concepts enables teams to coordinate actions and better support effective belay operations. Climbers must understand that if they rappel with a jerky flow or descend too fast, the Belay Person will not be able to keep pace and the system will lock up. If a Haul Team hits its stride and raises too fast, the Belay Person will fall behind or tire out. If haulers use a "heave-ho" style and develop a pulsing rhythm during a raise, the belay system will probably alternate between being too tight and too slack. When team members know how an effective belay must work, they will carry out their individual tasks in a manner that contributes to flawless belaying.

The basic premise of any rescue belay system is to seamlessly take over for main climbing supports when they fail and to safely limit any impact that results during the transition. To hold these desired attributes, backup systems must be able to immediately capture an accidental fall before the Climber picks up much downward speed and must provide sufficient cushioning without damaging the ropes. There are manufactured belay instruments designed to allow workers to move about in industrial settings that work automatically when a fall occurs. Most are not sturdy enough for rescue workloads or are not adaptable for over-the-side or up-climbing rescue situations. Belay systems that are specifically engineered for rescue work are just beginning to emerge on the market, but even these are not completely automatic for most over-the-side or up-climbing situations. The most reliable belay systems combine simple rigging and competent operators for effective backup.

There are many ways to skin this cat depending on what you're doing. This book will show how to use three basic belay systems that adapt very well to over-the-side and up-climbing rescue operations.

- **Tandem Prusik Belays:** This method hitches two anchored 3-wrap prusiks in tandem to the belay line. With a competent Operator, this rig is a very reliable means of providing fall arrest capabilities with built-in shock dampening qualities for over-the-side operations. Tandem prusiks cause minimal rope damage, even when catching severe falls. The tandem prusik belay will be considered the "best practice" choice for lowering, raising, and rappelling evolutions described in this book.

- **Münter Belays**: This technique capitalizes on the adjustability and holding characteristics of a Münter hitch that is tied directly onto the belay line. The Münter is usually tied onto an anchored compatible (HMS) carabiner, but it can also be hitched directly onto an anchor such as a round bar or pipe. Münter belays can be used for over-the-side operations, but they are usually used for overhead climbing situations in the rescue setting. Simple Münter belays are limited to single-person loads.

- **Traveling Self-Belays:** Climbers can protect themselves by moving their own belay attachments as they work. Some situations may require Climbers to manage their own belay attachments as they move vertically. Rapid intervention Climbers may need to use lines that are already over the side for their own fall protection as they rappel to help an injured teammate. Climbers may have to ascend up the lines they were lowered on if ropes become fouled or tangled. Traveling self-belays are movable attachments on fixed lines. Double lanyard attachments may also be considered to be traveling self-belays.

General Belay Rigging Considerations

Whichever belaying method is used, there are important rigging and operational considerations common to them all. The following points can affect all of the above-mentioned belay methods.

Independence: The safest belay systems are anchored to objects that are separate and independent from other parts of the rope rescue rigging. Optimally, the main support system and the belay system should each be connected to their own anchor objects. Fall-arresting measures that utilize independent anchors and rigging are referred to as "true belays." Avoid tying all of your gravity-defying eggs onto one basket. Huge objects that are obviously bombproof can be shared, but separate anchor attachments should be rigged for belay systems.

Military and law enforcement disciplines routinely use single ropes and employ backups that depend on the main support rope and anchor. The fall arrest method of pulling tension on a single rappel rope from below to stop an out-of-control Climber was commonly used in the fire service for many years. This "Fireman's Belay" technique is an example of a "conditional belay." Conditional belays rely on the integrity of the main support system for fall arrest measures. Fire service rescue organizations should only consider these kinds of belays as a last resort in very unusual conditions.

Ergonomics: Rig belays so that the Operator will be able to comfortably withstand the working conditions for the duration of the operation. Doing so greatly favors effective fall arrest if an emergency actually occurs. It's likely that things will not go well if a Belay Person is in pain or is fatigued because he or she has to crouch down or strain awkwardly to work the belay system. Assemble rigging that enables Belayers to safely stand or sit comfortably with a good view of the worksite and plenty of room to work. Forecast how the belay rigging might affect the Operator should a fall suddenly snap the rigging tight.

Vigilance: Fall arrest belays require constant attention. Whenever a Climber is connected to a belay system, the Belay Operator is considered on duty and expected to focus on the job at hand and to keep the rigging properly adjusted. This is true for staffed belays and traveling self-belays. When someone is assigned to a belay position, that person is expected to stay in place and ready to catch a fall without interruption until the Climber is off the belay. When using a traveling self-belay, a Climber must readjust the belay connection along with any movement of the main support system. It is not acceptable for Belayers to let go of tandem prusik or Münter rigging when a Climber holds position for a long time. Belayers using tandem prusik or Münter rigging must adopt a "smoke alarm" mentality and remain ready to arrest a fall for the duration of any vertical operation. Situations that warrant locking and tying off belay rigging can arise. In these cases, tandem prusik rigging can be set snug and then tied off in a way that maintains desirable shock-dampening characteristics. Münters can be mule-hitched. Traveling self-belays only require handling when the Climber needs to move.

Belay Vector: Think about the placement of the belay rope on the landscape and how it will affect the Climber should a fall occur. The path the rope takes from the belay device all the way to the Climber should be as direct as possible. Anticipate the shape the rope will take when it tightens under a load. If the belay line is straight and routes directly to the Climber, fall arresting will be much more effective. Straight, direct belays usually work more smoothly.

Directionals: Over-the-side belays routed through directional pulleys risk long falls if a pulley connection fails. Imagine a belay line threaded through a pulley that is anchored onto an overhead tree limb before it connects to the Climber. If the tree limb breaks while the Climber is over the side, he or she will experience a very long fall before the belay engages. The belay will eventually catch the fall, but the Climber may not survive the impact. The same is true of lateral directionals. Generally speaking, it is considered best practice to route a belay rope directly to the Climber without incorporating directional pulleys.

EXAMPLE: If the main climbing support line routes through a high directional mounted on a tripod, the preferred belay practice would be to place the belay rope on the ground where it goes over the edge and into a shaft. If the tripod fails, the belay would tighten and engage before the Climber could fall very far.

In some cases, conditions warrant using the inferior practice of routing belay ropes through directional pulleys to avoid hazards. Evaluate every situation, and place belays for the best possible fall arrest outcome.

It's important to remember how forces are affected as ropes wind through directional pulleys. Unless the angle in the rope created by a directional pulley is 120° or greater, forces on the pulley anchor will be amplified. Any shock load from arresting a fall would be greatest where the belay rope threads through a directional pulley. Picture a 200lb firefighter preparing to rappel from the tip of a fully extended aerial ladder as part of a demonstration at a public event. If the belay rope for that firefighter goes from a ground anchor and then up through a directional pulley hanging below the ladder tip, any accidental fall will put an amplified strain on the tip of the ladder. Yikes! Now suppose the firefighter stumbles as he or she transitions over the ladder tip to the rappelling rope resulting in a fall of one, two, or even three feet before the belay engages. Depending on the angle of the belay rope, the force at the pulley could easily exceed the capacity of the aerial ladder. Yikes again! A rope anchored to the ladder tip with a traveling self-belay would probably be a better choice for the demonstration.

Rope Length: You already know that life safety rope has a specified minimum amount of built in stretch. These minimum elongation properties are intended to provide cushioning for the purpose of protecting Climbers, equipment, and the rope itself. The amount of actual linear elongation depends on the length of the rope that is under tension. Without analyzing the obvious too closely, it stands to reason that longer ropes will stretch a longer distance and provide a bouncier, cushier ride for Climbers when compared to shorter ropes. Longer lengths of the same rope will absorb more impact forces than shorter lengths. Think of the bungee jumper leaping off a bridge with a long elastic cord tied to his ankles. Now picture him doing the same thing with a 5-foot bungee cord. This would not be good; he'd get pretty shaken up. The same principle is true of ropes used for belays. Whether the rope is a low-stretch life safety rope or a dynamic climbing rope, length affects the shock-absorbing performance.

When a Climber is at the edge of a cliff before a lowering operation, the belay line will be at its shortest length and at its lowest level of shock absorbing performance. The same is true when the Climber is near the edge after a raising operation, or at the beginning or end of an overhead climb. When the belay rope is short, it makes sense for the Belay Person to snug up the system a bit more. It should not be too tight, though. The Climber should understand the need for this and work through any inconvenience created by the tight belay line. Establishing belay anchors further away from the edge will lengthen the rope and add shock-absorbing ability.

Edge Hazard: Climbers standing next to the edge of a vertical drop while their belay line is at ground level create a severe hazard. People can feel a false sense of security standing near an edge when they're connected to a belay line. However, because the connection point on the Climber's harness is elevated 4 or more feet above grade, they would have to fall at least that far before the belay line would even begin to tighten. Factor in the shortness of the belay rope in those circumstances, and the result is a very nasty impact at the bottom of 6 or more foot fall. The same is true when a main climbing rope is routed through a high directional pulley on a tripod or A-frame with the belay placed on the ground. If the A-frame should fail while the Climber is maneuvering over the edge, a disastrous fall would result. In that case, the main support line(s) and the belay would bottom out at roughly the same time, making the impact felt by the Climber even worse.

The simplest remedy is to use practices that keep the belay connection on the harness as close to ground level as possible and snug up the belay line whenever the Climber is working on the edge. There are advanced rigging options for dynamic directionals connected to overhead anchors, but it's much simpler, and probably more effective, to adopt a body posture that's more appropriate for working at the edge. The method of leaning back on the ropes and doing leg presses on the sill of a window or cliff edge should be a thing of the past. Be smart about it, and kneel down at the edge to make those transitions to vertical. Use an action similar to getting on or off of a horse to transition safely over or up the edge of a vertical drop. Doing so keeps the belay connection on your harness at a safer level until you can move away from the hazard. It may sound a bit hokey, and may not be good for photos, but it works well and greatly influences safety.

Harness Connections: Belays should be attached to the appropriate rings or loops on the Climber's rescue harness. Prudent practice and OSHA regulations require that belays be connected to harness attachments that are separate from the main support rope attachment. Various attachment points on rescue harnesses are load specified. Some attachments are designed and placed for work positioning. Some are only suitable for carrying light objects like extra gear. However, most modern rescue harnesses have a number of full-weight capacity rings to choose from. In the vertical environment, the best choices for belay connections are full-strength attachment points that are above the Climber's center of gravity. Higher attachments on the harness will more favorably align the Climber's body position when the belay system arrests a fall. Sternum and dorsal attachments will cause the Climber's body to straighten out and take a more friendly 'feet down' position. Connecting belays to pelvic-level rings can cause the Climber's body to "taco" backwards upon impact. Obviously, this is not good. Some schools teach threading the belay through the sternum ring before connecting to the pelvic attachment.

Rigging belays in this way can cause unwanted compression at the impact of arresting a fall. Don't do it!

Because belay systems are not under tension during normal working conditions, the harness connection will tend to flop around quite a lot. This can become a nuisance for the Climber and cause carabiners to rotate, cross-load, and even unlock. Tying the belay rope directly onto the harness attachment ring reduces the nuisance and removes the problems associated with carabiner orientation. A figure-8 follow-through with a tight loop, or a double overhand noose tied directly onto the harness ring is a clean attachment and works very well. If frequent connecting and disconnecting from the belay is part of the job at hand, use an auto-locking carabiner to make the harness connection. To eliminate cross-loading, tie the belay rope to the auto-locking carabiner using a tight double overhand noose. Doing so will keep the carabiner spine properly aligned.

Communications: It's important to establish a set of basic belay-specific terms for confirming actions and alerting conditions that affect the fall-arresting system. The terms listed below are commonly used by many rescue disciplines. Whatever terms your team decides to use, they should be easily distinguishable and understood in difficult listening conditions.

- "On belay" or "I'm on belay": Announces to the Belayer and the team that the Climber is attached to the belay rope and in need of fall-arresting protection. The Climber usually calls out this command as he or she needs to approach the edge or move into climbing position. Think of the command as a question to confirm if the Belayer and rigging are ready. This command must be called out in a loud and clear manner to alert the entire worksite.

- "Belay On" or "Belay is on": Announcement from the Belayer that the fall-arresting system is staffed and ready to protect the Climber. It is almost exclusively used in response to the "On belay" inquiry from the Climber. This command must be called out in a loud and clear manner to alert the entire worksite.

- "Climbing": Announces to the Belayer and the team that the Climber is ready to go "hot" and take action to go over the edge or begin climbing up. This command must be called out in a loud and clear manner to alert the entire worksite.

- "Climb On": Announced by the Team Leader to grant permission to the Climber to move over the edge or to climb up. The Leader makes this announcement after confirming that the entire team is ready for the Climber to go hot. This command must be called out in a loud and clear manner to alert the entire worksite.

- "Falling": Announced by the Climber to alert the team that he or she is losing foot purchase and beginning to fall out of control. Once announced, the entire team should loudly repeat the command while taking action to brace and arrest the fall of the Climber. Parroting confirms comprehension and relays the message to anyone who may have missed or misunderstood the command.

Tandem Prusik Belays

Best practice for lowering, raising, or rappelling over the side. Because prusik hitches grab securely and slip when overloaded, they are perfect for belay rigging. Using prusiks in tandem to catch a fall is not about doubling the holding power of the rope-grabs. It's actually a little more complicated than that. It's less about boosting the holding power and more about backing up one prusik with another. Because they slip in overloaded conditions, this rigging concept enables one prusik to engage and slip to slow down the fall of the load just before the second prusik grabs the rope. Once the second prusik engages, the first prusik will be exposed to a lighter load and slipping will cease. Slightly slowing down the fall before the second prusik grips the rope will lighten the forces on the second prusik and subject the Climber to less impact.

Of course, this rigging concept can be overwhelmed if impact forces are extremely severe. But unless you're belaying an M1 tank, a couple of prusiks on a ½ inch life-safety rope will *catch* the load. The trick is to catch the falling Climber without scrambling his or her internal organs like an omelet. A good tandem prusik belay requires a competent Operator and a well-coordinated team to maintain conditions that are free of the potential for severe impact. The key ingredient here is to precisely manage belay line tension and slack. The prusik hitches and belay rope must be handled and manipulated in a way that maintains optimum tension. Optimum belay tension allows the Climber to move as needed without slack in the belay line. However, the belay system is not used to add support to the load under normal operating conditions. The belay line should appear taut without supporting or hindering the Climber. Belay ropes should not sag or droop. Drooping slack in the belay line will result in a drop exceeding several feet if the main line supports fail. A drop of several feet can create severe impact forces capable of damaging equipment and injuring Climbers, especially when the belay and main line ropes are relatively short (as would be the case at the beginning of a rappel, or the end of a raising operation). Whenever belay lines are short, there is less real rope elongation available to absorb shock. A good belay should engage before the Climber has a chance to drop more than a foot or so, even less when belay ropes are short.

Rigging Tandem Prusik Belays: To work properly, the prusiks must be rigged and handled precisely. Start with two prusik loops made from 8mm cord, one loop 16 inches long, and the other 22 inches long. Connect the two loops to a ½ inch life safety rope using 3-wrap prusik hitches. Make sure any bend knots on the loops end up midway between the hitch wraps and the loop ends. The shortest loop should be positioned on the rope so that it is closest to the anchor. The longer loop should be closest to the load (Climber). Orienting and aligning the hitches identically will make handling easier once operations begin. Tie the prusiks onto the rope so that the elbows on the hitches match each other. Avoid offsetting elbows (one up, one down). The hitches should be tight. Now clip both loops together with a general use "D"-shaped carabiner, and connect to the belay anchor. Orient the carabiner with the gate facing down to prevent unwanted rotation and cross-loading as the system moves with handling. With everything hitched and connected, pull a little false tension on the belay rope, and extend the prusik loops to make sure the rigging is correct. In this semi-tensioned state, the hitches should look identical and have a gap between them, but close enough together for easy handling. A gap of about 1 inch is ideal. Longer or shorter prusik loops can be used, but the size proportions must result in a gap between the hitches for proper belay performance. The belay station should now be ready for safety checking.

Handling Tandem Prusik Belays: Tandem prusik rigging is not a passive, or automatic, belay system. The system requires a well-trained, well-practiced Operator to safely arrest accidental falls. It's a mistake to regard the belay position as an easy assignment for personnel with superficial skills attained in the academy ten years prior. It's not a matter of just holding the prusik knots so the Climber can pull the rope down the hill. Tandem prusik rigging requires alert attention and good technique.

Lowering and Rappelling: Start by getting into position. Get close to the rigging and assume a stance that enables comfortable handling for the duration of the operation. Stack the standing line directly below the belay system. For lowering or rappelling, use whichever hand is closest to the anchor to grip both prusik hitches in a palm-down manner. Use that hand to gather the hitches together and pull the loops snug against the anchor and in line with the fall line. It's okay if the hitches butt together when handled this way. Now use the wrist of the gripping hand to rotate the prusik hitches upward 45° to 90° away from the fall line. Rotating the hitches out of alignment this way greatly improves fall-catching performance. With the prusiks held in position with one hand, use your other hand to grasp the belay rope in a palm-down manner on the Climber side of the rigging. Rotate this hand 45° to 90° as well to improve grip strength. Use this "downhill" hand to pull tension in the belay rope against the Climber. Both hands should now be a foot or so apart and pulling the Climber and the anchor connections toward each other. Finally, disengage thumbs forming a "false grip" to prevent injury should a fall violently snap the system tight. A small arch of rope should develop between both hands, and it should look like the Belayer has his or her hands on a steering wheel. Let's call this the "ready position."

When things get underway, the Belay Operator will feel increasing tension on the downhill hand as the Climber moves lower. It's up to the Belay Operator to decide when to pay out more belay line based on the amount of tension he or she feels on the downhill hand. Without letting go, quickly slide the downhill hand back toward the anchor to pull additional rope up and through the prusiks to pay out more line. This action should transition quickly from the ready position to pulling rope and then back to the ready position. Good form extends the belay rope in short segments to avoid accidentally paying out too much line. The weight of long lines can be mistaken for downward movement of the Climber. Extending the belay in short segments can help the Belayer better distinguish between Climber movement and heavy ropes.

Again, tandem prusik belay rigging is not a passive, or automatic, belay. In the past, it was common to see firefighters simply holding the prusik knots stationary while the Climber pulled the belay  line down the cliff. The problem with this practice is twofold. First, it requires the prusik hitches to be oriented in-line with the fall line to enable the rope to slide through the knots. Prusik hitches that are lined up this way are slow to engage and catch the rope when the Climber falls. Lined-up prusiks also require the Belayer to let go of, or even push the hitches downhill, to engage and catch a falling Climber. Second, it's nearly impossible to distinguish downward movement of the Climber from the weight of long heavy ropes pulling on the belay system when the hitches are simply held stationary. Using tandem prusiks as a passive belay with in-line hitches commonly results in severely drooping belay ropes. This is not good.

Raising: Start by getting into position. Get close to the rigging, and assume a stance that enables comfortable handling for the duration of the operation. Stack the standing line directly below the belay system. Assume the ready position, but hold the hitches with the downhill hand and grab the standing line with the uphill hand. It's important to rotate the hitches 45° to 90° out of alignment with the fall line. Use the uphill hand to pull up and through the prusik hitches to take up belay rope. When raising, the Belayer simply holds the rigging snug and pulls rope through as needed to keep the belay line taught.

Operating Tips: Belayers can develop severe muscle fatigue from the repetitive action of pulling up rope during long-duration raising operations. Slowing down the overall raising operation to a more sustainable pace can minimize problems with "arm pump." The raising operation can also be paused while the Belayer switches to the other side of the rigging to change hand positions. When extended long distances over the side, hanging ropes become quite heavy. It can be difficult to maintain good belaying form as ropes get heavier. Belayers can boost strength and increase raising stamina by pulling the prusik hitches uphill to take up rope and then quickly sliding the knots downhill while pulling slack through at the same time. This method should be reserved for times when ropes are heavy and difficult to manage. Another solution for dealing with heavy ropes during raising operations is to have a helper pull tension on the working section, downhill of the belay rigging.

Catching Falls: When held properly, tandem prusik belays will engage themselves instantly if the Climber suddenly drops. The belay rope and rigging will snap tight and pull out of the Belayer's hands. More gradual drops, as can occur if a Climber loses control during a rappel, may require the Belayer to quickly push the prusik hitches downhill (sometimes referred to as "throwing the knots") to engage them manually. EXAMPLE: throwing the knots downhill to engage the prusiks is the proper response to a "falling" announcement from a Climber even if the belay system doesn't snap tight.

Tying Off Tandem Prusik Belays: To preserve shock-absorbing characteristics, a small amount of slack should be adjusted into the standing line whenever tandem prusik belays are set snug and tied off. Do not make the mistake of setting the prusiks and then tying a mule hitch on top of them. Tying off this way does not allow the prusiks to work as needed. Another mistake is to pull the belay rope taut and then tie the standing rope tightly onto an anchor. The standing part of the belay rope must be tied off with about 2 feet of drooping slack between the tandem prusiks and the anchor. Doing this will allow the prusiks to engage to arrest a fall and then slip to dampen impact forces on the Climber.

Accidental Lockups: It's not uncommon for tandem prusik belays to occasionally over-tighten and lock up the hitches during lowering operations. This usually occurs when the Climber rappels or is lowered a little faster than the Belay person can pay out rope. To recover from a locked-up belay, simply raise the Climber enough to loosen the prusik hitches. This can easily be accomplished by pulling a perpendicular vector on the main lowering line. Stop the operation, and grab the main line at a mid-rope point, pulling it sideways. This kind of vector pull will raise the Climber a bit and relieve tension on the belay rope. When the belay is slackened, the prusik hitches can be released and the operation can continue. Load releasing hitches between the belay anchor and the belay rigging can be a remedy for severe lockups where a vector pull will not provide enough slack to loosen prusiks that are tightened rock-hard.

Tandem Prusik Belays - *Setup*

* 1/2" Life Safety Rope With 8mm Prusik Loops

* 16" And 22" Long Prusik Loops *(Before Hitching)*

* 1" Gap Between Hitches When Loops Are Extended

* Hitches Oriented The Same

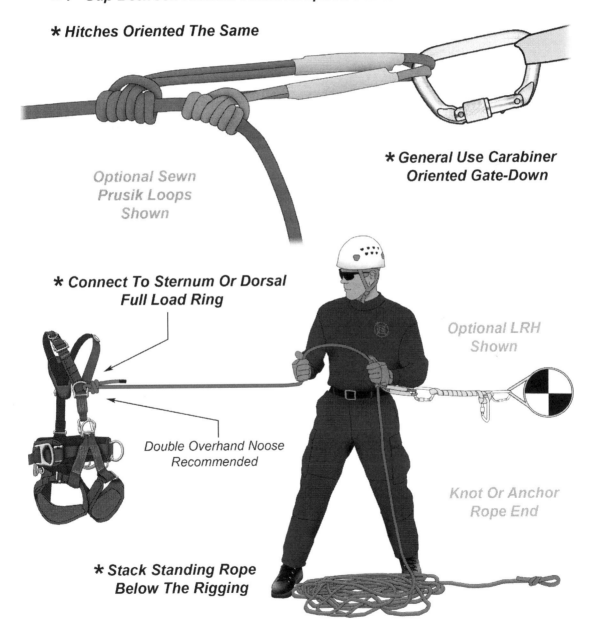

Optional Sewn
Prusik Loops
Shown

* General Use Carabiner
Oriented Gate-Down

* Connect To Sternum Or Dorsal
Full Load Ring

Optional LRH
Shown

Double Overhand Noose
Recommended

Knot Or Anchor
Rope End

* Stack Standing Rope
Below The Rigging

Tandem Prusik Belays - *Functional Grip*

LOWERING

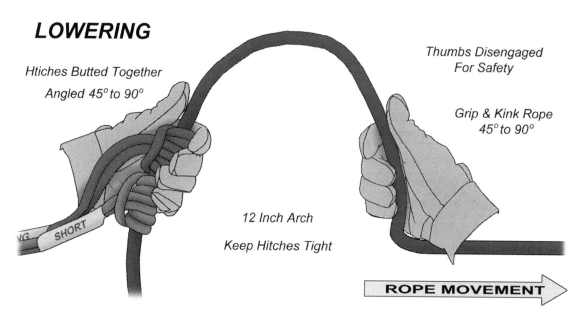

Htiches Butted Together
Angled 45° to 90°

*Thumbs Disengaged
For Safety*

*Grip & Kink Rope
45° to 90°*

SHORT

12 Inch Arch

Keep Hitches Tight

ROPE MOVEMENT

ANCHOR

CLIMBER

RAISING

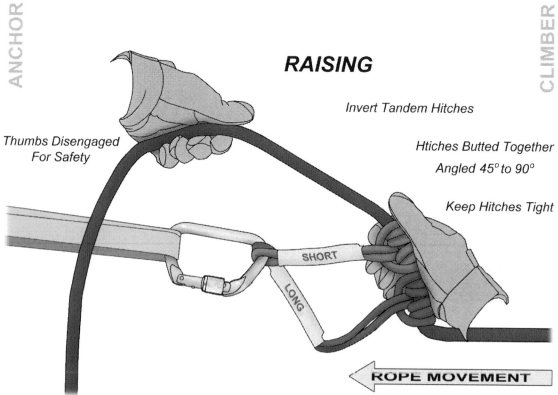

Invert Tandem Hitches

*Thumbs Disengaged
For Safety*

Htiches Butted Together
Angled 45° to 90°

Keep Hitches Tight

SHORT

LONG

ROPE MOVEMENT

Tandem Prusik Belays - *Basic Lowering*

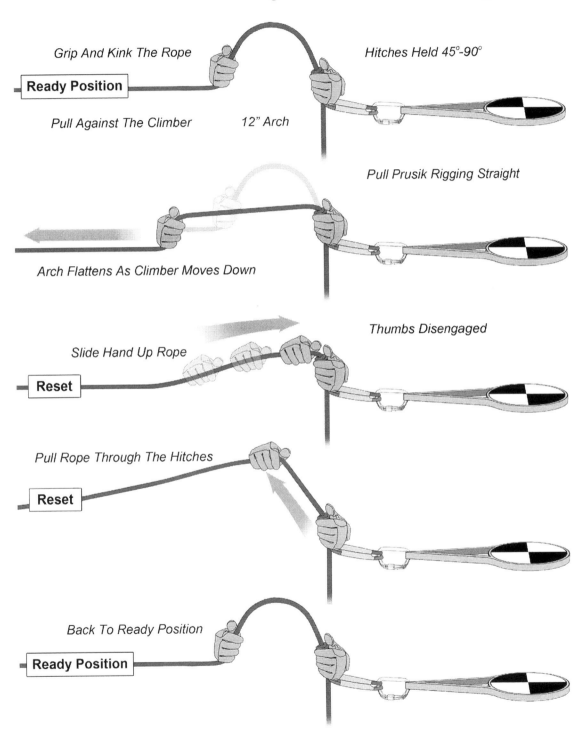

Grip And Kink The Rope

Ready Position

Hitches Held 45°-90°

Pull Against The Climber

12" Arch

Pull Prusik Rigging Straight

Arch Flattens As Climber Moves Down

Thumbs Disengaged

Slide Hand Up Rope

Reset

Pull Rope Through The Hitches

Reset

Back To Ready Position

Ready Position

Tandem Prusik Belays - *Basic Raising*

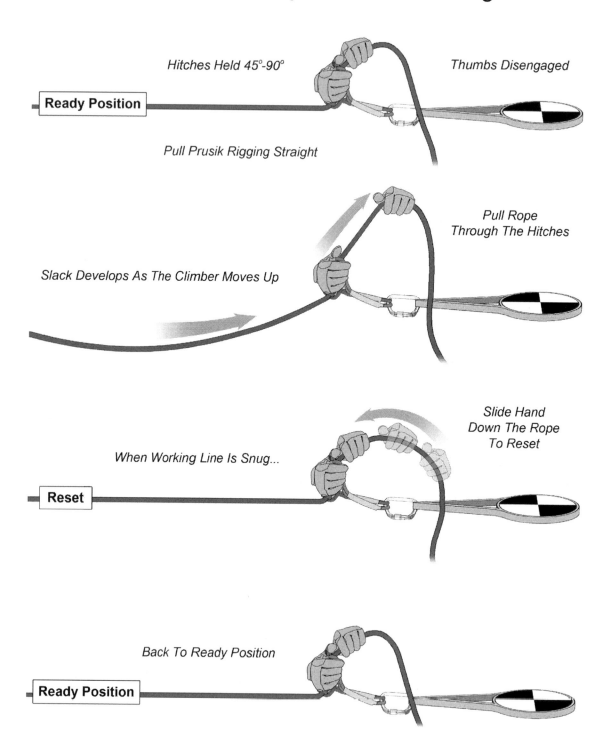

Hitches Held 45°-90°

Thumbs Disengaged

Ready Position

Pull Prusik Rigging Straight

Pull Rope
Through The Hitches

Slack Develops As The Climber Moves Up

When Working Line Is Snug...

Slide Hand
Down The Rope
To Reset

Reset

Back To Ready Position

Ready Position

Tandem Prusik Belays - *Catching A Fall*

Handling Technique And Hitch Orientation Is Critical

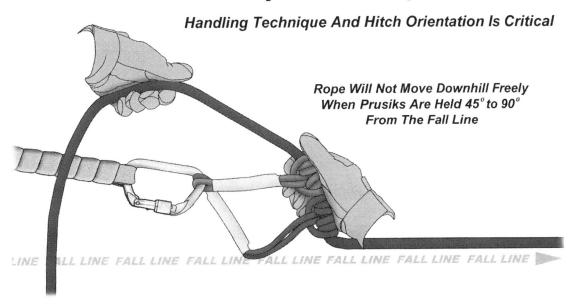

*Rope Will Not Move Downhill Freely
When Prusiks Are Held 45° to 90°
From The Fall Line*

LINE FALL LINE FALL LINE FALL LINE FALL LINE FALL LINE FALL LINE FALL LINE ▷

Properly Offset Prusiks Instantly Grip To Stop Unwanted Downhill Movement

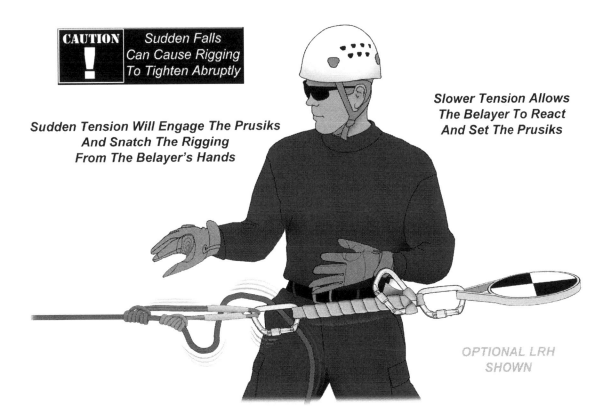

CAUTION ! *Sudden Falls Can Cause Rigging To Tighten Abruptly*

*Sudden Tension Will Engage The Prusiks
And Snatch The Rigging
From The Belayer's Hands*

*Slower Tension Allows
The Belayer To React
And Set The Prusiks*

*OPTIONAL LRH
SHOWN*

Tandem Prusik Belays - *Tying Off*

A Practical And Easy Method For Allowing The Belay Person To Go Hands-Free Without Additional Hardware

*   **Climber Must Remain Stationary**

*   **Remove Belay Line Slack - Set Prusik Hitches Tight**

*   **Mule Hitch Standing Rope Onto The Spine Of The Load Carabiner**

*   **Drooping Slack Between Prusik And Mule Hitches**

*   **Preserves Shock-Absorbing Capability - Allows Prusiks To Slip**

Rope Weight Will Likely Cause
The Carabiner To Invert
And Orient In A Gate-Up Position

Tandem Prusik Belays - *Inferior Practices*

WARNING The Belay May Be Slow To Engage, Or Even Fail To Engage When Tandem Prusiks Are Aligned With The Fall Line And The Climber Is Allowed To Pull Rope Through

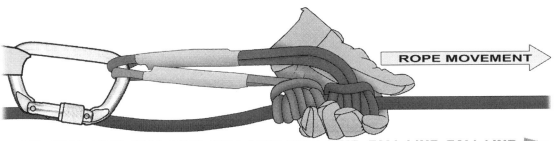

ROPE MOVEMENT

LINE FALL LINE FALL LINE FALL LINE FALL LINE FALL LINE FALL LINE

Incorporating A Minding Pulley Into Belay Rigging Unfavorably Aligns Tandem Prusiks With The Fall Line

Lowering Operations Require The Belayer To React And Release The Hitches Resulting In Longer Drops

Minding Pulleys Tend To Loosen The Prusik Hitches

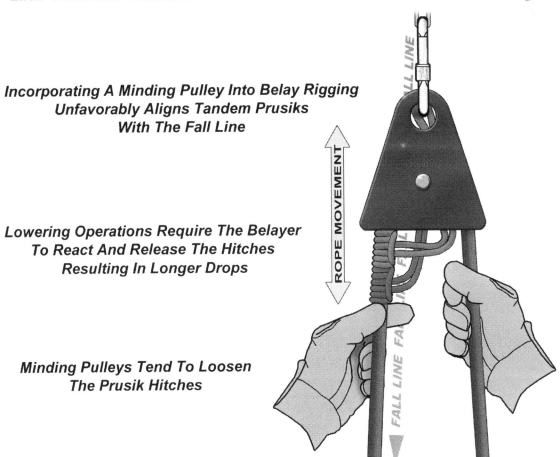

ROPE MOVEMENT

FALL LINE

Münter Belays

Best practice for use with dynamic ropes and running anchors during overhead climbing operations.

Due to the higher risk of arresting falls registering greater than 0.25 on the "Fall Factor Scale," low-stretch life safety ropes should not be used to belay overhead Rescue Climbers.

Münter belays can be used to back up over-the-side operations, but fire service rescuers usually reserve the tactic for overhead climbing situations. The Münter belay technique combines quick bi-directional adjustment of the belay rope with the ability to arrest the fall of a single Climber. The Münter is not suitable for 2-person loads.

When matched with a compatible (HMS) carabiner, the Münter hitch is perfect for the frequent slack and tension adjustments needed to protect an overhead Climber. With the Münter anchored to a solid object, the Belayer extends rope that threads through "running anchors" placed by the Climber as he or she moves upward. A running anchor uses a software loop and a carabiner to make a connection point on the structure so the belay rope can slide through. The highest running anchor will catch the rope and work as a directional if a Climber falls. The Münter hitch and runners allow the rope to run freely in either direction so long as the Climber is standing and the rope is slack. But with just a little tension on the working and standing sections at the same time, the Münter hitch cinches down to apply enough friction for the Belayer to hold and control the Climber. So as long as the Belayer doesn't let go of the standing line, the Münter will cinch down and catch a falling Climber. The Münter rig can then be used as a descent controller to lower the Climber as needed. Sounds easy.

A good Münter belay requires a competent, coordinated Operator and Climber duo to maintain conditions that are free of the potential for severe impact. The Münter hitch itself can be overwhelmed if falling forces are too great. The Münter hitch and belay rope must be handled and manipulated by both the Belayer and the Climber in ways that maintain optimum tension. Optimum belay tension allows the Climber to move as needed without excessive slack in the belay line. The Climber must also be mindful of the fall-arresting capacity of Münter hitches and the shock-absorbing capacity of dynamic ropes when deciding how running anchors should be placed as he or she proceeds. The higher a Climber moves above the last running anchor, the worse the Münter belays perform. This is especially true when the belay rope is short, as would be the case at the beginning or end of an overhead climb. In general, as overhead climbs progress, belays should be rigged in ways that will not allow the Climber to fall more than 25% of the length of the fall-arresting rope. That's the length of rope between the Münter hitch and the Climber. Working within this conservative 25% margin will expose the Climber, rope, and Münter hitch to tolerable impact forces if a fall occurs. When the Climber is close to the ground, the belay should thread through running anchors that are close together. As the climb proceeds and the belay rope lengthens, runners can be set further apart and still remain within the 25% margin of safety. This 25% limitation guideline corresponds with a score of .25 on the "Fall Factor Scale."

Rigging Münter Belays: Establish a waist-high anchor that provides plenty of room to work comfortably with a good view of the operation. Overhead operations should not place Belayers within the "drop zone" where they could be injured by dropped equipment or falling people. If a dropped pulley conks out the Belayer (bad enough in itself), the Climber will lose his or her protection. Locate the belay anchor so that the rope has some length to it when the Climber is close to the ground. The longer rope will improve fall arrest cushioning and can move the Belayer away from drop hazards. The added length also makes it easier for the Climber to place running anchors further apart on a structure that has few attachment options.

Connect the belay rope to the Climber's sternum or dorsal ring and then tie a Münter hitch onto the anchored carabiner. Stance is a matter of personal preference, but Belayers usually face the working line with their back to the anchor. Grasp the working line with one hand and the standing (braking) line with the other hand. Pull tension to straighten out the anchor attachments and position the carabiner and Münter close to the waist. The Belayer must not let go of the standing (braking) part of the rope. The standing rope should be stacked below the rigging and in front of the Belayer. The belay station and Climber should now be ready for safety clearance.

Handling Münter Belays: Münter rigging is not a passive, or automatic, belay system. A Münter belay must be handled in ways that maintain a firm grip on the standing rope. The system requires accomplished Operators and Climbers to safely arrest accidental falls. It's a mistake to regard the belay position in an overhead operation as an easy assignment for personnel with superficial skills. Münter belay proficiency should be developed and demonstrated in a clinical setting before personnel take this critical assignment with a live load.

As the Climber moves up and away from the anchor, the belay rope will obviously need to be extended. But as the Climber proceeds and rigs the rope with running anchors, frequent small adjustments of tension and slack will be necessary. Tension and slack must be precisely balanced to maintain good protection and allow the Climber enough mobility to work. The Belayer will have to pay out some rope whenever the Climber has to clip into a running anchor that is above his or her harness attachment. Once the rope is clipped in, the Belayer will then have to pull in rope to maintain proper tension until the Climber moves above the running anchor. As soon as the harness attachment passes the running anchor, the Belayer must carefully pay out rope again to allow the Climber to continue moving up freely. With a little practice, Belayers develop an ability to anticipate and react to Climber movements more precisely.

In overhead situations, simple commands exchanged by the Belayer and Climber can make climbing easier and belaying more effective. As belay ropes get longer and heavier on the Climber, communication becomes more and more necessary. Climbers and Belayers can fine-tune rope management by using the terms "slack," "tension," "climbing," "falling," "OK," and "stop." These terms are easy to distinguish from each other, even when listening conditions are difficult. The Climber may need adjustments in slack or tension to tie a knot, reposition the rope or to make a difficult maneuver easier to pull off. Plain language between the Climber and Belayer can certainly be used, but these simple terms work well and can be understood when the Climber is way up there.

Slack: If a Climber shouts this command, the Belayer should carefully extend the rope.

Tension: Means the Belayer should carefully pull rope in.

Climbing: Notifies the Belayer of impending movement, usually upward.

Falling: Announcement that the Climber is losing footing and that a fall is imminent. Belayer should brace and hold to catch or assist the Climber.

OK: Translates to "that's enough" or "that's good."

Stop: Command to cease an action immediately.

Catching A Fall: When a fall occurs, the Münter hitch will rotate itself and cause the working line to tension hard. The Belayer will have to brace and grip the standing (braking) strand hard to stop and hold the falling Climber. This may require using both hands on the braking strand of rope, or using the technique of leaning forward and partially wrapping the standing part around the Belayer's waist.

Münter Belays - *Setup*

* **For Use With Single-Person Loads Only**

* **Dynamic Rope Münter Hitched Onto Pear-Shaped (HMS) Carabiner**

* **Rigging Anchored Independent Of Belayer**

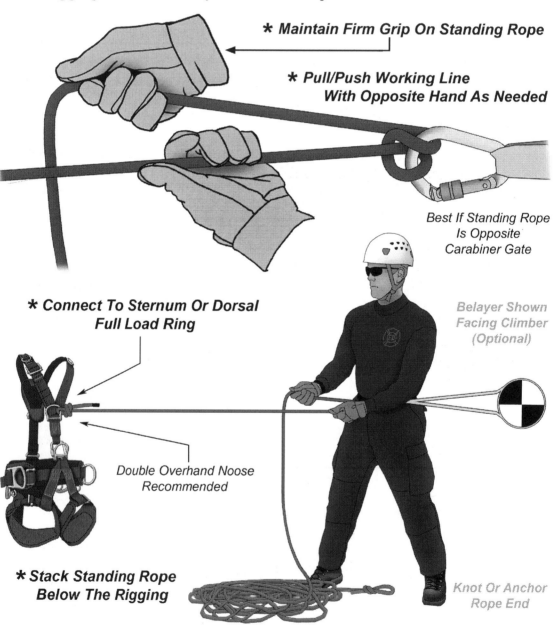

* **Maintain Firm Grip On Standing Rope**

* **Pull/Push Working Line
  With Opposite Hand As Needed**

*Best If Standing Rope
Is Opposite
Carabiner Gate*

* **Connect To Sternum Or Dorsal
  Full Load Ring**

*Belayer Shown
Facing Climber
(Optional)*

*Double Overhand Noose
Recommended*

* **Stack Standing Rope
  Below The Rigging**

*Knot Or Anchor
Rope End*

Münter Belays - *Extending Line*

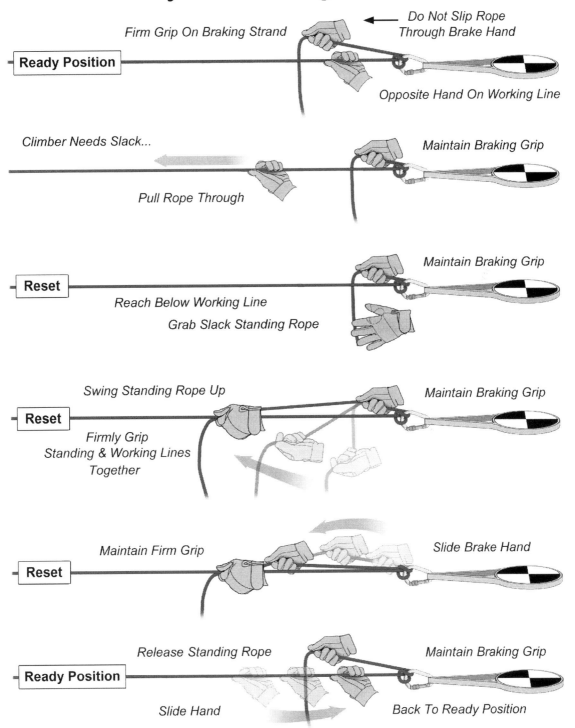

Ready Position
Firm Grip On Braking Strand
Do Not Slip Rope Through Brake Hand
Opposite Hand On Working Line

Climber Needs Slack...
Maintain Braking Grip
Pull Rope Through

Reset
Maintain Braking Grip
Reach Below Working Line
Grab Slack Standing Rope

Reset
Swing Standing Rope Up
Maintain Braking Grip
Firmly Grip Standing & Working Lines Together

Reset
Maintain Firm Grip
Slide Brake Hand

Ready Position
Release Standing Rope
Maintain Braking Grip
Slide Hand
Back To Ready Position

Münter Belays - *Retracting Line*

Ready Position

Firm Grip On Brake Strand

Firm Grip On Working Strand

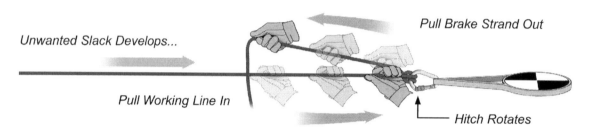

Unwanted Slack Develops...

Pull Brake Strand Out

Pull Working Line In

Hitch Rotates

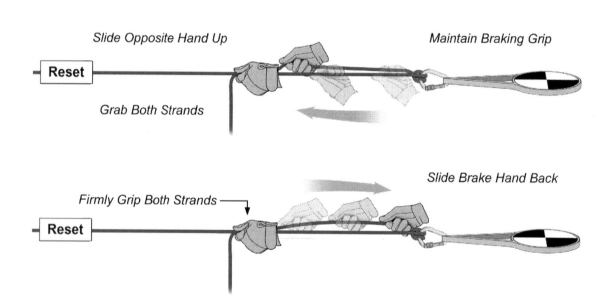

Slide Opposite Hand Up

Maintain Braking Grip

Reset

Grab Both Strands

Slide Brake Hand Back

Firmly Grip Both Strands

Reset

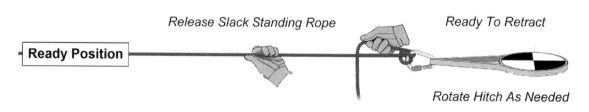

Release Slack Standing Rope

Ready To Retract

Ready Position

Rotate Hitch As Needed

Münter Belays - *Catching A Fall*

* ***Maintain Firm Grip On The Braking Strand***

* ***Step Forward And Lean Against Both Strands***

* ***Be Ready For A Second Fall***

* ***Wrap Braking Strand Against Hip***

* ***Use 2 Hands To Hold The Climber***

* ***Expect Pulsing Tension After Initial Impact***

The Climber Can Be Lowered Using The Münter Hitch For Descent Control

Münter Belays - *Tying Off*

* **Remove Slack From Working Line**

* **Form A Large Bight With The Standing Line** (Braking Strand)

* **Mule Hitch The Bight Onto The Working Strand**

Tying Off Münter Belays: A mule hitch is a suitable means to lock and tie off a Münter hitch. The mule can be applied and released while the lines are under full tension. The Mule is easy to tie whether the Münter is hitched onto a carabiner or a fixed object.

Münter Belays - *Inferior Practice*

✱ *Opening The Angle Between Strands Reduces Holding Strength*

✱ *Münters Are Unable To Sufficiently Support Belay Loads When The Braking & Working Strands Are Aligned*

✱ *Always Close The Angle And Hold Strands Parallel For Belay Loads*

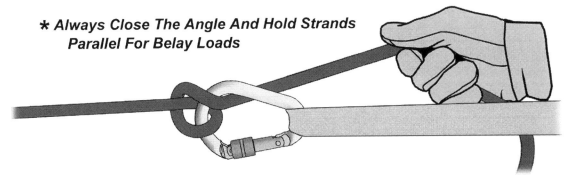

Self-Belays

Primarily used by fire service rescue teams as a back-up tool, belays that require Climbers to manage their own protection rigging are known as "self-belays." There are numerous self-belay methods and contraptions to choose from. *Vertical Academy* takes the basic 3-wrap prusik approach to minimize the need for special hardware, special rigging, or additional staffing. Attaching a cord loop onto a fixed life-safety line using a 3-wrap prusik hitch works very well as a self-belay for a single person load (single Climber). This tactic is also referred to as one form of a "traveling self-belay." There are at least two situations that justify learning and becoming proficient with traveling self-belays:

1. Rapid Intervention Incidents: If a Climber becomes incapacitated during an over-the-side operation, someone from the 7-person team will have to go down to assist. This can be accomplished using a pre-anchored rope to rappel down while using the original lines already over the side as a means of belay. As the Rapid Intervention Climber rappels down, he or she can use a traveling attachment on either of the original lines already over the side as the belay part of a 2-rope system.

2. Escape Ascending Incidents: If an over-the-side rope system severely snags or jams enough to seize up in terms of lowering and raising, the Climber may be able to ascend on the ropes to safety. To do this, the Climber will need to make a traveling belay attachment that can be moved as he or she ascends.

Rigging Traveling Self-Belays: Start by establishing a fixed half-inch life-safety line that follows the climbing route. During rapid intervention and emergency escape incidents, use lines that are already over the side. Attach a 8mm cord loop to the fixed line using a 3-wrap prusik hitch. Use a loop that is 22 to 30 inches long. Use an auto-locking carabiner to connect the loop to the sternum ring on the Climber's harness. Ideally, the length of the cord loop should allow placement of the prusik hitch at helmet level on the fixed line. Ensure the prusik hitch remains snug.

Handling Traveling Self-Belays: To maintain belay protection, the Climber must move the prusik rope grab appropriately as he or she moves up or down. The Climber simply pauses up or down movement long enough to reposition the prusik wraps on the fixed line as needed. Descent controllers that require the use of both hands can make rappels with prusik self-belays very cumbersome and slow. It is better to use one-handed descent controllers like brake bar racks or Rescue 8 plates.

Because this belay system aligns the prusik wraps with the fall line of the fixed rope, it is best to let go of the hitch after adjusting and tightening it. Pausing to readjust and set the prusik hitch ensures that the belay will engage instantly to catch a falling Climber. Once the belay has been repositioned, the Climber should remove his or her hand from the prusik wraps. The alternative of grasping the prusik wraps and pulling them along can work, but this requires the Climber to react and let go to engage the belay. Requiring the Climber to let go causes the belay to engage late and allows more force to develop when a fall occurs. A fearful Climber may even grip the prusik harder when a fall occurs, causing the belay to fail completely.

This belay system requires proper orientation of the prusik rope-grab relative to the sternum attachment on the Climber. A single 3-wrap prusik on a fixed line does not have the same stopping and shock-absorbing attributes as other belaying methods. This kind of self-belay rigging performs best when the prusik hitch is positioned at helmet level. As a Climber moves up, the belay prusik drops further and further away from helmet level and optimum performance. For this system to catch an accidental drop and manage shock adequately, the Climber must never position him or herself above the prusik rope grab on the fixed line. Climbers should keep the prusik wraps within the range between helmet level and waist level for the best balance of functionality and protection. Whenever a Climber is holding a position to work, the prusik hitch should be moved up to helmet level.

Rappelling: Start by placing the prusik hitch at waist level. Move down until the prusik wraps are at helmet level. Stop downward movement and reposition the prusik wraps back down to waist level. Set the prusik hitch tight before continuing down.

Ascending: Start with the prusik hitch at helmet level. Move up until the prusik wraps are at waist level. Pause movement, and reposition the prusik wraps back up to helmet level. Set the prusik hitch tight before continuing up.

Catching a Fall: With a prusik hitch of this kind on a traveling self-belay properly set, accidental falls or failures of the main rope system should be caught automatically. The less-favored practice of pulling the prusik attachment along during a rappel requires the Climber to react and release the hitch to engage the belay.

Traveling Self-Belays - *Setup*

* ✱ *8mm Cord Loop - 22 to 30 Inches Long*

* ✱ *3-Wrap Prusik Hitched Onto Fixed 1/2" Life-Safety Rope*

* ✱ *Attach To Harness Sternum Ring With An Auto-Locking Carabiner*

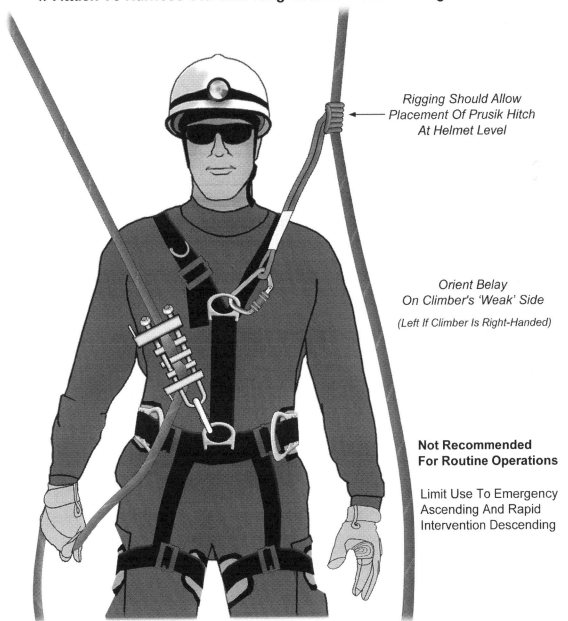

*Rigging Should Allow
Placement Of Prusik Hitch
At Helmet Level*

*Orient Belay
On Climber's 'Weak' Side*

(Left If Climber Is Right-Handed)

**Not Recommended
For Routine Operations**

Limit Use To Emergency
Ascending And Rapid
Intervention Descending

Traveling Self-Belays - *Descending*

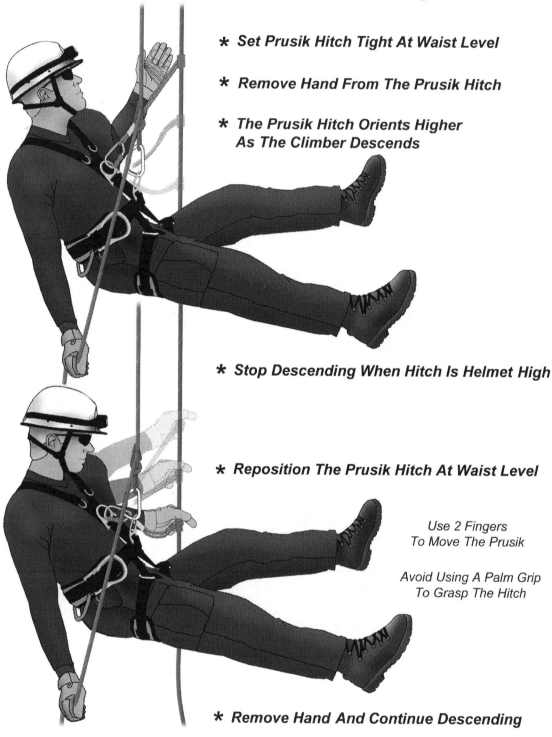

* **Set Prusik Hitch Tight At Waist Level**

* **Remove Hand From The Prusik Hitch**

* **The Prusik Hitch Orients Higher As The Climber Descends**

* **Stop Descending When Hitch Is Helmet High**

* **Reposition The Prusik Hitch At Waist Level**

Use 2 Fingers To Move The Prusik

Avoid Using A Palm Grip To Grasp The Hitch

* **Remove Hand And Continue Descending**

Traveling Self-Belays - *Ascending*

* Prusik Attachment
  Orients Lower
  As Climber Ascends

* Pause Ascending
  When Prusik Is At
  Waist Level

* Reposition Prusik
  To Helmet Level

CLIMBER

PRUSIK

* Use A 'Pinch Grip'
  To Move The Prusik

* Do Not Palm
  The Prusik Wraps

* Tighten The Prusik Wraps
  Before Continuing

Traveling Self-Belays - *Inferior Practices*

* *A Full Palm Grip Can Cause A Climber To Instinctively Grasp And Disable The Prusik When A Sudden Fall Occurs*

* *Better To Use A "Two-Finger" Pinch To Move The Prusik On The Fixed Line*

* *Pulling The Prusik Hitch Along While Descending Requires The Climber To React And Let Go To Engage The Belay*

* *Adding Reaction Time Allows A Climber To Fall Farther And Develop Higher Impact Forces*

Traveling Self-Belays - Tying Off

* Knot The Belay Line Below The Prusik Wraps

*** Set The Prusik Attachment 6 Inches Above The Knot
To Allow For Shock Dampening Slippage**

6"

Tying Off Self-Belays: In the extremely rare event that a traveling self-belay would need to be tied off, it's usually a simple matter of placing a knot in the rope just below the Climber attachment. It's important to preserve any shock-absorbing functionality by providing travel clearance for whatever rigging is used. In the case of prusik attachments, place the wraps of the hitch at least 6 inches above the knot in the belay line. Should the main vertical supports fail, the prusik hitch can engage and slip to dampen the impact of arresting the fall of the Climber.

Belaying - *Edge Transition - Best Practice*

* **Standing Upright At The Edge Creates Potential For a Long Drop Before The Belay System Can Engage To Arrest A Fall**

* **Be Aware Of The Belay Attachment To The Harness While Topside**

BELAY LINE

* **Stay Low To Keep The Belay Line Close To The Topside Surface While Climbing Over An Edge**

* **Use An Action Similar To Mounting And Dismounting A Horse To Move Over An Edge**

The Belay Line Will Not Tighten Until The Climber Falls Past Edge Level. Standing Upright Elevates The Belay Connection On The Harness To 4 Feet Or More Above The Topside Edge, Risking A Drop Of Approximately 6 Feet Or More Before The Belay Can Engage.

Belaying - *Edge Transition - Inferior Practice*

*** Standing Upright At The Edge Creates Potential For a Long Drop
Before The Belay System Can Engage To Arrest A Fall**

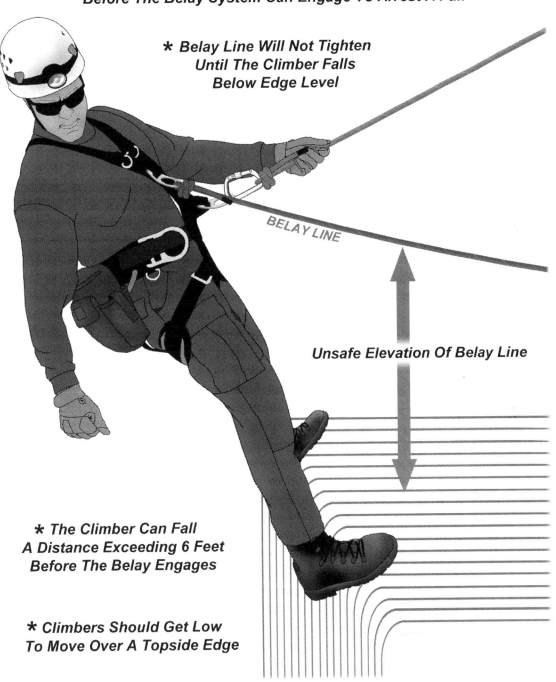

*** Belay Line Will Not Tighten
Until The Climber Falls
Below Edge Level**

BELAY LINE

Unsafe Elevation Of Belay Line

*** The Climber Can Fall
A Distance Exceeding 6 Feet
Before The Belay Engages**

*** Climbers Should Get Low
To Move Over A Topside Edge**

Belaying - *Rope Vector - Best Practice*

* Route Belay Lines As Directly To The Climber As Possible

* Belays At Topside Surface Level Will Instantly Engage To Arrest Falls

* Belays At Ground Level May Benefit From Topside Surface Friction

* Belay Integrity Does Not Rely On The Directional Supports

* Avoid Redirection Of Belay Ropes With Portable Anchors Such As Tripods And Multipods

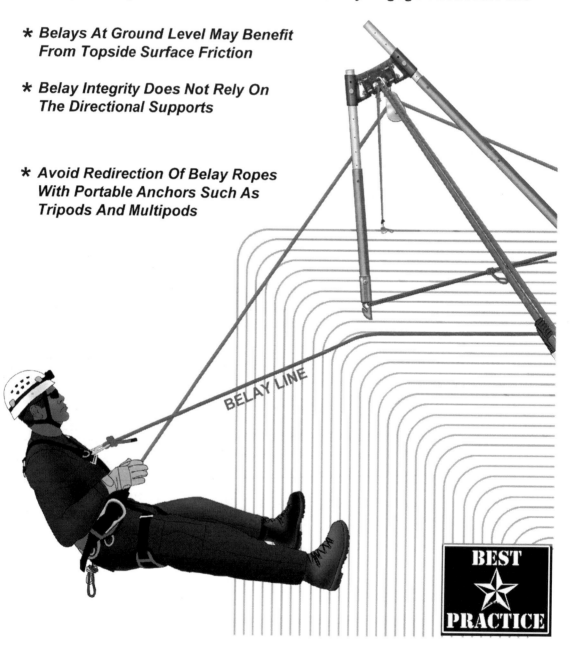

BELAY LINE

BEST ★ PRACTICE

Belaying - *Rope Vector - Inferior Practice*

* **Belays Routed Through Directionals Rely On Supporting Elements**

* **Redirected Belays Allow Climbers To Drop Greater Distances Should Supporting Elements Fail**

* **Long Drops = Severe Fall Arrest Impact**

* **Avoid Incorporating Directional Rigging**

REMEMBER
Route Belay Lines
Directly Over The Edge
Whenever Possible

BELAY LINE

Teaching/Learning Belay Skills

The serious consequences of belay errors warrant teaching/learning practices that are tightly controlled and structured. All elements of the various belays must be described and demonstrated by technically competent people using a sensible instructional order. Competency must be demonstrated under realistic testing conditions in a clinical setting before students belay live loads. Belay skills should never be developed through on-the-job training.

Introduction of belay concepts and technical information should begin with enhanced lecture techniques in an environment that encourages discussion. Lectures should be followed by "dry" demonstrations of belay rigging and practices performed by technically competent people. Dry demonstrations use an assistant to manually apply false loads for the purpose of showing belay system functionality. Students should then practice rigging and dry handling belays under close training supervision. Rigging and handling practice should be followed by full-weight demonstrations performed by technically competent people, including catching falls. Application of the content should have students assembling and handling belay rigging in realistic simulations that use full-weight loads. To confirm competency, student must demonstrate proficiency during realistic full-weight simulations.

TEACHING & LEARNING BELAY SKILLS - INSTRUCTIONAL ORDER

Instructor	Introduction	Introduction of belay concepts and technical information using enhanced lecture techniques.
Instructor	Demonstration	Dry demonstrations of belay rigging and practices performed by technically competent people.
Student	Application	Practice rigging and dry handling belay systems under close training supervision.
Instructor	Demonstration	Demonstrate catching falls using a full-weight mannequin.
Student	Application	Practice handling belay systems, including catching falls using a full-weight mannequin.
Student	Evaluation	Demonstrate proficiency handling belay systems and catching falls.
Student	Competent	Ready to belay live loads.

Simulating accidental falls for belay training can be accomplished using a basic pulley system and a load-releasing snap shackle. Snap shackles can be found at any sailing outfitter. Typical fire training tower facilities are perfect for these exercises. Anchor the pulley system high on the tower and attach it to the mannequin using the load-releasing shackle. Use a long tether to control the load-releasing shackle from ground level or from an upper floor window. Haul on the pulley system to move the mannequin up or down the face of a training tower as needed. A firm tug on the tether will disconnect the mannequin from the pulley system and allow it to fall free. Now, it's just a matter of rigging a belay for the mannequin.

Use dedicated equipment to assemble systems for belay simulation exercises. Forces generated during full-weight belay simulations affect the integrity of software and hardware enough to downgrade the equipment to "utility" applications only. Never suspend or belay a live load with equipment used for these kinds of simulations. All components used for full-weight belay simulations should be boldly marked and kept separate from working equipment caches.

Establish durable anchors, and attach belays to the mannequin(s). Repeated drop simulations will cause figure-8 and overhand knots to cinch down hard enough to make untying nearly impossible. A better method for attaching is to make several round turns around the chest of the dummy before tying a bowline knot. Using a carabiner to attach the mannequin is not recommended. This attachment method will usually untie without a problem after dozens of drops.

Depending on the facility, it may be necessary to use pike poles or ladders to recover and reattach the pulley system after the dummy disconnects. Strategically placing the rigging near windows or balconies can make recovery and resetting faster and easier. Important safety considerations include identifying the "drop zone" below the rigging and establishing appropriate rules for entering it.

As would be the case during a real vertical rescue emergency, a Leader should be assigned to direct the exercise. Staff the hauling system with several people, and assign a student to the belay position. The tether on the release mechanism will require an operator as well. The best-case situation places a supervising instructor with the student. At least one participant in the exercise should be assigned as a Safety Officer.

To carry out a simulation, the Leader directs the hauling staff to raise the mannequin using the "up" command. Move the dummy up at a realistic pace: not too fast, not too slow. To make the mannequin drop, signal the Release Controller to release the snap shackle. If all goes well, the mannequin should now be suspended on the belay line. Reconnect the pulley system, and haul the mannequin up to set up a fall during a lowering operation. You may need a ladder to reconnect the mannequin. The dummy will likely have to be raised to relieve tension on the belay prusiks. With everything in place, carry out a simulated fall while the mannequin is moving down at a realistic pace. The Leader directs the hauling staff using the "down" command. Create a fall by signaling the Release Controller as before.

Allow students to direct the release of the dummy at least once, but they must be able to catch falls without warning in order to prove competency. Hand signals between the Leader and the Release Controller will add the favorable element of surprise. It's good to simulate falls at various elevations to experience the effects of rope elongation on the belay systems when the ropes are both short and long. Observers and Belayers will notice differences in drop length and shock severity. Evaluate competency by assessing students handling techniques as well as their ability to cause the belay system to engage effectively.

Belaying - *Clinical Simulation Exercise*

* Rigging Disconnects Hauling System At Will

* Students Experience Realistic Fall Forces

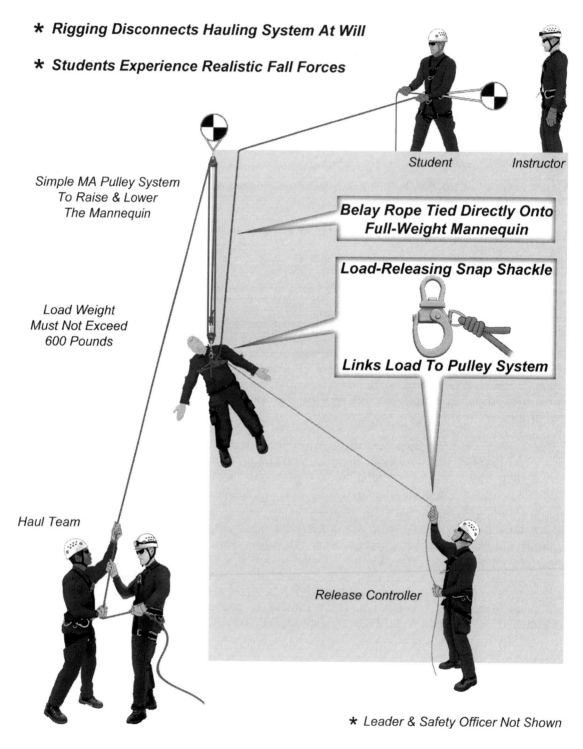

Student

Instructor

Simple MA Pulley System To Raise & Lower The Mannequin

Belay Rope Tied Directly Onto Full-Weight Mannequin

Load-Releasing Snap Shackle

Load Weight Must Not Exceed 600 Pounds

Links Load To Pulley System

Haul Team

Release Controller

* Leader & Safety Officer Not Shown

13 Rescue Baskets

Rescue Baskets

One of the most basic tools used by Rescue Teams is the rescue basket. Referred to as litters by NFPA, it's common for teams to have two or three versions of rescue baskets. Situations requiring the evacuation of non-ambulatory subjects can obviously occur almost anywhere. A basket perfectly suited for cliff rescues may not work well for confined spaces or snowy conditions. A wide variety of styles and features are available for just about any situation. This section will focus on the basic rigging elements for baskets well suited for vertical situations such as cliff rescues. Many of these rigging principles apply to all baskets. Be sure to study and practice instructions provided by the manufacturer of any baskets used by your team.

Desirable Features For Vertical Rescues

Baskets constructed of steel tubing are strong and easy on the hands for carrying, and the open design sheds soil that may fall in. Top rails that are larger in diameter make carrying over long distances easier. Fat top rails will need to be narrower where carabiner connections are expected. In some cases baskets are constructed with separate carabiner attachment points inside the rails. Look for baskets with spines that serve as skids on the bottom to allow for easy sliding on the ground. Baskets that taper toward the feet may be better for maneuvering through brushy areas. Plastic or wooden pallets fitted into the torso portion support riders better and can make moving an unconscious subject inside the basket easier. Mesh or fabric interior sheeting can help prevent snags and can help with carrying equipment.

Rescue Baskets - Desirable Features

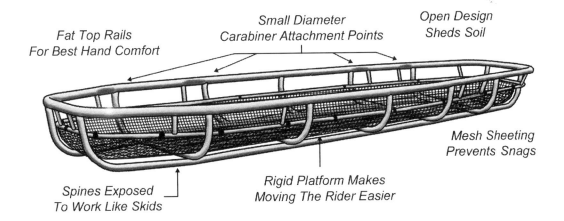

Fat Top Rails
For Best Hand Comfort

Small Diameter
Carabiner Attachment Points

Open Design
Sheds Soil

Mesh Sheeting
Prevents Snags

Spines Exposed
To Work Like Skids

Rigid Platform Makes
Moving The Rider Easier

Rigging Vertical Rescue Baskets

There are a few basic rigging premises for baskets used for vertical rescues that make work safer and easier. When rigged properly, a single Climber can safely take a basket over the side and get an unconscious rescue subject loaded and secured into it. Ignore some of these basic premises, and a second or even a third Climber may be required to go over the side to assist.

Do Not Connect Climber Directly To The Basket	Climbers should not use the basket as their connection point to the lowering/raising system. Connect independent of the basket to maximize mobility and to avoid accidentally pinning Climbers down if the basket is ever dropped or snagged.
Climber Able To Move Up And Down	Rigging should enable Climbers to easily ascend or descend on the rope system without help from the topside team for the purpose of making bridle adjustments, manipulating the basket, and loading the rescue subject.
Basket Adjustable In 3 Dimensions	The rope system must be connected to the basket in a way that allows for long axis and short axis adjustments up and down. Climbers must be able to raise, lower, and tilt the basket in any direction while over the side without help from the topside team.
Removable Bridle Legs	Rigging should allow Climbers to easily disconnect leg sections of the bridle to provide for clear access into the basket for loading.

Basket Bridles: There are many ways to configure rigging that connects the basket to a lowering/raising system and to address the minimum operating premises listed above. A very simple and well-functioning method is the basic four-legged spider strap bridle. This rigging provides four adjustable support connections that gather onto an anchor plate or ring. The spider strap system uses prusik rope grabs to adjust the length of each leg independently. Each leg is attached to the basket with a screw-locking carabiner for easy disconnection to provide an opening for loading. Screw lock carabiners are a good choice because auto-locking biners can be very difficult for the Climber to open if he or she is reaching from an awkward position. When extended fully, the distance between the rigging plate and the basket should be about 10 inches longer than the maximum length of the pick-off strap in your cache. With the basket connected to the bridle, the rigging plate or ring can be attached to the same rope system that supports the Climber. Simply fashion a small mid-rope loop knot, such as a directional 8, butterfly, or long-tailed bowline, where the basket should hang, and connect it there. Using a rigging ring can make this connection point more compact and improve topside clearance issues by eliminating the need for carabiners. Using screw links instead of carabiners can also improve compactness.

A downside to this basic bridle system is that the Climber will have to monitor the position of the carabiners that connect the leg ends and prusiks to the basket. Best practice is to position these carabiners so that the gates are facing inside the basket with the screw locks oriented to gravity. If the bridle system becomes completely slack, as it might when set down on a ledge during patient packaging, the carabiners can rotate out of position. This is not a deal breaker, but the gates will be exposed to potential impact and scraping, and the lock can vibrate open. The Climber will need to check and correct the orientation of these carabiners before suspending a life-load. Attaching the adjustment prusiks to the carabiners with a lark's foot hitch can minimize this problem. Some baskets are manufactured with attachment points that are inside the basket. Teams can fit their baskets with interior attachments by fixing short prusik loops onto interior strong points using prusik hitches. Adjust these prusik hitches to make the loops as small as possible.

Rescue Basket - *Basic Adjustable Bridle*

Shown Almost Fully Extended

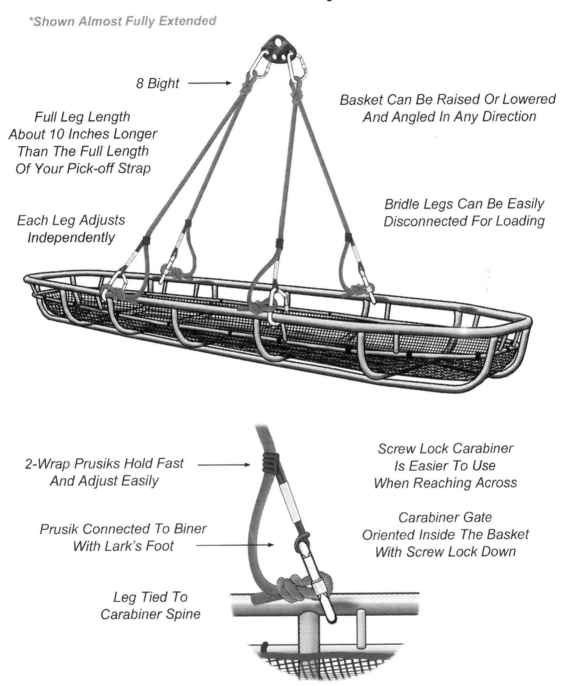

8 Bight

Basket Can Be Raised Or Lowered
And Angled In Any Direction

Full Leg Length
About 10 Inches Longer
Than The Full Length
Of Your Pick-off Strap

Bridle Legs Can Be Easily
Disconnected For Loading

Each Leg Adjusts
Independently

2-Wrap Prusiks Hold Fast
And Adjust Easily

Screw Lock Carabiner
Is Easier To Use
When Reaching Across

Prusik Connected To Biner
With Lark's Foot

Carabiner Gate
Oriented Inside The Basket
With Screw Lock Down

Leg Tied To
Carabiner Spine

* Carabiners May Side-Load When Bridle Is Fully Slacked - Check Biner Orientation Before Loading

Rescue Basket - Bridle Rigging Options

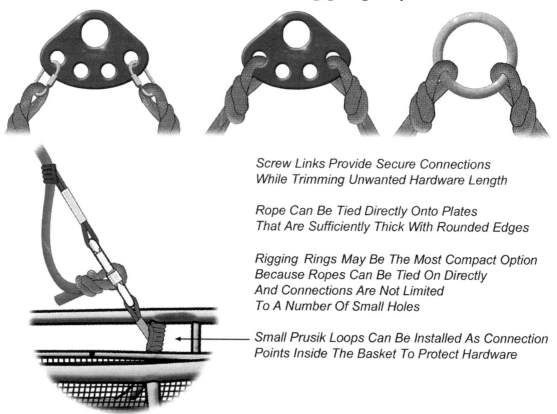

*Screw Links Provide Secure Connections
While Trimming Unwanted Hardware Length*

*Rope Can Be Tied Directly Onto Plates
That Are Sufficiently Thick With Rounded Edges*

*Rigging Rings May Be The Most Compact Option
Because Ropes Can Be Tied On Directly
And Connections Are Not Limited
To A Number Of Small Holes*

*Small Prusik Loops Can Be Installed As Connection
Points Inside The Basket To Protect Hardware*

Bridle Adjustments: The bridle can be attached to the basket with the legs placed wide apart, close together, or on one end, depending on the basket style. Rigging a wide bridle can add stability for a solid work platform when fully suspended. A narrow bridle can make manipulating the basket position easier for the Climber and may help with maneuvering in brushy areas. Attaching the bridle on the head end enables hauling in narrow or confined spaces.

Adjusting the hanging position of the basket is a matter of shortening or lengthening the legs of the bridle as needed. This sounds simple enough, but it can be nearly impossible to shorten or lengthen the legs of a basic bridle without exhausting the Climber when a human is riding in the basket. Adding an accessory mechanical advantage (jigger) to the basket rigging enables the Climber to hoist the load and to create bridle leg slack so that the prusiks can be loosened and repositioned easily. Clip a jigger onto the bridle bulkhead (rigging plate) so that it creates 4 to 1 mechanical advantage with a change of direction (4:1CD MA). The jigger will be much easier to use if the brake is on the traveling pulley. Use the jigger to hoist up anywhere on the basket to create slack on bridle legs. Conveniently, the 4:1CD jigger can be used for work positioning or picking off and hoisting rescue subjects into the basket.

Rescue Basket - *Accessory MA*

*Positioning A Jigger On The Bulkhead
For 4:1CD MA Enables The Climber
To Easily Slack The Bridle Legs
For Length Adjustment*

The Jigger Can Also Be Used For:
- *Climber Work Positioning*
- *Pick-off Maneuvers*
- *Patient Hoisting*

*Brake Placed On
Lower Block*

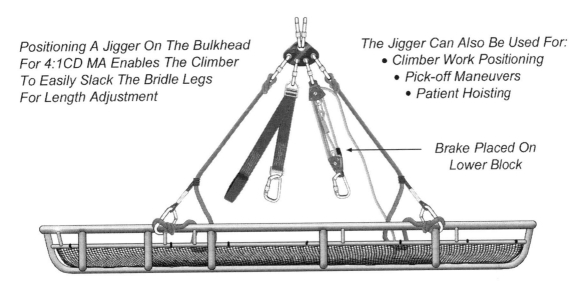

*A Pick-off Strap Can Be Clipped Onto The Rescue Subject
Allowing The Climber To Disconnect The Jigger
And Hold Position During Patient Hoisting Maneuvers*

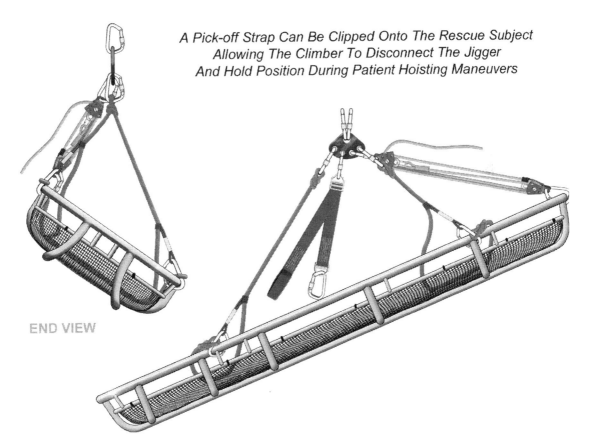

END VIEW

Rescue Basket - *Main Line & Belay Connection*

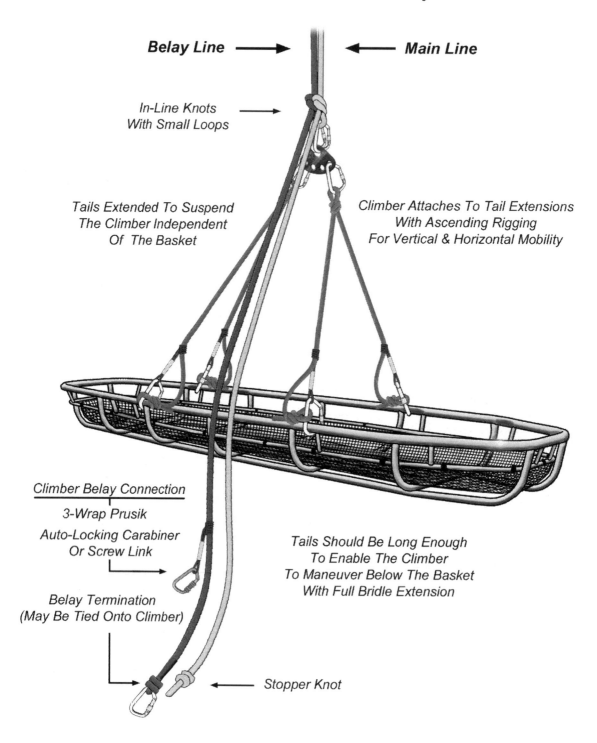

Belay Line ➡️   ⬅️ **Main Line**

In-Line Knots ➡️
With Small Loops

Tails Extended To Suspend
The Climber Independent
Of The Basket

Climber Attaches To Tail Extensions
With Ascending Rigging
For Vertical & Horizontal Mobility

Climber Belay Connection
3-Wrap Prusik

Auto-Locking Carabiner
Or Screw Link

Tails Should Be Long Enough
To Enable The Climber
To Maneuver Below The Basket
With Full Bridle Extension

Belay Termination
(May Be Tied Onto Climber)

⬅️ *Stopper Knot*

Main & Belay Line Tail Extensions and Climber Connections: The Climber connects to the rope system via long tails that extend from the inline knots that hold the rescue basket. The Climber attaches to the main line tail extension with rigging for ascending. The belay line connection uses a 3-wrap prusik and auto-locking carabiner or screw link clipped to the Climber's sternum harness ring. Attach the terminal end of the belay tail to the Climber's dorsal harness ring. This belay rigging requires the Climber to self-manage slack in the belay line tail as he or she moves up or down on the main line extension. Simply move and set the prusik hitch as needed to manage belay slack. The knot tails should be long enough to allow the Climber to position below the basket while the bridle is adjusted to full length. Attaching in this way enables a Climber to maneuver horizontally, up, and down independent of the basket and without help from the topside Team. These attachment methods provide enough mobility to reach and adjust any part of the basket and bridle assembly. This kind of maneuvering freedom is essential for securing and loading disabled rescue subjects using a single Climber. The adjustability of the basket bridle combined with the maneuverability of the Climber allows for very effective work positioning and subject hoisting. Free movement of the Climber also optimizes ergonomic advantage for transitioning over the edge or traveling on vertical topography. An additional benefit of this rigging is that a Climber can actually ascend all the way back to topside. If an emergency topside ascent is warranted, the bulkhead can easily be passed using the prusiks carried by the Climber.

For operating on inclines that are 45° or flatter ("low angle"), the basic bridle is converted to attach multiple Climbers without extending knot tails from the main and belay lines. The head rail of the basket is attached to the center hole of the gathering plate using a small webbing loop.

Rescue Basket - Connection Options

Directional 8	*Butterfly*	*Long-Tailed Bowline*

 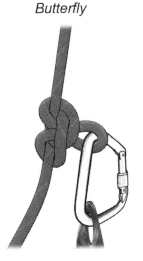 

*Single Line Shown For Clarity   *Make Loops As Small As Possible*

Rescue Basket - *Climber Connection*

* *Ascending System & Self-Belay Rigged Onto Tail Extensions*

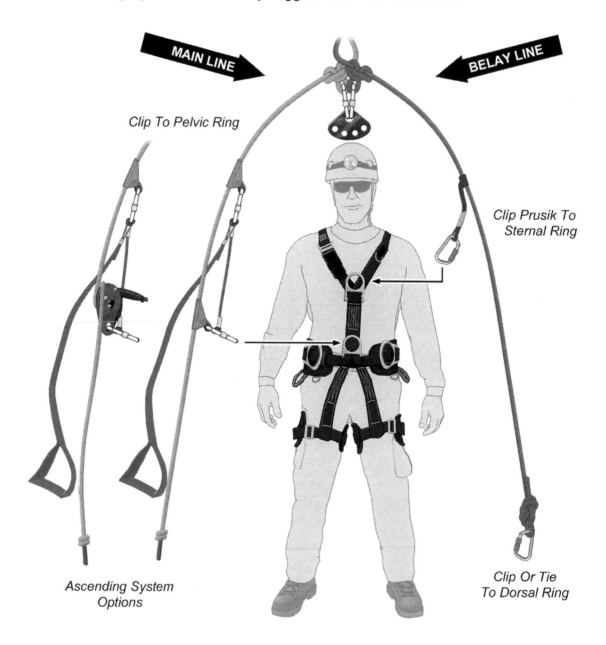

MAIN LINE

BELAY LINE

Clip To Pelvic Ring

Clip Prusik To
Sternal Ring

Ascending System
Options

Clip Or Tie
To Dorsal Ring

Move Prusik To Manage Belay Slack

- Bridle Conversion For Low Angle

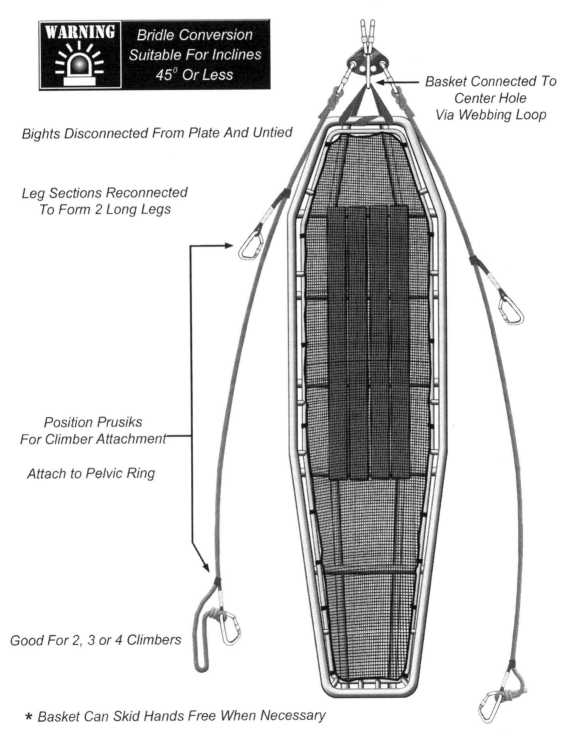

WARNING
Bridle Conversion
Suitable For Inclines
45° Or Less

Basket Connected To
Center Hole
Via Webbing Loop

Bights Disconnected From Plate And Untied

Leg Sections Reconnected
To Form 2 Long Legs

Position Prusiks
For Climber Attachment

Attach to Pelvic Ring

Good For 2, 3 or 4 Climbers

* Basket Can Skid Hands Free When Necessary

Basket and Climber Positioning

The relative positions of the basket and the rescue Climber greatly affect operating efficiency when working over the side. The position of the basket can either facilitate or impede movement and loading. The same is true for the position of the Climber on the main line and belay tail extensions. Vertical orientation of the Climber and basket can either improve or hinder stability, access to the subject, or loading ergonomics. It's common during training sessions to watch rookie Climbers take shortcuts and attempt to rely on brute strength to maneuver around the basket and load the subject. Time compression (the feeling that things are taking too long to do) can make anybody feel rushed and cause them to rationalize that adjusting the basket before proceeding isn't worth the time it takes. This usually results in jerking movements, rough handling of the subject, and bouncing loads on the overall system. It also results in a worn out Climber. With a little practice, Climbers learn that trimming the basket rigging properly results in smoother operations that take less time and energy in the long run.

Travel Position: Used while moving up or down on vertical or steep faces during over-the-side operations. The bridle is trimmed with short legs that orient the basket close to the bulkhead, tilting away from the cliff face and toward the Climber. The long axis of the basket is level. The short axis is angled at about 45° or more. The Climber is positioned on the tail extensions so that the closest (lower) rail is chest high. The Climber can optimize solid foot contact by leaning back until his or her body is nearly perpendicular with the main line. When everything is trimmed this way the Climber has good leg clearance to walk on or fend off the cliff face while still able to reach the interior of the basket. Foot contact with the face will be lousy if the basket is rigged too low, or if the Climber is riding too high and more parallel with the main line. You don't want to be forced to tiptoe lightly on the face because the basket is banging into your shins. Poor foot contact means less control. Tilting the basket to 45° reduces the horizontal profile and causes rocks and soil to fall out automatically. The travel position is beneficial whether the basket is empty or loaded and makes handling heavy loads easier. Using this method on surfaces that are less than vertical enables the Climber to hold the load close to his or her own center of gravity for stronger control. The basket can be easily rotated 90° on the horizontal plane to pass through narrow areas when needed. To transition up and over abrupt topside edges with a loaded basket in travel mode, the Climber need only press in the standing position until the basket is level with the horizontal surface where topside workers can then disconnect it and take over. Consider the travel position as the default setup for beginning and finishing over-the-side basket operations.

Keel Position: When the Climber is positioned below the basket. The bottom of the basket is referred to as the "keel." Usually used in preparation for initial contact with the rescue subject, the keel position provides the Climber with a cleaner work area and a high anchor point for hoisting and loading. When the Climber is low on the tail extensions, the bulkhead will be higher overhead. This provides more room to extend the length of a jigger for better hoisting and subject loading. The keel position enables the Climber to access the bottom of the basket to disentangle snags that would otherwise be out of reach. The keel position can be used to quickly shrink the horizontal profile to fit through tight spots like cracks and slots. Climbers can take refuge deep in the keel position and use the basket to shield them from rock fall when moving through crumbly terrain.

Loading Position: Used when moving the rescue subject into the basket. The primary intent is to optimize the Climber's lifting and hoisting ergonomics to make loading easier and smoother. With the bridle length adjusted at whatever level is needed, the Climber positions on the tail extensions with his or her torso above the basket. It can be beneficial to keep a foot in the ascending rigging (foot loop) and/or one knee in the basket for added stability. Keeping the foot strap loaded maintains rope tightness to help manage elasticity and provides the Climber with something to push against when lifting. Putting one knee in the basket can prevent unwanted rotation and provide additional lifting support. The loading position usually involves disconnecting at least one bridle leg for better loading clearance. It may be necessary for a Climber to get into or even stand up in the basket to anchor a jigger up high or position for a strong pull. Do whatever is necessary as long as it is safe.

Fanny Position: Used to negotiate cornices, overhangs, and difficult edges. The bridle is adjusted to medium length with the short axis of the basket perpendicular to the main line or angled toward the face. The Climber takes a position inside the bridle sitting against the rail closest to the face. The basket rail should not act as the main support for the Climber. The Climber should be suspended from the tail extensions with his or her fanny against the basket rail. Grab the same rail with both hands and use leg pressure to push the basket away from the face. This orientation enables the Climber to keep his or her feet in firm contact with the face as it transitions to a cornice or overhang. The Climber will be able to maintain foot contact on surfaces that are well overhead or below an overhang. To transition up and over abrupt topside edges or parapets, continue raising until the Climber is high enough to scramble out of the bridle and onto the topside surface. With the Climber on the ground, continue raising the basket topside.

Vertical Position: Used to operate in narrow vertical cracks, shafts, channels, and confined spaces. The bridle is connected to the head or torso-level basket ribs (strong points) as needed to orient the long axis parallel with the main line. The Climber positions on the tail extensions as needed and either straddles the basket or hangs dependant without making foot contact on vertical surfaces. Rigging this way creates a very small horizontal profile and makes transitioning edges and hatches very smooth. The Climber has the option to ascend up above the bridle bulkhead to exit through very small hatches to prevent being blocked by a basket clog. When hauling up to topside edges or openings, the topside team will be presented with a large section of the basket above the edge for easy handling. Using the vertical basket position requires bomber internal lashing to securely hold the subject in any dimension. Make sure the lashing system you use will hold the subject fast. With regular practice, the method shown in the diagram uses three sections of webbing and is quick and easy to apply.

Low Angle: Used for faces that are 45° or flatter. The basic bridle is reconfigured to create two long legs that serve as attachment points for two, three, or four Climbers. Do this by untying the bights connected to the gathering plate and then reconnecting the ends to form the two long legs. Position the prusik hitches on the legs for attachment points. Connect to the head rail of the basket using a small webbing loop clipped to the center hole of the gathering plate. The main and belay lines terminate at the plate and do not extend to each Climber for low-angle operations. Connect the prusik attachments to pelvic harness rings. Climbers manually carry the basket but can allow the basket to skid on the ground hands free when needed. It's important that Climbers lean back on the rope system for good footing and optimum lifting posture.

Rescue Basket - *Functional Positions*

Travel Position

- *Bridle Adjusted Short*
- *Basket Tilted To Climber*
- *Rail Chest High*

Keel Position

- *Climber Low On Tails*
- *Basket Out Of The Way*
- *Access To Basket Keel*

- Best Leg Clearance

- Basket Will Shed Rocks & Soil

- Smaller Horizontal Profile

- Best For Final Approach

- Basket Clear Of Subject

Rescue Basket - *Functional Positions* *(cont.)*

Loading Position

- *Bridle Adjusted Long*
- *Climber Above Basket*
- *Standing In Footstrap*

Fanny Position

- *Bridle Adjusted Medium*
- *Climber Sitting On Rail*
- *Press Away From Cornice*

CORNICE

- Good Hoisting Ergonomics

- Good Access Clearance

- Easy Foot Contact Above Basket

- Good For Negotiating Abrupt Edges

Rescue Basket - *Functional Positions (cont.)*

Vertical Position

- *Bridle On Torso Or Head Ribs*
- *Climber Positioned As Needed*
- *Subject Lashed In Securely*

Low Angle

- *Bridle Untied - Two Long Legs*
- *Basket Attached Via Web Loop*
- *Prusik Loops As Attachments*

45° Or Less

- Small Horizontal Profile

- Good For Confined Spaces

- Move Prusiks To Adjust Position

- Climbers Lean Back On Rope

- Up To 4 Climbers

- Option - Skid Basket Hands Free

How Loading The Basket Works

The real work begins once a Climber equipped with a rescue basket reaches the rescue subject. It's relatively easy to move a person into a rescue basket when he or she is stranded on a cliff face but still mobile enough to sit up on his or her own. Workers completely suspended on ropes are also pretty easy to load into rescue baskets. But moving an *immobile* rescue subject into a basket is tough to do by yourself, even when you're on level ground. Doing it alone in a vertical environment when the subject is in danger of falling is nearly impossible to do unless you're well rigged and well practiced. Sending multiple Climbers over the side complicates and delays operations unnecessarily. Rescuers should embrace the adjustability and nimble mobility that the basic bridle system provides and use a jigger (accessory mechanical advantage system) to do the heavy lifting.

A good default loading tactic in vertical situations is to use a 4:1 CD jigger to hoist the torso of the immobile rescue subject just enough to slide the basket underneath. For this maneuver to work well, the Climber must consider several key positioning elements as he or she approaches the rescue subject.

1. The Climber must get close enough to quickly harness and connect the subject.

2. The bulkhead (gathering plate) must be positioned high enough to hoist with the jigger.

3. The Climber should anticipate rope stretch that will occur as the system takes on the additional weight of the rescue subject during hoisting.

To deal with these elements, the Climber should approach at quarter-speed while deep in the keel position and direct the team above to stop lowering as soon as the subject is within adequate reach of the pick-off rigging. Remember, the team topside controls the level of the bulkhead via direction from the Climber. The Climber controls his or her own vertical position on the tail extensions. The longer the rope system, the more rope stretch and rebound will be a factor. Standing up on a foothold or ledge during loading may cause the bulkhead and basket to spring up because of rope elasticity. If the rope system is spongy and elastic, the hoisting jigger will pull the bulkhead down significantly before the subject lifts. Unwanted rope stretch and rebounding can be minimized if the Climber keeps the rope system tight by sitting down in their harness and/or leaving a foot in the ascending rigging until the subject is in the basket.

Once the basket rigging is in good position, the Climber should immediately harness and connect the subject using the pick-off strap. If using an improvised harness system, begin with the chest harness, and connect the pick-off strap until the seat harness is in place and ready. Place head and eye protections on the subject, and carry out any medical treatment that is immediately necessary. Next, extend the jigger, and connect it for hoisting the weight of the subject's torso. The jigger can be anchored anywhere on the bulkhead, including the loop of the main line knot. If main line rope stretch is excessive, the jigger can be anchored to the main line above the bulkhead via a 3-wrap prusik rope grab. Hoist with the jigger until there is just enough clearance to move the basket in place. Extend the bridle legs enough to position the basket below the subject. It's usually best to disconnect one bridle leg for loading clearance. Now use the jigger to lower the subject into the basket. Be sure to adjust the pick-off strap as needed. Once the subject is lashed into the basket the jigger can be disconnected and used to slack the bridle legs for adjustment. The bridle should be adjusted for the travel position before raising or lowering.

Rescue Basket - *Loading The Subject*
* Non-ambulatory Subject - Precarious Narrow Ledge

Spine Immobilization
Equipment Not Shown
For Clarity

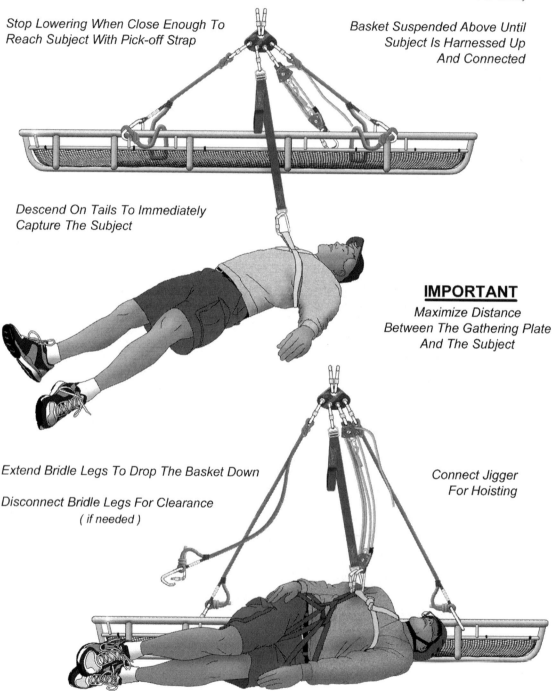

Stop Lowering When Close Enough To
Reach Subject With Pick-off Strap

Basket Suspended Above Until
Subject Is Harnessed Up
And Connected

Descend On Tails To Immediately
Capture The Subject

IMPORTANT

*Maximize Distance
Between The Gathering Plate
And The Subject*

Extend Bridle Legs To Drop The Basket Down

Disconnect Bridle Legs For Clearance
(if needed)

Connect Jigger
For Hoisting

Rescue Basket - *Loading The Subject (cont.)*

＊ *Non-ambulatory Subject - Precarious Narrow Ledge*

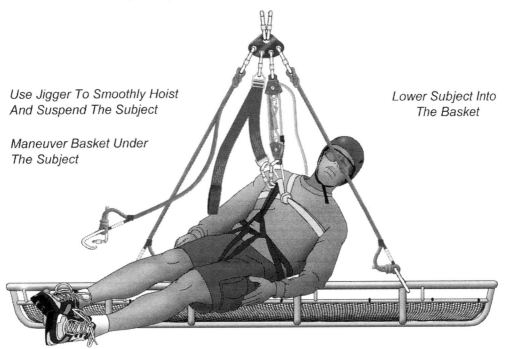

Use Jigger To Smoothly Hoist And Suspend The Subject

Maneuver Basket Under The Subject

Lower Subject Into The Basket

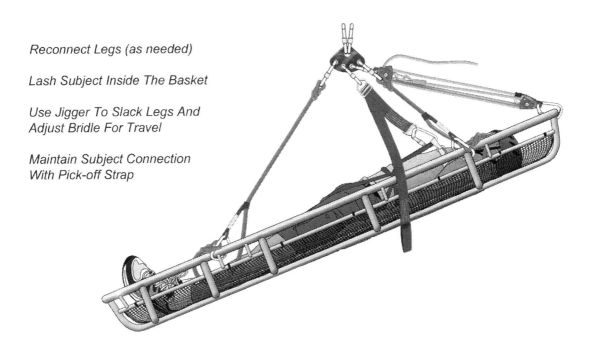

Reconnect Legs (as needed)

Lash Subject Inside The Basket

Use Jigger To Slack Legs And Adjust Bridle For Travel

Maintain Subject Connection With Pick-off Strap

Rescue Basket - *Internal Lashing*

* Extraordinarily Secure At Any Angle

Subject Wearing Improvised Harness

Larks Foot Hitches Chest & Seat Harness

Tie Off To Pull Chest Down & Seat Up

Snuggly Lace Subject In

Round Turn + 2 Half-Hitches

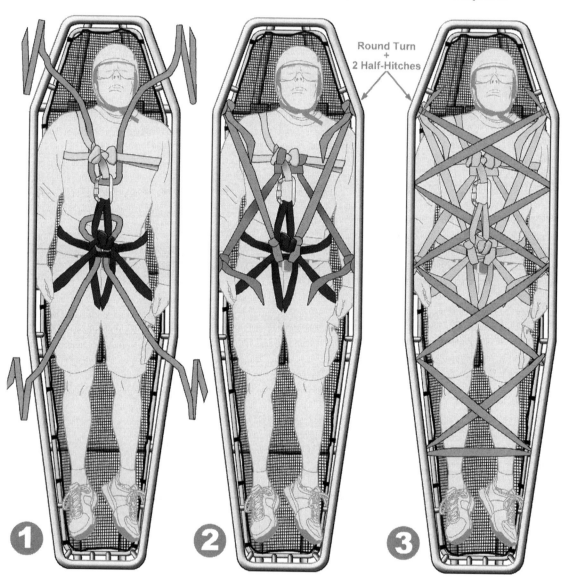

1 *Hitches Should Surround Attachment Points*

2 *Tie Webbing To Strong Points Below The Top Rails*

3 *Thread Strong Points Below The Rail*

*Subject Attachments Exposed

Internal Lashing - Securing the Rider: Any system used to belt the subject inside the basket for vertical operations needs to hold fast in any dimension. There is plenty of potential for tilting the basket in just about any direction when maneuvering through brush or around obstacles. Relying on the pickoff strap attachment alone is usually not an adequate option. Prefabricated belt systems can work well, but check during practice sessions to make sure the subject will remain correctly positioned inside when the basket is angled severely. Many restraining belt systems allow the rider to slip out when the head or foot of the basket is tilted down. It can be very difficult to maneuver safely and effectively when the subject's head or feet are extending out of the basket after slipping.

Webbing can be used to quickly improvise restraining lashing that is very secure on any axis, including vertical or inverted. This usually involves capturing the torso of the subject and securing it against the long dimension of the basket. Then, a shoelace method of lashing is used to secure the subject against the short dimensions of the basket. Improvised restraining lashing can be integrated with any harness the subject is already wearing, including improvised harnesses applied by rescuers. It's fun to test your system by lashing a team member in and positioning the basket upside down and vertical (at ground level over a soft surface, of course).

Practice: Rigging and using rescue baskets for vertical recoveries as described above requires adequate instruction and practice. Never send a Climber over the side with the intent to make a basket recovery, whether during a training session or real emergency, before they've demonstrated an ability to carry out the maneuver in a realistic but low elevation setting. It usually takes several tries to get it down. Repeat training sessions until Climbers can load subjects smoothly and securely, and then configure the bridle for travel before completion. Practice the skill regularly using a full-weight mannequin that is precariously placed in a variety of positions (supine, prone, sitting, etc.).

NFPA STANDARDS - LITTER PERFORMANCE

Litters shall be tested for strength and deformation as specified in Section 8.12, Litter Strength Test, and shall withstand
a minimum load of 11kN (2473 lbf)
Without failure or deformation of the structural element of more than
50mm ± 5mm (2 in. ± 0.2 in.)

---

14 Climbing Up

Climbing Up

It's not difficult to imagine a rescue situation with a subject clinging high up on a transmission tower, antennae tower, stadium light pole, or other elevated structure. Everything from trees to carnival rides constitutes potential overhead rescue hazards. Every firefighter knows that life-threatening emergencies happen overhead. Sometimes these situations exceed the reach of aerial ladders and require Rescuers to climb up. Firefighters can employ techniques used by rope access workers, recreational climbers, linemen, and arborists to safely climb up and work overhead.

Climbing up, commonly referred to as "lead climbing," should be considered an advanced skill. As with any low-probability, high-risk circumstance, you must possess the necessary skills even though they are rarely put to use. If you don't have the requisite skills, the consequences can be extreme. Careful training and practice in a clinical setting is a must for developing lead climbing rescue proficiency for both individuals and teams. An ability to safely climb up to access an overhead rescue objective is an invaluable capability that is worth the training and practice effort when you show up to the rare lead climbing rescue scene.

Climbing up may seem intuitive and easy at first glance. And it's true, the basic mechanics of grabbing onto and moving up an object like an antennae tower can be relatively easy as long as there are enough handholds and footholds. But climbing efficiently while protected from falls requires some technique and forethought. Overhead operations demand a completely different fall protection paradigm. As Climbers maneuver overhead, they must establish and adjust their own belay protections. If connected to a belay rope, Climbers must anchor directionals to whatever they're climbing on and thread the rope through them as they progress. Those using double lanyards must carefully connect, disconnect, and reconnect their lifeline as they move. Either way, it's an entire dimension of difficulty added to the tricky task of climbing up and lowering a rescue subject safely to the ground. Both methods require careful attention to factors that make or break fall protection success.

Climb Smart: Going up to get someone down requires a rational plan of attack. It's hard to develop a good plan without sizing up the situation first. Just like getting a good look and sizing up a burning house before taking firefighting action, it's important to survey the situation, assess climbing route options, and consider methods for fall protection and evacuation of the rescue subject. Taking a good look before you go is the first step to climbing smart.

Look for climbing routes that present the best footing and belay connection availability. Consider how belay ropes will lace up through running anchors as the climb progresses. You can even pre-plan and count running anchor connections before beginning the climb. Favorable resting spots, escape routes, and drop shelters can be identified from the ground before starting. It may be necessary to climb routes that are better protected from high wind. It is very important to remember that the rescue subject can fall before Climbers reach them. Choose a route that will be clear of a falling or jumping rescue subject whenever it's possible to do so.

Fall Protection: Once the climbing route and evacuation tactics are figured out, establish a fall protection plan. This usually means using the techniques that are most familiar to the team. EXAMPLE: though a given situation may be perfectly suited for fall protections that use double lanyard connections, the team may not be equipped properly for or familiar with the technique. Choosing and applying a fall protection method that the team practices regularly is usually the best option.

Double Lanyard Fall Protection: Best used for climbing permanent, plumb-mounted access ladders on buildings, towers, and poles, personal double lanyard fall protection methods are quick to deploy and intuitive to use. Double lanyard techniques are also well suited for use with difficult climbing situations that would cause belay ropes to tangle or drag heavily. With no need for ground support, Climbers are not limited by the length of a belay rope. At the same time, if a Climber becomes fatigued or disabled, he or she cannot be lowered on a belay rope controlled from the ground.

Manufactured double lanyard rigging must be applied properly for safe fall arrest protection. Double lanyard arresters must have adequate shock-absorbing characteristics built in. Shock absorbers should be checked regularly and immediately before use to make sure they are in good condition. In some cases, absorbers have expiration dates. Connect lanyards onto the climbing medium carefully to make sure there is adequate clearance below should the absorber fully extend when a fall occurs.

Lead Belaying: Well suited for climbing tower structures, trees, and rock faces, Lead belays arrest falls using a dynamic rope that is handled by someone below. In some circumstances, lead belays are controlled from above or lateral of the Climber. This guide will focus on manmade structure applications of lead belay techniques. The Climber contributes to the integrity of this system by strategically fixing directionals (running anchors, or "runners") onto the climbing medium as the belay extends. The Climber also follows a route and maneuvers within a safe working range for the lead belay rigging. Runners should be carefully placed to minimize rope friction and arrest falls efficiently. Rope length, fall distance, clearance below, and rope drag are all important considerations when placing running anchors for lead belays. Running anchors are usually removed by the Climber(s) as he or she climbs down.

Work Positioning: At some point, overhead Climbers will need to let go and stand hands-free to get some work done. The main (primary) support for the person climbing is the structure itself. The Climber maintains primary support by simply standing up and hanging on. Letting go and leaning back results in a fall. A professional Climber would, of course, be protected by a secondary connection of some kind which would capture the fall. But this secondary (belay) connection should never be used to support work positioning. In other words, do not let go and lean back on belay connections. Doing so abandons fall protection back-ups and alters the belay rigging to the only support for the Climber.

There are rigging techniques that safely use the belay rope to add a work positioning function, but using a "flip line" is a simple and practical work positioning solution used by linemen and arborists. Think of an adjustable strap on your harness that you can wrap around structural elements to anchor off with. Going up with a flip line enables Climbers to quickly tie off, lean back, and let go whenever they want. With a little practice, you'll never want to climb up without a flip line on your harness.

Double Lanyards

Double lanyard setups allow Climbers to establish and manage their own fall protection as they move about. Manufactured rescue versions are made up of two large auto-locking hooks connected to the ends of two yoke straps or dynamic ropes that are joined by a single point harness connection. Two single lanyards can be used for the same purpose. Lanyard lengths are made to accommodate the reach of the user, usually 2 to 2.5 feet. Most of these types of manufactured lanyards are fitted with shock absorbers or are intended for use with shock absorbers. Typical absorbers are made from folded strapping that is sewn in place with tear-away stitching that is engineered to dampen shock by controlled destruction. Double lanyard fall protectors are usually used while climbing structures like plumb vertical ladders, towers, bridges, catwalks, ledges, etc.

The basic premise for using double lanyard fall protection is to leapfrog the hooks to maintain connection with the structure as the Climber moves about. The Climber uses the structure for support, and the lanyard provides fall protection backup if he or she falls. This process can be applied to vertical or horizontal maneuvers.

It's important to understand that double lanyard fall protectors are designed to function properly for specific types of falls. Absorbers used with lanyards that meet OSHA and ANSI standards are tested with 220lb weights free-falling 6 feet. To perform adequately, the resulting peak impact force must not exceed 15kN, the deceleration distance must be no more than 42 inches, and total extension must not exceed 51 inches. Lanyards must be connected so that the absorber will engage before the Climber falls the maximum 6 feet. There must also be enough fall clearance below to allow the absorber to extend fully. Any interference with these fall paths will inhibit the absorber's ability to adequately dampen impact forces.

Climbers must work within the safe functioning limits of double lanyards and shock absorbers. Connection points with the structure and connection to the harness and body position must be well coordinated. The sternum ring is usually the best harness connection choice. Connecting to the sternum ring works well ergonomically and favorably aligns impact forces with the Climber's long axis if a fall occurs. To keep accidental fall distances within engineering limitations, the Climber should maneuver so that the sternum harness connection point is never higher than 2 to 2.5 feet above the structure connection point. The structure connection point should not allow the hook(s) to slide vertically as the Climber maneuvers up. If the structure connection is not fixed in the vertical dimension, then there is potential for fall distances exceeding 6 feet and impact forces that can overpower the equipment and severely injure the Climber. Unconnected hooks should remain free. Whenever one hook is not connected to the structure, it should never be hooked to a harness ring or strap for convenience. Doing so will hinder the functionality of the absorber. Best practice is to keep the hook free by slinging it over a shoulder, holding it in a free hand, or stowing it in a compatible loose holster.

Double Lanyards - *Vertical Climbing*

Connect High To Anchor Off

Sling Free Hook Over Shoulder While Climbing Up

When Anchor Is Waist-high -Connect High Again

Disconnect Bottom Hook -Continue Climbing

*Connect Waist-high And Reverse Order To Down-Climb

WARNING Do Not Connect Free Hook To Harness

Avoid Connections That Allow Hooks To Slide Up **WARNING**

Lead Climbing Rigging

Let's focus on rescue situations with someone stranded high on a large structure like a transmission tower. Towers usually have some kind of permanently mounted access ladder, but Climbers will usually need to use the structural components for their support as they traverse toward their objective. The long distances between and angular configuration of structural elements on these towers can make double lanyard fall protection measures difficult. Climbing up with a lead belay for fall protection (lead climbing) is a good choice for transmission towers.

Survey and plan a climbing route up the tower and estimate how many running anchors will be necessary. The Climber should carry a few extra runners for flexibility and to deal with accidental drops. If a lot of runners are needed, they can be gathered together using a cord loop (known as a rack) and carried like a shoulder bag. The Climber should be outfitted with a flip line.

Establish a belay anchor with a Münter compatible carabiner. Locate this "belay station" outside of the area (zone) where objects might fall from above. Climbers may accidentally drop equipment or dislodge loose objects as they work. It's always possible that the rescue subject can fall before Climbers reach them. Arrange the belay so the Climber will not tangle in the rope if he or she falls. If a falling Climber lands on the rope, it can disable much of the shock-absorbing characteristics of the belay rigging.

Tie the dynamic belay rope to the sternum ring on the Climber's harness, and Münter hitch it to the anchor attachment. The belay system is now ready to extend and arrest an accidental fall. The belay system and Climber are now ready for safety clearance.

As the Climber moves up, he or she should make anchor attachments for carabiners that will be used as directionals for the belay rope. Deciding where and how to place these directionals (running anchors, or "runners") is a matter of belay functionality. The first running anchor should be placed low on the tower to keep the ground-level section of the belay rope oriented horizontally as the Climber moves up. This horizontal orientation is ergonomically favorable for the Belay Operator and enables efficient handling when a fall occurs. At the start of a climb, when the Climber is close to the ground, the belay rope "in play" is at its shortest. The phrase "in play" describes the length of rope between the Münter hitch and the Climber. The rope in play is the section that is available to stretch and decelerate the Climber before stopping a fall. Remember, a long fall on a short rope results in severe shock impact. Keeping falls short relative to the length of the rope in play is a matter of life and death. Place running anchors so that no fall exceeds 25% of the length of belay rope that is in play. It's important to understand that this 25% guideline is the MAXIMUM limitation, not the ideal. At the beginning of a climb, when the rope is short, running anchors will be fixed close together if this safety guideline is followed correctly. Falls can be safely arrested with running anchors placed further apart as the rope in play extends.

Fall Factor Scale: Limiting fall distances to 25% of the belay rope that is in play relates to measurements on the "Fall Factor Scale." This Fall Factor Scale is used to practically quantify and forecast the shock energy that the rope and Climber are exposed to during fall arrest events. The scale measures fall arrest characteristics on calibrations from zero to two. Zero equates to no shock and two equals maximum shock. The 25% limit equates to a figure of 0.25 on the Fall Factor Scale. Fall factors are simple to calculate by dividing the actual distance of a fall by the length of the rope in play. The actual fall distance depends on how high the Climber moves above the highest running anchor. If the Climber looses his or her footing while he or she is positioned below the last running anchor, the actual fall distance should be zero if the lead belay is working properly. If a fall occurs from a position ten feet above the last running anchor, the Climber will drop ten feet and then pass the running anchor by another ten feet before the rope tightens and begins to stretch. The actual fall distance in this example would be twenty feet. So, if a Climber takes a 20-foot fall with 100 feet of rope in play, the fall factor figure will be 0.20 on the scale (20 ÷ 100 = 0.20). When 100 feet of rope is in play, the Climber can fall as far as 25 feet and remain within our 25% safety limit guideline. When 50 feet is in play, the fall limit is 12.5 feet (that's 6.25 feet above the highest runner). You can only drop a little over 6 feet if the rope in play is 25 feet out. That's only 3 feet above the highest runner.

Forecasting how an anchor attachment will perform under a heavy load is critical. Anticipate how the anchor choice will hold the attachment components if the Climber (you) takes a fall. Will the runner stay in place when it gets loaded? Will the runner slide down or sideways when it gets loaded? When poorly placed, runners slide out of position during an arrest event and total fall distances will be increased. This kind of circumstance is referred to as "Via Ferrata." Measurements can exceed 2.0 on the Fall Factor Scale under Via Ferrata conditions. Via Ferrata falls can be fatally serious whether using lead belays or lanyard belays.

The principles measured by the Fall Factor Scale apply to other types of belays, including slings and lanyards. Fall distances have the same effects on sling and lanyard belays without the benefit of a long dynamic rope to absorb shock energy. Proper lanyard placement and rigging with shock absorbing links are necessary for safe lanyard or sling fall protections. REMEMBER: Controlled destruction links extend the length of the sling or lanyard to absorb shock when a fall occurs. Maintain adequate clearance below to allow shock absorbers to extend as necessary to arrest falls.

Heavy Climbers: The size of a Climber does not change measurements on the Fall Factor Scale, but weight does affect the shock absorbing performance of dynamic ropes. To comply with UIAA standards, dynamic ropes must arrest falls without exceeding 12kN of impact force. UIAA uses a load of 80kg (176lbs) to fall test and grade dynamic rope performance. Lighter Climbers will experience less rope stretch to decelerate and arrest a fall. Heavier Climbers will stretch and strain the rope more to arrest a fall. Different sized Climbers on the same rope may experience more or less actual impact discomfort during a fall arrest event. It's possible that arrested falls with the same Fall Factor figure are better tolerated by lighter or heavier Climbers, depending on the length in play and grade of the belay rope. Generally speaking, heavy Climbers will experience more impact discomfort than lighter Climbers during fall arrest events with higher Fall Factor figures. Climbers weighing in above 176 pounds when geared up should be more cautious and conservative when placing running anchors for the belay system. Limit potential fall distances for heavy Climbers to Fall Factor Scale figures of 0.20 or less as the belay extends.

Impact Force Amplification: It's important to consider how a fall event will distribute impact forces over the entire lead belay system. While dynamic ropes can be relied upon to limit impact on the Climber, other parts of the system may be exposed to forces that are over the 12kN limit established by UIAA. Forces will be amplified where directionals are anchored. The 12kN safety figure is the result of military testing to determine survivable impact forces relevant to parachute and ejector seat performance. While the rope stretches to limit impact on the Climber to 12kN, forces will be directionally amplified at the top running anchor. Theoretically, this directional amplification can be as much as double the force the Climber experiences during a fall event. But because pulleys are not used for running anchors, friction at the carabiner limits this directional amplification to about 66%. Even so, a 66% increase in the impact generated by arresting the fall of a heavy Climber can overload some running anchor attachments and rigging. A hard fall arrest that nears 12kN of impact on the rope can develop 20kN at the top runner. That's a lot of force. Consider how this phenomenon might contribute to equipment failure when placing running anchors. Will a huge pulling force cause the structural anchor you're considering to cut the webbing of your runner? Heavier Climbers should place runners more conservatively to shorten potential drops and/or use beefier equipment for running anchors.

Friction: Friction develops as the belay rope slides through the carabiner of a running anchor. Severity of friction depends on the angle of direction change and contact pressure between the rope and the carabiner. Climbers experience this kind of friction as "drag" on the overall functionality of the belay system.

Drag accumulates as running anchors are added. Drag can build up enough to make climbing difficult as the rope becomes harder and harder to pull through the running anchors. Drag also suppresses the shock-absorbing qualities of the rope that is in play. Each running anchor adds a small dose of friction. Each dose of friction slightly inhibits the ability of the rope to slide freely through the runners. It becomes harder and harder for the rope to slide freely through the collective running anchors as multiple doses of friction accumulate. Drag restricts desirable rope stretch in the same way.

As running anchors are added to the overhead system, the Belay Operator below feels less and less pull sensitivity from the Climber. Similarly, in a fall arrest event, the Belayer experiences less shock load as running anchors are added to the system because the Climber is partially supported by the aggregate drag. On the other end, the Climber experiences more shock during a fall arrest event because drag from multiple running anchors suppresses rope movement and stretch.

Theoretically speaking, drag effectively shortens the rope that is in play. Theoretically shortening the rope in play reduces fall arrest cushioning for the Climber and skews Fall Factor Scale calculations. It's important to consider drag when placing running anchors. Placement of running anchors should allow as much free rope movement as possible. Running anchors will create less belay drag when they line up and allow the rope to run in a straight line. Friction will accumulate very quickly if the belay rope follows a runner path that zigzags or serpentines.

Drag, and theoretical rope shortening, will also develop quickly if too many runners are used. It may seem conservative and safe to simply place a running anchor every two feet along the entire climbing route. But this approach can create so much friction that it becomes impossible to climb up and may suppress desirable rope stretch too much. It's best to take a "Goldilocks" view of running anchor placement, that is "not too many and not too few." Combine your understanding of friction, rope performance, and fall arrest principles to place running anchors in a way that is "just right." Develop a good feel for anchor placement, rope handling, and dealing with pulling rope up through sticky runners by practicing lead belays under realistic conditions on a regular basis.

Clearance Below: Fall Factor considerations are meaningless if you fall onto a hard surface or rigid object before the belay rope tightens and begins stretching. The belay rope can't help you if your potential total fall distance is twenty feet while you're climbing above a harpoon-like antennae that is only fifteen feet below. Place running anchors sensibly to prevent contacting hard objects on the way down during a fall event. There may be plenty of rope in play to allow wide spans between running anchors, but it is necessary to place additional runners as you climb above objects that obstruct the fall arrest path below. Pay attention to clearance below, and fix running anchors to limit potential total fall distances as needed.

It will sometimes be necessary to crowd running anchors very close together while maneuvering above a hazard that blocks fall arrest clearance below. In these instances, you can use a "leapfrog" technique to manage friction and conserve equipment. Place runners close together as you climb above the hazard. After extending the rope and clipping into the last runner, disengage or remove lower runners that are within reach. Doing this will reduce overall belay friction and can conserve equipment for later use. Runners must be replaced in reverse leapfrog fashion on the way back down.

Fixing Running Anchors: Assemble runners using webbing or cord loops and screw-lock carabiners. Vary loop sizes as needed for compatibility with the climbing medium. Consider the climbing medium and the risk of software damage when choosing between webbing and cord. Screw gate carabiners are much easier to lock and load with one hand during lead climbing maneuvers. Type 1 (non-locking) carabiners are commonly used for belays in recreational climbing, but require rigging techniques that will not be described in this book. Clip runners onto a webbing or cord loop (rack) slung over the neck and one shoulder. Adjust the size of the rack so that runners are within easy reach of either hand.

At each point on the climbing route where a running anchor is necessary (anchor spot), the Climber will have to stop, grab a runner from the rack, fix it to the climbing medium, and then clip and lock in the belay rope. Evaluate every anchor spot closely to make sure the runner will hold its position throughout the climb and during a fall arrest event. Look for anything that may cut the software or interfere with rope movement. Rig runners so they hang at least six inches long on the anchor spot to optimize functionality. Runners that choke the carabiner tightly against the climbing medium can create friction hot spots and reduce shock durability.

While it seems simple, it actually takes some practice to develop the coordination and hand movements necessary for attaching a runner to an anchor spot and then clipping in the belay rope. Instead of using a flip line to tie off and let go each time, it's far better to develop an ability to establish a running anchor using only one hand. Start by learning to remove a runner from the rack with either hand, one at a time. Reach the hand through the runner loop before grabbing the carabiner to unclip it from the rack. Doing this positions the loop around the wrist like a large bracelet to prevent fumbles and accidental drops. With the loop on the wrist, raise the carabiner above and behind the anchor spot, and drop it. The weight of the biner will snug the software and wrap the anchor spot. Now grab the carabiner below the anchor spot with the same hand, and pull it through the software loop to form a lark's foot hitch. The runner should now be snuggly fixed. Using the same hand, reach down low and grab the belay rope. Pull rope up to create enough slack to reach and load the running anchor. It may be necessary to make a couple pulls on the belay rope to obtain enough slack. Use a finger of the other hand, or your teeth, to temporarily hold a droop of slack while making a second pull. Drape the belay rope loosely in the pit of your hand between the thumb and forefinger. Grab the carabiner with all four fingers on the spine and the thumb pressing the rope against the gate. Squeeze the carabiner until the gate opens and the thumb and rope pass through. Now reposition the hand to screw down the lock. This technique will work well on the open structural elements found on towers, bridges, and ladders. Practice adaptations of this technique on a variety of climbing medium.

Lead Climbing - *Personal Gear*

✱ Items Carried By 1st Climber Up

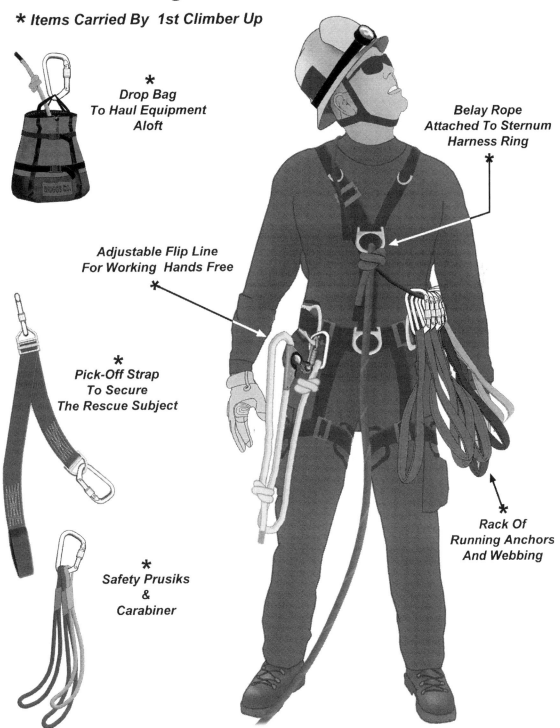

✱
Drop Bag
To Haul Equipment
Aloft

Belay Rope
Attached To Sternum
Harness Ring
✱

Adjustable Flip Line
For Working Hands Free
✱

✱
Pick-Off Strap
To Secure
The Rescue Subject

✱
Rack Of
Running Anchors
And Webbing

✱
Safety Prusiks
&
Carabiner

Lead Climbing - *Fixing A Running Anchor - One Hand*

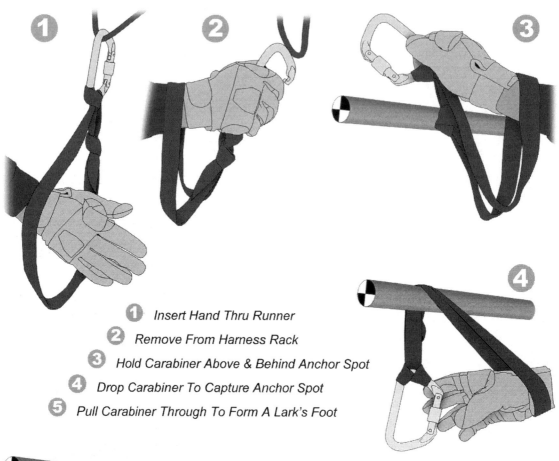

1. Insert Hand Thru Runner
2. Remove From Harness Rack
3. Hold Carabiner Above & Behind Anchor Spot
4. Drop Carabiner To Capture Anchor Spot
5. Pull Carabiner Through To Form A Lark's Foot

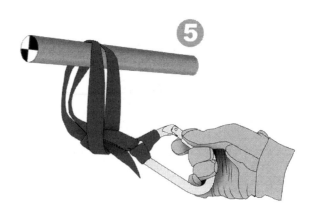

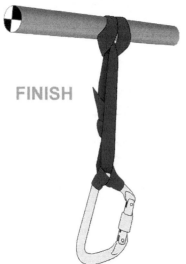

FINISH

Lead Climbing - *Clipping A Running Anchor - One Hand*

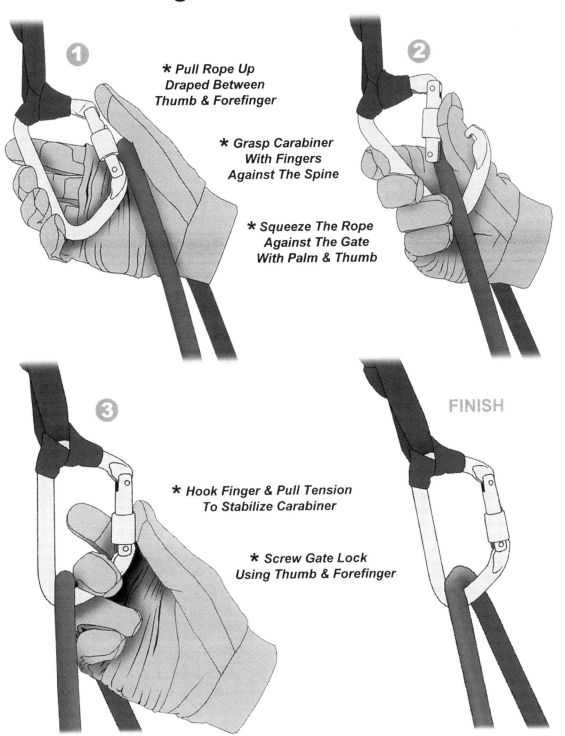

1

* **Pull Rope Up Draped Between Thumb & Forefinger**

* **Grasp Carabiner With Fingers Against The Spine**

* **Squeeze The Rope Against The Gate With Palm & Thumb**

2

3

FINISH

* **Hook Finger & Pull Tension To Stabilize Carabiner**

* **Screw Gate Lock Using Thumb & Forefinger**

Lead Climbing - *Fall Factor*

* Tethered By A 10 Foot Lanyard   *** Fall Distance ÷ Lanyard Length**

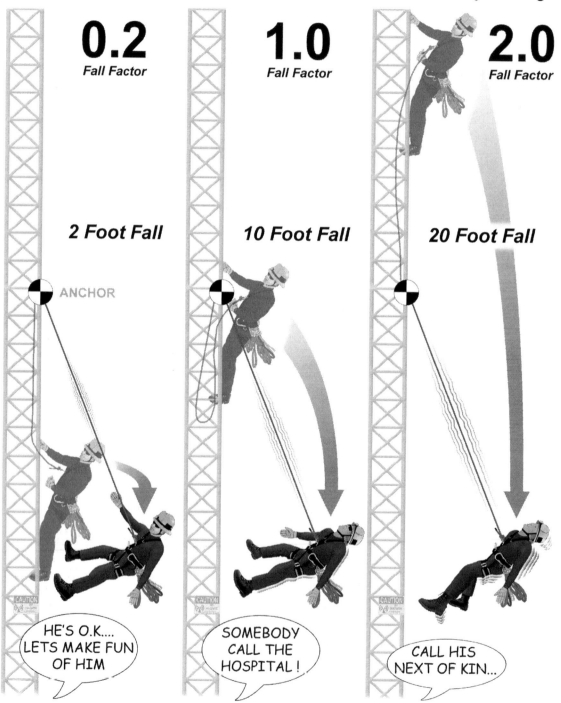

Lead Climbing - *Fall Factor & Running Anchor Placement*

* 50 Feet Of Rope In Play *** Fall Distance ÷ Rope In Play**

Running Anchors
Dangerously
Far Apart

Potential For Severe
Fall Impact

Up To 12 Foot Fall   **20 Foot Fall**   **40 Foot Fall**

0.25   0.4   0.8
Fall Factor   *Fall Factor*   *Fall Factor*

Running Anchors   *Running Anchors*
Arranged To Maintain   *Arranged*
0.25 Fall Factor   *Too Far Apart*

Impact Potential
Exceeding
0.25 Fall Factor

BELAY
STATION

Lead Climbing - *Base Rigging*

*** Establish Belay Station
Outside Of Drop Hazard Area**

*Greater Rope Length Between
The Belayer & Climbing Vector
Improves Fall Factor Conditions
At The Beginning Of The Climb*

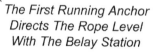

*The First Running Anchor
Directs The Rope Level
With The Belay Station*

*Belay Tightly While The Rope Is Short
And The Climber Is Close To The Ground*

*** Place Running Anchors
Close Together
To Maintain 0.25 Fall Factor**

*** Place Running Anchors
Further Apart
As Rope Extends**

*** Place Runners
To Route The Rope
As Straight As Possible**

Lead Climbing - *Friction Considerations*

* Create A Smooth-Running Belay As You Climb

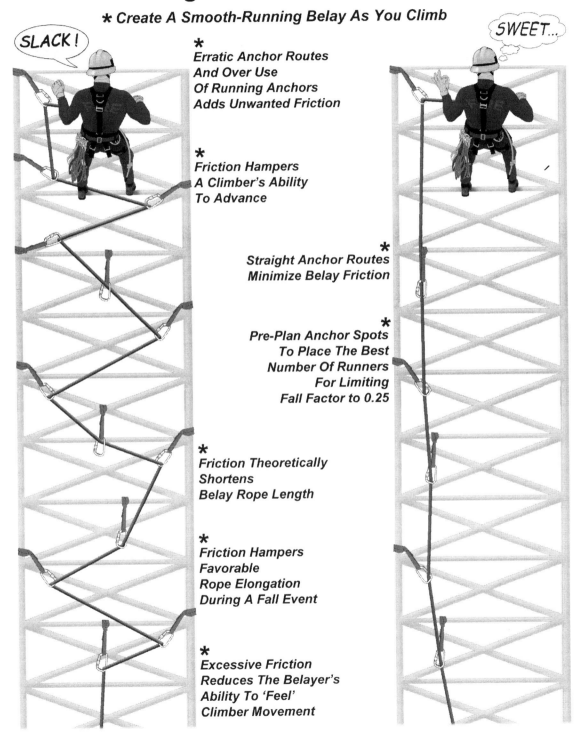

* Erratic Anchor Routes And Over Use Of Running Anchors Adds Unwanted Friction

* Friction Hampers A Climber's Ability To Advance

* Straight Anchor Routes Minimize Belay Friction

* Pre-Plan Anchor Spots To Place The Best Number Of Runners For Limiting Fall Factor to 0.25

* Friction Theoretically Shortens Belay Rope Length

* Friction Hampers Favorable Rope Elongation During A Fall Event

* Excessive Friction Reduces The Belayer's Ability To 'Feel' Climber Movement

Following Climbers: Sometimes more than one person is needed overhead for an operation. Sometimes the subject is located higher than ropes will reach. In cases like these, lead belay methods can be used to provide fall protection for an additional following Climber. Simply stated, two Climbers can use the dynamic belay rope in a "leapfrog" or "inchworm" fashion to maintain fall protection. Climbing profiles that require these techniques are referred to as "multi-pitched" by the recreational climbing community. A "pitch" is roughly a single rope length.

If the first Climber (Lead Climber) runs out of rope or equipment before reaching the subject, he or she can anchor off and handle the rope to belay a following Climber. The following Climber is known as the "Second." After securely tying off, the Lead Climber can establish an overhead belay station using the same rope. With the overhead belay established, the rope can be disconnected from the bottom anchor and attached to the Second Climber's harness. It usually makes good sense to pre-attach the bottom end of the rope if the Belay Operator is the Second Climber. The Lead Climber operates the belay while the Second climbs up. The Second Climber removes and collects runners as they are encountered. The Second can climb up beyond the overhead belay station in leapfrog fashion, or tie off and assume belay duties allowing the Lead Climber to continue up in inchworm fashion. In either case, the belay anchor will likely have to be adjusted or moved to maintain Münter hitch functionality before climbing above the overhead belay station.

Climbing Down: All of the techniques and safety considerations are the same while climbing down. For a single pitch operation, the running anchors will have to be disconnected, removed, and collected as they are encountered. Multi-pitched climbs will require replacing and connecting to runners any time a Climber is moving down from an overhead belay station. These runners must be placed for the benefit of the Climber who will follow at the end of the downward pitch. Pay careful attention to Fall Factor considerations for the belay system when choosing anchor spots during multi-pitch down-climbs.

Overhead Evacuation

The rescue subject will eventually have to be moved to the ground. There are two basic strategies for moving an overhead rescue subject safely to the ground: overhead-based lowering systems and ground-based lowering systems.

Ground-Based Lowering Systems: Rope systems that are anchored at the same level to which the rescue subject must be moved (usually ground level) are ground-based lowering systems. These types of rigs are anchored below and routed through a high directional for the purpose of lowering overhead rescue subjects. The lowering function is controlled from below. The ground-based approach can be a means to lighten the load carried by Climbers on their way aloft. Ropes controlled from below must be at least twice as long as the distance between the anchor and the rescue subject. Basing the lowering system controls on the ground make it much more practical to add and use rescue subject belay rigging.

Overhead-Based Lowering Systems: Rope systems that are anchored overhead for the purpose of lowering a rescue subject are overhead-based lowering systems. These lowering systems are controlled by personnel working aloft. Anchoring overhead is necessary when available ropes are not long enough for a lowering system that is controlled at ground level. Overhead control is also necessary when ropes are not long enough to lower the subject all the way to the ground. In some cases, overhead-based lowering systems require Climbers to carry all the equipment needed for evacuating the rescue subject. Basing the lowering system controls overhead make it more difficult to add and use belay rigging for the rescue subject. Two-rope techniques that include belay rigging usually require two Rescue Climbers positioned overhead. For this reason, overhead-based lowering systems are sometimes rigged using a single rope approach out of necessity. Rig overhead-based lowering systems to include belays whenever possible.

Hauling Equipment Up: Climbers carry up any equipment needed to capture and secure the subject. There are several options for getting the additional lowering ropes and related equipment aloft:

- Climbers carry ropes and equipment to the top and drop the ropes from above.
- Climbers carry equipment and pull rope ends as they move up.
- Climbers use a small diameter pilot line to haul the rope ends and equipment up.

Tag Lines, Deflecting Track Lines & Deflection Blocking: Tower profiles are often tapered and covered with obstacles that obstruct plumb lowering routes. Winds can adversely affect load stability and cause unwanted contact with the tower. Some means of stabilizing and adjusting the lowering vector will almost certainly be necessary for most tower rescue operations.

Tag Lines: Tag lines use a tail of rope that reaches personnel below to stabilize and move the rescue subject away from obstacles on the way down. Tag lines can be rigged during ground-based and overhead-based operations. Tag lines can be rigged using a separate rope or by extending the tail of the lowering line until it reaches ground level. Personnel below pull tag lines to adjust the position of the rescue subject as lowering progresses. Deflect the load out of plumb no more than necessary to clear obstacles. Keeping the rescue subject close to plumb reduces the hazard of slamming hard against the structure if tag line control is fumbled. It is always best practice to deflect the load out of plumb no more than necessary for clearing obstacles. Tag lines can be added to track line and deflection block rigging.

Deflecting Track Lines: Track line techniques use a separate (additional) rope to establish a stable lowering vector that clears obstacles on the way down. Track lines can be rigged during ground-based and overhead-based operations. Rig track lines by anchoring a rope on both ends to create a lowering vector that clears obstacles. Form a short pigtail on the lowering line where it attaches to the rescue subject. A short lanyard can be used if a pigtail is not rigged. Clip the pigtail onto the track line with a carabiner (and optional pulley). The rescue subject will now follow the vector of the track line as lowering progresses. Track lines usually do not need to be rigged tight. Tighten track lines just enough to clear hazards while keeping the rescue subject as close to plumb as possible. The more the load is offset out of plumb, the greater the hazard for slamming the subject hard against the tower if the track line fails. Tracks can even be rigged on a plumb vector to counter wind forces on an otherwise clear lowering path. Track lines can be rigged with the ability to adjust tension and change the degree of deflection as the lowering operation progresses. This adjustability enables the team to clear large obstacles and then return the subject to a safer vector that is closer to plumb.

Deflection Blocking: This technique is used to stabilize and automatically draw the rescue subject away from obstacles as a ground-based lowering operation progresses. Deflection block rigging uses the actual lowering rope as a track vector to stabilize and direct the rescue subject away from obstacles on the way down. Deflection blocking will not work with overhead-based ops. Assemble deflection block rigging by including a short pigtail or lanyard at the end of the lowering rope before attaching the subject. Once attached to the lowering rope and belay, use a carabiner (and optional pulley) to clip the pigtail onto the working line between the high directional and the ground anchor. As the lowering operation progresses, the load will ease away from the tower. The degree of deflection will depend on where the lowering rope is anchored at ground level.

Securing & Connecting the Rescue Subject: At the top of the climb, the rescue subject will have to be captured and secured before the Climber can assemble the evacuation rigging. This is usually a matter of quickly harnessing and connecting the subject to the structure. Once the subject is connected to the structure and protected from falling, the operation has reached an important "situational improvement" milestone. Rescuers have made the situation much better.

Start by fixing a runner near the subject. Put a harness on the subject, and clip to the runner. If you will be using an improvised harness, start by forming the chest portion and clipping onto the runner. Then apply and integrate the improvised seat harness. Avoid over tightening the connection between the harness and the structure. Protect the subject's head with a helmet. The subject should now be protected from falling and ready to ride the lowering system. Use this approach for alert and strong subjects as well as unconscious or non-ambulatory subjects.

It may be advantageous in some situations to integrate a pick-off strap or jigger MA between the runner and the harness for adjustability. If the subject is suspended on a rope or strap, it may be necessary to use a small block and tackle to release him or her. If the subject is already wearing a harness, quickly check the waist belt, chest portions, and attachment rings to assess usability. Make sure the harness in place was not damaged during the accident to which you are responding. Use the harness in place if it appears undamaged and sturdy enough to continue full suspension.

Assembling The Lowering System: Whether using ground-based or overhead-based methods, the first part of rigging a lowering system is establishing stout anchor attachments. Use durable, cut-resistant anchor straps to make stationary attachments for the main lowering line and belay ropes. Place abrasion and cut protection as needed.

Start by fixing anchor attachments directly above the rescue subject. These anchors are all that is needed unless a track line is used. Ideally, anchors should be close enough to reach while providing enough lifting clearance. If the subject is lowered using an overhead-based system, position these high anchors for easy handling of descenders and belay devices. Attach any needed equipment such as pulleys, brakes, or descenders.

Haul up ropes (if needed) and thread them into the directionals or anchored devices. Tie a carabiner to the end of the belay line using a double overhand noose, and clip it to the subject harness. Tie a figure-8 on a bight with a 24-inch tail onto the end of the main lowering rope. Connect the lowering line to the subject harness. Tie a figure-8 on a bight on the end of the tail to form a pigtail that can be used as a deflection attachment. Ropes can be pre-rigged (pre-tied) for these applications before they are hauled up. Complete a remote safety check on all the attachments and connections. The subject should now be ready to evacuate.

With safety checks complete, move the subject into position, and have him or her put weight on the lowering system. Direct the ground team to pull tension on a ground-based system if lifting assistance is needed. The ground team can easily lift the subject by making a perpendicular vector pull on the span of the main line. Disconnect the subject from the runner. Clip the pigtail onto the working section of a ground-based lowering line between the high directional and the ground anchor. If a separate track line is rigged up for an overhead-based system, clip the pigtail onto it. Fix tag lines as needed. The subject can now be lowered.

Rescue Baskets: If a rescue basket is needed, it's usually best to have the ground team send it up on the lowering system. This is simply a matter of assembling the lowering system and then sending the end back down to the ground team. The basket can then be connected and sent up untended by the Ground Team. It will be necessary to use tag lines or deflection rigging. Climbers then use routine basket rigging to move and tie in the subject. In some circumstances, the basket can be used as a scoop to capture and secure a suspended rescue subject. The basket can be loaded and lowered back down untended or with a Climber if lowering is controlled from below. If long ropes are not available, baskets may have to be hauled up by Climbers. Compact spine-immobilizing harnesses can sometimes be used as lightweight alternatives to baskets.

Multi-Pitch Lowering: Multi-pitch lead climbing methods are used to access subjects positioned higher than available ropes can reach. The same multi-pitch approach can be used in reverse to lower subjects to the ground. Subjects can be lowered to the full length of a rope and then secured to the tower until Rescuers reposition and set up for another lowering pitch. Multi-pitch lowering is laborious and slow, but it can effectively evacuate subjects from extremely high positions.

Lead Climbing - *Top Belay Rigging*

✱ Belaying A Following Second Climber From Above

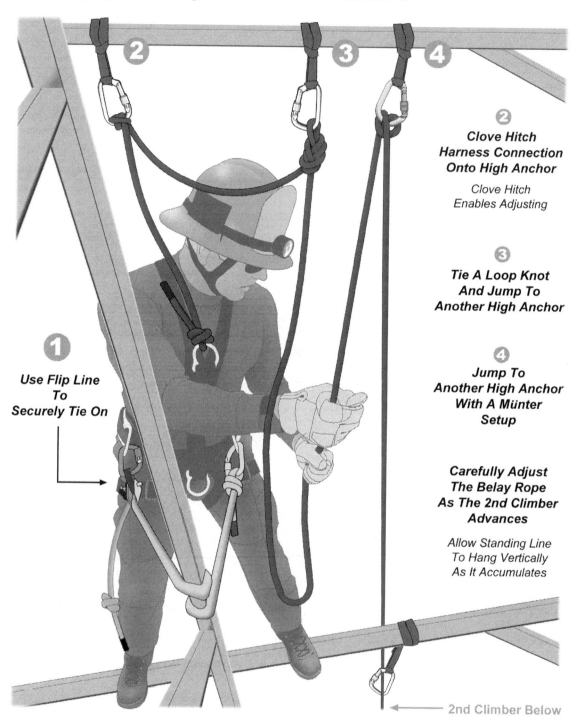

②

**Clove Hitch
Harness Connection
Onto High Anchor**

*Clove Hitch
Enables Adjusting*

③

**Tie A Loop Knot
And Jump To
Another High Anchor**

④

**Jump To
Another High Anchor
With A Münter
Setup**

**Carefully Adjust
The Belay Rope
As The 2nd Climber
Advances**

*Allow Standing Line
To Hang Vertically
As It Accumulates*

①

**Use Flip Line
To
Securely Tie On**

2nd Climber Below

Lead Climbing - *Top Belay Rigging*

* Belaying A Second Climber Advancing Overhead

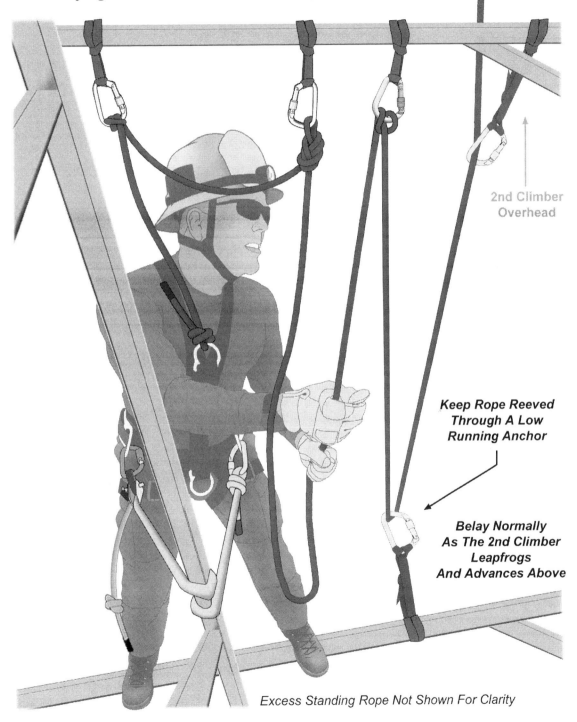

2nd Climber
Overhead

**Keep Rope Reeved
Through A Low
Running Anchor**

**Belay Normally
As The 2nd Climber
Leapfrogs
And Advances Above**

Excess Standing Rope Not Shown For Clarity

363

Deflection Rigging - *Tag Lines*

* Attach An Addition Line Or Extend A Long Tail As A Means Of Guiding The Load From Below

Tag Lines Can Be Used Along With Other Forms Of Deflection Rigging For Added Control

BELAY NOT SHOWN FOR CLARITY

* Manually Guide The Load Away From The Tower As Lowering Progresses

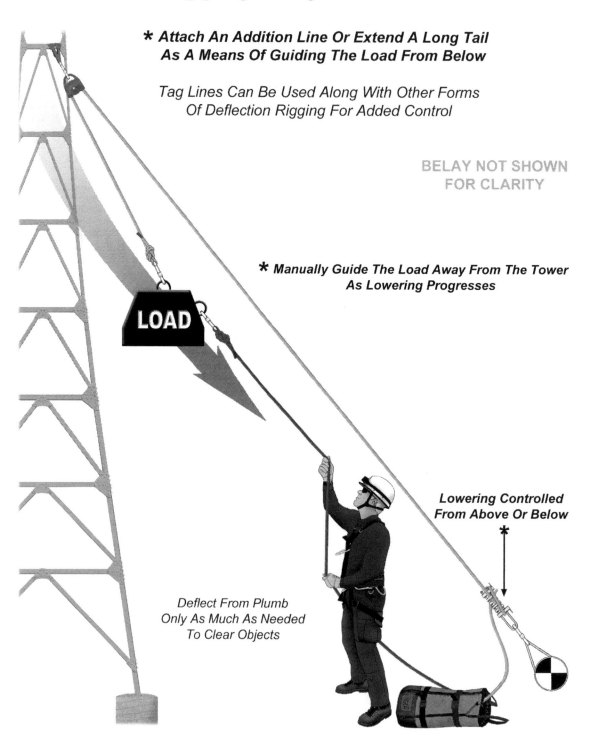

LOAD

Lowering Controlled From Above Or Below

Deflect From Plumb Only As Much As Needed To Clear Objects

Deflection Rigging - *Deflection Track Line*

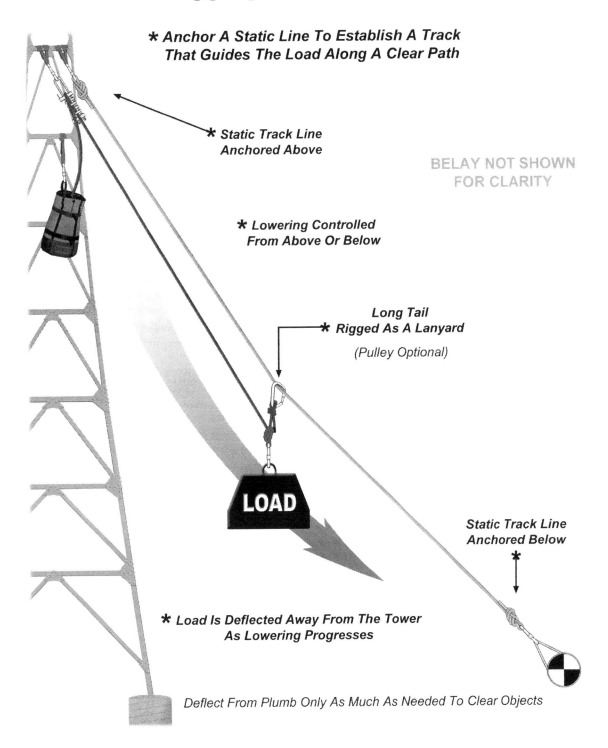

*** Anchor A Static Line To Establish A Track
That Guides The Load Along A Clear Path**

*** Static Track Line
Anchored Above**

BELAY NOT SHOWN
FOR CLARITY

*** Lowering Controlled
From Above Or Below**

**Long Tail
* Rigged As A Lanyard**

(Pulley Optional)

**Static Track Line
Anchored Below
***

LOAD

*** Load Is Deflected Away From The Tower
As Lowering Progresses**

Deflect From Plumb Only As Much As Needed To Clear Objects

Deflection Rigging - *Deflection Block*

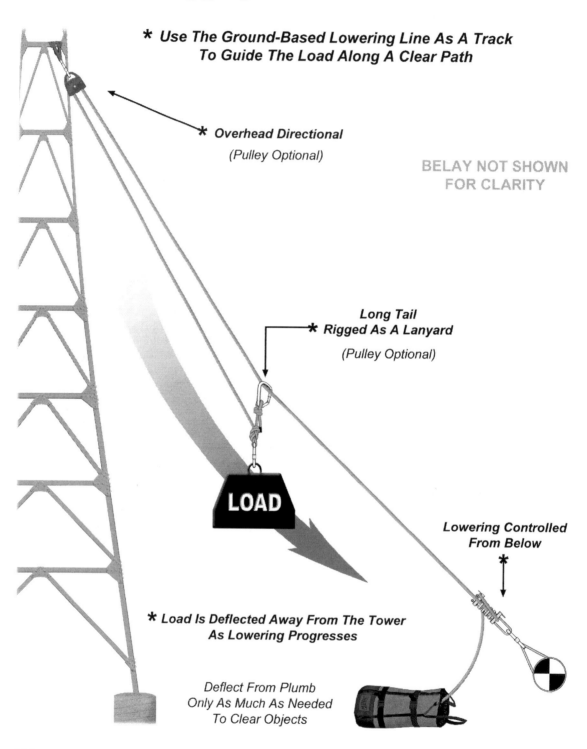

*** Use The Ground-Based Lowering Line As A Track
To Guide The Load Along A Clear Path**

* Overhead Directional

(Pulley Optional)

BELAY NOT SHOWN
FOR CLARITY

**Long Tail
* Rigged As A Lanyard**

(Pulley Optional)

LOAD

**Lowering Controlled
From Below**
*

*** Load Is Deflected Away From The Tower
As Lowering Progresses**

*Deflect From Plumb
Only As Much As Needed
To Clear Objects*

Overhead Ops - *Trespasser Pick Off*

✱ Improvised Harness - Ground Based Lowering - Deflection Block Rigging

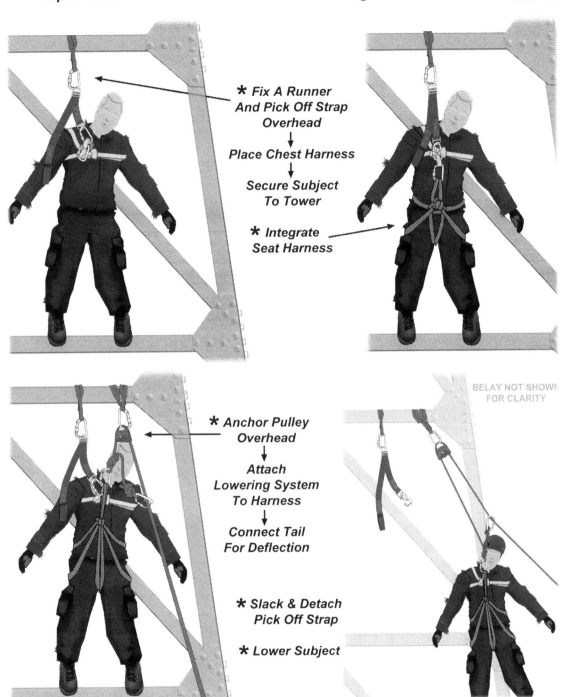

✱ Fix A Runner And Pick Off Strap Overhead

↓

Place Chest Harness

↓

Secure Subject To Tower

✱ Integrate Seat Harness

✱ Anchor Pulley Overhead

↓

Attach Lowering System To Harness

↓

Connect Tail For Deflection

✱ Slack & Detach Pick Off Strap

✱ Lower Subject

BELAY NOT SHOWN FOR CLARITY

Teaching & Learning Lead Climbing Techniques

Introduce overhead climbing and belay concepts thoroughly with enhanced lectures and dry demonstrations in a classroom setting. Formally evaluate apprentices to confirm understanding of Fall Factor Scale principles and fall protection measures. Expose apprentices to climbing and belay demonstrations carried out by competent persons. Allow apprentices to practice and demonstrate belay technique competency using a simulated horizontal climbing route at ground level. Use a chain link fence or staircase as a simulated horizontal climbing route. Permit practice sessions on vertical climbing routes after apprentices demonstrate lead climbing and belay competency at ground level. Always connect conventional belays to students while they practice lead belay techniques. Connect a tandem prusik belay system to a Climber's dorsal harness ring while they practice fall protection placement along a vertical climbing route. Select an easy climbing route, like a ladder, to start out and progress toward more difficult climbing challenges. After apprentices develop and demonstrate climbing and lead belay competency, allow practice on vertical routes without using additional fall protections. Involve apprentices in exercises that use lowering systems to evacuate full-weight mannequins from overhead. As mastery develops, practice multi-pitch belay techniques.

TEACHING & LEARNING UP-CLIMBING SKILLS - INSTRUCTIONAL ORDER

Instructor	**Introduction**	Introduction of up-climbing and belay concepts and technical information using enhanced lecture techniques
Instructor	**Demonstration**	Dry demonstrations of up-climbing and belay practices performed by technically competent people
Student	**Application**	Practice rigging and dry handling up-climbing and belay systems horizontally under close training supervision
Instructor	**Demonstration**	Physically demonstrate up-climbing & belaying techniques
Student	**Application**	Practice vertical up-climbing and belay methods while on full belay
Student	**Evaluation**	Demonstrate proficiency with up-climbing and belay techniques
Student	**Competent**	Ready to up-climb and belay in the field

Lead Climbing - *Training Exercises*

Dry Handling - Horizontal Vector

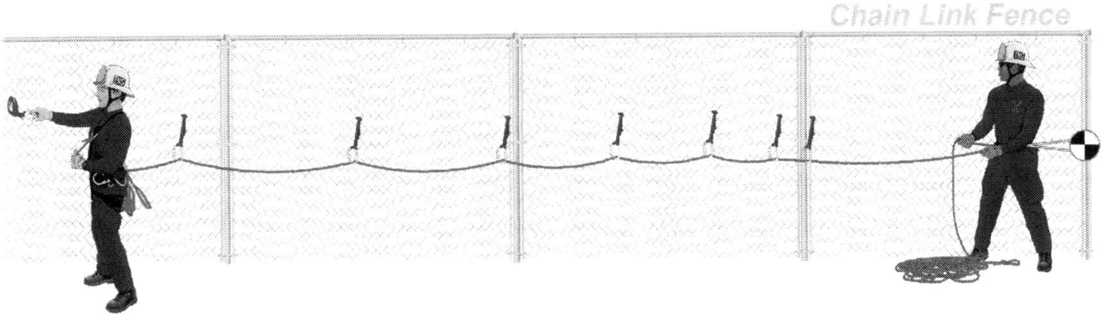

Chain Link Fence

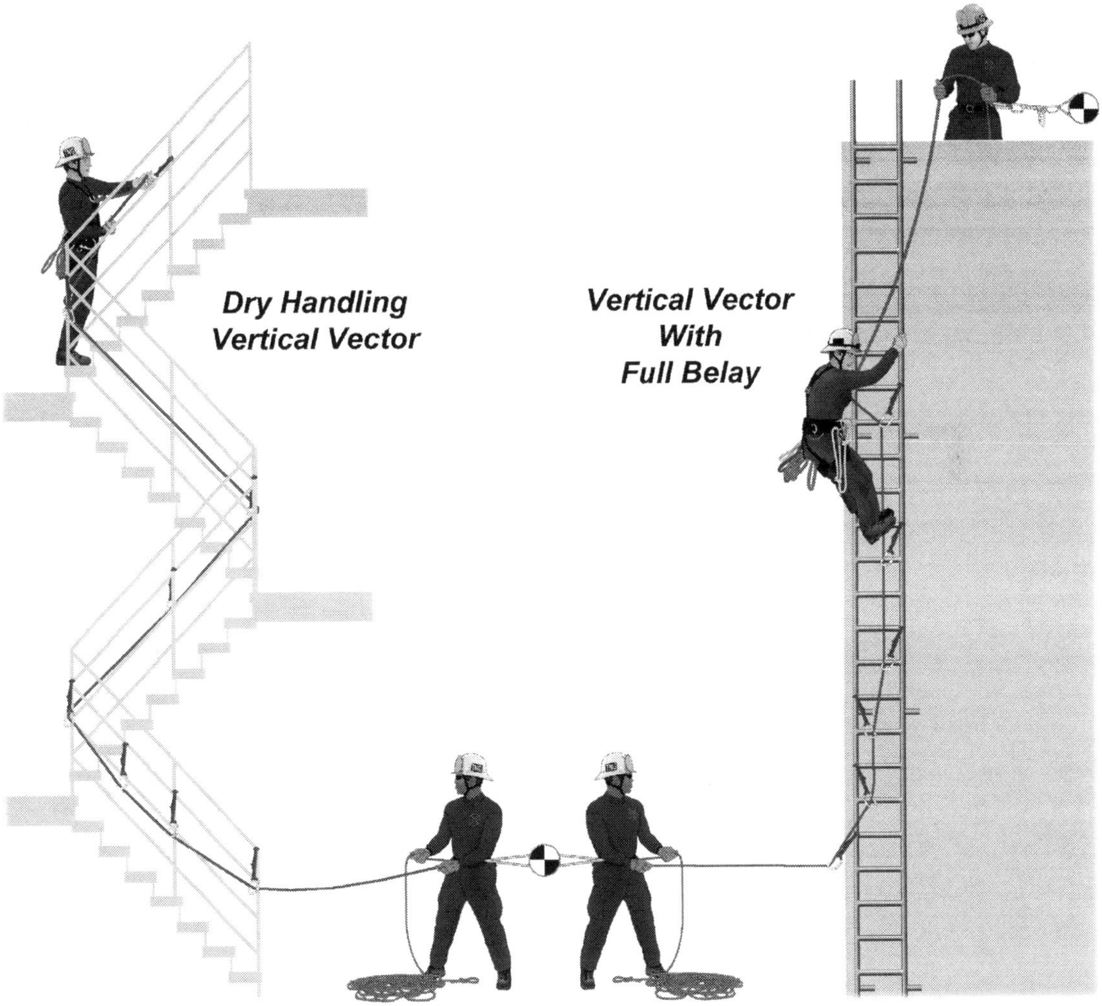

**Dry Handling
Vertical Vector**

**Vertical Vector
With
Full Belay**

Regular Practice: Overhead operations seem straightforward and easy to understand, but climbing up, placing protection, and evacuating a rescue subject is difficult to do. Realistic practice is essential for developing and maintaining competence and proficiency. The persistence of real world conditions like wind, tangled ropes, fatigue, hot steel, etc. tends to bog down overhead climbing ops. Lead climbing skills degrade quickly. Regular practice in realistic conditions perfects skills and abilities for dealing with adverse real world difficulties and leads to smooth overhead operations in the field.

Energized Equipment Safety

Towers and poles are usually erected to support utility lines, lighting, or antenna equipment. The hazards of working near electrical equipment are well known to most, but familiarity with antenna emissions may be less common. Radio and microwave antennae emit energy that can be harmful to human health. Climbing in the proximity of electrical and antenna equipment requires an adequate understanding of precautionary personal safety measures.

High Voltage Safety Precautions: Electrical energy measuring as low as 50 volts can cause death. Electrical transmission and distribution lines always carry voltages significantly higher that 50 volts. The International Electrotechnical Commission identifies 1000-volt alternating circuits, and 1500-volt direct currents as "High Voltage." High voltage can spark across a significant air gap to electrocute a Climber or rescue subject.

Controlling proximity to high voltage electrical equipment is a matter of life and death. The first, and best, step to controlling high voltage proximity is safety education. Establishing an operating standard for working in the presence of electrical hazards is critical. Operating regulations established by OSHA identify safe working distances from various electrical energy sources.

OSHA 1910.269(I)(10) table R6 establishes basic "Minimum Approach Distances" (MADs) for working near live electrical equipment. Based on the information in this table, a good default MAD for initial encounters with electrical equipment during first responder incidents is 15 feet. MADs can be adjusted tighter as technical clarification improves during an incident. OSHA establishes regulations identifying MADs for application under varying conditions such as altitude and over voltage. Understand that damaged equipment can create electrical hazards that are not apparent. High voltage from damaged equipment can be conducted on insulating materials, mechanical parts, vegetation, and in the soil.

OSHA Minimum Approach Distances - Voltage		
Nominal Voltage - Kilovolts Ground to Phase	Feet	Meters
0.5 to 1.0	Avoid Contact	Avoid Contact
1.1 to 15.0	2'- 1"	0.64m
15.1 to 36.0	2'- 4"	0.72m
36.1 to 46.0	2'- 7"	0.77m
46.1 to 72.5	3'- 0"	0.90m
72.6 to 121	3'- 2"	0.95m
138 to 145	3'- 7"	1.09m
161 to 169	4'- 0"	1.22m
230 to 242	5'- 3"	1.59m
345 to 362	8'- 6"	2.59m
500 to 550	11'- 3"	3.42m
765 to 800	14'- 11"	4.54m
Reference: OSHA Table R6 [1910.269 (I) (10)]		

The second best step to controlling electrical hazards proximity is attention to signage. Various standard and regulatory associations and agencies establish signage laws and recommendations for high voltage safety.

 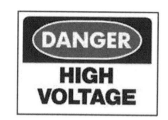  

In general, OSHA requires warning and danger signage at least 12 feet from any place that contains high voltage equipment. Twelve feet plus the 2 to 3 feet between the sign and the person reading it creates a MAD of about 15 feet. Firefighters can provide their own signage in the form of fireline tape and/or traffic cones to establish exclusion zones.

Preplanning for fixed installations can greatly improve worksite safety and efficiency. Visiting and mapping out high voltage equipment hazards can allow rescue companies to fine tune MADs before an incident occurs. In some cases, safe access paths can be mapped out ahead of time. Identifying switches and breakers that can be safely manipulated may allow firefighters to de-energize equipment before technical specialists arrive.

Lock-Out, Tag-Out Measures: Switching circuits off to provide safe access requires assurances that the switch remains in the off position. The physical means of placing locking equipment on breakers and switches allows personnel to turn their attention to the rescue problem without the worry of constant monitoring. Never move into a de-energized high voltage area unless accessible switches and breakers have been properly locked up and/or tagged. If locks are not available, post a guard.

Technical Specialists: As with any other emergency incident, safety and efficiency can benefit greatly from civilian personnel who possess related technical expertise. It makes good sense to seek out and mobilize electrical technicians as soon as an energized hazard is identified at a worksite. Tech Specs can advise teams about safe travel routes, safe working distances, and they can sometimes de-energize equipment.

Hot Sticks & Clean Throw Lines: In some extreme situations, properly-trained personnel may be able to safely use insulated "hot sticks" (poles with grabbing and cutting functionality) and insulated throw lines to manipulate energized switches, breakers, wiring, or people. These tools require high levels of technical expertise to be used safely.

Radio Frequency (RF) and Microwave Emission Safety: Determining whether a potential health hazard could exist with respect to a given transmitting antenna is not always a simple matter. Signal frequency, radiating power, and exposure times all play a role in worker safety at antenna worksites. Preplanning first responder safety precautions for permanently installed antenna hazards is best. Various standard and regulatory associations and agencies establish signage laws and recommendations for radio frequency and microwave safety. Look for signs to gather information and follow any directions they provide.

In general, transmitting antennae are either omni directional or directional, meaning they either emit energy in every direction or in the form of a relatively narrow beam. Omni directional antennae are sometimes referred to as "whip" antenna but are often more complex than a simple whip style. Determining the emission patterns of modern antennae can be very difficult for people who don't work in the industry. Worksites with multiple antennae can complicate matters even further. Seek out and secure RF and microwave emission technical specialists any time firefighters have to climb towers or work on roofs with antennae.

RF and microwave emission safety is managed, on the most basic level, by controlling antenna proximity and duration of exposure. Establish default operating safety standards for first responders entering RF and microwave worksites. All personnel should at the very least be able to recognize conditions that present emission hazards and understand the need to keep their distance and minimize their exposure. Safety personnel should establish exclusion zones, minimum approach distances, and predetermine exposure limits at all energized worksites, then monitor and record exposure times as part of the overall operation. Plan routes that allow Climbers to minimize emission exposure. Consult with technical specialists to develop pre-planned actions and guides in advance of any actual response.

> *A Reasonable Default Practice For Firefighters Pressed Into Working Within Areas Identified By Emission Hazard Signs Is To Limit Exposure To 6 Minutes And To Maximize Distance From Antenna Hardware Until Technical Specialists Can Provide More Information*

The six-minute benchmark is based on Code of Federal Regulations (47 CFR 1.1310) and FCC requirements for protecting technical workers. Controlling access and limiting exposure time will require protocol identical to "Permit-Required Confined Space" operations. Protective clothing, protective shields, and dosimeters are used in the technical field. These types of safety measures may make good sense for jurisdictions with numerous severe RF and microwave hazards.

Lock-Out, Tag-Out Measures: Switching circuits off to make access safe requires assurances that the switch remains in the off position. Placing locking equipment on breakers and switches allows personnel to turn their full attention to the rescue problem. Never move into a de-energized RF or microwave area unless accessible switches and breakers have been properly locked up and/or tagged. If locks are not available, post a guard to prevent switching.

15 Team Competency

Team Competencies

A playbook made up of a handful of basic rope techniques and evolutions can prepare teams to safely and effectively handle most vertical rescue incidents. Standardizing and regularly practicing this small quiver of basic operations will enable teams to access and transport subjects from almost any vertical rescue situation. Adding evolutions to the playbook for specific special hazards will be a cinch as team competency develops toward technical level expertise. The following techniques and evolutions, in combination with scene management and safety practices described in previous chapters, empower teams to place a Rescue Climber over the side, below grade, or overhead to capture and relocate a stranded subject. Think about the hazards within your own response area, and consider the relevance of the team competencies described below.

General Topside Layout

Lowering and raising techniques for various over-the-side operations are more alike than different. Almost any incident that requires 2-rope lowering and/or raising can be set up using the same basic worksite layout. The trick is to keep a compact footprint without hampering workflow. A compact layout enables team members to communicate more easily and keep an eye on everything topside. Using a worksite blueprint that can be applied to a wide variety of situations simplifies matters and reinforces competency.

Anchor the main lowering/raising line as close to the fall line as possible in an area with a clear and level haul field. Orient the standing section of the lowering/raising system away (opposite) from the area where the belay is set up. Doing so makes it possible to closely route the belay line parallel with the main line without fouling up the Haul Team. Think about fashioning a corridor between the main and belay lines that maintains access to the edge to avoid rope vector hazards. Anchor travel-restricting fall protection for people working at the edge. Locate these leashes outside of rope vector hazards.

Lay out rapid intervention rigging close to the group in a way that makes it easy to "grab and go." A good location can be toward the rear of the access corridor, between the main and belay lines. It's also a good idea to position the forward cache of equipment used to assemble the rope systems close to the worksite. Placing the cache behind the main and belay anchors is often a good choice because it puts the equipment close by without getting in the way.

Extra personnel not involved in lowering or raising the Climber can be a real obstruction if they're allowed to wander on the worksite. Whenever possible, standardize the practice of establishing a safe "observation spot." Observation spots are a good way of dealing with all the curious chiefs who show up for a look. People will cooperate and watch from a predetermined observation spot if the view is good. If they can't see what's going on over the side, chiefs won't stay where you want them.

Compressed Topside Layout

Small or narrow worksites can make it tough to construct a 2-rope system with all the favorable nuances listed above. It's often necessary to redirect ropes topside to make everything fit and maintain efficient functionality. This usually involves anchoring a directional pulley to reroute the main line 90 degrees or so. This topside configuration functions as normal, but the redirected main line creates a substantial vector hazard area that personnel should not occupy. In cases like this, the standing section of any hauling pulley system should pull from the uphill side of the vector hazard.

Imagine working on the shoulder of a roadway that patrol personnel want to keep open because of heavy traffic. Apparatus parked parallel along the shoulder can serve as main, directional, and belay anchors. Anchoring the main line onto one vehicle and routing the rope through a directional pulley anchored to another vehicle located above the fall line creates a nice long haul field for the pulley system. This technique provides workers with a decent workspace without having to go into the roadway. The belay can be anchored above the fall line, close to the directional pulley for the main line. Belay functionality is usually not affected by the size of a worksite.

Pulley Systems for Hauling

The ability to recognize, assemble, and use the most appropriate pulley system for any given application is an important competency. Teams must be operationally proficient with a variety of pulley systems used for hauling to be able to adapt as needed in the vertical rescue environment. Along with all simple mechanical advantage pulley systems, teams can adapt to just about any over-the-side hauling situation using the pulley systems diagramed below. Consider the need to haul loads up to 600 pounds with the staff you have on hand. Remember, the act of hauling should be carried out smoothly. Build in enough mechanical advantage to avoid rhythmic "heave-ho" bursts of hauling effort that can cause rock fall and compromise rigging integrity.

3:1 Z-Rig: This pulley system can be viewed as the "backbone" for most over-the-side hauling rigs. Easy to recognize and assemble, the Z-Rig provides a 3:1 theoretical mechanical advantage. Mechanical advantage degrades with pulley friction. For most operations that haul a Climber and a rescue subject, the Z-Rig does not create enough mechanical advantage for a 3-person Haul Team to work smoothly. The Haul Team will need to be staffed with more than three people if a Z-Rig is used for hauling a heavy rescue package topside. Fortunately, Z-Rig hauling power can be easily boosted by minor rigging changes that can take place while the system is still "hot." Mechanical advantage can be increased to as much as 9:1 using the rigging methods diagramed below.

5:1 Complex: This pulley system is simply a Z-Rig with the standing section routed through a traveling pulley that is grabbed onto the second leg. The third pulley can be added while the system is fully loaded. So if a Haul Team misjudges and finds that a 3:1 Z-Rig isn't providing enough mechanical advantage, it can be quickly converted to a 5:1 complex pulley system. The downside to this hauling rig is that the two traveling pulleys converge toward each other as the load raises. This shortens the stroke length, making resetting more frequent.

6:1 Compound (unsynchronized): This rigging adjustment significantly boosts the mechanical advantage of the Z-Rig by compounding a 2:1 onto the 3:1. Attaching a separate 2:1 pulley system onto the Z-Rig develops a theoretical compound mechanical advantage of 6:1. The diagram below anchors the 2:1 to the same point as the Z-Rig creating an unsynchronized pulley system. The illustration also shows the option of rigging up using the end of the rope from the Z-Rig. Because the 2:1 pulls its load at a faster rate than the 3:1, the 2:1 will bottom out (2-block) before the 3:1. While the unsynchronized rigging is quicker and easier to set up, synchronizing the stroke and rope lengths will make your hauling operation go smoother and faster.

6:1 Compound (synchronized): With the same power as the unsynchronized, a 6:1 compound with the stroke lengths of the 2:1 and 3:1 synchronized to bottom out at the same time will make raising operations smoother and faster. This rigging is recommended any time the size of the worksite allows it. It should be understood that the anchor used for the 2:1 in this rigging does not have to be bomber as if it was supporting a life-load. Strain on the anchor that supports the 2:1 section of this rigging will be much lower than the anchor holding the 3:1 section. Simply sinking a single picket into the ground to anchor the 2:1 section may be all that is necessary. The illustration shows the option of rigging up using the end of the rope from the Z-Rig.

9:1 Compound: Very similar in appearance to the unsynchronized 6:1 compound, the 9:1 compound is simply a Z-Rig with a 3:1 compounded onto it. The standing section of the Z-Rig is threaded through a pulley anchored at the same point. This rig is easy to create from a Z-Rig that is fully loaded. Synchronizing the stroke and rope lengths of both 3:1 sections using two separate anchors is the better option when initially rigging up. The 9:1 compound makes hauling heavy vertical loads smooth and easy for a 3-person Haul Team, but the load will be raised very slowly.

Hot Change-Overs
Over-the-side operations will sometimes require converting from lowering mode to raising mode, or vice versa. Operational competency with over-the-side ops depends on the ability to lower a Climber and then haul him or her back topside. Making this conversion without supporting the weight of the Climber and/or rescue subject is a rarity. Teams must become proficient with converting a lowering system while the operation is still "hot." Carrying out a hot change-over should be relatively quick and smooth without changing the position of the Climber. Practice this maneuver as a team until it becomes just another routine task during over-the-side ops.

Over-The-Side Operations
Sending a Climber over the edge to access a rescue subject is the meat and potatoes of the vertical rescue discipline for most jurisdictions. Also described as top-down ops, routine over-the-side access problems are challenging and require a well-practiced team. The following basic evolutions enable responders to access, capture, and relocate vertical rescue subjects stranded below the edge. While the descriptions seem straight forward, carrying out these evolutions takes a great deal of coordination and discipline. In the real world, everything from weather to soil types to insect infestations exist to foul things up for the Climber going over. Realistic and regular practice is the only way to develop team competency with working over the side in the real world. Practice these evolutions for rescue basket recoveries and ambulatory pick-offs. Place the rescue mannequin in various positions of difficulty to develop the competency necessary for operational level performance. Consider the relevance of the following over-the-side evolutions for your own response area.

Lower-Capture-Lower: The boilerplate vertical rescue tactic would have to be lowering a Climber over the edge, capturing the subject, and continuing down to the bottom. This strategy makes the most sense any time there is adequate access below to transport the rescue subject and Climber. Several factors make this approach simpler to carry out. In many cases, this over-the-side evolution can be executed without having to set up a high directional at the edge. The main rope system remains in lowering mode from beginning to end. Consider this operation as the "go to" default whenever conditions permit.

Lower-Capture-Raise: Some situations prevent capturing the subject and lowering to the bottom. Rising tides, rushing rivers, or stands of poison oak are only a few examples of hazards that force converting from lowering mode to raising. The need to convert from lowering to raising is a bit more complex and equipment intensive. Hauling a Climber and rescue subject topside is very difficult to do without rigging a high directional at the edge. Setting up a portable anchor, if one is needed, is a pretty extensive step in the setup process. Converting the lowering system to a raising system complicates things a little more. Teams that practice regularly figure out how to economize high directional setup time and carry out smooth and fast hot change-overs. Lowering and then raising can easily become just another routine evolution with enough practice.

Rapid Deployment: Teams may wish to up their game as they develop expertise and refine their performance. It is possible to safely get a Climber over the side for a lower/raising operation before setting up a high directional at the edge. The Climber transitions the edge to go down while Haul Team members gather and assemble a portable anchor in preparation for the raising part of the evolution. The main line can be retrofitted with a high directional using an accessory block and tackle once the portable anchor is set up. A well-practiced team can easily place a portable anchor and incorporate the main line before the Climber is ready to go up. These tactics may shave overall time in gaining access to a rescue subject in danger of falling from a precarious perch. This strategy can also streamline workflow when staffing is short while waiting for additional resources to arrive.

Rappel Down–Haul Up: Similar to the rapid deployment evolution described above, rappelling down to access the subject can streamline workflow even further with fewer personnel. In a dire emergency, this evolution can get underway with as few as three people on scene if self-belay skills are used. A topside belay can be used if a fourth person is on scene. A downside to this method is that it's limited to pick-off operations where a rescue basket is not used. Carrying a rescue basket over the edge during a rappel is far too cumbersome and unsafe. As the Climber makes contact with the rescue subject, he/she locks off and ties off the descent control device. With the descender secured, the Climber uses pick-off techniques to capture the rescue subject. While the Climber works, topside personnel fill in operational positions as they arrive and prepare for lowering or hauling up as necessary. If the Climber is ready to pick off the subject before topside personnel are ready, he/she can use rappelling techniques to continue down if the bottom is accessible. These kinds of operations obviously require a great amount of skill and understanding to be carried out safely. In other words, a lot of practice in a clinical setting is necessary to perfect these advanced operations.

BE CAREFUL: Rappelling down with limited staff on scene can increase risk tremendously. Consider arrival times of additional personnel and resources carefully before committing to this evolution in the real world. Weigh the risks and benefits of sending a Climber over the side while the only available Backup Climber is en route.

Climb Up–Capture–Lower: A competent team must be able to send a Climber up vertical structures to capture and relocate a rescue subject. Structures where ladders won't work—such as towers, bridges, light poles, and cranes—are all potential vertical rescue venues. Team members should preplan their hazards and develop climbing and belaying skills needed to go up and get someone down. Accessing the subject is only one major part of these evolutions. Teams must also practice capturing and relocating the rescue subject to a safe location, usually to vehicle transportation at ground level. Practice climbing up and relocating subjects via pick-off and rescue basket recoveries. Incorporate various types of deflection rigging to lower the subject along a clear route. Work on more advanced tactics and strategies using multi-pitched climbing and lowering methods as competency develops. While these evolutions are rarely used in the field, they are invaluable when the need arises.

Vertical Entry And Extraction: Confined space and trench rescue disciplines usually require some level of rope rigging for vertical transportation. The stereotypical scenario for these rescues involves the use of some kind of simple pulley system supported by a tripod or multi-pod. Vertical rescue belays are useful for these operations, and winch cable systems can be supported/backed up using ropes and pulleys. Erecting a portable anchor over an access hole and clipping on a pre-rigged simple pulley system is very fast and adaptable. Develop proficiency using simple pulley systems for lowering. Practice various entry and extraction protocols using basic rope methods and challenge your team by simulating difficult portable anchor placements. Anticipate conditions that may interfere with safe resultant force angles affecting the stability of the portable anchor. Get used to belaying snuggly to compensate for the small amount of rope in play during short lowers and raises. Practice setting up and operating safely in the cramped worksites around entry holes.

Rapid Intervention: As is true at the scene of an interior structure fire, hanging a Rescue Climber out there should never occur without a backup plan ready to launch. Any time a member has committed their center of gravity over the edge or overhead, a Backup Climber (Climber 2) should be ready to deploy the instant something goes wrong. Best-case scenario in an emergency involving the initial Climber is to have a standardized backup plan already established. Standardizing backup actions familiarizes everyone with how things should go and encourages personnel to practice rapid intervention maneuvers regularly. In our 7-person Vertical Rescue Team structure, it makes the most sense to use a member of the Haul Team to fill the position of Backup Climber. The Backup Climber should have a clear understanding of his or her mission and possess the skills necessary to competently carry out that mission.

The Backup Climber must also be harnessed up and equipped before Climber 1 goes hot. Identify which anchor is to be used for the backup rigging ahead of time. Anchor the rigging ahead of time if it makes sense. A basic approach to accessing Climber 1 is to anchor a separate rappel line for Climber 2 and using any of the existing lines already over the side for traveling self-belay rigging. If a Mayday situation arises and the Leader deploys Climber 2, all other operational positions should stop and hold whatever they're doing until advised to do otherwise. During this time, the Backup Climber sets the rappel rope and rigs the traveling self-belay. The rappel rope can be dropped over the edge or carried in its bag as Climber 2 goes down. It may be necessary to bypass hardware and/or knots in the rigging on the way down. Climber 2 should carry additional prusiks and carabiners to maintain connection with the belay rope while passing obstacles. Climber 2 goes through safety protocol as normal before transitioning the edge and rappelling down.

Climber 2 uses whatever methods are necessary to secure and care for Climber 1 after making contact. It may make good sense to load Climber 1 into the rescue basket intended for the original rescue subject. It may be necessary to load both the subject and Climber 1 into the basket. If a basket was not part of the original rescue effort, pick-off methods can be used. If the situation is severe for both the rescue subject and Climber 1, it may be best for Climber 2 to stabilize the situation and wait out the arrival of additional resources. In any of these cases, rapid action to access Climber 1 can be achieved very easily by a well-practiced Backup Climber.

Team Competency - *General Topside Layout*

✱ *General Setup Strategy For Over-The-Side Operations* *Raising & Lowering*
✱ *Facilitates Compact Work Site For Easy Communication & Teamwork*

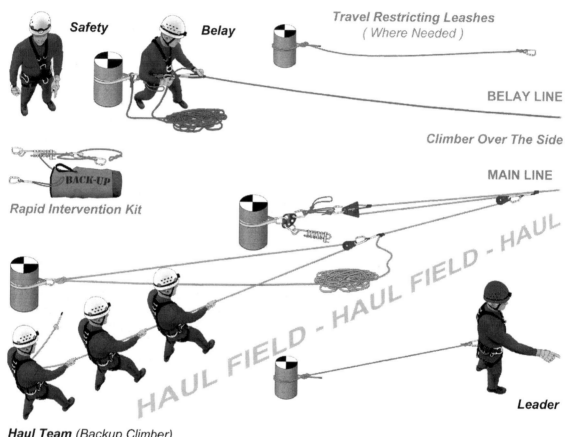

Safety   **Belay**

Travel Restricting Leashes
(Where Needed)

BELAY LINE

Climber Over The Side

MAIN LINE

Rapid Intervention Kit

BACK-UP

HAUL FIELD - HAUL FIELD - HAUL

Leader

Haul Team (Backup Climber)

- **Belay** - *Belay Line Vector Directly Over The Edge To The Climber*

- **Haul Team** - *Clear Haul Field Oriented Opposite Belay Rigging - 1 Member As Backup Climber*

- **Leader** - *Clear View Of All Topside Members - View Of Climber Desired*

- **Safety** - *Wandering Position - Clear View Of All Topside Members - View Of Climber Desired*

- **Rapid Intervention** - *Kit In Place And Ready To Deploy - Backup Climber Haul Team Member*

- **Travel Restriction** - *Identify Exclusion Zones - Provide Fall Preventing Leashes Where Needed*

- **Equipment Cache** - *Locate Closely Behind Belay & Haul Team*

Team Competency - *Compressed Topside Layout*

* Tight Worksites Often Require A Perpendicular Haul Vector

* Rig A Horizontal Directional To Position The Haul Field As Needed

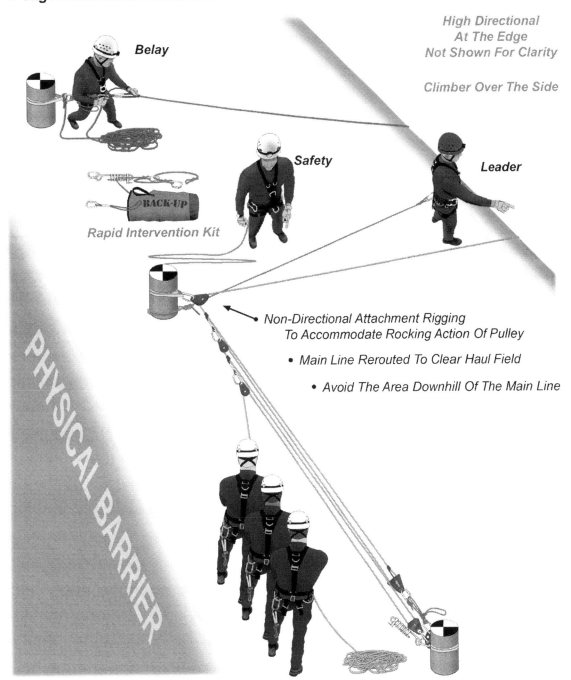

*High Directional
At The Edge
Not Shown For Clarity*

Climber Over The Side

Belay

Safety

Leader

Rapid Intervention Kit

BACK-UP

*Non-Directional Attachment Rigging
To Accommodate Rocking Action Of Pulley*

- *Main Line Rerouted To Clear Haul Field*

- *Avoid The Area Downhill Of The Main Line*

PHYSICAL BARRIER

Team Competency - *Pulley Systems*

✶ *Pulley Systems Well Suited For Over The Side Ops* - 3-Person Haul Team

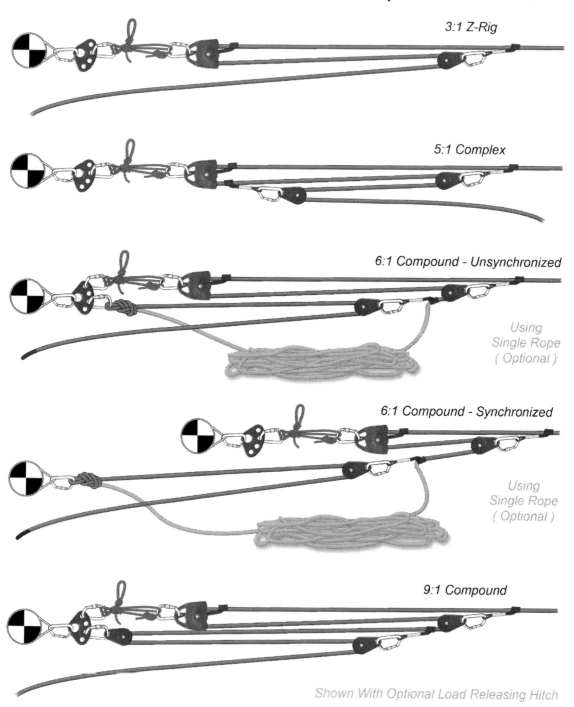

3:1 Z-Rig

5:1 Complex

6:1 Compound - Unsynchronized

*Using
Single Rope
(Optional)*

6:1 Compound - Synchronized

*Using
Single Rope
(Optional)*

9:1 Compound

Shown With Optional Load Releasing Hitch

Team Competency - Lowering To Raising Conversion

* Transition From Lowering The Climber To Hauling The Climber Topside

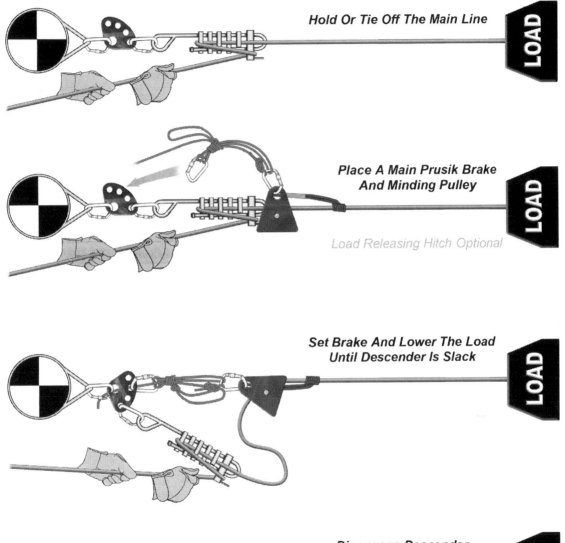

Hold Or Tie Off The Main Line

LOAD

Place A Main Prusik Brake And Minding Pulley

LOAD

Load Releasing Hitch Optional

Set Brake And Lower The Load Until Descender Is Slack

LOAD

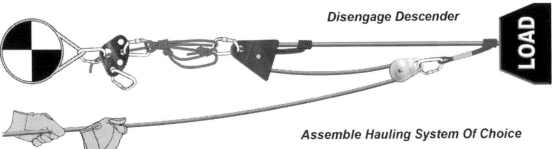

Disengage Descender

LOAD

Assemble Hauling System Of Choice

Team Competency - *Lower-Capture-Lower*

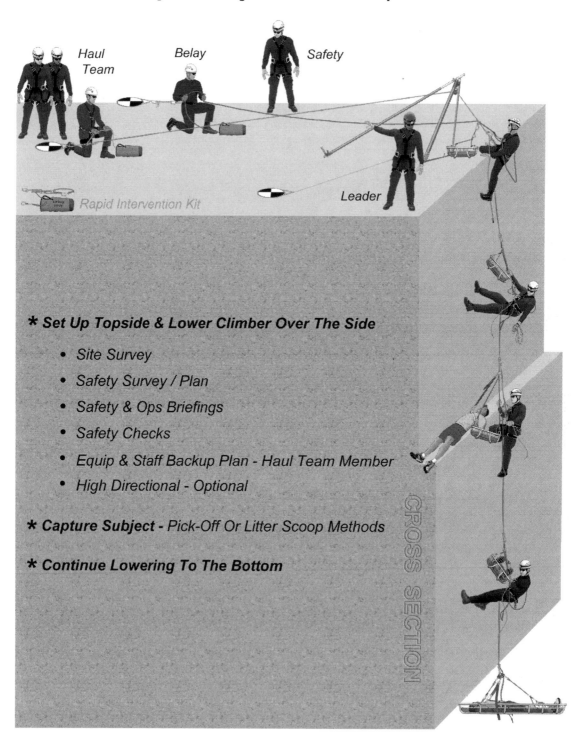

Haul Team

Belay

Safety

Rapid Intervention Kit

Leader

CROSS SECTION

* Set Up Topside & Lower Climber Over The Side

- *Site Survey*
- *Safety Survey / Plan*
- *Safety & Ops Briefings*
- *Safety Checks*
- *Equip & Staff Backup Plan - Haul Team Member*
- *High Directional - Optional*

* Capture Subject - *Pick-Off Or Litter Scoop Methods*

* Continue Lowering To The Bottom

Team Competency - *Lower-Capture-Raise*

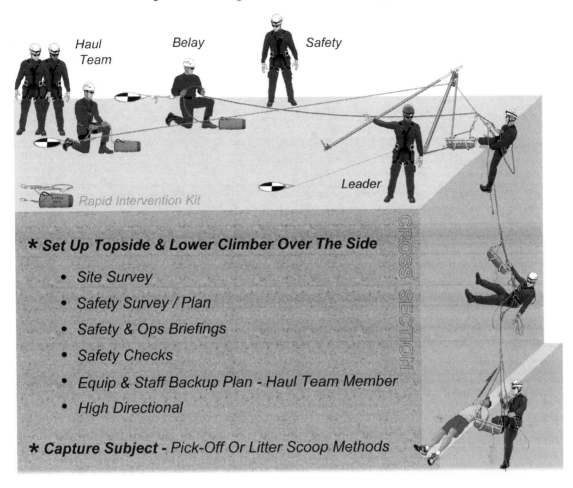

Haul Team

Belay

Safety

Rapid Intervention Kit

Leader

CROSS SECTION

✱ Set Up Topside & Lower Climber Over The Side

- *Site Survey*
- *Safety Survey / Plan*
- *Safety & Ops Briefings*
- *Safety Checks*
- *Equip & Staff Backup Plan - Haul Team Member*
- *High Directional*

✱ Capture Subject - *Pick-Off Or Litter Scoop Methods*

✱ Change To Raising System - Haul Climber Topside

Team Competency - *Rapid Deployment*

✴ Deploy The Climber Without Waiting To Set Up A High Directional

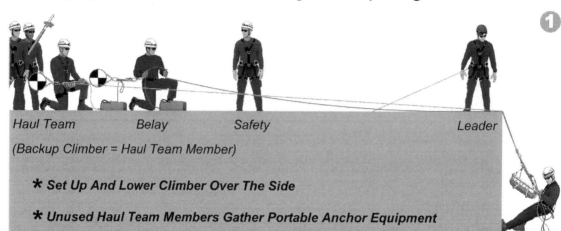

Haul Team   Belay   Safety   Leader

(Backup Climber = Haul Team Member)

✴ Set Up And Lower Climber Over The Side

✴ Unused Haul Team Members Gather Portable Anchor Equipment

**✴ Place Portable Anchor For High Directional At The Edge
While Climber Holds Position To Capture The Subject**

✴ Anchor The Directional Pulley With An Accessory Block & Tackle

✴ Use The Block & Tackle To Lift The Main Line

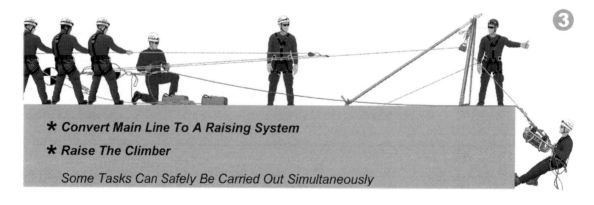

✴ Convert Main Line To A Raising System

✴ Raise The Climber

Some Tasks Can Safely Be Carried Out Simultaneously

Team Competency - *Rappel Down - Haul Up*

✳ *Rapid Deployment & Access While Team Sets Up Haul Rigging*

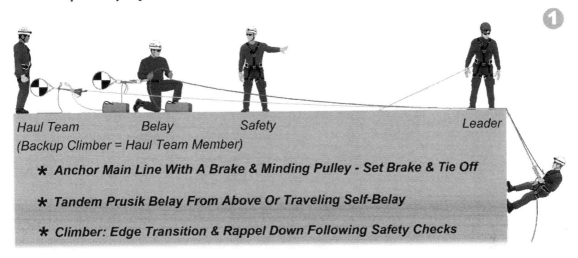

①

Haul Team   Belay   Safety   Leader
(Backup Climber = Haul Team Member)

✳ *Anchor Main Line With A Brake & Minding Pulley - Set Brake & Tie Off*

✳ *Tandem Prusik Belay From Above Or Traveling Self-Belay*

✳ *Climber: Edge Transition & Rappel Down Following Safety Checks*

②

✳ *Assemble Raising System & High Directional At The Edge*

✳ *Climber: Lock & Tie Off Descender Before Pick-Off & Raising*

③

✳ *Haul Climber Topside Upon Command*

Limited To Pick-Off Tactics For Securing & Moving The Rescue Subject

Team Competency - *Climb Up-Capture-Lower*

* Shown: Ground-Based Lowering & Belay Using Deflection Block Rigging

Leader, Safety & Additional Haul Team Members
Not Shown For Clarity

* Alternative: Overhead-Based Lowering

* Alternative: Overhead-Based Belay

* Alternative: Climb Up - Double Lanyard

* Alternative: Two Climbers Overhead

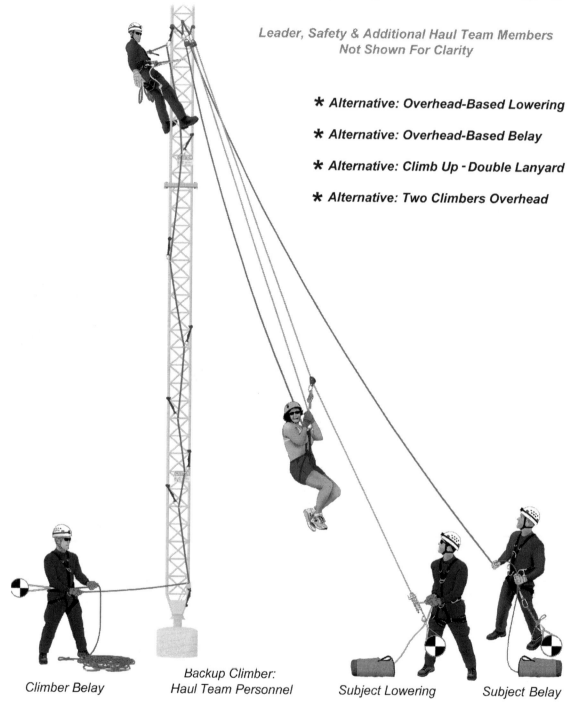

Climber Belay

Backup Climber:
Haul Team Personnel

Subject Lowering

Subject Belay

Team Competency - *Vertical Entry & Extraction*

✱ Portable Anchor - Simple MA For Lowering & Raising

- **Outfit Workers With Travel Resticting Leashes Wherever Needed**

- **Establish Stabile Anchor Above The Entry Point**

- **Rig A Simple Block & Tackle With A Brake As The Lowering/Raising System**

- **Establish Direct Belay** *(No Directional Pulley)*

- **Tend The Brake & Reverse Stroke To Lower**

- **Closely Monitor Resultant Force Angle**
  Created By Directional Pulley

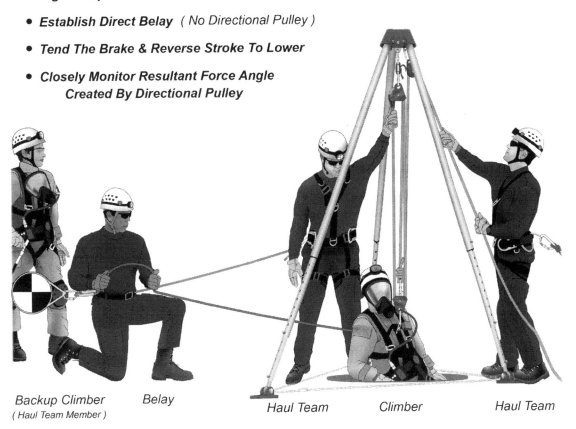

Backup Climber   Belay   Haul Team   Climber   Haul Team
(Haul Team Member)

- **Attach Main & Belay Lines To Appropriate Harness Rings As Necessary**

- **Rigging Can Be Used In Conjunction With Cable Winch Accessories**

- **Extract Rescue Subject Using Pick-Off Techniques Or Separately On Haul System**

- *Simple 5 to 1 CD Mechanical Advantage Shown*

- *Leader And Safety Not Pictured For Clarity*

- *Confined Space Rescue Support Personnel & Equipment Not Shown For Clarity*

Team Competency - *Rapid Intervention*

* Quickly Deploy Backup Climber - Simple Pre-Rigged Equipment Cluster

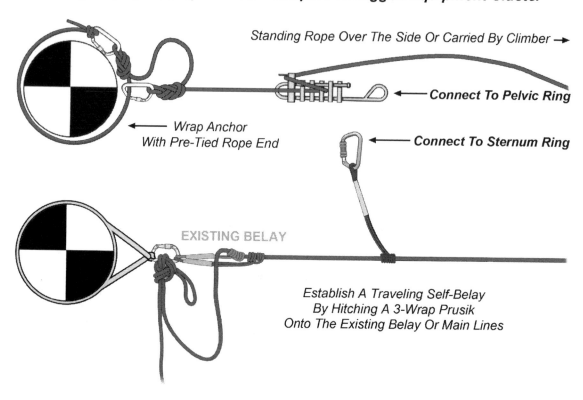

Standing Rope Over The Side Or Carried By Climber →

Connect To Pelvic Ring

← *Wrap Anchor*
With Pre-Tied Rope End

Connect To Sternum Ring

EXISTING BELAY

Establish A Traveling Self-Belay
By Hitching A 3-Wrap Prusik
Onto The Existing Belay Or Main Lines

- *Securely Anchor The Pre-Rigged Rapid Intervention Kit*

- *Establish A Traveling Self-Belay Using The Belay Or Main Lines Already Over The Side*

- *Extend The Standing Line Over The Side, Or Attach Bag Of Rope To Backup Climber*

- *Connect Backup Climber - Carry Out Safety Checks*

- *Transition Edge And Rappel Carefully To Avoid Sending Falling Rocks Toward Climber 1*

- *Use Separate Prusik Loop To Pass Knots And Rigging As Needed*

- *Secure Climber 1 - Load Into The Rescue Basket Already In Place* (For Example)

- *Backup Climber Connects To Original Rigging*

- *Carry Out Remote Safety Check Before Disconnecting From Backup Rigging*

- *Team Hauls Climber 1 And Backup Climber Topside*

Glossary

2 Blocks, 2 Blocked - Jargon describing a pulley system that is fully bottomed out; pulleys close together.

A-Frame - Rigid A-shaped portable anchor, usually for placing a high directional pulley.

Accessory - Specialized or extra equipment used to supplement the functionality of other equipment.

AHD - Artificial High Directional; usually associated with a portable anchor.

AHJ - Agency Having Jurisdiction.

Aid Climbing - Technique that uses equipment and fasteners to move vertically.

Anchor - Object used to fasten a rope system securely stationary.

Anchor Attachment - Equipment used to connect anchor objects and rope systems together.

Apprentice - Person learning a trade or skill from an employer or professional authority.

Arm Pump - Concentrated, disabling fatigue in the arms.

Artificial High Directional - (*see Portable Anchor*).

Ascender - Jargon describing mechanical ascending devices; mechanical equipment used to climb a fixed rope.

Attachment Point - Locations on Life Safety Harnesses suitable for full-weight support.

Auto Locking Carabiner - Connector with a gate that closes and locks automatically; requires manipulation to unlock and open.

Auxiliary Equipment - Specialized tools and equipment that fine-tune or improve performance.

Axis - Imaginary line about which a body rotates or aligns.

Back-tie, Back Tying - Rope techniques that connect anchors together to add support; weak anchor object supported by connecting it to a strong anchor object.

Backup Climber - Person assigned with lowering or climbing up to assist or rescue the primary Climber; Climber 2; carries out rapid intervention actions.

BCCTR - British Columbia Council of Technical Rescue.

BCDTM - Belay Competence Drop Test Method established by the British Columbia Council of Technical Rescue (BCCTR).

Belay - Stopping a fall while climbing.

Belay Device - Equipment that adds friction to a rope to stop a fall.

Belay System - Rigging assembled to stop a fall while climbing.

Belayer - The person controlling the belay system; title of an operational position among members of a 7-person vertical rescue team.

Bend - Term used to identify tying methods for joining rope ends together.

Best Practice - Favored method among multiple choices for doing something.

Bight - Sharp hairpin turn of rope.

Biner - Slang term for "Carabiner" (*see Carabiner*).

Block and Tackle - Simple pulley system that is portable.

Block Creel - Technical term describing rope construction methods using continuous unbroken fibers from end to end.

Bollard - Short, thick post that is well anchored.

Bolt, **Climbing Bolt** - Mechanical device inserted into a tight fitting hole for the purpose of securing a climbing anchor.

Bomber, Bomber Anchor - Slang for 'Bomb Proof'; jargon describing an anchor choice or anything as being far stronger than necessary.

Braking Hand - Term used to identify which hand holds and controls the braking function.

Bridle - Straps, rope, or cord configured to attach to and support a bulky object onto a single point.

Bulkhead - Term adapted in this book for rigging or auxiliary equipment that strongly gathers rigging elements; gathering plates or rings, head of a tripod, or multi-pod.

Cable - Metal rope; often used with industrial winch accessories for portable anchors.

Cache - A collection of equipment of the same type that is stored together.

Cadence - Rhythm; a modulation or inflection of the voice.

Camming - Counterforcing pressure; torquing mechanics principle applied for the purpose of creating grip or purchase.

Carabiner - Mechanical connector used to join vertical rescue cache components together.

Caution Tape - Warning sign configured into a rolled up line of plastic tape (*see Fireline Tape*).

CE - A European standard marking, compulsory on new personal protective equipment.

Center of Gravity - The average location of the weight of an object.

Chaining, Chaining Hazard - Describes when hardware objects are connected together in succession without a swivel, creating a torsion strain.

Chock - Anchoring equipment used to wedge and hold between rock surfaces.

Cinch - A firm grip, or something easy to do.

Cleaning - The process of removing running anchors from a climbing route.

Climber - Title of the worker suspended over the side or climbing up; identifier given to a person assigned to an operational position on a 7-person vertical rescue team.

Clinical Setting – Highly-controlled and appropriately setup work or training environment.

Command - Verbal communication relaying information to direct action; select words chosen for standard communication on vertical rescue worksites.

Comparative Measurement - Empirical method of testing mechanical advantage of pulleys systems; measuring by observation.

Competency - The ability to do something successfully or efficiently.

Complex Pulley System - Pulley system that is neither simple nor compound.

Compliant - Meeting or in accordance with rules or standards.

Compound Pulley System - Rigging that arranges components so that pulley systems haul on other pulley systems to compound mechanical advantage.

Continuous Filament Fiber - NFPA; fiber of indefinite or immeasurable length.

Contour - An outline of a natural feature such as a hill or cliff.

Cord - Small diameter rope.

Cordelette - A section of 7 to 9 millimeter rope.

Cornice - Architectural: decorative overhang; architectural name given to overhanging natural features, such as overhanging cliff faces.

Counterbalance - Weight that balances another weight.

Critical Angle - Jargon identifying 90° angles as the maximum safe vector created by load-sharing rigging.

Cross-Load - Unwanted lateral or perpendicular loading of a device.

D-Ring - Metal ring shaped like a "D".

Daisy Chain - Sewn webbing sling with multiple loops.

Debrief, Debriefing - Discussion about a completed mission or undertaking.

Decommission - To remove something from duty or service.

Default - A pre-selected option.

Deflect, Deflection - Directing away from; altering the path of gravitational pull; guiding along a hazard-free path.

Descender (Descendeur) - Jargon for Descent Control Device (*see Descent Control Device*).

Descent Control Device - NFPA: An auxiliary equipment item, a friction or mechanical device utilized with rope to control descent.

Design Load - The amount of weight or force that an item or component is engineered to securely hold.

Designator - Term used to describe a name or title give to a person assigned with a particular objective, responsibility, job, or task.

Direct Anchor Attachment - Rigging method that uses the Life Safety Rope itself to attach to an anchor object.

Direct Brake Placement - Describes the functional placement of a hauling system brake so that it supports the full weight of the load when set.

Directional - Describes an anchor and hardware (usually a pulley) combination rigged to alter the tension vector of a rope.

Distributing - Term used to describe the division of and distribution of load forces; a form of load sharing; distributing anchor attachments sometimes referred to as self-equalizing or self-adjusting when rigging is configured to support a dynamic load.

Dorsal - Anatomical location high on the back between the shoulder blades.

Double Lanyard - Manufactured fall protection device that combines rope and hardware to form a yoke with two large locking hooks; used for fall protection; highly engineered; usually integrated with shock absorbing components.

Drag, Rope Drag - Reduction in rope motion caused by contact with an object or surface; friction.

Dress, Dressed - Jargon describing how neatly a knot or hitch is tied; well dressed, or poorly dressed.

Drop Hazard - Possibility of falling objects from above.

Drop Tests - Scientific methods that expose equipment to impact loads by creating and measuring varying falling conditions.

Drop Zone - Area below a vertical worksite that exposes people to the hazard of falling objects from above.

Dry Rope - Ropes treated with coatings that improve water-repelling characteristics.

Dynamic Rope - Ropes engineered for climbing belays that stretch and absorb impact energy.

Edge - Worksite landmark where the topside surface ends and the vertical face begins; edge of a cliff.

Edge Protection - Any measure of protecting rope, software, and rigging from abrasion and cutting.

Edge Transition - The act of maneuvering across the edge from the topside surface to the vertical surface, or from the vertical surface to the topside surface.

Elbow - Term that identifies an exposed turn of rope on a knot or hitch.

Elevator Tails - Extended knot tails as part of rescue basket Climber connection rigging.

Elongation - NFPA: The increase in length, expressed in a percent of the original length, that occurs in a sample of new rope when tested; General: The amount of extension of an object when stressed.

End-To-End Load Straps - NFPA: Straps with end connection points meant to be loaded in end-to-end fashion, including, but not limited to, pick-off straps, load-releasing straps, or vertical lifting straps.

Equipment Loop - One name given to the light duty loops on a life safety harness designed to carry lightweight equipment.

Ergonomic - Intended to provide optimum comfort and avoid stress or discomfort.

Escape - Relocating from a hazardous environment; ascending after becoming stuck on a rope system.

Etrier (Etrie') - French term describing a software ladder or foothold system.

Exclusion Zone(s) - A defined area; geographical area that requires personnel to use appropriate fall protections before entering.

Eye - Pre-sewn end loop; connection hole.

Face, Climbing Face - General term to identify a climbing surface.

Fail-safe - Devices that protect in the event of failure.

Fall Factor - NFPA: A measure of fall severity by dividing the distance fallen by the length of the rope used to arrest the fall.

Fall Line - Imaginary topside force vector that leads directly over the edge toward the climbing objective; the straight line the rope system must follow to access the rescue subject.

Fall Protection - Measures taken to prevent or safely arrest accidental falls.

FEMA - Federal Emergency Management Administration.

Figure 8 - Term used to describe a group of knots suitable for rescue work that resemble the shape of the number eight.

Fireline Tape - Warning sign configured into a rolled up line of plastic tape (*see Caution Tape*).

Fixed Leg - Section of rope within a pulley system that remains stationary.

Fixed Line, Fixed Rope - Length of rope that is anchored and not intended to move; often used to grab and/or tie on to for support.

Flake - Rock formation that is thin and flat, often with sharp edges.

Flaking - A method for organizing a length of rope in a temporary location for the purpose of paying out.

Flip Line - Software configured for use as an adjustable waist-level attachment for work positioning.

Floating Anchor - Rigging that arranges anchor connection points above ground for the purpose of optimizing ergonomics or to overcome issues related to clearance.

Floating Anchor Attachment - Rigging that connects an anchor object with a rope system in a way that elevates it off the ground.

Focused - Rigging methods that collect and direct the strength of two or more anchor points forward to a single stationary point are known as focused.

Follow-Up Program - NFPA: The sampling, inspections, tests, or other measures conducted by the certification organization on a periodic basis to determine the continued compliance of labeled and listed products that are being produced by the manufacturer to the requirement of this standard (1983-2012).

Following Climber - Term sometimes used in overhead operations where the Lead Climber is followed by a second Climber.

Foothold - Feature on a climbing face where a Climber's foot is placed for purchase; feature of some kinds of climbing equipment intended to work like a stirrup for standing.

Fray - To become unraveled or worn at the edge.

Fulcrum - The point where a lever is supported and pivots.

Full-Weight Mannequin - Human shaped training prop weighing 165lbs or more.

Gain - Knot tying term used to describe the size/gauge of a loop.

Gathering Plate, Ring - Hardware made of solid materials used to focus strong rigging connections.

Gear Loop - Light duty loops on life safety harnesses intended to secure a small personal cache of equipment; usually on the waist belt portion.

General Use - NFPA: One design of equipment item or manufactured systems designed for general use loads, technical use loads, and escape based on design loads that are calculated and understood; General: 2-person load not to exceed 600lbs.

Gin Pole - Portable anchor comprised of a single compression strut supported by some form of guying.

Golden Angle - Jargon identifying rope vectors that create a 120° angle resulting in equal force distribution at the apex and both ends.

Guy, Guying - Rope or cable used to laterally support a vertically standing object; method of stabilizing a standing object with laterally fixed lines.

H.I.P. - Harness Induced Pathology; phrase identifying a causal relationship between injuries or maladies and prolonged suspension while wearing a harness.

Hardware - NFPA: Non-fabric components of protective clothing or equipment including, but not limited to, those made of metal or plastic.

Harness - NFPA: Life Safety Harness. An equipment item; an arrangement of materials secured about the body used to support a person.

Haul Field - Location, area where a Haul Team works a pulley system.

Haul Team - Title of the subgroup of a 7-person Vertical Rescue Team tasked with assembling and operating the main lowering and raising systems.

Haul Team Leader - Title of the person assigned to direct the actions of the Haul Team subgroup in a 7-person Vertical Rescue Team.

Hauling - The action of pulling a rope to move a load (object or person); operating a pulley system.

Hazard - Any potential source of danger.

Hazards Assessment - Analysis to determine features within a jurisdiction that present a hazard with potential of requiring fire and/or rescue response and mitigating action.

Heave-Ho - Phrase describing the action of bracing and pulling hard to develop hauling inertia.

High Directional - Term given to any rigging that alters rope tension in a vertical direction; pulleys anchored overhead.

High Line - Rope anchored at both ends in a horizontal, or near horizontal, orientation for the purpose of traversing.

H.I.P. – (HIP) Harness induced pathology; injury or illness caused by prolonged suspension in a harness.

Hitch - Rope arranged to hold onto an anchorage in a gripping manner.

Hobble, Hobbling - Methods of containing skate forces by tying legs together.

Horn, Rock Horn - Conical shape in a rock or other solid object that is suitable for anchoring.

Hot Change-Over - Converting rigging while under a "hot" life-load (*see Hot*).

Hot, Going Hot - Jargon describing conditions where a rope system is supporting a human life; *"We're going hot," "The operation is still hot."*

Impact Load - NFPA: Sudden application of force.

Improvised Harness - An arrangement of webbing secured about the body used to support a person.

Indirect Anchor Attachment - Rigging method that uses materials other than the Life Safety Rope itself to attach to an anchor object.

Indirect Brake Placement - Describes the functional placement of a hauling system brake so that it supports less than the full weight of the load when set.

Input Force - Force applied to work a lever or pulley system.

IRATA - (I.R.A.T.A) The Industrial Rope Access Trade Association

Jam - Any condition that causes a raising, lowering, or belay rope system to become stuck and immovable.

Jigger - Jargon describing any small auxiliary block and tackle.

Jurisdiction - The territory or sphere of activity over which the legal authority of a court or other institution extends.

Keel - Bottom aspect.

Kern - Interior portion of a kernmantle rope.

Kernmantle Rope - Rope with a core of filaments encased inside a woven sheath.

kN - Abbreviation of kilonewton; 1,000 Newtons; metric calibration for measuring energy.

Knot - Functional formations of tucks, ties, and bindings to create loops or stoppers in rope or cord.

Labeled - NFPA: Equipment or materials to which has been attached a label, symbol, or other identifying mark of an organization that is acceptable to the authority having jurisdiction and concerned with product evaluation, that maintains periodic inspection of production of labeled equipment or materials, and by whose labeling the manufacturer indicates compliance with appropriate standards or performance in a specified manner.

Labeling and Information - Specifications for label style and content.

Lanyard - Rope, cord, webbing, or strap fashioned as a means of keeping an object within reach; short length of software attached to equipment to prevent dropping.

Lashing - Secure, tight wrapping or binding.

Lead Climber, Leading Climber - Person climbing up and placing fall protection (belay) rigging along the route as he or she progresses.

Leader - Title of the person assigned to manage and direct the actions of a 7-person Vertical Rescue Team.

Leapfrog - Jargon describing the action of maneuvering over or passing another Climber; following Climber moves up and past the Lead Climber.

Life-Load - A human being supported by any rope system.

Life Safety Harness - NFPA: An equipment item; an arrangement of materials secured about the body used to support a person.

Life Safety Rope - Rope dedicated solely for the purpose of supporting people during rescue, fire-fighting, other emergency operations, or during training evolutions.

Light Use - Term describing equipment being used to support a single person load of 300lbs or less; term used in NFPA 1983-2006.

Line - NFPA: Rope when in use.

Listed - NFPA: Equipment, materials, or services included in a list published by an organization that is acceptable to the authority having jurisdiction and concerned with evaluation of products or services, that maintains periodic inspection of production of listed equipment or materials or periodic evaluation of services, and whose listing states that either the equipment, material, or service meets appropriate designated standards or has been tested and found suitable for a specified purpose.

Litter - NFPA: An apparatus, also called a stretcher, designed to secure, protect and transport a patient vertically or horizontally.

Load - A weight or source of pressure borne by someone or something.

Load Limiting - Measures taken to ensure rigging will not be exposed to forces able to break equipment, disable systems, cause equipment failure, or injure people.

Load Releasing Hitch - Connection rigging that serves to lengthen under a load for the purpose of relieving tension.

Load Sharing - Rigging techniques that support a single load using multiple anchors.

Load-Bearing Attachment Point - NFPA: Point on a harness or escape belt that is used for connection to an anchor system that will provide full support and fall arrest for the designated load.

Load-Bearing Connector - NFPA: An auxiliary equipment system component; a device used to join other system components including, but not limited to, carabiners, rings, quick links, and snap-links.

Lock, Lock Off - State of stability in the off position; mechanisms that prevent operation; act of putting in a locked state.

Low Angle - NFPA: Refers to an environment in which the load is predominantly supported by itself and not the rope rescue system (e.g., flat land or mild sloping surface); General: Slopes up to 45°.

Low Stretch Rope - NFPA: Ropes with elongation characteristics between 1% and 10% under load at 10% of MBS (*see Static Rope*).

LRH - Load releasing hitch.

Lumbar - Relating to the lower part of the back.

MA, Mechanical Advantage - The ratio of the working force exerted by a mechanism to the applied effort.

MAD - Minimum Approach Distance; prescribed distances for managing exposure to radiating or arching electrical hazards.

Manipulative - Term used to describe physical activity of handling something or participating in an exercise that requires physical effort.

Mantle - Exterior sheath of a kernmantle rope; a climbing move (technique) for positioning.

Manufactured System - NFPA: Preassembled system sold as a unit by the manufacturer and tested as a complete assembly.

Manufacturer - NFPA: The entity that directs and controls any of the following: compliant product design, compliant product manufacturing, or compliant product quality assurance; or the entity that assumes the liability for the compliant product or provides the warranty for the compliant product.

Mechanical Advantage, MA - The ratio of the working force exerted by a mechanism to the applied effort.

Melt - NFPA: A response to heat by a material resulting in evidence of flowing or dripping.

Minimum Breaking Strength (MBS) - General: Measurement benchmark in tensile testing that identifies the force needed to break a material or piece of equipment; NFPA: The result of subtracting three standard deviations from the mean result of the lot being tested using the formula in 8.2.5.2.

Moderate Elongation Laid Life Saving Rope - Rope constructed of laid fibers with maximum elongation characteristics of 25% under a load 10% of the maximum load; often found in fall protection systems.

Multi-Pitch(ed) - Sections of actual climbing on routes with multiple belay stops; often determined by the length of the belay rope.

Multi-sheaved - Pulley configured with more than one sheave.

Multiple Configuration Load Straps - NFPA: Straps with end connection points that can be configured in multiple loading,

including, but not limited to, end-to-end, basket, and choker configurations.

Multipod - Portable anchor system that can be configured in a variety of forms.

Münter - Noun: Adjustable hitch used to create friction to support or lower a load; Verb: Act of manipulating a rope that is tied with a Münter hitch to support or lower a load.

Non-Working - Not involving movement.

Noose - Adjustable, self-tightening loop in a rope that is tied with overhand knots.

Nut - Anchoring equipment used to wedge and hold between rock surfaces (*see Chock*).

Nylon Chainsaw - Jargon used to describe how a running rope cuts or melts a stationary object or surface.

Observation Spot - Geographical location identified as a safe place to view a vertical rescue operation; usually used for those not participating as part of the rescue party.

Offset - Rigging, active or passive, used to deflect suspended loads carried by a rope away from hazards.

OLEA - Odd Load, Even Anchor; memory aid.

Operational Level - Level of expertise; ability to use tools, to assemble and operate systems as taught.

OSHA - Occupational Safety and Health Administration.

Parrot - To exactly repeat verbal communication out loud.

Passive - Without active response or resistance.

Pelvic - Anatomical location; frontal region at waist level.

Personal Use - Term formerly used in NFPA standards publications to identify application of a single person load; 300lbs.

Picket - Pointed steel bar sunk into the ground to establish an anchor.

Picket System - Multiple picket anchors connected together to support a load.

Pigtail - Jargon describing a short end of rope in rigging that is used for connecting or retaining.

Pitch - Section of a climbing route between a belay station and the overhead Climber; usually limited by the length of the belay rope.

PMP - Pursik Minding Pulley.

Portable Anchor - NFPA: A manufactured device with rigid arms, legs, or both designed to support human loads.

Positioning Attachment Point - NFPA: Point on a harness or belt that is used for connection to an anchor system that will support a person's weight for work at height.

Practice - The actual application or use of an idea; a customary, habitual, or expected procedure.

Proof Load - NFPA: The application of force to a material as a nondestructive test to verify the performance of that material.

Protection - Measures of varying application intended to prevent an unwanted outcome.

Prusik (Prussik) - Noun: A form of hitch used as a rope grab. Verb: The act of manipulating a prusik hitch to capture rope movement progress; ascend a rope using prusik hitches.

Pulley - A wheel designed to support movement of a rope, cable, or belt along its circumference.

Pulley System - Any assembly of pulleys and rope for the purpose of creating mechanical or practical advantage.

Purcell - Cord, or cord loop, arranged for adjustability and/or slippage as a lanyard or shock absorber.

Rack, Gear Rack - Sling draped around the torso or belt used to carry a small cache of equipment while climbing.

Raising - Term used to describe the process of moving a rescue load up; hauling up a rescue load.

Rapid Intervention - Response without delay to make access and take mitigating action to assist a coworker in distress.

Rappel, Rappelling - Moving down along the length of a rope equipped with a friction device that controls the rate of descent.

Recon - Short for reconnaissance; reconnoiter; preliminary survey or search.

Red Flag Condition(s) - Extreme or severe state of risk; potential for serious unwanted outcome; conditions that should be recognized as dangerous.

Rescue Basket - NFPA: Litter; an apparatus, also called a stretcher, designed to secure, protect, and transport a patient vertically or horizontally.

Rescue Subject - Person or animal in need of rescue.

Rescuer - Any person involved with accessing, helping, treating, and/or transporting a person or animal in need of rescue.

Reset, Resetting - (Pulley systems) The act of fully extending a bottomed out (2-blocked) pulley system.

Responder - Any person with the responsibility to react to public emergency calls for assistance by going to the location to take mitigating action.

Resultant, Resultant Force, Resultant Angle - Reduction of multiple forces to a single force vector.

Rigger - Title given to any person assigned the responsibility of assembling vertical rescue systems.

Ring - An auxiliary equipment component; an ungated load-bearing connector.

Rope - NFPA: A compact but flexible, torsionally balanced, continuous structure of fibers produced from strands that are twisted, plaited, or braided together and that serve primarily to support a load or transmit a force from the point of origin to the point of application.

Rope Bag - Fabric sack with varying features used to contain and deploy rope.

Rope Grab - NFPA: An auxiliary equipment device used to grasp a life safety rope for the purpose of supporting loads; includes ascending devices.

Route - A way or course taken in getting from a starting point to a destination.

Runner - Length of webbing or cord used to connect components of a climbing safety system; also called a sling.

Running Anchor - Component of a lead climbing belay system; an anchor attachment the dynamic belay rope runs through as a Climber progresses.

Safe Working Load - (SWL) is the load that a lifting device such as a crane, a cherry picker, or a lifting arrangement can safely lift, suspend, or lower.

Safety Check - Systematic inspection to confirm rigging and safety systems are assembled and installed properly.

Safety Factor - Factor of safety; the ratio of the breaking stress of a material or structure to the calculated maximum stress when in use.

Safety Officer, Safety - Title of the person assigned to manage safety practices and procedures as part of a 7-person Vertical Rescue Team.

Second, Second Climber - Title sometimes used in overhead operations where the Lead Climber is followed by an additional Climber; the Lead Climber is followed by the Second Climber.

Self Arrest, Self Arresting - Function of some types of auxiliary mechanical devices that automatically detect and stop a fall; mountaineering term for using an ice axe to stop a downhill slide.

Self-Belay - Backup fall-arresting techniques used by a Climber; a belay operated by the Climber as he/she progresses.

Self-Destructive Action - NFPA: Interaction of materials in a manner that leads to deterioration; General: principle used in the function of some types of shock absorbing equipment.

Self-Equalizing - Anchor rigging technique that adjusts automatically and equally distributes a load among multiple anchor points.

Sheave - A wheel with a groove for rope to run on.

Shock Load - Forces that are sudden and severe (*see Impact Load*).

Simple Pulley System - Rigging with rope and hauling pulleys that are attached directly to a load item.

Skate Force - Phrase used to describe force vectors that cause something to lose purchase.

Sling - Length of webbing or cord configured as a loop and used to connect components of a climbing safety system.

Snap Link - NFPA: An auxiliary equipment system component; a self-closing, gated, load-bearing connector.

Snug - Moderately tight, or close fitting.

Soft Link - Software connection feature rigged to twist or bend.

Software - NFPA: A type of auxiliary equipment that includes, but is not limited to, anchor straps, pick-off straps, and rigging slings.

SPRAT - Society of Professional Rope Access Technicians.

Stacking - Method of piling up rope in a temporary location in a manner that enables one end of the rope to pay out easily without snagging or knotting.

Standard - An idea or thing used as a measure, norm, or model in comparative evaluations.

Standing End - The inactive end of a rope or cord.

Standing Part - Knot-tying term; part of the rope or cord not engaged with a knot or hitch, or supporting a load; the part of the rope or cord that remains stationary as a knot is tied.

Standing Section - Segment of a length of rope that is not supporting a load or engaged in a knot or hitch; the balance of rope.

Static Rope - NFPA: Ropes with elongation characteristics between 1% and 10% under load at 10% of MBS, and 45% elongation while supporting 75% of MBS.

Static System - Systems that anchor a span of rope on both ends.

Sternum - Breastbone; term for anatomical location between the nipples.

Sticht, Sticht Plate, Sticht Hole - A friction device or feature used with rope to belay or support a load; named after Franz Sticht.

Stokes Basket - Brand name used ubiquitously to describe rescue baskets (*see Rescue Basket, Litter*).

Stopper, Stopper Knot - Knot tied onto a rope or cord for the purpose of blocking the progress of rope-grabbing auxiliary equipment; to prevent rappelling off the end of a rope.

Strap, Strapping - Woven material in the form of a long, flat strip.

Strategy - A plan of action or policy designed to achieve a major or overall aim.

Stretcher - Equipment in the form of a lightweight, portable bed used to move non-ambulatory people; sometimes used as a term to describe litters or rescue baskets.

Suspend - Hang; supported in free air by a rope.

Synthetic - Man-made.

Taco - Slang term used to describe the unwanted severe bending of rigid equipment or human posture.

Tactic(s) - Actions carefully planned to achieve a specific end.

Tail - Rope tail; short section of rope or cord protruding from a knot or hitch.

Task Book - Document used to record an individual's training effort and accomplishments for the purpose of competency or completion.

Team - A group of people with a common goal or mission; 7-member group of personnel trained for vertical rescue work.

Technical Specialist - Person possessing relevant expertise in a subject relative to an operation or job.

Technical Use - NFPA: One design of an equipment item or manufactured systems designed for technical use loads, and escape based on design loads that are calculated and understood.

Technical Use Loads - Loads weighing up to twenty 20kN (4,496 lbf).

Thread - To insert and pull rope or cord through something, such as a pulley; linear strand of fibers used for sewing.

Tie Off - Tucks and ties in a rope that serve to prevent operation, slipping, or unlocking.

TMA - Theoretical Mechanical Advantage.

Topside - Term used to describe the worksite surface during an over-the-side vertical rescue incident.

Torque - Tendency of a force to rotate about an object on an axis.

Torsion, Torsional - Twisting of, or the effect of twisting, an object due to an applied torque.

Training Timeout - Any pause during a training event to emphasize or reinforce an important, relevant, or timely point of information.

Travel Restricting - Physical means of limiting walking access to a measurable distance or area.

Travel-Restricting Leash - Rope, cord, or strap rigged for the purpose of travel restricting; a form of fall prevention.

Traveling Pulley - Pulley within a pulley system that moves as the system is operated; part of a pulley system that is not stationary.

Traveling Self-Belay - Self-belay rigging that is manipulated and operated by a Climber as he or she moves on a rope.

Triangle Of Death, Death Triangle - 2-point anchor rigging infamous for developing excess force enough to cause attachment rigging to fail

Tripod - Portable anchor configured with three adjustable legs hinged together.

Tyrolean - (*see Highline*).

UIAA - International organization that develops and maintains safety standards for climbing equipment; Union Internationale des Associations d'Alpinisme.

USAR - Urban search and rescue.

Vector - Geometric measure of magnitude and direction.

Vertical - Direction aligned with the direction of the force of gravity, as materialized with a plumb line.

Via Ferrata Hazard - Name given to circumstances that lead to fall protecting anchor attachments sliding out of position enough to be dangerous.

Victim Extrication Device - NFPA: A device to be secured about the body of a victim in a harness-like manner to provide support in a head-up or horizontal configuration for the purpose of lifting and transporting the victim with life safety rope.

Virgin Fiber - NFPA: Fiber that is new and previously unused.

Waist - NFPA: The area above the hips and below the xiphoid process.

Webbing - Woven material in the form of a long strip; can be of flat or tubular weave.

Work Positioning - Maneuvers and rigging used to alter or secure a Climber's position while supported by a rope or when standing on a vertical worksite.

Working End - Term identifies the end of a rope closest to the load it supports; also the end of the rope used to trace through tucks and ties to form a knot or hitch.

Working Part - Segment in a length of rope or cord that makes up the body or loop of a knot; also refers to the segment of rope contained inside the workings of pulley systems; sometimes interchangeable with working section.

Working Section - Segment in a rope length between the load and anchor, or between the hitch and the anchor; also can describe the segment between the load and gripping hands.

Z-Rig - Mechanical advantage pulley system that resembles the letter "Z."

Made in the USA
Lexington, KY
25 January 2018